MENTAL DISABILITIES
AND
CRIMINAL RESPONSIBILITY

HERBERT FINGARETTE
ANN FINGARETTE HASSE

Mental Disabilities and Criminal Responsibility

UNIVERSITY OF CALIFORNIA PRESS
BERKELEY · LOS ANGELES · LONDON

University of California Press
Berkeley and Los Angeles, California
University of California Press, Ltd.
London, England
Copyright © 1979 by
The Regents of the University of California
ISBN 0-520-03630-1
Library of Congress Catalog Card Number: 77-91756
Printed in the United States of America

1 2 3 4 5 6 7 8 9

This book is lovingly and appreciatively dedicated to

LESLIE FINGARETTE

CONTENTS

PART IV   *Current Controversial Defenses: The Addictions and Their Rationales*

PART V   *The Disability of Mind Doctrine: A Proposal*

APPENDICES:

PREFACE

This book concerns itself with mental disabilities, of whatever kind, as they affect criminal responsibility. The book is so organized as to be useful in two ways: as a systematic commentary on current law in the area, and as an exposition of a proposed unifying doctrine. The book as a whole constitutes an argument in depth for the proposed doctrine.

Parts II, III, and IV of the book, if taken separately, are independent contributions to the systematic understanding of current legal doctrine on criminal law defenses that, respectively, completely exculpate the accused (e.g., insanity, unconsciousness, automatism), partially exculpate the accused (e.g., intoxication from alcohol or other drugs, diminished mental capacity), or have as yet erratic exculpatory force (e.g., addiction to alcohol or other drugs). Over the past few years, about half of this material has appeared in independent articles in law reviews in the United States and England.[1] Much of that previously published material has been substantially revised for this book, however.

1. The material in Chapters 2, 3, 4, 5, 6, 15, and Appendix I is hitherto unpublished. Of this material, Chapters 2, 3, 4, and 5 were primarily the responsibility of H. Fingarette. Chapter 6 was primarily the responsibility of Ann F. Hasse. Chapter 15 and Appendix I were shared responsibilities.

The material in Chapter 7 appeared, in slightly different form, as "Drug Intoxication and Criminal Responsibility—Old Dilemmas and a New Proposal," by Ann F. Hasse in 16 *Santa Clara Lawyer* 249 (1976).

The material in Chapter 8 is a substantially revised version of an article entitled,

We became increasingly aware as we pursued our inquiry that we were repeatedly grappling with a single, recurring source of conceptual confusion that feeds much of the controversy and creates the acute sense of dissatisfaction so evident in the area of law dealing with criminal responsibility. Correspondingly, we came to realize clearly that the real inspiration and motivation for the development of the common law in this area lay in certain basic intuitions, moral and legal, that have never been elaborated explicitly and as a coherent doctrine.

These intuitions emerge in topic-specific form in each of the separate studies alluded to above. However, in order to orient the reader, we have introduced them in Chapter 1.[2] They are later brought together systematically and developed in depth in Part V (and in the Appendices). In Part V we present a statement of a proposed legal doctrine—which we have called the Disability of Mind (or D.O.M.) doctrine—and which we believe to be no more than explicit formulation in adequate legal terms of the basic intuitions underlying the thrust of the common law in this area. Though a part of this material, too, was published independently, it has been substantially re-edited. Chapters 14 and 15 contain important new material added to respond to the principal queries we have received about earlier versions. Appendix I further develops the new ideas. It consists of a set of suggested Model Jury Instructions for the D.O.M. doctrine. Appendix II is, with minor editorial changes, a reprint of an article[3] arguing the D.O.M. doctrine in the context of English criminal law. It appeared a few

---

"Keeping Wolff from the Door: California's Diminished Capacity Concept," by Ann F. Hasse, in 60 *California Law Review* 1641 (1972).

Chapters 9, 10, 11, and 12 constitute a drastically reorganized and re-edited presentation of materials that appeared in two articles by Herbert Fingarette in 83 *Harvard Law Review* 793 (1970) and 84 *Yale Law Journal* 413 (1975), under the titles, respectively: "The Perils of Powell: In Search of a Factual Foundation for the 'Disease Concept of Alcoholism,' " and "Addiction and Criminal Responsibility." The latter study was supported by PHS Research Grant #1 RD3 MH 25193-01, NIMH (Center for Studies of Crime and Delinquency).

2. Some of the material in Chapter 1, a slightly different earlier version of Chapter 13, and much of the material in Chapter 14 appeared in "Disabilities of Mind and Criminal Responsibility," 76 *Columbia Law Review* 236 (1976) by H. Fingarette. The material in Chapter 14, though basically taken from the preceding article, has been substantially re-edited and has had significant new material added.

3. Appendix II is a re-presentation, with only stylistic editorial changes, of "Diminished Mental Capacity as a Criminal Law Defence," by H. Fingarette. It appeared in the English law journal, 37 *Modern Law Review* 264 (1974), and it

years ago and is an earlier version of the D.O.M. doctrine. Therefore it is not consistent in all respects with the later form, but we believe the differences are easily identified and may serve to show not only how the doctrine developed, but also its adaptability to rational revision with increasing experience and reflection.

Though each chapter in the book was authored by one or the other of the individual co-authors, the work as a whole may be viewed as a joint product. For in each case basic ideas were discussed at length in the early writing stage, and drafts were discussed jointly and in detail. Even at the stage when the senior author was writing some of the earlier relevant studies whose results appear here or elsewhere, the drafts were extensively discussed to the mutual profit of both of us.

In ways that will be evident to the careful reader, but which are too complex to state fully here, the earlier book by the senior author—*The Meaning of Criminal Insanity*[4]—is the predecessor to the present work and is conceivable as a part of the total project which the present work consummates. We can only note here that the section of the present book that deals with the insanity defense is much narrower than the earlier book in scope, being focused on very central conceptual issues of direct relevance to the theses of the present book. Moreover, the material presented here represents a significant advance over the earlier book in the depth, precision, substantive insight, and even the orientation with which these issues are treated here.

This book owes more to Leslie Fingarette than we can possibly say here. We constantly turned to her to transform our innumerable, extensive, and often indecipherable drafts of work-in-progress into clean copy instantly ready for our continuing use, and hers also was the very large job of producing final copy for the printer's type. She was an unfailing source of moral support and of keen editorial candor. She was our companion throughout this venture.

---

presents the main theses of the D.O.M. doctrine developed systematically in relation to English criminal law. There are some differences in the formulation as compared to that in Chapters 1 and 13, which represent later versions of the doctrine. The reader is referred to a note at the beginning of Appendix II.

4. Berkeley: University of California Press, 1972, 1974 (paperback edition).

PART I

The Disability of Mind Doctrine: A New Proposal

1

The Argument of the Book
and the Proposals

The issue of concern in this book is the criminal responsibility of the offender suffering a disability of mind. Our central datum has been the fact that mental disability has a distinctive bearing on culpability because it can negate responsibility. That this should be so has been a deep and persistent intuition of common men and the common law over the centuries. But the law that has developed in this area is a thicket of confusion and controversy, lacking any rational ground plan.

The present study constitutes a fundamental analysis of the key concepts of legal doctrine in this area. Two complementary approaches serve this end: first, the major current doctrines are analyzed in their own terms; then, a unitary doctrine that can replace the present multiplicity and confusion of doctrines is expounded. The "new" doctrine proposed— which we call the Disability of Mind (or D.O.M.) doctrine—is not an invention of ours but is a synthesis of insights gained from the analyses of current doctrines.[1]

1. Some of the ideas herein were adumbrated in a much narrower context in Fingarette, *The Meaning of Criminal Insanity* (1972). An early attempt at explicit formulation of a generalized doctrine along these lines was formulated in the context of English law—see Fingarette, 1974. The concepts and the doctrine have since then undergone intensive rethinking. Analysis of other areas of mental disability law have revealed a deeper pattern and a more ubiquitous one. Basic new insights have led to

3

The core of D.O.M. doctrine is the body of valid intuitions and motivations that we found to underlie the legal and moral thinking in this area.

Our concern has been to answer a question that, surprisingly, has rarely been addressed in fundamental terms:[2] *Why* should mental disability affect criminal responsibility? The point of thinking through this fundamental question is to lay a systematic conceptual basis for doctrinal reform.

The desirability of a unified and realistic basic doctrine for assessing the criminal responsibility of the mentally disabled is apparent. In current criminal law the issue of mental disability, once introduced, becomes linked with a confusing multiplicity of special defenses, legal doctrines, and procedures and forms of verdict, the latter often linked in a logically erratic way with post-verdict dispositional issues, all of which can vary from one jurisdiction to another.[3]

For example, where a defense is based on "absence of specific intent" because of gross intoxication, the distinctive substantive doctrine, trial and pre-trial procedures, and ultimate disposition will be fundamentally different from those that obtain in a defense of insanity.[4] Thus, in the case of the *M'Naghten* test for insanity, the decisive findings are the presence of mental disease and lack of understanding of the nature of the act. But in the case of intoxication, *neither* of these issues is normally raised. Instead, the crucial question is whether that legal will-o'-the-wisp—"specific

---

revision and refinement of earlier formulations. The present statement offers what we believe to be a much deepened and simplified version, significantly improved over the earlier attempt, and in this case expressed primarily and for the first time in the context of U.S. law rather than English law. Moreover, we have now been able to develop this in the context of systematic analyses of current criminal law doctrine in specific areas such as insanity, intoxications, addictions, and diminished mental capacity. These critiques in each case reveal the underlying need for a new doctrine, and adumbrate its nature in regard to the area of law covered in the chapter. Part V and Appendix I develop the new doctrine systematically, both in theory and in regard to practical language and implications.

2. See H. Morris (1976), 74–75.

3. For an overview of these issues, see generally Goldstein (1967), especially chaps. 8, 10, and 12; and Brooks (1974), especially chaps. 5 and 6.

4. For background on the comments that follow, compare the insanity defense (see references in note 3 supra) with the defenses based on intoxication (see Part III) and addiction (see Part IV). See Fingarette (1970), (1972), (1974), and see also "Intoxication," in Hall (1960), 529.

intent"—was present. And yet, in either case the essential reason for any mitigation or exculpation that may be warranted is the same: an irrational condition of mind at the time the crime was committed. True, there are also important differences between the two kinds of cases—but why should *utterly* different doctrines be used?

Indeed, with respect to gross intoxication itself, there are various possible bases for defense strategy. Depending on jurisdiction, special circumstances, and the defense attorney's ingenuity, the defense may be based on "absence of specific intent," "diminished mental capacity," "unconsciousness," "insanity," or "involuntariness due to addiction." Each such strategy, whether or not associated with intoxication, calls for its own peculiar tactics and associated legal doctrines. Each could result in different post-verdict dispositions from any of the others, ranging from immediate and complete freedom [5] to lengthy involuntary commitment in either a hospital[6] or a prison.[7] Insanity and intoxication illustrate, but are far from exhausting, the list of confusing defense options available under current law.

In understandable reaction to this miasma of ad hoc legal doctrine and evidentiary confusion, contemporary reformers have proposed radical surgery: Remove the entire issue of mental disability from the trial process. Leave the matter instead to post-verdict assessment and dispositional decisions by experts. Let the behavior, not the mental state or condition of the actor, be at issue in the trial.

There are variant forms of this basic proposal. Some, for example Lady Wootton,[8] propose that *all* evidence as to mental condition, even the usual evidence of *mens rea,* be considered only after the trial—the trial itself being devoted purely to finding whether the relevant physical act was committed. Others, for example Professor Hart,[9] propose that the usual specific elements of *mens rea* (intent, malice, and so forth) be dealt with, as is now the case, during the trial process, but that what are now "general defenses," such as insanity, should instead be matters for a post-trial phase of medical assessment and disposition.

Such reforms, whatever their procedural efficiencies or inefficiencies, infringe in fundamental ways on the principle that justice requires the

5. In a successful defense of unconsciousness, involuntariness, or automatism.
6. In a successful defense of insanity.
7. In a successful defense of diminished mental capacity.
8. Wootton (1963), chaps. 2, 3, and 4.
9. Hart (1968), chap. 8.

defendant to have the right to present at his trial a complete defense to an accusation of criminal guilt. Absence of *mens rea*—whether "specific" or "general"—is a defense that is fundamental in common law. [10]

Even less extreme versions of the proposed reforms, such as Professor Hart's, deny this right. In "compromising," his suggested reform fails to come to grips with the problems posed by the "in-between" lines of defense based on such conditions as intoxication, addiction, and automatism. [11] Moreover, Hart's view creates a fundamental and inherently insoluble problem: What if the general condition of mind—to be assessed only in a later forum—affects substantially one of the specific elements of *mens rea* that must be assessed during the earlier forum, i.e., the trial? [12] Hart's proposal requires a jury to ignore the basic condition of mind of the defendant in assessing, for example, the defendant's intent or belief. Yet the whole point of the concept of insanity is that it constitutes a condition of mind that crucially affects the nature or existence of the person's beliefs and intentions!

Fundamental legal principle must always limit what we do for the sake of "efficiency"; and these reforms, proposed as improvements in efficiency, conflict with fundamental principles of justice. Nevertheless, the fact remains that the current concepts and doctrines have justifiably engendered a ubiquitous sense of dismay among medical and legal professionals who deal with these issues.

In the present work we argue for the adoption of a new doctrine, a unitary and realistic one, which we call the Disability of Mind doctrine (D.O.M.). We hold that this doctrine expresses the distinctive moral and legal basis for lessening or negating criminal responsibility where there is mental disability. The D.O.M. doctrine is founded on the premise that, whatever the cause, the condition that directly justifies ascribing nonresponsibility, insofar as this is justified at all, is the defendant's irrational condition of mind in committing the offense. This proposition is a distillation of what the analyses in the chapters on specific defenses will show to be a basic intuition. Even though it has remained unexpressed, it has

10. Kadish (1968).

11. I.e., defenses that can plausibly be argued, in the contemporary context, to establish either a generalized mental derangement or an absence of some specific element of the alleged crime such as "specific intent," "deliberation," "voluntariness," or "knowledge."

12. For the problems raised, see Goldstein (1967), at p. 222; Wasserstrom (1967). See also Jacobs (1971). An excellent brief review of the situation is in Brooks (1974), at pp. 309–312.

inspired and motivated the common law in this area, and has remained fundamental to the thinking of the common man.

Specifically, the D.O.M. doctrine, which is systematically set forth in the last chapter of this book, is derived from three linked intuitions: (1) Someone whose behavior has its source in a deranged mind is not in that respect acting as a responsible person, and cannot in justice be judged morally culpable, in that same respect, for harms committed. (2) However, if such a person, while still responsible, culpably produced that derangement of mind, as for example in the excessive use of drink or drugs, that originating responsible act should be placed in the balance in assessing the ultimate culpability of the offender. (3) Regardless of culpability, if a disability of mind is found to have been the source of criminally prohibited behavior, the person so disabled should be subject to post-verdict mental examination and, where suitably shown to be necessary, subject to medical or other supervision under appropriate legal and social policies.

The legal procedure implied in principle by the three propositions lies roughly midway between the practice as it is at present and the practice as it would be under the previously discussed proposals to abolish *mens rea* defenses. That is, mental conditions bearing on guilt and responsibility remain matters for determination in the trial; but questions of future welfare and safety are completely separated for resolution after each trial in which any degree of criminal nonresponsibility because of D.O.M. is found.

Such a doctrine is in substance readily comprehensible and readily applicable by the juryman because the doctrine is rooted in common sense, both as to facts and intuitive concepts. Therefore the jury can actively use their critical intelligence rather than relying unduly on expert evidence or floundering among arbitrary legal technicalities and "constructive" legal interpretations of the facts in ways that flout common sense.

The doctrine here called the Disability of Mind (or D.O.M.) doctrine is entirely general and unitary. It covers all the legal rubrics mentioned earlier. Indeed, it covers *any* mental pathology whether temporary or chronic, whether self-induced or not, and whether it has an identifiable physical origin or not.

The D.O.M. doctrine expresses only the basic legal issues and, tacitly, the deep moral intuitions that underlie these. It is not expressed in terms of, and therefore not tied to, any particular medical theory, doctrine, outlook, or fashion of the moment. But it is hospitable to the best medical knowledge of the time, present or future, even while it systematically discourages the usurpation by medical experts of the role of jury or judge.

That the D.O.M. doctrine is not an invention but a crystallization of the truly underlying intuitions is essential to our argument. Certainly the basic datum—that mental disability does have a distinctive, inherently mitigating effect—is deeply rooted in the common law. It is, after all, a familiar feature of the common law jurisdictions that psychoses, neuroses, "character disorder," congenital mental defect, malfunction of body or traumas affecting the mind, intoxications, addictions—in short, all forms of impairment of the powers of mind—may mitigate or negate the criminal culpability of the afflicted person.[13] It is significant that this common sense and common law tradition has persisted through centuries, and in spite of often dramatic changes in intellectual fashions in law, philosophy, and medical psychology.[14] Such persistence suggests, rightly, that in this area of law and morality the basic concepts that govern must indeed be few, simple, coherent, and powerful.

Unfortunately, however, in the course of history no unified doctrine emerged as the courts faced, case by case, a central dilemma: (a) What criterion must be used to identify responsibility-negating mental disability? (b) How is the criterion to be kept narrow enough to exclude common flaws of mind and character—greed, selfishness, cruelty, and impetuousness—that generate many of the very criminal inclinations that the criminal law intends to hold us responsible for curbing? There was no coherent and unified response to this dilemma. The case-by-case approach to the reform of the older, more rigid laws, though moved obscurely by the underlying intuitions, led the judges to achieve the intuitively desired ends through either of two inappropriate kinds of doctrinal response.

On the one hand, the judges sought to achieve the solution by reliance on fashionable new extralegal doctrines, as in the unwarrantedly optimistic

13. Many of these conditions, as affecting criminal responsibility, are discussed in detail and systematically at various points in the chapters that follow, and in *The Meaning of Criminal Insanity* (supra, note 1). There is, of course, a very large literature on mental disability. Since this chapter presumes that current law as developed in the preceding literature is inadequate, and is aimed at elucidating an alternative, new doctrine, there is no need nor pretense here to do more than note a few basic references. (Detailed analyses of current law and its inadequacies are to be found in the chapters that follow.) See: Goldstein (1967); Dix (1971); Fox (1963); Edwards (1958); Rose (1970); Baumgartner (1970); Lunter (1972); Hall (1960), "Intoxication," chap. 14; Fingarette (1970); Fingarette (1975).

14. For historical treatments of the Anglo-American law pertaining to mental disabilities and criminal responsibility, see generally: "Lunacy and Idiocy: The Old Law and Its Incubus" (1951); Weihofen (1954); Biggs (1955); Guttmacher (1961); Platt and Diamond (1966); and Lewinstein (1969).

reliance in *M'Naghten* on the nineteenth-century medico-philosophical concept of "mental disease." [15]

On the other hand, the judges often sought the intuitively desired result by ad hoc use of traditional legal principles having relevance to special features of the early cases, but having only peripheral relevance to the basic issues. Specifically, it was convenient and seemed promising to argue that if the mental derangement resulted in lack of some requisite criminal intent, or in absence of voluntariness, or in absence of some requisite "mental elements" such as premeditation or deliberation or knowledge, then it is the absence of that particular mental element of the crime that is the ultimate ground for full or partial exculpation.[16] As new cases arose, unforeseen implications of these precedents emerged—including the fact that too often the relevant mental element was obviously *present* in cases where the defendant seemed nonculpable to common sense, and often was so found by the jury in spite of legal doctrine. In such cases it was commonly the very gross irrationality of mind that led the defendant to *want* to commit an act that would otherwise never have been committed. The attempts to modify, generalize, limit, redefine, and in general to patch and paste, led to the proliferation of confusing and confused doctrines and troublesome terms of art that now abound. "Specific intent," "general criminal intent," "unconsciousness," "knowledge of the nature of the act," "knowledge that it was wrong," "capacity to conform behavior to the requirements of law," "automatism," "pharmacological coercion"—these and more are strewn about the pages of the legal literature in this area, every one of them assigned paradoxical meanings and used arbitrarily.[17]

15. *M'Naghten's Case* (1843). In view of the many and persistent attacks in recent years on the very concept of psychiatry as a medical or scientific discipline, it may be worth re-emphasizing here that the remarks in the text are *not* intended to be, or to imply, a radical attack on the foundations of psychiatry. The criticism in the text is directed to one particular concept, "mental disease"—a concept that has no systematic role in psychiatric doctrine, and is not found in the official *Diagnostic and Statistical Manual of Mental Disorders*, 2nd ed. (1968) of the American Psychiatric Association. This phrase has nevertheless been central to the legal tests of criminal insanity in England and the United States ever since *M'Naghten's Case*. See chap. 1 in Fingarette (1972).

16. The substantiation of this analysis is presented in detail in regard to each major area taken up in Parts II, III, and IV.

17. For a full discussion in connection with lack of criminal intent, ignorantia, and involuntariness, see Part II infra; for a full discussion of "absence of specific intent," see Part III infra; for a full discussion of "pharmacological coercion" and related notions, see Part IV infra, on the addictions.

What probably helped to confuse matters further here was the premature introduction, by justifiably concerned jurists, of a logically separate question that should arise only *after* there has been a finding of a disability of mind. That subsequent question is: Was the defendant culpable as to the origin of the mental disability? It is in regard to this latter question, and not the question whether the offender was mentally disabled, that insanity and gross intoxication, for example, contrast sharply and call for different responses by the law. The overreaction of pressing the subsequent question prematurely has obscured a basic analytical distinction, and confuses the issues beyond all hope of rational repair. It is central to the doctrine of Disability of Mind presented here to maintain the simple two-step analysis: the D.O.M. doctrine gets us to recognize simply and straightforwardly that insanity and gross intoxication are alike in being conditions of irrationality at the time of the offending act; and it also systematically makes us recognize that the two cases differ significantly as to ultimate culpability because of the differences in the *origin* of that irrationality. And with regard to all the other mental disability conditions, this two-step analysis called for by the D.O.M. doctrine serves similarly to clarify the basic issues.

The confusion in the development of mental disability law has been even further compounded in recent times simply because mental disability is now an area where so many learned specialties intersect. Law, moral philosophy, medical psychology, sociology—these and other specialties make claims to relevant expertise. Therefore individual specialists inevitably feel to some degree like strangers to concepts of mental disability imported from other disciplines—as indeed the laymen of the jury may feel, frustrated by the legal conundrums. In the face of this, modern legal reasoning in this area has often reflected either excessive antiscientific rigidity and parochialism, or, at the other extreme, a lack of confidence in its own genius and a continuation of the tendency to excessive hospitality to the latest fads and theories in other professions such as the social sciences and medicine.

One of the consequences is an ambivalent attitude, deeply rooted in the law, toward the psychiatrist or psychologist as expert witness—an ambivalence that is inevitably mirrored in these experts' attitudes toward the law. Legal doctrines today, often enough in spite of the wishes of all concerned, have encouraged the "tyranny of the experts" in the courtroom. This is because, depending on the legal theory adopted by defense counsel, the mental incapacity may be defined in different ways, and in any case includes reference to the medical-looking term, "mental disease." These nuances of definition must then be settled during the trial. As things now stand, expert testimony reflects either of two unhelpful tendencies: either it moves into depths and nuances of diagnosis and of technical terminology that easily leave a jury stranded; or it achieves pseudo-clarity by allowing expert witnesses to offer a sequence of medical-sounding clichés that conform verbally to legal formulas but provide no factual insight to the jury.[18]

Reassessment of fundamental doctrine that can lead to such tensions and confusions is very much in order. Surprisingly, although a large literature has grown out of the controversies over the insanity plea and over intoxications as bases of defense from criminal charges, very little of it goes to the analysis of the conceptual foundations—questions of basic meaning, or of the rationale for having such defenses at all. Moreover, there is to our knowledge no fundamental inquiry of this kind that covers both the general concept of mental disability and also the full range of special forms of it, and that does this with specificity and depth in relation to a full repertoire of the relevant doctrines in law. That, however, is the scope—as we felt it *had* to be—of this book.

The criminal law must be liberated from the inherited pseudo-solutions that have generated past and present confusion—and, in the end, therefore, injustice. The problems are ripe for a return to the basic common law principles centering around the notion of responsibility, which lies at the heart of the criminal law in all common law lands. The practical alternative to such a fundamental clarification and rejustification seems, in the current atmosphere, to be the tendency toward abandoning as too troublesome the very notion of individual responsibility as the basis of our law.[19]

No one can hope to resolve within the range of one book all of the many controversies and confusions that have arisen in this area of law. But if it is true that these are in good part reflections of certain basic conceptual confusions lying at the heart of current criminal law mental disability doctrine, then fundamental clarification ought to provide a ground plan for rational reconstruction of the law in this crucially sensitive area.

18. For a classic discussion of these problems as faced by a frustrated court, see *Washington v. U.S.* (1967).
19. A classic analysis of the alternatives is presented in H. Morris (1976) in chap. 2, "Persons and Punishment."

PART II

Current Complete Defenses:
Their Rationales

2

Introduction and Overview

In this part of the book, we shall concern ourselves with mental disability as a defense that completely exculpates the accused from all criminal charges.

In the criminal law it has consistently been held that the mere existence of some mental incapacity is not, per se, exculpatory.[1] Even in insanity the

1. It should be noted that since *M'Naghten*, every test of criminal insanity in England and the U.S. has included the requirement of "mental disease," but no test has been satisfiable *merely* by a showing of mental disease. Wechsler (1955, p. 373) has said: "Is it the law that mental disorder *ipso facto* establishes irresponsibility? Could anyone embrace it as the law without assuring himself that the term disorder would imply the relevant impairment of capacity? As courts and commentators have repeated to the point of tedium, the criteria are addressed to the question of when disorder or defect should be accorded the specific legal consequence of a defense to criminal conviction, with the specific differences in dealing with the individual that this specific legal consequence entails. Thus the criteria are not concerned with the indicia of diagnosis of disease; they are concerned with the *effects* that a disease must have on the defendant if it is to work the exculpation claimed." "Though [the law] has always used the concept of mental disease as a point of departure, the central issue has been relating the medical part of the formula to the social functions which could alone justify exemption from criminal responsibility" (Goldstein, 1967, p. 89). In England also it has been authoritatively said, "There is no *a priori* reason why every person suffering from any form of mental abnormality or disease, or from any particular kind of mental disease, should be treated by the law as not answerable for

15

mental incapacity, if it is to be exculpatory, must meet the "core requirement of a meaningful relationship between the mental illness and the
incident charged." [2]

This correct thesis has usually been confused, however, with invalid
claims as to the nature of the relationships. The aim of this chapter is to
explore in depth—and refute—the usual claims as to the nature of that
"meaningful relationship" between illness and act. This will be done
against the background of a different conception of the relationship—a
conception that was set out in Chapter 1 and that we maintain is the valid
one.

What do "valid" and "invalid" mean here? In this area of law the basic
response of the common law has in our view been (tacitly) guided by
certain basic intuitions, but these intuitions have been unexpressed or
ill-expressed in the legal concepts and doctrines invoked. These intuitions
can be rationally defended, but because of confusion about their nature
they have not been so. Our aim in this book is to express such concepts
and doctrines, and to display explicitly the ground for the claim that they
have been tacitly operative and are defensible in depth. If our claim is true,
then the doctrine in question is a valid doctrine in common law. On the
other hand, much of the prevailing terminology and doctrines in terms of
which the law in this area has explicitly been rationalized have not been
truly operative. These concepts and doctrines are verbally invoked although they are not rationally defensible, are rarely analyzed in depth, and
are genuinely applied only occasionally and eccentrically. These we call
invalid doctrines. By examining in some depth the current concepts and
doctrines, we shall not merely show that they are invalid, but also reveal
specifically why and how they are necessarily the source of so much of the
confusion and controversy that permeates this area of law today; and we
shall then see the way out of the morass.

Since so much of the relevant comment in the literature has been in
connection with the insanity defense, it is appropriate to use that defense
as the primary focus of discussion in Part II of this book. Nevertheless, the
implications of the analysis are far more general, as will be seen in Parts III
and IV.

What, then, is that crucial relation in insanity between the mental
illness and the offense charged, that is essential to establishing nonculpabil-

---

any criminal offence which he may commit, and be exempted from conviction and
punishment" (Royal Commission, p. 99).

2. *U.S. v. Brawner*, p. 983.

ity? We shall begin with a very brief overview of common opinion, of some initial troubling questions that arise, and of a first sketch of a ubiquitous pattern of fallacious reasoning in this area.

The following illustrates a reasonably orthodox contemporary interpretation of the criminal insanity test:

The two main components of the rule define ①mental disease, ②the *consequences* thereof *that exculpate* from responsibility. . . .
The *second component* completes the instruction and *defines the ultimate issue*, of exculpation. . . .[3]

The assumption is, then, that the "ultimate" ground of exculpation lies not in the concept of "mental disease" itself but in some independently identifiable condition that such a disease may (or may not) produce.

What is that exculpatory condition in insanity? In its most general form it was well captured in *State v. Jones:*

The real ultimate question to be determined seems to be, whether, at the time of the act, he had the mental capacity to entertain a criminal intent—whether, in point of fact, he did entertain such an intent.[4]

Thus, combining the theses quoted, we have the position that a mental illness may be related to the alleged offense in that it incapacitates the person from having criminal intent with respect to that offense; and it is this absence of criminal intent that defines the ultimate exculpatory issue. If mental illness does produce such an exculpatory consequence, then the mental condition in toto, i.e., the mental condition as including the incapacity for criminal intent, is of course exculpatory, and is, by definition, criminal insanity. But if the mental illness does not have as a consequence an incapacity for criminal intent with regard to the incident charged, then no matter what the illness or how severe, there exists no

3. *Ibid.*, p. 991.
4. *State v. Jones* (1871), p. 382. See also: Comment, "Admissibility of Subjective Abnormality to Disprove Criminal Mental States," p. 233: "Insanity is a complete defense because it indicates the defendant's incapability of forming a criminal intent" (Kadish and Paulsen, 1969, p. 589). This point of view is substantially reasserted, in explicit terms, in the recently proposed Senate Bill S.1, The Criminal Justice Reform Act of 1975, par. 522: "*Insanity.* It is a defense to a prosecution under any federal statute that the defendant, as a result of mental disease or defect, lacked the state of mind required as an element of the offense charged. Mental disease or defect does not otherwise constitute a defense." It follows from the various other provisions of S.1, as applied in relation to par. 522, that it is intent or knowledge that is the "required" state of mind.

ground of exculpation (and therefore this is, by definition, *not* "criminal insanity").

This "answer" poses a further question: In what, specifically, consists this absence of criminal intent? What does "criminal intent" mean here? Though systematic analysis is rare, three main sorts of "answers," i.e., apparently relevant formulas, constitute a persistent refrain in the common law countries. (1) The defendant at the time of the act did not know or truly understand the nature of his act. (2) He did not know or appreciate that he was doing something wrong, or illegal, or criminal. (3) What he did was done involuntarily (he was unable to conform his conduct to the requirements of law).[5]

Each of these so-called exculpatory conditions requires systematic analysis. We shall see that not only does each one fail in its own way to do the job here that it is supposed to do, but all share a certain basic pattern of error.

As a preliminary, however, it will help to set the inquiry into a basic perspective. The next section will therefore concern, generally, the peculiar role in law of inquiries directed to assessing an individual's mental

5. After having extensively explored these three, below, we shall take up briefly a few remaining and possibly relevant meanings of "criminal intent." The latter meanings can be readily dealt with once these principal candidates have been placed in perspective. They are of relatively minor significance. The only possible rationale of major significance that has been proposed in addition to the three basic rationales here formulated is the one suggested by the New Hampshire and *Durham* tests of insanity. In brief, they require merely that the offending act have been caused by something labeled "mental disease" (*State v. Jones*; *Durham v. U.S.*). It might seem, then, that in this test it is not some further and ultimately exculpating condition, but the label "mental disease" itself that does the principal exculpatory job. This interpretation, though plausible, is probably not correct, as is made evident in the line of cases subsequent to, and elaborating on the meaning of *Durham*. The District of Columbia Court of Appeals found itself forced to go beyond the label "mental disease," and in *dicta* in *Carter v. U.S.* (pp. 615–616), Judge Prettyman explained that "the simple fact that a person has a mental disease or defect is not enough to relieve him of responsibility for a crime," there being the need to "keep constantly and clearly in mind the basic postulate of our criminal law. . . . If a man [is so deranged] . . . in respect to an act . . . [that he] is not a free agent, or not making a choice, or unknowing of the difference between right and wrong . . . he is outside the postulate of the law of punishment." This view was formally fixed into the definition of "mental disease" in the *Durham* context by means of a reference to "impaired behavior controls" due to mental abnormality (*McDonald v. U.S.*, p. 851). This brings the issue, in substance, into the third category in the text above, the category of "involuntariness."

capacity or incapacity—his *personal,* individual condition of mind, as contrasted with inquiries into the specific and *impersonally* defined elements of the act, such as knowledge and voluntariness, that are usually essential in establishing criminal culpability. After this, we shall better be able, in Chapters 3 and 4, to take up the analysis of specific mental elements of *mens rea* and their purported relevance to exculpation in insanity.

II

With the great exception of defenses based on mental incapacity, the focus in the criminal law is paradigmatically on the act, not the individuality of mind or personality of the actor.[6] It is, in principle, for his criminal act and not for his peculiarities of mind or personality that a person is punished.[7] With exceptions that do not affect this fundamental principle, the definition of the criminal act therefore typically describes a specific behavior and mental state independently of the individuality of the actor: "*Whoever* breaks and enters with intent to commit a felony...."

"Criminal act" is, of course, an abstract concept. An act cannot exist independently of an actor. Nevertheless, acts can, in the abstract, be identified and classified independently of the individuality of the actor, as, e.g., an act of "shooting," or "breaking and entering," or "intentionally causing death."

There are at least apparent exceptions in the law to this central concern with the acts as impersonally defined. But except in defenses based on mental incapacity, the important apparent exceptions do not concern the individuality of mind of the defendant. They rest either on the actor's "status" or on the context of the act, each in turn defined in terms of abstract, objective categories and not tied to the individual personality, or mind, of the actor. For example, it can be criminally relevant that the defendant was a police officer in performance of his duty, or a person legally married at the time of a second marriage ceremony, or a person with prior theft convictions who was discovered under certain circumstances that, against this background of prior thefts, are incriminating. In

6. Fitzgerald says: "Nor is the law in general concerned with what a man is, but only with what he does, since he may choose what he does, but not what he is" (1961, p. 5).

7. For a recent and systematic discussion of the issues here, see the probing analysis of H. Morris (1968).

none of these cases, though personal status is at issue, is the essence of the inquiry directed to probing the actor's concrete individuality or personal life history (except as to the highly specific and impersonally defined acts mentioned).

Since criminal acts include mental elements, one can never exclude the possibility that there may be occasion to inquire into the personality or individuality of mind and character of a defendant. But the crux of the matter is that—except in insanity—such inquiry is not engaged in routinely or for its own sake. Such inquiry is occasional and always instrumental, needing to be carried forward only enough to permit inferences to the issue of ultimate interest: were certain quite specific, impersonally defined behaviors and mental states constituting the criminal act in fact present? Thus, for example, learning that the particular defendant has repeatedly shown himself to be unusually frightened and awkward in dealing with firearms may give some basis for inferring whether in the case in question he fired the gun by accident, as he claims, rather than with intent. Here, ultimate interest in the defendant's personal trait of fearfulness is nil. It could well turn out that there is completely adequate evidence, indeed better evidence, having nothing to do with the personality of the defendant, as to whether he fired the gun by accident or design. In these cases the pattern of evidence is relatively simple, and the inference to be drawn is relatively direct and self-evident in relation to the factual situation claimed.[8]

8. The simplicity of the evidentiary structure in the paradigmatic legal judgments of involuntariness is typical: the defendant's arm was pushed or physically constrained to move as it did by someone else; the defendant fainted, or fell in an epileptic seizure (see note 7, Chapter 4 infra). Coercion, often viewed as a kind of involuntariness, shows the same typical simplicity in the facts: the defendant was ordered to act as he did by a gunman (see note 17, Chapter 4 infra). Moreover, in each type of case, given the essential facts, the inference to involuntariness is normally so *immediate*, so natural, that unless challenged by further unusual circumstances, the judgment is spontaneous.

In ignorance or mistake the structure of the evidence is usually slightly more complex (see Chapter 3, infra) but still notably simple in comparison to the facts that establish insanity. Some examples illustrate this point:

The defendant heard someone strange moving about at night in his house, took it to be a burglar, thrust his sword into a small room where he heard the noise, and killed—as it turned out—a servant's friend who had been invited to come to the house by the servant (*Levett's Case*). The pattern of the essential facts to be proved is simple, and its significance, if proved, is patent.

The defendant had caused injury when he aimed and pulled the trigger of a weapon that he had, shortly before, unloaded and put safely away; for without his

In contrast to all this, the insanity defense focuses interest squarely and for its own sake upon the individual character of the defendant's mind: It is *necessary* to make a judgment that goes well beyond the facts related to the particular offense, a judgment about this particular person, the make-up of *his* mind and personality in its concrete individuality.[9] The final judgment on this is not instrumental to some further and primary factual inference; it is, as factual finding, conclusory. Whereas, on the contrary, any specific items of behavior, or specific mental states such as intent, knowledge, or deliberation that are here of interest, are so only instrumentally. In this context, inquiry into the defendant's acts or into particular states of mind merely serve to evidence or to help illuminate what we really want to know about—i.e., the pattern in which his particular mind was functioning at the time. Here the pattern of evidence is typically complex, and the relation between it and the conclusion to be inferred is often one that reasonable men can differ on, even if the constitutive facts are as claimed.

---

knowledge or consent, it had in the meantime quite unpredictably been used by someone else and left loaded. This, too, is a mistake of fact—a simple pattern of fact, a pattern whose import is self-evident (cited at p. 74, *Russell on Crime*, 1964). Here the mistake as to whether the gun was loaded was thought to be reasonable, and the defense succeeded on the facts as cited. But for a discussion of the complexities that can now arise in such a case in England, see Smith and Hogan, pp. 59, 150 (1973). If the mistake claimed concerns the consequences foreseen to follow from the act, rather than the circumstances at the time (a tenuous distinction), the mistake need not even be reasonable (in England).

The defendant came to the city, had never learned (and had no reason to believe) that there was a local law requiring her to register with the police as an ex-felon. She did not register (*Lambert v. Calif.*). Again the essential pattern of facts to be proved is simple. And the conclusion to be inferred—that she was in fact ignorant of the law—lies on the face of the evidence (though the *defense* will of course be ignorance of law, not of fact).

In all these cases, though we are interested in the facts about mental states, we learn little about the individuality of the actor—it is enough if we find a very few, very simple mental "facts" whose legal significance is perfectly intelligible independently of the actor's individual personality.

9. "[Supposing the accused to have presented an insanity defense:] now his mental life is wide open. His life history can be presented in elaborate detail—his school problems, his prior aberrational behavior, his experiences with psychiatric clinics and mental hospitals. The search becomes one for information regarding what the accused was *really* thinking when he committed the crime, how he was *really* functioning, rather than for inferences drawn from his acts at the time of the crime" (Goldstein, 1967, p. 19).

In the light of such radical contrasts and differences as those brought out up to this point, certain questions emerge vividly. What connection, sufficient to justify applying the same doctrines, is there between the uses of "involuntariness" and "ignorance" in act-oriented contexts that present simple situations whose significance is immediately apparent, and the uses of these same words in the personality-oriented, factually complex, and highly inferential context of insanity? We think the answer is: None— except for the very general point that in each case something has gone wrong for the purposes of responsible conduct. The connections usually claimed are expressed on high metaphysical or psychological levels of abstraction. We are asked to assume that in all these cases, the ultimate and invisible fact is that "The will is overcome," or "*True, real* understanding is lacking."

The confusion at issue consists in this: In insanity the true topic of inquiry is the soundness or faultiness of the individual mental *setting* out of which particular states of mind emerge; but the legal analyses we are offered make it seem as if the topics of interest are the particular mental states themselves, and most especially whether the states are absent or present. The obvious *presence,* in many cases, of these ordinarily inculpating states, along with our intuitive realization of the unsoundness of the individual mental setting in which they were generated, and of the consequent lack of responsibility, leads to use of the confusing verbal device of saying that the particular inculpating mental state is only "superficially" but not "really" or "truly" present, not enough so to count in establishing culpability. But this verbalism, while it may achieve the intuitively desired result, leaves the issues unanalyzed.

It is no accident that these verbal maneuvers, which work by retreating into pseudo-philosophical and psychological vagueness, subsequently plague legal analysis. It is no accident that substantive and procedural principles of law applicable to ignorance and involuntariness generate unending controversy when applied in the radically different context of inquiry into mental incapacity.

The above preliminary remarks are intended to set a background and a stage for the detailed demonstration, in Chapters 3 and 4, that ignorance and involuntariness are usually not relevant to insanity, and that in any case the exculpatory force of mental disability has very different and independent roots.

3

Insanity and Ignorantia

I: IGNORANCE OR MISTAKE OF FACT VIS-A-VIS "NOT KNOWING THE NATURE AND QUALITY OF THE ACT"

Of the set of alternative conditions satisfying the *M'Naghten* test for insanity, the first is that the defendant "did not know the nature and quality of the act."[1] According to the theory here being examined, it is this latter phrase that defines an "ultimate" ground of exculpation, that specifies the required "meaningful relationship" that relates the mental illness to the offense alleged.[2] Our task here is to seek to discover and to assess the reasons why it should be an ultimate ground of exculpation in insanity. We shall find that the theory fails, and that the analysis finally leads in quite a different direction to the true ground of exculpation.

In referring to the rationale for this aspect of the *M'Naghten* test, the Discussion in the American Law Institute's Model Penal Code has this cryptic remark: "The individual could not, by hypothesis, have employed reason to restrain the act; he did not and could not know the facts essential to bring reason into play."[3] The single illustration offered is of the "madman who believes that he is squeezing lemons when he chokes his wife." The intuitively obvious madness in the illustration tends to

1. " . . . labouring under such a defect of reason, from disease of the mind, as not to know the nature and quality of the act he was doing, or if he did know it, that he did not know what he was doing was wrong" (*M'Naghten's Case*, p. 210).

2. See notes 2 and 3, Chapter 2, supra.

3. ALI Model Penal Code, Section 4.01, p. 156.

remove any inclination one might have to quibble about the form of words used. But analysis—hitherto largely absent—is of the essence in our project here.

There are two quite different concepts embodied in this cryptic Discussion comment on the import of "not knowing the nature and quality of the act." One concept is, in effect, "not being able to use reason effectively." The second is "not knowing the essential facts." The complete statement suggests that it is the former, the incapacity to use reason in governing the act, that is most basic.[4] And this, of course, is in substance what we here also urge as central. But the Model Penal Code Discussion implies that in speaking of "not knowing the nature and quality of the act," the *M'Naghten* test proposes as the more *immediate* basis for this failure to employ reason that the defendant "did not know the essential facts." And indeed in *M'Naghten* the phrase, "not know the nature and quality of the act," and other language related to delusions do seem to suggest that we are dealing here with what has been called a " 'mistake of fact' rule."[5]

It is the view that we are dealing here with something in the nature of "mistake of fact"[6] that will be examined below. The analysis will proceed in two stages: first, an examination of "ignorance or mistake of fact" taken in a straightforward way[7] to see if it is relevant to insanity; and second, an examination of the claims that ignorance or mistake in some "deeper" sense of these words is at stake.

The Model Penal Code example, in which the madman thinks his wife is a lemon, would thus illustrate a mistake of fact. But does it? If in these matters we have been left so largely to our intuition, ought we not, perhaps, to have used our intuition fully? While it is intuitively evident that such a man cannot act responsibly having such a belief, is it not

4. Perkins (1957) says: "The essence of M'Naghten is that for mental disease or defect to incapacitate it must be of such a degree as to leave the person irrational—that is, no rational person lacks criminal capacity by reason of insanity" (p. 751). Perkins elsewhere cites, in connection with not knowing the nature and quality of the act, the illustration of Stephen, "a man who thought his homicidal act was 'breaking a jar' . . ." (p. 748).

5. Perkins (1957), p. 754.

6. *R. v. Tolson*, p. 181: "Honest and responsible mistake of fact stands in fact on the same footing as absence of the reasoning faculty, as in infancy, or perversion of that faculty, as in lunacy. . . ." See *Russell*, p. 73.

7. For a general discussion of *ignorantia facti* and the doctrine *ignorantia facti excusat*, see: Hall (1960), chap. 10; Perkins (1939); Keedy (1908).

counter-intuitive to call his delusion a "mistake of fact"? He is *mad*, not *mistaken*.[8]

Normally, if we see something as a mistake, then we tacitly exclude madness. "Mistake" implies at least a certain minimum capacity for rationality, and a specific fault (due to ignorance, misinformation, misapplication, etc.) in the exercise of that capacity. Insofar as we speak of madness, the very thing we mean to say is that this is *not* a case of a specific fault in the exercise of a capacity, but something more basic—a grave defect or lack of the mental capacity itself. The specific capacity in question is that of rational conduct. That is the reason why if someone strangles his wife believing she is a lemon, there is at most an absurd humor in saying that "he made an error." Such a person has *lost his reason*.[9]

If the insanity defense is to be reasoned about at all, then, it is essential to see at the outset that it is likely to be a distinctive defense whose real significance lies in its *contrast* with such defenses as ignorance or mistake[10] that presuppose the basic capacity for rational conduct.[11]

8. Sayre (1932), in his careful analysis of the different forms of *mens rea*, is quite clear on the issue that "The criminal state of mind ... of the insane person ... differ[s] from that of the sane adult acting under a mistake of fact" (p. 1026). Sayre shows how the mistake of fact defense arose in the context of *reasonable* mistake, thus contrasting with the unreasonableness inherent in the case of insanity.

9. "Infants under seven and lunatics are exempted from criminal responsibility, because they have not the power of reasoning. One who commits a criminal act under mistake of fact has a defense, because he has wrong or insufficient *data* for reasoning" (Keedy, 1908, p. 81).

10. Hall, quite uncharacteristically, fails to see this point in his discussion of mistake: "In mistake, e.g., knowledge of the material facts is just as absent as it is in the case of feeble-minded persons and psychotics, and the accompanying intention is not a *mens rea*" (1960, p. 107). Norval Morris (1968), who opposes the insanity defense, also treats insane delusion as "mistake of fact," thus in effect making the innocence or guilt of the defendant rest on the question of the particular content of his delusions rather than on the condition of mind in which he becomes and remains subject to delusion. Morris says: "There was no doubt of Hadfield's brain damage nor of his gross psychological disturbance. He did, however, clearly intend to kill the king. He had the insane *mens rea* for murder and treason. I do not regard the phrase 'insane *mens rea*' as a contradiction in terms. Had his psychological disturbance led him to think that he was discharging the blunderbuss to start the performance on the stage, or to burst a balloon, he would have lacked the *mens rea* for murder and treason" (p. 521). This makes "justice" a derivative of madness, an Alice-in-Wonderland approach.

11. There are cases where it is difficult to draw the line between grossly faulty use of a capacity and lack of the capacity. This does not make the distinction less

We can now consider several important and more specific legal objections to viewing insanity as a matter of ignorance or mistake of fact. These objections, though valid independently, can be seen to have their deep roots in the preceding general observations on "madness" and "mistake."

If an ultimate exculpatory element in insanity *were* ignorance or mistake about a fact material to the criminality of an act, that ignorance or mistake would, in itself, normally establish absence of *mens rea*; recourse to the legal complexities of the *"insanity"* defense would then be superfluous.[12] Any attempt to show the utility of the defense in spite of this initial superfluity leads into a tangle of conceptual underbrush in which only thorny paradox grows. A very brief excursus will reveal this.

There is a suspect but nevertheless real tendency in U.S. and English courts to hold as a matter of law that mistake of fact must in general be *reasonable*.[13] In this view, *insane* "mistake" or "ignorance" presumably would *not* exculpate, and the theory of insanity we are examining would thus fail.

---

important, but it does help explain why judgments on borderline cases can differ so. For there is, at this borderline, an element of the pragmatic in the decision: For what *purpose* are we making the decision, and in what context? How little ability should we demand to be present if we are to count it as a faulty use of minimal capacity rather than an absence, for practical purposes, of any capacity? In criminal insanity, the context is criminal condemnation; and the practical decision is made, in effect, by a jury of citizens representing the community concern with respect for the laws against crime. See the discussion in Chapter 1 at notes 60–63, supra.

12. Indeed, it is for this reason that Norval Morris (1968) opposes introducing it: "In a few cases moral non-responsibility is so clear that it would be purposeless to invoke the criminal process. Accident, in its purest and least subconscious, accident-prone form, is a situation where there is little utility in invoking the criminal process. The same is true where a person did not know what he was doing at the time of the alleged crime. But in these situations there is no need for the M'Naughten or Durham rules, because they clearly fall within general criminal law exculpatory rules. The actor simply lacks the *mens rea* of the crime. It thus seems to me that, within the area of criminal responsibility and psychological disturbance, all that we need is already achieved with existing, long-establishing rules of intent and crime . . ." (pp. 520–521). It is his attention to the logic of this position that leads him to arrive at, and accept, what we have referred to as the Alice-in-Wonderland doctrine that guilt or innocence depends on the particular content of the madman's delusion—whether it happens in law to justify or excuse his act, supposing it true, or whether not (see note 10, supra).

13. See, for example, the summary conclusion in Perkins (1939): "If no specific or other special mental element is required for guilt of the offense charged, a mistake

However, it has very plausibly been held that an absolute requirement of reasonableness is unjustified, and that the ignorance or mistake need only be "honest." The criterion of reasonableness is then viewed merely as a rebuttable test of the bona fides of the belief.[14] In this view, the reason for introducing insanity would be precisely to rebut the presumption implicit in the test and to show that the "mistake" or "ignorance" was indeed bona fide in spite of its unreasonableness.

---

of fact will not be recognized as an excuse unless it was based upon reasonable grounds" (p. 56) [citation omitted]. This remark is reaffirmed verbatim in Perkins (1957). Hall (1960) says: "Not the defendant's erroneous perception of the facts, but the facts 'as they reasonably appeared to him' determine whether he is criminally liable" (p. 33, citing *Nalley v. State*, p. 671). But see note 23, infra. But Keedy (1908) at times takes a view along these lines: "In order that the defendant may escape criminal liability because he acted under an insane delusion it is clear that the standard of an ordinary, reasonable man cannot be applied, because the definition of delusion indicates that the belief of the defendant is not in accord with the impression which would ordinarily be obtained from the situation by the use of the senses. A man acting under an insane delusion is not an average, reasonable man. This seems to illustrate further the contention that a mistake of fact need not necessarily be reasonable in order to be a good defense" (p. 88). This confusion of delusion with mistake also arises in the *M'Naghten* answers to the effect that an insane delusion as to existing facts should be treated as, in effect, a mistake of fact—an approach that elsewhere Keedy had seemed (at pp. 87–88) to reject.

14. In England and in the U.S., the situation as to whether reasonableness merely has an evidentiary role in establishing sincerity, or is in itself required, is confused. The tendency seems in both countries to favor the latter view. In England, the latter view is supported by *R. v. King*. But, *per contra*, it was said in *Wilson v. Inyang* (p. 803): "If he has acted without any reasonable ground, and has refrained from making proper inquiry, that is generally very good evidence that he is not acting honestly. But it is only evidence." So also says *Russell*, p. 75. See generally: Kenny (1966), p. 59; and Smith and Hogan (1973), pp. 148–151.

In the U.S. the requirement of reasonableness, where no "specific intent" is at issue, seems to be one of law rather than evidence. *Hill v. State*, p. 946; 2 A.L.R. 509, 518 (1915). On the other hand, where a "specific intent" is at issue, as the intent to steal in larceny, even an unreasonable but sincere belief that the property is one's own serves as a defense, though the belief be mistaken (*Stanley v. State*). However, the most logical approach would seem to be that expressed by Kadish (1965): "Mistake of fact exculpates when it negates a state of mind required by the definition of the crime, not otherwise. Thus any mistake is a defense when the crime requires intention or knowledge; only a reasonable mistake is a defense when the crime requires negligence." See also Keedy (1908) at pp. 84–85, who takes the same position as expressed by Kadish.

Merely to show that a mistaken belief about a material fact is bona fide, however, will not always suffice to exculpate, for there are surely ways in which unreasonable but bona fide beliefs may develop other than from insanity, and some of these, e.g., such a belief arrived at through gross negligence, could establish *culpability*.[15] We must therefore ask, why is an unreasonable but bona fide "mistake of fact" nonculpable if insane?[16] Perhaps the answer is that insanity establishes the unreasonable mistake as *non*-negligent? But it is hornbook law that the standard of negligence is objective. What care would the reasonable and prudent man take in the circumstance to avoid mistake? The insane person is by definition unreasonable in just the respects that involve his "mistakes"—these are the very manifestations of his insanity. It might seem then, paradoxically, that by the objective standard he is necessarily negligent! The equally absurd alternative is to speak of the care that would be exercised by "a reasonable and prudent man with the defendant's capacities," i.e., in this case an irrational reasonable man.[17]

15. See, e.g., Kadish, note 14, supra.

16. Hall (1960), after saying that "an actual mistake of fact is not sufficient" [to excuse], "the requirement of reasonableness being additional," then remarks that "only rarely is there even a hint that a court will permit consideration of serious incapacities, falling short of insanity" (p. 366). Keedy (1908), however, in effect makes the distinction that we think is central—the "lunatic" does not have "the power of reasoning," whereas one who has a mistake-of-fact defense has it by virtue of having "wrong or insufficient data for reasoning" (p. 81, emphasis in original).

17. Hart (1961b, pp. 46–48) says that to avoid such confusion we should ask two questions here: "(1) What *would* the reasonable man with ordinary capacities have done in these circumstances?" "(2) *Could* the accused with his capacities have done that?" (emphasis in original). But what sense does the latter question have in relation to the insane? They often do have the capacity to *do* what the reasonable man would—but the insane person, because of his insanity, may *choose* to do otherwise. One might take Professor Hart's formula in a different way and say that the insane person lacks, by definition, the mental capacity necessary to act reasonably, and therefore, in *that* sense, could not do what a reasonable man could do. The answer to question 2 thus being in the negative, the insane person would not be negligent, by virtue of his insanity, according to this test. So we might conclude that this confirms the hypothesis being examined in the text above—that the insanity defense is at bottom a way of exculpating by establishing mistake of fact that, although unreasonable, is honest and not negligent. But while this might work in a verbalistic way, the substance of the matter here does not rest on a showing that this person exercised adequate care, which is what a finding of absence of negligence normally means, but on a showing of irrationality, i.e., that concepts of care are beside the point for such a person.

Perhaps an insane "mistake" exculpates because it is an *involuntary* mistake. This approach takes us, for practical purposes, to the relation between the concept of insanity and that of involuntariness, a relation that we shall explore at length in Chapter 4. Suffice it to say here that this move effectively abandons the element of mistake or ignorance as the *ultimately* exculpatory element in insanity, and it shifts this role to the purported element of involuntariness.

Finally, in an attempt to escape this quagmire, one might argue simply that the concept of insanity is introduced, in addition to the exculpatory mistake, because insanity per se establishes that the mistake is in turn nonculpable. That is, the claim would be that the mere fact of mental impairment, as source of the mistake, makes the mistake nonculpable.

This approach takes us full circle and begs the fundamental question. For the theory we are assessing held that mistake or ignorance of fact is what ultimately exculpates in cases of insanity where the accused does "not know the nature of the act"; whereas now the exculpatory force of the mistake or ignorance is ultimately based on the fact that it originates in the mental impairment in insanity. And indeed this, we maintain, is the beginning of wisdom here—the recognition that mental disability introduces a distinctive and irreducible exculpatory condition.

The irrelevance of the "mistake of fact" interpretation of *M'Naghten,* when "mistake of fact" is taken in a straightforward and not some "deeper" sense, is also attested in another and more practical way: insanity trials rarely, if ever, concern defendants who claim to have suffered any confusion analogous to the wife-is-a-lemon example.[18] On the contrary, it is usual in insanity trials, for example in the case of homicide, that the defendant cognitively recognizes that he has a gun, that it can kill a person, and that he has no legal justification for doing so, yet shoots the victim.[19] In a few cases, notably those in which hallucinatory drugs are at

18. Fitzgerald (1962), p. 136, says: "Of the two tests laid down by the M'Naghten Rules the first is such that it is doubtful whether it would apply to anyone. The accused must be suffering from a defect of reason due to a disease of the mind such that he did not know the nature and quality of his act. The examples usually given of this are the case of a woman sawing off her child's head thinking it is a loaf of bread, and the case of a man strangling a woman thinking he is squeezing a lemon. According to the leading authorities on medical jurisprudence the existence of such forms of insanity is nothing but a legal fiction." Brooks (1975) discusses the situation at pp. 142–143, and concludes, more cautiously, that such cases are "not common."

19. The Royal Commission Report on Capital Punishment notes in this connection that "An insane person may therefore *often* know the nature and quality of his

issue, the defendant may have been deranged or befuddled in such a way that he did not know—in the usual sense of that word—that it was, for example, a human being rather than a snake he was strangling.[20] But such drug-intoxication cases do not usually establish *insanity*.[21] In insanity, *scienter* in the usual legal sense is rarely what is at issue.

This is a point at which the temptation to speak of a "deeper" kind of "not knowing" cannot be suppressed, and we shall turn to this aspect of the issue now. When, in criminal law contexts not involving mental incapacity, we speak of "knowledge," what is at issue is "knowledge" in that ordinary sense whose antonyms are "mistake," "ignorance," "error." Thus, murder is usually accomplished by hitting a person, or shooting him, or knifing him, or poisoning him; and therefore, correlatively, mistake and ignorance (in non-insane contexts) would then be, for example: believing (on non-insane grounds) that the gun is not loaded, or that the substance is a sleeping pill rather than a concentrated poison.

There is nothing philosophical, speculative, abstract, or complexly inferential intended in calling such beliefs mistaken. The court may lack adequate evidence as to the fact, or adequate evidence as to what the person believed to be fact. But the meaning of the claim of mistake, and the sorts of evidence that would suffice, present no fundamental conceptual problems. If the defendant claims he did not know the gun was loaded, his use of "know" is essentially that of the prosecution in its claim that he did know. The crucial task normally centers on applying the accepted tests to the evidence in the particular case.

When, however, the purportedly insane offender is spoken of as not "knowing" the nature of his act, there is usually a shift to a radically different context and a radically different use of the word "know," and therefore "deeper," and in truth radically different tests for "knowing." Unfortunately, the claim that the insane person did not "know" the nature and quality of his act in some deeper sense of "know" is rarely, if

---

act and that it is wrong and forbidden by law, but yet commit it as a result of the mental disease" (p. 80, emphasis added). The Utah Supreme Court interpreted not knowing the nature of the act in this way: " ... did not know he had a revolver, that it may be loaded, or that, if discharged, it may injure or kill" (*State v. Kirham*, p. 860, cited by A. Morris, 1968, pp. 606–607, with the comment that "only a few psychotics" can meet such a standard).

20. E.g., in *R. v. Lipman.*

21. See, generally, the discussion of drug intoxication in Part IV, infra.

ever, made clear.[22] This shift to another kind of "knowledge" is usually plainly signaled, though not explained, by the common resort to qualifying adverbs—the question now becoming whether the defendant "not only knew but fully understood," or whether he "*really*" knew, or whether he "not only knew but also *appreciated*" what he was doing. Another sign of the shift in usage is the claim that this is a kind of "knowledge" that the psychiatrist is specially qualified to identify, a kind of knowing that the layman will often fail to identify or be unlikely to appreciate.[23]

Whatever *this* concept of lack of knowledge is, and whatever its validity or importance in other contexts, we cannot ignore that the tests that reveal it are acknowledgedly different from those ordinarily used in connection with mistake or ignorance of fact. Indeed, the defense usually *acknowledges* tacitly and in effect that the defendant may have known what he was doing so far as the usual and allegedly "superficial" tests of knowledge go.

22. The reader will find handily collected a wide variety of such idioms as have been used in the present context in Hall (1960), p. 521, note 48, and in Goldstein (1967), pp. 49–58. These include phrases such as the following: "appreciation"; "realization"; "normal evaluation"; "adequate feeling"; "significant and appropriate experiencing"; "the true significance of his conduct is not appreciated"; "understands" enough to enable him to judge of "the nature, character, and consequences of the act charged against him"; "more than mere knowledge that the act is being committed; there must be an appreciation of the factors involved in the act and a mental capacity to measure and foresee the consequences of the violent conduct"; "real insight"; and "to realize with full emotional clarity." See also Fingarette (1972), chap. III, pp. 145–152.

23. Goldstein (1967) summarizes the matter: "The bulk of the critics [of *M'Naghten*] . . . distinguish . . . the law's meaning [of 'know'], from what they describe as the 'psychiatric' meaning—which they take to connote a fuller, deeper knowledge, involving emotional as well as intellectual awareness" (p. 49). One writer has said, for example: "With what was then known the psychological aspect of the 'act' part of the crime concept was adequately described in 1843 as the knowledge of the nature and quality of one's act. Literally applied, this is entirely too restrictive in 1961. We have become sophisticated! Today, in psychiatric terms, we should have to describe it as behavior emanating predominantly from the conscious-preconscious sphere of the human psyche, subject to the control of relatively healthy superego" (Mueller, 1961, p. 106). He adds: "To correctly incorporate the findings of depth psychiatry, the word 'know' as defining only a surface knowledge on the level of verbal response, should have been changed to something more expressive of the participation of preconscious and unconscious forces in human behavior" (*ibid.*, p. 112).

Unfortunately for this line of argument, it is logically obvious that if evidence of "knowledge" in a certain common sense of that term is incriminating, then evidence that knowledge in a *different* sense was absent does not constitute a rebuttal. Rhetorical adjectives such as "superficial" and "deeper" affect the logic not at all. The only way in which absence of the psychiatric or "deeper," "truer" kind of knowledge could justifiably exculpate would be if the presence of such "deeper" knowledge were *also,* in common law or by statutory requirement, an essential element of inculpation, or its absence a recognized excuse. No one has ever demonstrated such a thesis; indeed, it does not appear that this crucial issue has even been recognized or discussed.

In our attempt here to take these concepts seriously and analyze their substantive implications, we shall seek to do what the proponents of these notions have never done—i.e., to make explicit the legally relevant meaning of this "deeper knowledge" in relation to the insane person.

One apparently promising type of remark often made by psychiatrists and echoed in law literature is that this defect in knowledge, undiscovered by the usual legal tests of knowledge, consists in lack of "adequate feeling," in cognition not "fused with affect," or in absence of "full emotional clarity." [24] This kind of answer, however, directed as it is to feelings and emotions, is not relevant to the immediate inquiry, since it bears mainly on failure to "know the act is wrong" or to "appreciate the *criminality* of the act." We shall explore this dimension of the insanity tests in Section II, but at present our concern is with the possibility that criminal insanity can consist at times in some "deeper" unawareness of *fact.* If the defendant plans the act, uses effective means to his end, and shows by his actions and words a mastery of the pragmatic and intellectual, nonmoral aspects of his conduct, it is difficult to see how absence of "full emotional clarity" (whatever that obscure phrase may connote) is essential for his *factual* knowledge.

As a practical matter, the insanity defense that is seen with any frequency and that could imaginably be construed as centering on mistaken apprehension of fact is the defense based on insane delusion, i.e., insanely false *beliefs.*

Typically it is these delusory beliefs that are revealed by using the "deeper" tests of knowledge, for these delusory beliefs are about what may be called background questions—the supposed secret motives or unobservable powers of other persons, or the supposed great schemes or

24. See note 22, supra.

satanic conspiracies or divine projects that constitute the unobservable larger or cosmic context of the local conduct at issue.[25] But such background beliefs—*whether true or false*—would not normally serve in criminal law to exculpate. Even if sincere, they could, in general, be relevant only to sentencing. Hence, it is not the fact that there are such supposed "morally justifying" background beliefs, or motives arising out of them, or that the beliefs are false, that has exculpatory force.

When we do allow exculpatory force to such a background of false beliefs, beliefs normally irrelevant to exculpation, what we require is their rootedness in mental derangement. This exculpatory condition is distinctive and essential, and it is neither reducible to nor translatable into terms of specific "mistaken" or false beliefs, for these alone would *not* exculpate in this context.[26] It is the well that is poisoned, not the cup. But the language used—"he doesn't *really* understand what he's doing"—while innocent and serviceable enough in itself, is highly misleading in a legal context. For in this context there does exist a familiar doctrine that ignorance-or-mistake can exculpate, whereas there does not yet exist any developed legal doctrine of mental disability as, per se, a distinctive exculpatory ground when it renders the individual criminally irrational in his conduct.

In dealing with the phrase, "quality of the act," there is a temptation to introduce the moral dimension. One might suppose that the reference to the "quality of the act" could be a reference to something more than bare "fact." This possibility has been carefully excluded from the preceding discussion. In English case law, and in some U.S. case law, it has been held that this phrase refers only to the physical qualities of the act.[27] Fortunately we do not have to delay to debate the question; it will take care of itself in the next sections, in which the "knowledge of wrong" criterion is explored.

25. Among the classic cases along these lines are *M'Naghten's Case, Hadfield's Case*, and *People v. Schmidt*.

26. The nonsense of the "mistaken belief" approach is evident in the *M'Naghten* rule "which ordains that a man suffering from an insane delusion must be judged as if the facts were what he imagined them to be. . . . As the law stands, the [*M'Naghten*] Rules demand that the accused show method in his madness. It has been well said that he must be reasonable in his unreason, sane in his insanity" (Fitzgerald, 1962, pp. 137–138).

27. *R. v. Codere*, pp. 26–27. *People v. Roche*, Trial Tr. 488–489; *People v. Horton*, Trial Tr., 1088, 3262–63. But, taking a contrary view, see: *State v. Essen*, p. 521; *Schwartz v. State*. See discussion in Hall (1960), p. 483.

II: "NOT KNOWING THE ACT IS WRONG": MORAL IGNORANCE

The "knowledge of wrong" clause of the insanity tests is probably the operative one, i.e., the one foremost in the jury's mind, in the great preponderance of successful uses of the insanity plea.[28] To common sense it has an intuitive exculpatory implication that seems undeniable; and this fact must be accounted for by any satisfactory analysis of the meaning and rationale of the plea.

Paradoxically, however, this clause—so immediately plausible to common sense—no less immediately appears implausible as a ground of exculpation when viewed in the light of accepted principles in modern criminal law. Phrases such as "not knowing" or "not appreciating" that the act is "wrong" or "criminal" can plausibly be taken in either or both of two senses: they may refer, in effect, to ignorance or mistake of the law, or to ignorance or mistake as to the moral wrongness of the act, or to some combination of both. But independently of the insanity plea (or infancy), ignorance or mistake as to the moral quality of the act is not a criminal law defense,[29] and this seems even more emphatically true in connection

28. Although statistics are hard to come by here, several indicators attest to the predominance of this clause in successful use of *M'Naghten*: (1) the evidence of the rarity of a successful use of the alternative clause concerning knowledge of the "nature and quality of the act" (see section I, and especially text and note supra at n. 18); (2) the fact that *M'Naghten* is quite commonly alluded to as the "right-wrong" test; (3) the fact that most of the attempts to replace the word *knowledge* with presumably more adequate concepts are directed to questions of emotional-ethical "appreciation" rather than intellectual-perceptual validity (see note 22, supra); and (4) the fact that the increasingly widely adopted ALI Model Penal Code test focuses on "appreciating the criminality of the conduct" and capacity to "conform conduct to law," and drops explicit mention of the knowledge of the *nature* of the act. In regard to the "ability to conform" or "loss of free will" class of insanity defenses, as compared to the knowledge of wrong, the comparative frequencies are less easy to show, but in any case it should be noted that many states do not allow a defect-of-will insanity defense at all, nor has English law accepted such a doctrine.

29. Sayre (1932), in his classic study of *mens rea*, traces the evolution of criminal concepts from the early days of common law when moral judgments were explicit in applying these concepts, to the modern situation in which, whatever the moral roots of our concepts, the criminal law concepts themselves have become technical, nonmoral concepts (pp. 1016–26). Only the insanity defense, among the ones he discusses, still retains an explicit reference to moral concepts (pp. 1004–07). Hall (1960), who disagrees in certain fundamental respects with Sayre, nevertheless holds, in substance, that in regard to the concept of *mens rea* in modern law, arriving at a verdict will not, generally, require the making of moral judgments or direct, explicit

with ignorance of the law, which the ancient maxim explicitly precludes as an excuse.[30]

This leaves matters puzzling. *If* insanity does establish ignorance of wrong or of law, then this fact, far from explaining why insanity exculpates, itself requires further explanation as a basis for exculpation. Since our present quest is to clarify and make explicit the true basis of the insanity plea, we shall consider both possible meanings of the clause—ignorance of law and ignorance of morality—to see whether the paradoxes can be resolved and whether these concepts can be shown to have the ultimate exculpatory force in insanity.

Before we undertake this task, however, it should be noted that the earlier remarks about "knowledge" in a "deeper" sense[31] apply, *mutatis mutandis,* in connection with the knowledge of wrong (or "appreciation of criminality") at issue here. For nothing significantly novel emerges in this connection if one qualifies "knowledge" by speaking here of "emotional" knowledge, or "knowledge fused with affect," or "significant and appropriate experiencing," or knowledge "assimilated by the whole personality."

All these phrases, vague as they patently are, represent attempts to express the intuited fact that these cases *contrast* with cases of not knowing law or morality in the ordinary sense, the sense of "know" whose contraries are "mistake," "error," "misinformation," or lack of informa-

---

invocation of moral standards. Crimes, he says, are defined "objectively," so far as the mental state goes, in terms of the "voluntary commission of a proscribed harm." That the harm in question is legally proscribed is, ultimately, rooted in an ethical judgment. But when it comes to applying law so created, "neither the offender's conscience nor the personal code of ethics of the judge or jury can be substituted for the ethics of the penal law"—an ethics built into the principle of *mens rea* in a way that is "objective"—i.e., defined (for ethical reasons) in specific *non*-ethical terms such as intent, knowledge, and negligence (as "objectively" defined). (See his discussion in [1960], chap. III, and especially his conclusions at p. 104.) There are, perhaps, a few exceptions, aside from the insanity defense, where a judgment of criminal guilt calls for explicitly adverting to moral standards and the defendant's attitude in relation to them in doing the allegedly criminal act, e.g., criminal allegations against minors whose age is between the current minimum below which criminal culpability is absolutely excluded by law and the current minimum below which a defense of infancy cannot apply; and allegations of criminal libel, where, once again, one finds there are special reasons to justify explicit use of a moral test, such a test being generally atypical of modern law.

30. See text and notes 42 to 45, infra.

31. From text at note 21, supra, to end of Section I.

tion of any sort. For, in connection with knowledge of wrong, analogously to knowledge of fact, it is not uncharacteristic that there is no claim to error, i.e., lack of information about the moral code or law.[32] In the usage related to insanity, the point of the qualifying phrases is plainly to express awareness that something more radical is amiss—*in spite* of the presence of knowledge (in the usual sense) that the act is contrary to law and to commonly accepted moral values.

Here, analogously to the case of "not knowing the nature of the act," there is an intuitive judgment that this person's response to moral issues is that of one whose mind is irrational, and that such a person cannot be held morally responsible. Of course, in everyday English the judgment that there is this mental disability can be expressed idiomatically by saying he does not grasp "with full emotional clarity" that his act is wrong, doesn't "appreciate the criminality" of his act, doesn't "assimilate his knowledge into his total personality."[33] The legal mind, inclined on principle to seize upon traditional formulas, may take the familiar key word "knowledge," or its close cousins, as the clue to the relevant legal doctrine. Thus moral intuition is satisfied because exculpation is allowed; and the lawyer's felt need for a traditional formula is appeased, because of the availability of an idiomatic use of "know"—an idiom that here has as its real point to express the intuition that knowledge, in the ordinary, non-idiomatic sense, is *not* at issue here.

Let us, however, put aside the shift to a "deeper" sense of the words, and turn back to the basic theme here—that we have to do ultimately with *some* form of ignorance or mistake of morals or of law. What makes this approach even feebler is the fact, as has been suggested, that the traditional formulas at issue here are generally *in*culpatory in law, and not, as in the mistake of fact situation, exculpatory. Where else in the law would the claim of ignorance of morals, or ignorance of law, serve to exculpate? It is a paradox that the analytical legal minds should have felt at rest in announcing that what ultimately exculpates in insanity is some kind of unawareness of criminality! Surely this ought to be a challenge to begin inquiry, not end it. In keeping with the resolution of these pages, we shall at once begin such inquiry. We turn first to examine the issue in terms of a lack of *moral* "knowledge"; then we shall examine it in terms of ignorance of law.

32. See notes 18 and 19, supra.
33. See note 22, supra.

It has been said by one distinguished scholar that although "in modern times criminal liability is no longer based upon a moral standard when the wrongdoer is deemed to be sane, . . . [in] the case of persons who have set up the defense of insanity a moral criterion is still observed. . . ."[34] Another distinguished scholar says, "Insanity, which robs one of the power to make intelligent choice between good and evil, must negative criminal responsibility if criminality rests upon moral blameworthiness."[35] It has indeed often been asserted that the criminal law is rooted ultimately in the moral values of the society;[36] even more specifically, that the technical concept of *mens rea* in the law itself was, in its origins, a moral standard—the "wicked mind"—and that it still retains vague overtones of elements of that standard.[37]

These theses, even if true,[38] do not respond to the question we pose here, however. For although some form of moral standard may lie in the background, or may constitute the root, or may somehow pervade the assessment of criminal culpability,[39] such a standard is not directly

34. J. W. C. Turner (1936), p. 35.

35. Sayre (1932), p. 1004.

36. See note 29, supra. Also note the following: "[T]he early criminal law appears to have been well integrated with the mores of the time . . ." (Hall and Seligman, 1941, p. 644). "[C]rimes are also generally sins . . ." (Holmes, 1963, p. 100). "If as our legal moralists maintain it is important for the law to reflect common judgments of morality, it is surely even more important that it should in general reflect in its judgments on human conduct distinctions which not only underly morality, but pervade the whole of our social life. This it would fail to do if it treats men merely as alterable, predictable, curable or manipulable things" (Hart, 1968, p. 183). "It is not the penal statute that renders an act corrupt and wrongful. On the contrary, it is because of the vice in the act that the people forbid it by statute" (*People v. McLaughlin*).

37. For an extended study of the relation of *mens rea* to moral values, see Sayre (1932).

38. Of course, these theses are here broadly and vaguely stated, with no attempt at the refinement that would be necessary to refine them for purposes of serious discussion of them. But, as the text that follows indicates, we need not seriously discuss them here—they merely suggest lines of thought that are likely to occur to one at this point, but that are seen to be, upon further reflection, irrelevant to the question before us here.

39. The situation is well expressed in the Report of the Royal Commission on Capital Punishment: "Responsibility is a moral question; and there is no issue on which it is more important that the criminal law be in close accord with the moral standards of the community. There can be no pre-established harmony between the criteria of moral and of criminal responsibility, but they ought to be made to

applied—except, apparently, in the insanity defense.[40] Our question therefore still remains: Why does the law make this exception?

The natural line of answer is that insanity constitutes that special case where there is not merely a failure of moral discrimination but a positive incapacity of mind to make such discrimination. Insanity "robs one of the *power* to make intelligent choice. . . ."

But in saying even this much, we have already been compelled to abandon the theory which we set out initially to examine. That theory was that the mental illness in criminal insanity is not per se essential to exculpation, that it engenders some specific *independently* identifiable condition which defines the ultimate legal ground of exculpation. Under the hypothesis stated just above, however, we are told that what is ultimate is not merely failure to discriminate good and evil, but the mental disability.

One might argue that at least it takes *both* concepts—that there exists a mental disability, and that the disability essentially concerns the discriminating of good and evil. Let us, then, pursue this hypothesis in order to identify more specifically the scope of the disability as essential to absence of criminal responsibility.

Does *any* mental incapacity to make moral discriminations tend to exculpate? Surely not. For it might reasonably be said of a morally perverted person that he is no longer mentally capable, even assuming he once was so, of making moral discriminations. The career gangster or

---

approximate as nearly as possible. The views of ordinary men and women about the moral accountability of the insane have been gradually modified by the development of medical science, and, if the law cannot be said to have always kept pace with them it has followed them at a distance and has slowly adjusted itself to their changes. It is therefore proper and necessary to enquire from time to time whether the doctrine of criminal responsibility, as laid down by the common law and applied by the courts, takes due account of contemporary moral standards and of modern advances in medical knowledge about the effects of mental abnormality on personality and behavior" (p. 99). This, of course, is not at all to say that moral standards are invoked directly in the typical judgment of guilt or innocence, or that the defendant's moral judgment of his conduct as wrong is a necessary condition, generally, of his being guilty in law.

40. Turner (1936) adds later to his comment quoted in the text at note 34, supra: "It was stated above that in modern times criminal liability is no longer based upon a moral standard when the wrongdoer is deemed to be sane. The case of a wrongdoer who is insane has presented problems which cannot be said yet to have been solved" (p. 48).

criminal—the "hired gun," the inveterate swindler or forger, the longtime drug hustler, the professional gambler-cheater—these may be persons so inured to crime, so perverted or dulled, so selfish or callous, as a result of their life of crime, that they are mentally incapable of acting on the moral discriminations that concern the criminal law.

One is inclined to say at once—and correctly—"That is not what we mean; that is not the right sort of incapacity." For we do not consider the incapacity that arises out of chronic moral depravity as exculpatory—quite the contrary. But then it follows that mental incapacity to discriminate morally is not, per se, what has exculpatory force. Something more specific yet seems to be at issue. Can we express, then, that specific kind of mental incapacity to discriminate morally that is at issue in insanity, and that *does* have some kind of ultimate exculpatory implication?

Is it not because phrases like "insanity," "mental illness," "mental derangement," "mental disease," and "unsoundness of mind" point to a lack of capacity for rationality rather than to depravity that they carry exculpatory implications? Mere lack of capacity for moral discrimination is not what ultimately is exculpatory; but when irrationality of mind, rather than ingrained depravity or moral apathy, is the reason for that incapacity, then indeed it does seem pointless to ascribe moral or criminal responsibility in that respect.

The concept of irrationality and its exculpatory import need analysis and receive it elsewhere.[41] It is in any case sufficiently familiar and traditional in this context, however, to warrant our exploring the import of the thesis stated above, rather than pausing to analyze the word itself. The coherence of legal doctrine that at once emerges in the light of this thesis is substantial. The impairment of capacity for governing conduct rationally embraces within one concept the traditional (and conceptually troublesome) insanity clauses such as lack of "knowledge of the nature of the act," lack of "knowledge of the wrongness of the act," and lack of "free will" or of "capacity to conform to law." These phrases all can be seen as attempts to express aspects of one central phenomenon: the serious impairment of the power to engage in conduct governed by reason.

Thus, in summary, the analysis of the theory that insanity ultimately exculpates in criminal law because it entails failure of moral judgment cannot be supported. Even common sense sees lack of moral perception as exculpatory only in those cases where common sense tacitly and intui-

41. Chapter 14, infra; and Fingarette (1972), chap. IV.

tively looks behind the moral failure and sees that the failure is rooted in irrationality, in the incapacity for rational conduct. Otherwise, failure of moral discrimination is positively *in*culpatory.

III: "NOT KNOWING THE ACT IS WRONG": IGNORANCE OF LAW

We have now seen that mere failure to distinguish good from evil, or even incapacity to do so, is neither in law nor in common sense an independent and ultimate ground of exculpation. Each requires a finding of irrationality before exculpation can ultimately be justified. We turn now, therefore, to the other interpretation that might prima facie be suggested by the thesis that it is insane absence of "knowledge of wrong" or "appreciation of criminality" that exculpates. This is, of course, the idea that we can understand the ultimate exculpatory ignorance in insanity as, specifically, ignorance or mistake of *law*.

Of course, the first obstacle to this interpretation is the ancient and still viable maxim, *Ignorantia juris neminem excusat* ("Ignorance of the law is no excuse"). Here again, then, the theory of exculpation in question seems to fly in the face of the law. There are, however, exceptions to this maxim, or—if one prefers to put it otherwise—the maxim needs to be expressed more restrictively before it can serve as a *rule* rather than a suggestive principle.[42] Can it be that when we take these necessary qualifications into account, insane unawareness of criminality would fall outside the scope of the maxim? Would such unawareness be, moreover, positively exculpatory?

A quick review of the exceptions to the maxim will reveal that insane unawareness of law, *if* viewed as "ignorance" or "mistake," could not be an exception but, on the contrary, would be typical of that very *ignorantia* to which the maxim is centrally directed and which is declared *non*-exculpating.

One class of exceptions to the maxim includes, characteristically, mistakes about property law, and it can be illustrated as follows: Since larceny requires that one (knowingly) take another's property, I am not guilty of larceny if, because of my misunderstanding of the law of property, I take someone else's property in the bona fide belief that title had been transferred to me. This mistake of law *does* serve as a basis of

---

42. For systematic discussions of this issue, see: Perkins (1939); Hall and Seligman (1941); Keedy (1908); Stumberg (1937); Hall (1960), pp. 376–408; and Winfield (1943).

defense to a criminal charge.[43] Distinctive of this class of exculpable exceptions is the fact that the ignorance in question is ignorance of law as to some material *element* of the crime. It cannot excuse to be ignorant of the law defining the very offense alleged, e.g., the law that defines and prohibits larceny.[44]

The insanity plea typically does not present facts suited to be included in this major category of exceptions to the maxim. For in the typical successful insanity defense, where the defendant argues that because of mental disease he did not know (or appreciate) the wrongness (or criminality) of his act, the law in question is typically the very law defining the alleged offense. The insane homicide, for example, is defended as having lacked appreciation of the criminality of homicide, the very offense charged.[45]

Lambert[46] typifies another important category of exceptions to the maxim. The successful defense in *Lambert* was based on ignorance of the very law that defined the crime alleged. Virginia Lambert, an ex-felon, did not know of the law requiring an ex-felon to register upon residing three or more days in Los Angeles. The Supreme Court declared that ignorance

43. "If *A* thinking he have title to the horse of *B* seiseth it as his own this makes it no felony but a trespass because there is a pretense of title" (Hale, *Pleas of the Crown*, p. 508. See Perkins, 1957, p. 817).

44. Perkins (1939) presents the following summary and representative quotations: " 'It is very true,' said the Alabama court, 'that to constitute a crime there must be both an act and an intent. But, in such a case as this, it is enough if the act be knowingly and intentionally committed. The law makes the act an offence, and does not go farther and require proof that the offenders intended by the prohibited act, to violate the law.' The same idea has been repeated in different forms. The intent to commit crime 'is not the intent to violate the law but the intentional doing the act which is a violation of law.' It is an intent to do what the law calls a crime, whatever the actor himself may call it. A word of caution, however, may well be added at this point. If for guilt of a particular offense, some special mental element is required, such as that the prohibited deed be done 'corruptly,' the law itself does not apply the label 'crime' to such a deed in the absence of the required mental element. Hence the innocent intent to perform such a deed in the bona fide belief of its propriety is not an intent to commit crime" (p. 40).

45. Indeed, if the case were one of theft, and if there were a claim of mistake of the kind indicated in the text, e.g., a mistake as to ownership of an item of personal property taken by the defendant, this mistake would serve as defense to a theft charge, and there would be no need of the insanity defense. In any case, it is plain that the insanity defense can succeed, will exculpate completely, even if the "mistake" in question concerns (as it almost always does) the very crime charged.

46. *Lambert v. California.*

of that law *was* an excuse because Lambert's failure to register, though
contrary to a police regulation in this case, was an act essentially innocent
in itself (*mala prohibita* rather than *mala in se*), and because there was not
adequate notification to the defendant of her statutory duty to register,
and finally because failure to register was a "passive" omission rather than
positive commission of an act. All of this is, typically, in direct contrast to
the insane defendant's criminal acts. Criminally insane acts are typically
acts that embody a blatant and generally acknowledged wrong, *malum in
se*—killing, arson, rape, assault, larceny—crimes of commission rather than
omission. It is with crimes such as these that *Lambert* was expressly meant
to contrast.[47]

Here lie the boundaries of the maxim, then, unchallenged by the
courts: at one pole, a law may be so minor and buried in regulatory
material, and directed to "acts" that are so passive and on their face so
harmless and innocent, that even "strict liability" will not overcome the
exculpatory force of bona fide ignorance of that law; and at the other
pole, the law may be directed to an act so universally recognized as illegal
and immoral, so paradigmatically purposeful and *malum in se,* that the
excuse of ignorance or mistake as to the law simply cannot be entertained.
In the trial of criminal insanity, the crime at issue and the criminality or
law of which the defendant was purportedly insanely unknowing are
characteristically at the latter pole.

The supposition was discussed in Section I that the specific role of a
showing of insanity might be to show the *nonculpability of origin* of some
ignorance or mistake of fact. This approach has even less plausibility here,
for the distinctive force of the maxim "Ignorance of the law is no excuse"
lies largely in the fact that it declares such ignorance to be non-excusing
even if it was nonculpable.

Since, in any case, the defendant invoking this clause typically acknowledges that he *did* know that his act was contrary to law, the theory that it

47. Hall (1960) says of the "simple valuations expressed in penal law" that "it
does not require a college education or extraordinary sensitivity to understand that it
is wrong to kill, rape, or rob" (p. 96). Hall, Livingston, and Seligman (1941) say in
this connection: "But a defendant's mistake as to the content of the criminal law
itself (i.e., whether certain acts are criminal) would not ordinarily affect his moral
guilt. For the early criminal law appears to have been well integrated with the mores
of the time, out of which it arose as 'custom.' . . . Accordingly, from the earliest cases
to the time of Blackstone, no *general* defense of mistake of law was recognized" (p.
644).

is "ignorance of law" that ultimately exculpates in the typical case of insane "not knowing the act was wrong" fails utterly.

It must be concluded [48] that the insanity defense *cannot* derive its exculpatory force from the general *mens rea* defenses of ignorance or mistake of law (or of fact).

It was early held that ignorance or mistake of fact establishes a kind of "involuntariness" in law. We shall explore at length, immediately below, the involuntariness concept in relation to insanity. It can be said at once, however, that the preceding discussions have shown that at least "involuntariness" rooted in ignorance or mistake is not at issue in insanity. This is so since, as we have now seen, there is no such mistake or ignorance in the first place.

In summary, the basic truth about the "not knowing" and "not appreciating" clauses is that they do not in themselves express an ultimately exculpatory ground. Rather, they in turn derive such exculpatory significance as they do have in the insanity context from the reference back to their source in mental disability, in that more radical condition of mind that amounts to impairment of capacity for rational control of conduct. The full and distinctive significance of this condition of irrationality, which makes ascriptions of localized error, mistake, or ignorance pointless, has been lost from sight because the *words* of the idioms have been suggestive of the legal language of "ignorance."

48. There are other categories of exceptions to the maxim that ignorance of the law is no excuse, but they are of little interest here, being plainly irrelevant to the insane person's unawareness of the criminality of his conduct. Such exceptions include, for example, certain cases where the law is unclear, where official but erroneous advice as to the law has been given, where a specific knowledge of, or intent to violate, the law is required as an element of the crime, etc. These exceptions are reviewed in detail in Perkins (1939).

4

Insanity and Involuntariness

I

The insanity defense and other exculpatory claims based on mental malfunction are at times discussed as if their exculpatory force lay ultimately
in establishing that the behavior was not voluntary.[1] "Involuntariness" is,
of course, a standard, general defense.[2] If insanity, or some major form of
it, entailed (nonculpable) involuntariness, this would be a ground for
exculpation. But it is the thesis of this study that insanity involves an
independent ground of exculpation, and it is the thesis of this chapter
that, in any case, involuntariness is typically *not* entailed by insanity.

1. See, generally, *State v. Harrison* (1892), annotated; *State v. Maish* (1947),
annotated; Keedy (1952); Weihofen (1954), pp. 81 ff.; Davidson (1956); and Goldstein (1967), chap. 5, with listing of relevant cases in note 1. A representative
statement is H. L. A. Hart's: "What is crucial is that those whom we punish should
have, when they acted, the normal capacities, physical and mental, for doing what
the law requires and abstaining from what it forbids, and a fair opportunity to
exercise these capacities. Where these are absent as they are in different ways in the
varied cases of accident, mistake, paralysis, reflex action, coercion, insanity, etc., the
moral protest is that it is morally wrong to punish because 'he could not have helped
it' or 'he could not have done otherwise' or 'he had no real choice' (1961, p. 45). In
Brawner, Judge Leventhal said: "The concept of lack of 'free will' is both the root of
origin of the insanity defense and the line of its growth" (p. 29). One is compelled to
add that this is a highly dubious historical reading.
2. Some would refer to the claim of lack of voluntariness as a *mens rea* defense,
some as denial of the *actus reus*. Fitzgerald, in his discussion of "Voluntary and

44

The concepts of voluntariness and involuntariness have been the subject of legal and philosophical controversy, and the usage of these and related terms in law is notably variable.

One can, of course, speak very generally about the "will," and about frustrating the will, or rendering it inoperative, destroying its power, overcoming it, or simply about its absence in relation to certain behavior or occurrences. All this is general, vague, and irreducibly metaphorical and

---

Involuntary Acts" (1961), stresses the "very important distinction between what a man does voluntarily and what he does under compulsion, duress, necessity . . ." and, by contrast, a "totally different distinction: the distinction between normal conduct and involuntary movements of the body, such as the beating of one's heart, spasms, what one does in sleep, etc. In these cases there is no question of choice at all." Fitzgerald adds immediately, however, that "the voluntary act theory blurs this important difference . . ." (pp. 12–13). A full discussion of various kinds of involuntary behavior due to physical disorders and lapses of consciousness, and in relation to criminal liability, is found in Fox (1963). For further discussions, generally, of duress and related defenses, see: Hall (1960), chap. 12; Newman and Weitzer (1957); *Russell* (1964), pp. 86–95; *State v. Lee*, annotated; *R. v. Hudson* (1971). An advantage of seeing the involuntary act as a case of no *actus reus*, as viewed by proponents of this view, is that involuntariness establishes the defense even in cases of strict liability (*Kilbride v. Lake* [1962], discussed in 25 *Modern Law Review* 741 [1962]). Among those holding that involuntariness is now held in law to preclude the *actus reus* are Williams (1961), p. 12: "An act is a *voluntary* movement" (emphasis in original). However, Williams (1961) adds his opinion later that the "requirement of will" could "just as well be put on the ground of absence of *mens rea*" (p. 14). Perkins (1957) says: "An act must be a willed movement. . . . This is essential to the *actus reus* rather than to the mens rea" (p. 660, emphasis in original). Hart (1968) says in connection with "cases of unconsciousness, automatism, reflexes and the like" that "both the ordinary man and the lawyer might well insist . . . that in these cases there is not 'really' a human action at all and certainly nothing for which anyone should be made criminally responsible however 'strict' legal responsibility may be" (pp. 106–107). The ALI Model Penal Code places voluntariness within the *actus reus* rather than the *mens rea* (Sec. 2.01). Hall (1960), on the other hand, speaks of "Mens rea, a fusion of cognition and volition [as] the mental state expressed in the *voluntary* commission of a proscribed harm" (p. 104, emphasis in original). Fox (1963) calls this "one of the most difficult areas" (p. 642). At bottom, however, the issue of direct concern to us here will not be the distinction between involuntariness and *non*voluntariness, or the classification of involuntariness as relevant to the *actus reus* or to the *mens rea*, but whether the sorts of facts that can show involuntariness *or* nonvoluntariness (which acknowledgedly *can* serve as defenses) are the sorts of facts at issue in insanity or other defenses based on mental disabilities that are "psychogenic." We shall see that only where the mental disability is identifiably rooted in physical disability is there overlap.

idiomatic in ways that are immensely difficult to analyze with a clarity adequate to the purposes of the law. Such idioms, though used at times in the law, are notable sources of confusion and controversy.

If one seeks a precise legal definition or analysis of the concept, one seeks in vain.[3] In one of the more recent systematic and quasi-authoritative approaches, the American Law Institute's Model Penal Code, there is presented[4] merely a list of categories of nonvoluntary acts. Moreover, the list is not systematic but logically heterogeneous, consisting of three specific items and one very general catchall. The latter in effect substitutes the "effort or determination of the actor, conscious or habitual," for the traditional term "the will," and says that a bodily movement not a product of such effort or determination is not voluntary. If these words in the Model Penal Code version had an established or specified meaning that would enable us to discriminate issues in the problems we face here, the formula might be justified. But when we turn to the relevant portion of the Model Penal Code test of insanity, we are faced with paradox. How are we expected to view an insane person who is characterized as lacking "substantial ability to conform his behavior to the law"?[5] Is that person to be viewed as one whose act was not voluntary, i.e., "not a product" of his "conscious or habitual effort or determination"? But such a reading of

3. Fitzgerald (1961, p. 28) in his analysis of the topic concludes that "The common quality connecting all these types of [involuntary] behavior would seem to be inability to control one's bodily movements. . . ." But he earlier (see note 2, supra) distinguished involuntary from nonvoluntary behavior (see notes 7 and 15, infra). Moreover, he does not include insanity (or such medical categories as "functional" psychoses) among the sources of conduct that is not voluntary (or involuntary). Finally, he stresses that the way the law treats or should treat involuntariness, especially in relation to *liability*, will depend upon the purposes and principles of different branches of law (pp. 27–28). Thus his analysis purports to provide a definitive answer only in relation to a certain subclass of "involuntary" actions. The problem of providing a generalized account of "involuntariness" is certainly not solved in the Model Penal Code (see infra beginning at note 4).

4. At sec. 2.01 (2): "The following are not voluntary acts within the meaning of this section: (a) a reflex or convulsion; (b) a bodily movement during unconsciousness or sleep; (c) conduct during hypnosis or resulting from hypnotic suggestion; (d) a bodily movement that otherwise is not a product of the effort or determination of the actor, either conscious or habitual."

5. Where resulting from "mental disease." See the ALI Model Penal Code test of insanity, Sec. 4.01: "A person is not responsible for criminal conduct if at the time of such conduct as a result of mental disease or defect he lacks substantial capacity either to appreciate the criminality of his conduct or to conform his conduct to the requirements of law."

the words is quite strained. The fact is that the criminally insane act is one that typically seems more naturally describable as a "product of conscious or habitual effort or determination" than the contrary. On this natural reading of the voluntariness test, however, the conduct, though it might be held insane in the terms of the Model Penal Code definition, is in the terms of that same Code plainly voluntary. This leads in turn to the conclusion that what is distinctively exculpatory about insane "incapacity to conform to the requirements of law" is *not* (contrary to what the words suggest) involuntariness. Rather, it must lie somewhere else in the concept of mental malfunction. Whatever meaning "incapacity to conform" may have here (and it now becomes mysterious), that meaning cannot be "not voluntary."

Of course, the Code might be taken to require that in such cases of insanity it should be a matter of legal "construction" that the act "manifested no conscious or habitual effort or determination." In the latter case the "involuntariness" in insanity would not be a fact demonstrated by analysis of the concepts but a doctrinal dogma arranged by an ad hoc and patently inappropriate reading of the words to achieve the desired verbal result.

Turning from the Model Penal Code to the common law, one finds that the terms *voluntary* and *involuntary* have been used in a variety of ways whose links have not always been made clear or explicit. One early use has already been mentioned: "[I] n some cases *ignorantia facti* doth excuse, for such an ignorance many times makes the act itself morally involuntary."[6] We shall pass by this use as irrelevant, without further comment beyond that contained in Chapter 3.

Beyond this, "involuntariness" is used on occasion in the criminal law in reference to physical compulsion, epileptic seizures, somnambulism, "unconsciousness,"[7] necessity, coercion or duress in connection with

6. Hale, *Pleas of the Crown*, p. 42.

7. As an early example of physical compulsion amounting to involuntariness, Turner cites Hale, *Pleas of the Crown*, at p. 434, where the situation is one in which "*B* holds a weapon and *A*, against *B*'s will, seizes his hand, and the weapon, and therewith stabs *C* . . ." (Turner, 1936, pp. 31, 37). In regard to epilepsy, see: *People v. Decina*; and *People v. Freeman*. In regard to sleepwalking and somnambulism, see the discussion in Fox (1963); see also *Fain v. Comm*; *Bradley v. State*. On "unconsciousness," see generally Fox (1963); *People v. Hardy*; and *People v. Freeman*. See also the Model Penal Code at 2.01 (2) quoted in note 4, supra, as well as the cases included under the rubric of "automatism," etc., in the Model Penal Code Discussion at pp. 120–123.

criminal defenses,[8] and coercion in connection with police maltreatment in obtaining confessions or admissions.[9]

Under such circumstances one may well wonder whether anything can be lost by still another extension of the use of *involuntary*. Why not also include behavior that is the result of mental malfunction or disease, or at least such behavior if the disease can be shown to have caused an "irresistible impulse," or a "loss of self-control," or an "incapacity to conform behavior to the requirements of the law"? Indeed, these latter idioms seem on their face to imply involuntariness.

No attempt will be made here to present a definitive generalized analysis of the meaning of *voluntary, nonvoluntary,* or *involuntary* in legal usage or in any other usage.[10] Fortunately, the needs of the present inquiry can be met by adopting a different and more pluralistic strategy.

8. See note 74, infra.

9. "The trial court found that the tax payments were made by respondents involuntarily under duress, coercion, and compulsion . . ." (*Crown Zellerbach Corp. v. State*, 1941). Here the court is plainly using the word *involuntarily* in the sense (as we define it) of *nonvoluntary*—an example of the ambiguous usage that is so common. Not only in civil law, but in such criminal law contexts as that of receiving confessions, the language of voluntariness shifts in meaning to accord with context, and *involuntariness* is used to include what we have called *nonvoluntariness*. Thus in *Rogers v. People* (1939) the court said, "The authorities are not in accord as to when . . . evidence is given voluntarily and when involuntarily. Surrounding facts and circumstances receive a different interpretation in different jurisdictions" (p. 456). And more specifically, for example, it was said that "A plea of guilty is involuntary when made under such inducements as would cause an innocent person to confess guilt" (*Pennington v. Smith*, pp. 812–813, citing *Wigmore on Evidence*). Such a test of involuntariness is plainly different from (and weaker than) that used, for example, in the defense of coercion.

10. The Model Penal Code makes no pretense of a systematic or unitary definition of nonvoluntariness of behavior for purposes of assessing criminal responsibility. According to the American Law Institute, *Model Penal Code*, Proposed Official Draft (1962), Article 2—General Principles of Liability, Section 2.01 (2), the following are not voluntary acts:

    (a) a reflex or convulsion

    (b) a bodily movement during unconsciousness [coma?] or sleep;

    (c) conduct during hypnosis or resulting from hypnotic suggestion;

    (d) a bodily movement that otherwise is not a product of the effort or determination of the act or, either conscious or habitual. . . .

For brevity, we use common usage and refer hereafter to both nonvoluntary and involuntary behavior as involuntary; where the distinction is relevant, however, this will be noted explicitly. See note 2, supra, for these distinctions.

The inappropriateness of attributing the exculpatory force of insanity to involuntariness can be demonstrated, without such a general theory of voluntariness, by showing the following: (1) The language and idioms of "loss of control," though at times aptly used in relation to insane conduct, are idioms that are perfectly consistent with the act's being legally *either* involuntary *or* voluntary. Since the idioms are entirely ambiguous on this issue, their frequent use in connection with insane conduct does not of itself imply that insane acts of this kind ought to be classified as involuntary. (2) The substantive evidence sought in connection with insane "loss of control" conduct is of a radically different kind than that sought in all other criminal law contexts where involuntariness is at issue. One can, for example, use the single word *involuntary* to characterize both an epileptic seizure and an insane homicide. But the evidence in each case is so different in nature and logical structure from the other as to strongly suggest that one is using a single word to do duty for what, from the standpoint of criminal law, are two very different grounds of exculpation. (3) The relation between the two notions "involuntariness" and "insanity" has been expressed often in a (putative) medical context, in which the "disease model" and related metaphors and analogies have suggested a close connection between the two; yet "involuntariness" and "insanity" are notions of law, rooted not in medicine but in the common law conception of man, and (as it happens) the two notions are not closely related at all in sound legal usage.

II: THE IDIOM OF "INVOLUNTARINESS" AND THE LAW

There can be no "proof" that a word ought not to be usable in a certain way; on the other hand, insofar as the rules for use of a key word are grounded in reason and are not arbitrary, the aim of this section is to illustrate how the use of idioms of loss of self-control do not systematically imply nonvoluntariness or involuntariness in the context of assessing criminal responsibility.[11] This is important to realize because there is no doubt that idioms of loss of self-control are doubtless often used, *and used*

---

11. For an analysis of these issues in the same spirit as the following, see Fingarette (1972), pp. 158–172. Though there is a certain overlap between that discussion and the present one, the present discussion differs in (a) being briefer in analysis of the idiom and language aspects, and (b) going much farther in setting the issues in the larger perspective suggested by (2) and (3) in the preceding paragraph of the text above.

aptly, in connection with insane conduct. This idiomatic usage unquestionably encourages the tendency to think that the conduct is in a relevant legal sense not voluntary. This, in turn, seems to provide an easy and direct answer to the question, "Why are the insane not responsible?"

Fortunately, we need only explore a few clear-cut illustrative uses of such idioms in order to make explicit what have, tacitly, been the relevant elements of meaning when we use these idioms.

"I couldn't help myself" is used aptly, for example, in situations ranging from the most obviously voluntary to the most obviously involuntary. At one extreme: *"I couldn't help myself* from doing it; it gave me such pleasure because the child seemed so eager to have the toy, and was so delighted when I gave it to her." No court would consider this to amount to involuntariness in defense against a larceny charge. At the other extreme: *"I couldn't help myself*; his sheer strength forced my arm back." Assuming the facts as stated, this is a clear case of involuntariness. The idiom "I couldn't help myself" thus provides no basis, per se, for distinguishing in the context of criminal responsibility the voluntary from the involuntary. It takes only a reasonable fluency in the language to imagine a number of illustrative and apt uses of this idiom, ranging along the spectrum from the most obvious through the intermediate and borderline cases of involuntariness and voluntariness in criminal law.

"I lost control—I couldn't prevent myself." Was it because I had found his ideas so unpalatably snobbish and racist that at last I had become annoyed enough to respond with a personal insult that provoked a fight? It is, then, perfectly proper English, and quite apt, to say that I lost my self-control. But what I did was plainly voluntary in law in the context of assessing criminal responsibility. Or did I "lose control" in the sense that I was dizzy and faint, physically unable to keep from falling and injuring a bystander in my fall? In that case my behavior was, in that same legal context, involuntary. One might add, by way of legally relevant illustration of this same idiom, the case of provocation. Provocation, as a successful defense in homicide, establishes three facts: (1) the defendant, having been provoked, "lost his self-control"; (2) he was criminally responsible for at least voluntary manslaughter; and (3) by necessary implication from the second fact, his action was, in law, voluntary (though in part excusable).[12]

It is unnecessary to explore here every variant of these idioms. The principle is clear; the variety of illustrative uses and minor linguistic

12. Perkins (1957), p. 42. *Archbold* (1973), pars. 2501–2509.

variants is indefinitely large. The essence is that these idioms are in fact entirely ambiguous on the issue of voluntariness in law; in themselves, even assuming they are aptly used, they have no weight with respect to the assessment in law of voluntariness.

It may seem that the preceding discussion of the idioms of informal, lay discourse is misdirected. The law, one might argue, should rely on the presumably unambiguous terms of medicine or science generally, not on the common idiom. Do not "mental disease," "irresistible impulse," and "compulsion" necessarily imply "involuntary"? As to this it should be recalled that the reliance on medical terms to settle legal issues in the area of mental malfunction has been criticized again and again by the courts.[13] And related to this is the fact that the common law concept of the voluntary derives from the common store of morally oriented notions about human conduct, not from technical and esoteric notions of science. Nevertheless, the implications of this more esoteric terminology will be explored after we have reviewed the typical structure of evidence in insanity, and have compared it with the structure of evidence in all other criminal law assessments of involuntariness.

III: INVOLUNTARINESS: THE NATURE OF THE EVIDENCE

It has already been briefly noted in Chapter 2, and it will be only slightly elaborated here, that in every criminal law use of "involuntariness" as a defense—excepting, of course, the uses we here question—the evidentiary structure of fact is simple and its significance immediate. The coma, the epileptic seizure, the faint, the use of superior physical force to compel, the clear and believable threat of imminent grave injury—these are very different forms of externally or internally caused, physically or psychically grounded, authentic involuntariness in law. But they all share in this: once the few simple and (in principle) observable elements essential to the defense are established, their significance—the exculpatory involuntariness they manifest—typically lies on their face. Of course, the court may on occasion lack direct eyewitness proof of the facts; or the significance of the facts may on occasion be challenged by reference to exceptional

13. For example, Judge Leventhal took note of this persistent problem in *Brawner*, when he said, "A principal reason for our decision to depart from the Durham rule is the undesirable characteristic . . . of undue dominance by the experts giving testimony" in what, he said, were essentially ethical and legal questions. The underlying problem, he said, was identified, with stress on different facets, in the cases of *Carter, Blocker,* and *Washington (Brawner,* pp. 981–982).

circumstances. But the model, and in real life very often the actuality, is one in which a few simple observations have an import that is self-evident.

The situation is just the contrary where the person is conscious but irrational, as in insanity. Here the structure of fact that establishes the condition is in principle complex. In insanity the data required for a model proof derive from many sources, times, and places, and are provided by expert testimony in addition to lay testimony. If only a few simple observation reports are available, they are almost necessarily ambiguous as to the presence of insanity. Even where there is agreement as to these facts, as is often the case, immediacy of inference to a conclusion of insanity is the exception, and probably suspect, rather than the rule in a well-conducted criminal trial.[14] The judgment of insanity requires thoughtful deliberateness, since it is an overall assessment of complex characteristics and workings of a man's mind. The judgment of involuntariness is typically in profound contrast: Was the defendant in a coma? Was there an order backed by a gun at his head? Was he physically constrained by some person or thing?

Such general considerations as the preceding suggest that when we have to do with what we may call insane defects in self-control, we are dealing with something substantively very different from any of the things we deal with in connection with the usual defense of involuntariness.

The same point can be viewed from a slightly different and revealing angle. Viewed from the standpoint of involuntariness as strictly conceived[15] in criminal law, the conduct one sees in insanity seems to be a model of *voluntary* conduct. It is (typically) purposeful, intentional, and

14. The *facts* are always complex, but unfortunately they can too often be alluded to in certifications or in testimony that consist merely of a few conclusory labels. For example: "We conclude as the result of our examinations and observations [which are not in any form presented] that Mr. Kent is mentally competent to understand the nature of the proceedings against him and to consult properly with counsel in his own defense. It is our opinion that he is suffering from a mental disease at the present time, Schizophrenic Reaction, Chronic Undifferentiated Type; that he was suffering from this mental disease on or about June 6 and 12, and September 2, 1961; and the criminal acts with which he is charged, if committed by him, were the product of this disease. He is not suffering from mental deficiency" (quoted in Arens, 1974, pp. 64–65).

15. That is, movements under physical compulsion or while in a coma, rather than conduct influenced by threats or other psychological pressures. "There is, it is true, a very important distinction between what a man does voluntarily and what he does under compulsion, duress, necessity, etc. . . . But there is a totally different

effectively executed; it is often premeditated, planned, and prepared; and it is not infrequently tenaciously and ingeniously pursued in spite of external obstacles.

The facts in some instances of insane criminal conduct, particularly in some types of paranoid states or agitated, destructive depressions, suggest a wilfulness reaching passionate and stubborn intensity. But passionate intensity has not in itself served in criminal law as proof of involuntariness. On the contrary, passionate wilfulness may evidence a morally culpable failure of "self-restraint," and it generally establishes in law the *voluntariness* of the act, not its involuntariness.

In sum, in the above comparisons of involuntariness and insanity, the structure of fact and inference, and the substantive nature of the facts, all reveal dramatic differences, *not* similarities, as soon as we turn from words and idioms to look at the concrete realities.

It has been stressed in the immediately preceding discussion that the insane "loss of self-control," by contrast with the strictly involuntary act, is very often aware and purposeful—but then, so also are certain acts that are *"non*voluntary," i.e., acts done under coercion, necessity, and provocation.[16] Can we not infer, then, that awareness and purposiveness may be compatible with action that is not voluntary, and is so in some either fully or partly exculpatory sense?

Here we must bring to bear in a more specific way the earlier general remarks made in reference to simplicity and complexity. In coercion, necessity, and provocation, the integrity of mind of the defendant is not challenged; his mind is not internally analyzed and characterized in its complex inner relationships. He is viewed, in impersonal terms, as the "standard" reasonable man, the citizen responsible to law. However, in this group of defenses an immediate, urgent, readily identified, and highly defined motive to unlawful conduct, peculiar to an objectively defined situation, becomes legally relevant. It becomes legally relevant because its

---

distinction: the distinction between normal conduct and involuntary movements of the body, such as the beating of one's heart, spasms, what one does in sleep, etc. In these cases there is no question of choice at all. Now the voluntary act theory blurs this important difference . . ." (Fitzgerald, 1961, pp. 12–13). "Defences like duress or coercion refer not to involuntary *movements*, but, as Austin himself emphasized, to other, quite different ways in which an *action* may fail to be voluntary; here the *action* may not be the outcome of the agent's free choice, though the *movements* of the body are not in any way involuntary" (Hart, [1961b], p. 37). See note 2, supra.

16. See note 15, supra.

immediacy, extreme intensity, and universal efficacy is such that *any* person, i.e., any *reasonable* and *law-abiding* person, may be expected to succumb at least momentarily.[17] If we speak here of the victim's "will" being "dominated," or momentarily "overcome," even though he intentionally acts as he does, it is because, set over against this isolated intent arising out of a rare and isolated motive, we ascribe to him the "standard" mind and will, the mind and will of a law-abiding and rational person, i.e., the mind of the man who understands the law and wills not to defy it. Here, then, as in the cases of coma or physical restraint, we have simple, immediate, impersonally defined circumstances whose significance leaps to the mind's eye. There is no essential analysis of the internal complexities and individuality of the mind and personality of the defendant.

What becomes of the concept of nonvoluntary conduct when the presumption of the rational, responsible person no longer holds, when the mind is internally in fundamental disarray, when it can no longer respond rationally to circumstance (and, in particular, to law)? We can now see that to speak of a lack of voluntary conduct here is to wrench the concept from its very roots, to apply a concept that in *every other* criminal law use presumes an integral, "standard" mind faced with impersonally defined constraints. To shift to the context in which the supposition of the rational mind itself is questioned is in effect to shift to a context in which "voluntary" and "nonvoluntary" no longer have their usual application, for now a basic *precondition* of their usual use is lacking. Of course, the

17. Provocation, if it existed, must be such as would provoke a reasonable man, not merely the defendant personally, if it is to serve in mitigation (*Rivers v. State* [1918]; *R. v. Lesbine* [1914]). With regard to duress, the repeated refrain is that this excuses only where the apprehension is "well-grounded" (*D'Aquino v. U.S.* [1951]; *R. v. Hudson* [1971]). And see also a recent case dealing with the rare defense of necessity, related as it is in the present context to the defense of coercion: *U.S. v. Kroncke* (1972). See generally, on coercion, *State v. Lee*, annotated. See note 1, supra. Fitzgerald's formulation is somewhat different from ours, but the implication in the present context is the same. He says: "Duress is similar to necessity. The accused is faced with a choice of breaking the law or being injured by the person coercing him to break the law. It differs from physical compulsion, where the accused has no choice. In duress the accused's plea is that he had *no fair* choice" (1962, p. 126). See also on this point Smith and Hogan (1973, pp. 164–168); here the element of choice, and hence the distinction from physical compulsion, is also stressed, but the lack of courage rather than the lack of "fair" choice is remarked. The point made, in effect, is that the choice of refusing to obey the threat calls for more courage than people ordinarily possess; hence the excusing force of coercion in non-homicide crimes.

words could be *given* some new and partially analogous meaning in this new context. No one has ever clearly done this in the law, because the issue has remained obscure. Moreover, such a verbal move would be likely to continue to obscure the fundamental differences between nonvoluntariness and irrationality. It would seem far more helpful to mark the radical differences by using different terms rather than to purchase a specious terminological economy by use of radically ambiguous language.

IV: INVOLUNTARINESS: "DISEASE" MODELS AND METAPHORS

The tendency to become preoccupied with certain analogies between irrational behavior and nonvoluntary behavior has been vastly reinforced by certain pseudo-analogies that easily take root. The chief of these is probably the pseudo-analogy based on viewing the concept of "mental disease" as a reference to a reified "external" cause acting "on" the mind.[18] The power of this apparently scientific model, and of related pseudo-analogies, has been so pervasive that it is essential to explore the issues in order to dissolve the illusions.

The problems to be raised here can become perhaps overly complex— too much so in the end for the needs or interests of lawyer and judge. Indeed, this is the very fact that is basic to the present thesis. For it is the argument of this chapter that in criminal law the assimilation of insanity to involuntariness and nonvoluntariness is rooted, at best, in dubious, immensely complex and obscure connections, and is therefore bound to remain a locus of trouble for the law.[19] It is hoped that the analysis that follows does throw light upon the issues. Yet if the reader sees the

18. "When the disease is the propelling, uncontrollable power. . . . If his mental, moral, and bodily strength is subjugated and pressed to an involuntary service, it is immaterial whether it is done by his disease, or by another man, or a brute or any physical force of art or nature set in operation without fault on his part" (*State v. Pike*, p. 441). "If some controlling disease was, in truth, the acting power within him which he could not resist, then he will not be responsible" (*Reg. v. Oxford*, p. 950).

19. It should be noted that we have been discussing insanity here, not disabilities of mind in general. There are disabilities of mind whose manifestations include behavior that in law is, quite strictly speaking, involuntary. Some of these are included at times in the category "unconsciousness" or "automatism." This would include bodily movements without mental content or meaning, but due to brain damage, such as arteriosclerosis or "stroke," or to physical brain trauma, or to epileptic convulsion, or to syncope, or to brain tumor, or due to neural pathology resulting in uncontrollable movements, or due to incapacitating effects of drugs or to

magnitude of the shift, and the conceptual tangle into which it quickly leads, then the most essential point has been made.

It often seems to be tacitly assumed that once one introduces the concept of "disease," and links certain conduct to disease, this at one stroke establishes involuntariness [20] in the disease-related behavior. Commonly, those who rely on this presupposition seem to have either of two forms of the presupposition in mind.

One, the more general, amounts usually to the supposition that if an act is the "product" or "effect" or "symptom" of a "mental disease," then that is not a voluntary act—the "victim" of the disease "can't help behaving as he does." [21] The variant form of the presupposition makes a narrower claim. It is acknowledged that mental disease per se need not render behavior involuntary, but it is asserted that *some* forms of mental

---

physiological pathology, etc. Not all so-called unconsciousness or automatism, however, is of this kind: the performance of a complex and purposeful course of conduct over a substantial period of time while in an "epileptic fugue state" is *not* in the strict sense involuntary behavior, though it may be viewed as a disability of mind that precludes responsible conduct while in that condition. While there are, then, some forms of disability of mind (but *not* usually "insanity") that are associated with involuntary behavior in the strict sense, the legally central feature of interest is the existence of the disability of mind, not the involuntariness (see Chapter 4; and Chapter 5, Section II). The reasoning here, in short, is akin to that by which we refuse to hold an infant guilty of crime: We do not absolve of criminal guilt because of some (infantile) mistake of fact, or involuntary motion, or nonvoluntariness of an act, any of which may have existed; we absolve of criminal responsibility because of the underlying condition of infancy, which makes these and other infantile incapacities so likely in relation to adult norms, as to take the infant, per se, out of the domain of the criminally responsible. Thus, to summarize: Involuntariness in the strict sense, and in the sense relevant to assessing criminal responsibility, is not typical of insanity, nor of mental disabilities generally, but it does occur in some mental disabilities. But even when involuntary behavior does occur by reason of mental disability, it is the *latter* condition that should be of principal interest in assessing criminal responsibility. The involuntariness then has peripheral or at most evidentiary interest, and is not, as in other contexts, the very ground of exculpation.

20. Here we shift back to the use, as is common in this context, of "involuntary" to mean both "involuntary" *and* "nonvoluntary." This usage causes confusion in many discussions of "involuntary conduct due to mental disease." We shall attempt to disentangle the relevant issues as we go; but it would not be appropriate to distort the views we are to discuss by building in at the outset a distinction that the proponents of these views do not make.

21. This, of course, is one way of viewing the rationale of the *Durham* test. See also Judge Leventhal's remark in *Brawner*, quoted in note 1, supra, in which the position stated in the text above is implicit. This notion, that an act "produced" by

disease do in fact produce certain specific symptoms: "compulsive" behavior, or "irresistible impulse," or some form of "incapacity to conform" behavior to the law.[22] Each version will be considered in turn.

What is it about "disease" that suggests that, in general, its manifestations are involuntary? When involuntariness pertains to physical disease, involuntariness is paradigmatically illustrated by the flushed face, fever, running nose, and sneezing of the person with an acute "cold," or by the thrashings of the epileptic in the grip of a *grand mal* seizure. In each case the demeanor and movement in question is plainly—paradigmatically—not voluntary. What test of involuntariness are we using here? In each case the demeanor or behavior is taken to be the physical effect of influences which do not in any decisive way include guidance of the mind. Intent, purpose, will—all are, as it were, bypassed.[23]

In this context we can distinguish a derivative sense of "voluntary" that has relevance to the criminal law. The running nose of a person with a cold might be called *indirectly* voluntary—that is, although the person cannot stop it or start it by a direct "effort of will," as in the case of raising his arm, standing up, uttering a word, or kicking his leg, he can, if he wills, stop it "indirectly" by swallowing a decongestant agent. The swallowing of the pill is directly voluntary, and the cessation of the runny nose then is, indirectly, voluntary. This distinction, though rough-and-ready in its way, is useful in the context of assessing the exculpatory value of a defense of involuntariness, since the defense may fail, at least partly, if the behavior was even indirectly voluntary.[24]

"mental disease," or merely by "disease," is perforce involuntary, is crucial in many of the arguments designed to show the nonresponsibility of the addict for acts committed as part of the pattern of his addiction. Some of the themes here taken up are therefore taken up again, infra, in Part IV, but in relation specifically to addiction rather than insanity. The basic issues remain the same, however: the thesis that we deal in these contexts with entities scientifically identifiable as "diseases," and that these disease-entities can cause certain acts, and that these acts are in a reasonable legal sense "involuntary"—all this is pervaded with error and confusion.

22. See generally, Keedy (1952); Davidson (1956); A. S. Goldstein (1967), chap. 5. And see Part IV, infra, on the addictions, especially at Chapter 9, Section III. See also *Smith v. U.S.* (1929), annotated.

23. I.e., strict involuntariness. See text and notes at note 2, supra.

24. Thus the failure of a diabetic to take his prescribed doses of insulin and to follow his prescribed diet will preclude a defense of involuntariness or automatism in England (*R. v. Quick* [1973]). For discussion and citations pertaining to this issue in U.S. law, see Part IV, infra, on addictions, especially Chapter 9, Section II. And see *People v. Decina* (1956).

Once we have this distinction, the combinations and permutations are many. For example, a person may by directly voluntary steps cause it to be that he ultimately does not develop a certain disease; or if he does get the disease, he may by directly voluntary steps avoid causing undue subsequent harm to himself or contagion to others. The avoidance of the disease or of the harmful effects, then, is *indirectly* voluntary. Failure to take such steps could be punishable in law.[25] The test of voluntariness suggested earlier seems consistently applicable in all this: if the guidance of the mind could enable avoidance of the harm, directly or indirectly, then the harm, if produced, may for purposes of the law be viewed as produced voluntarily.

Physical diseases are the acknowledged model from which the notion of "mental disease" is supposedly derived.[26] But it would appear on the face of things that the symptoms and other harmful effects of mental disease are in a very different category with respect to voluntariness. In cases of physical disease we can reasonably expect that the person will use his mind to bring about whatever he can, directly or indirectly voluntarily, to avoid, limit, or eliminate both symptoms and disease. But mental disease is a disorder wherein the person's mind cannot be relied on for help; for it is the mind that is incapacitated in this view, and incapacitated in just the respects where we would have wished to rely on it. The person whose "mental disease" leads him to a criminal impulse often cannot be expected to take steps, directly or indirectly, voluntarily to control and contain or eliminate this impulse. The presumption is that his mental disease (or its "symptom") consists, among other things, just in his having such desires or in his mental incapacity to see that such acts are to be avoided.

Related to this is the fact that there is not here that paradigmatic lack of influence by the mind that is the mark of the involuntariness of the symptoms and effects of a physical disease. Quite to the contrary, the influence of the mind in "mental disease" and insanity is not only present but is *the* substantial and decisive influence on the criminally offending conduct, the "symptom." If there were not a decisive influence of the mind, it would not be called a "mental" disease; it would be called a physical disease that among other things renders the mind inoperative and the conduct, therefore, involuntary.

Lacking the distinctive features of physical disease that relate to voluntariness and involuntariness, mental disease would seem to be no basis for

25. See Chapter 9, Section II, infra, on addictions.
26. See Fingarette (1972), pp. 20–21.

a claim of involuntariness. The defender of the "involuntariness" thesis might be tempted to say, by way of response, that although there is a mind guiding the behavior here, the mind guiding this behavior is not a healthy mind but a *diseased* one, and for this reason alone the mental influence on the behavior should be discounted, and the behavior therefore viewed as not willed. The question is, why should that mental influence be discounted? It ought not to be enough merely to invoke the *word* "disease"—though this is done and has tended to cut off further analysis. If we are to understand the issues, we need to understand the legitimate force here of the word "disease." There is, in truth, no escape from the substantive question—what is there about a "diseased" mind that, in spite of the purposiveness of the conduct and often the skill of its execution, renders that conduct involuntary?[27]

There is no answer to this question. Or perhaps one should answer that there is indeed a feature of a disordered mind that can justify exculpation—i.e., irrationality—but there is no common law principle justifying the characterization of this feature as "involuntariness"—for, in any usual criminal law sense of the word, it is not appropriate.

One might, as a last resort, speak in terms of familiar but vague notions like the "will," and say that if at least it is the *will* that is "diseased," and not merely the mind generally,[28] then the mere fact that the will is "diseased" renders the behavior not voluntary. But the question remains—

27. One might think that the argument in *State v. Jones* avoids the voluntariness issue: "[N]o man shall be held accountable, criminally, for an act which was the offspring and product of mental disease. Of the soundness of this proposition there can be no doubt. Thus far all are agreed; and the doctrine rests upon principles of reason, humanity, and justice, too firm and too deeply rooted to be shaken by any narrow rule that might be adopted on the subject. No argument is needed to show that to hold that a man may be punished for what is the offspring of disease would be to hold that he may be punished for disease. Any rule which makes that possible cannot be law" (p. 395). But this argument, as it turns out, tacitly relies on the assumption that mental disease entails involuntariness (see the discussion on addictions in Chapter 9, Section II, infra), and this assumption is precisely what is in question here.

28. This kind of assumption seems to be tacit in the leading Supreme Court case on the point, *Davis v. U.S.* (1897), which declares that there is insanity where there is "such a perverted and deranged condition of the mental and moral faculties" that the defendant's "will . . . has been otherwise than voluntarily so completely destroyed that his actions are not subject to it . . ." (p. 378). Here, of course, there is the double notion, when taken in the modern legal context, that not only the mind generally is diseased, but that specifically "the will" is "destroyed." Yet the person is spoken of as having performed "actions"—presumably purposeful, coordinated be-

why should behavior that *is* willed, even though the will be "diseased," be called *in*voluntary? This seems to be a corruption of language in order to achieve a desired conclusion, since it is natural and usual to hold that behavior, if *willed,* is voluntary. Indeed, it is not to be denied that it may be relevant to exculpation that the "will" is "diseased." But we shall quickly lose from sight whatever it is about such a will that negates responsibility for the conduct if at the outset we describe the conduct as *un*willed![29] This way lies total confusion. If, on the other hand, we acknowledge that the conduct is willed, but willed by a diseased will, we have to ask why *this* (rather than involuntariness) should make the conduct in that respect nonculpable.[30]

There is, as mentioned earlier, another, narrower form of the argument designed to establish that disease of the mind produces nonvoluntary conduct. In this second and qualified form of the argument, it is not the existence of "mental disease" per se, not even "diseased will" per se, that renders the conduct involuntary. It is the purported fact that, in some cases, mental disease can produce as a particular symptom an "irresistible impulse" or a "compulsion" to act in a certain way regardless of whether the act is criminally prohibited. Here the claim is not that the impulse is nonvoluntary merely by virtue of being diseased; it is that this particular symptom is a distinct effect or manifestation of the disease, and can be judged by *independent* criteria to amount to a compelling, irresistible inclination to act in a certain way.[31]

---

havior. Does this not imply "will"? It is crucial in this context to see that there are two different ways in which the word *will* is used—to refer to behavior that is meaningfully purposive, "governed behavior," and to refer to behavior that is not merely governed but *rationally* governed. Our thesis is that where there is insanity, the will, in the sense of purposefully governed conduct, is typically present, but not the rational will. It is *rational* will that is central to the issue of criminal responsibility.

29. A good example of the attempt to press this false analogy is A. Morris's remark in the context of the case of a person suffering melancholia who killed his family. Morris says: "We do not hold that a man is rightfully blamed for his acts when he has no power over them. . . . In such a situation, lacking volition, his 'acts' are akin to a muscular spasm. . . . We hold him blameless" (1968, p. 612).

30. Our answer here and throughout, of course, is that "disease," when it has a valid role in exculpating, is an obscure and pseudo-medical reference to irrationality. The will, as formed by a mind that lacks capacity for rationality in some respect, is the will of a person who cannot justly be held responsible in that respect.

31. It is presumably something of this sort that Kenny intends in saying: "In cases in which a man is able to show that his conduct, whether in the form of action

Here again, in spite of the temptation to speak of involuntariness, if we do so we face a profound paradox. For the person who acts "compulsively," or under the sway of some "irresistible" impulse or mood or passion, is one who is *absolutely intent upon* acting in a certain way. He will not allow himself or anyone else—if he can help it—to divert him from *his* purpose. It is the peculiar intensity and single-mindedness with which he *wills* to act in a certain way that strikes us. No *other* motive or wish that he brings to bear leads him to temper or put aside his purpose. If, as we are supposed to do here, we leave aside any claim that this is involuntary *merely* because it arises out of mental disorder, by what other, independent criterion could such conduct be classed as involuntary? On the face of it, one would see "compulsive" conduct as an expression of (stubborn) "will" *par excellence.*

Of course, there is in some of these cases something odd, something that can at times be responsibility-negating, in the mental condition underlying such single-mindedness and obstinacy, such persistence, such absolute undissuadability. That this is so is both true and important. For such a will may be irrational. But on what grounds should we characterize this irrational will as an *absence* of will?

If, however, one argues that the "will" has been "overthrown," this quickly generates familiar controversies of a "metaphysical" rather than an empirical kind. What is the "true" will? Is an irrational commitment a "false" will? And by what independent computation or other criteria do we determine that this "true will" was not "strong" enough to resist the irrational impulse or resolution rather than having been lax in not using its available "power" to resist? One expert says one thing; another says otherwise. Some, understandably, wash their hands of all such debate.[32]

---

or of inaction, was involuntary, he must not be held liable for any harmful result produced by it; . . . cases of this kind would arise where a man, through no fault of his own, falls upon and injures or kills another; or where the like harm results from his walking in his sleep; and in some cases of insanity, intoxication, or automatism" (*Kenny*, 1966, p. 30).

32. "The Witness [a psychologist as expert witness]: 'At this time, this last test, there was no evidence on any tests that showed this boy had any feelings of conscience or regret; he was completely swallowed up with thoughts of hostility, of vengeance, of being captured, and escape, and electrocution, and all etcetera, associated with his personal life.' "

"The Defense: 'Mrs. Kirby, doesn't this make him identifiable easily as a bad boy, as a sick boy?' "

Commonly the experts do not differ about some objective measurement or specific observation of this particular defendant. Dispute arises because they adhere to competing psychological doctrines, or because they have different attitudes toward the justice or future therapeutic efficacy of criminal conviction of the defendant. Differences in expert opinion often amount to a covert expression of such differences. A jury, asked to assess the strength of a mysterious "inner" and "true" will, can only look to the experts. The question is not factual in the way it would be if one were dealing with such a paradigmatic form of irresistibility as compulsion by a superior external physical force, or coercion with a shotgun at the head. In such cases, objective measurement assures us that the one force is greater than any counterforce the defendant's muscles could exert, and common experience assures us that a reasonable man of good will could not fairly be expected to ignore the threat and disobey. There is no question in these latter cases of covert rivalry among speculative doctrines, or of covert and conflicting philosophies as to the justice of punishing the defendant, all masquerading as quantitative medical assessment of "resistibility."

No doubt, one of the chief influences in perpetuating the assimilation of some of these forms of "compulsive" conduct to "involuntariness" is the explicit or tacit background metaphor of the person as victim: we view him *as if* he were being subjected to a superior external force.

There can be benefits from such an approach—but not to the law. There can be dangers from such a way of speaking—and particularly so for the law. A few words may bring out the issues here.

From the private standpoint of the person himself, characterizations in terms of being "compelled" or "irresistibly driven" may genuinely and

---

"The Witness: 'No, because of the difference in the strength of the ego from the two dates shows that this boy has lost control, voluntary control of his behavior' " (quoted by Arens, 1974, p. 211).

Since the only evidence one has of the "strength of the ego" is just the behavior and thought processes already described, the phrase constitutes a preferred redescription of it rather than an independently identifiable fact. This sort of interchange naturally enough leads to statements such as Lady Wootton's: "[A] volitional test raises practical difficulties far more formidable even than those involved in a purely cognitive formula [for insanity].... [I]f I assert that I have an uncontrollable impulse to break shop windows, in the nature of the case no proof of uncontrollability can be adduced. All that is known is that the impulse was not in fact controlled; and it is perfectly legitimate to hold the opinion that, had I tried a little harder, I might have conquered it." From this Lady Wootton concludes that it is "impossible" to devise a test of "volitional competence" which can be "objectively established" (1968, pp. 1026–27).

helpfully reflect the subjective sensation of inclinations to incompatible lines of conduct. The idiom reflects one's frustration that one is not acting on one's own reasonable and nobler inclinations, but instead acting on an inclination that, even as one indulges it, one judges to be less admirable, less in keeping with one's ideas of prudence, or decency, or morality. This language expresses one's desire to resist being identified, by oneself or by others, with the inclination that one in fact follows. It is also a way of expressing both self-exculpation and self-condemnation: What I do is contrary to what I approve. Yet by condemning what I do, I reveal that there is another, better side of me, a side of me that aspires to the higher, even while I follow the lower.

Such talk may truly be part of a moral battle, genuine or self-deceptive, in one's attitude to oneself and one's conduct. Yet such subtle and inner "battles," conceived in various idiomatic and metaphorical terms, significant though they may be in one's personal life, are obviously not the proper subject matter of judgments of culpability with respect to criminal law. However important, however authentic or self-deluding they may be from the standpoint of morality or religion, however fascinating and useful such modes of analysis may be to the novelist or the psychologist, such "internal tensions" and "battles" constitute a different order of subject matter for analysis than anything the law can legitimately concern itself with.

The criminal law is concerned not with what the person, with one metaphorical "part" of himself, would wish that he would elect to do, while with another metaphorical "part" of himself he finally does otherwise.[33]

Nor does it materially change matters to invoke, again in this context, the magic word "disease," and to view the "disease" as an actual entity, interior and yet "alien" to the person, but somehow exerting a "superior

33. "When we say that [an alcoholic] appellant's appearance [drunk] in public is caused not by 'his own' volition but rather by some other force, we are clearly thinking of a force that is nevertheless 'his' except in some special sense. The accused undoubtedly commits the proscribed act and the only question is whether the act can be attributed to a part of 'his' personality that should not be regarded as criminally responsible. Almost all of the traditional purposes of the criminal law can be significantly served by punishing the person who in fact committed the proscribed act, without regard to whether his action was 'compelled' by some elusive 'irresponsible' aspect of his personality" (Concurring opinion of Mr. Justice Black, *Powell v. Texas,* p. 540). Justice Black is, of course, not referring to the case of one who is actually carried into the street by someone else, since in that case " 'he' does not do the act at all . . ." (*ibid.*).

force." This is all metaphor, and unacceptable in this context, because there is no "entity" to be identified—not even psychiatrists today think of mental disease as an "alien entity" that "causes" certain effects by virtue of superior psychological "force."

If "disease" merely means something like malfunction of the mind, and if the metaphor of "alien forces" is abandoned, then the issue is radically shifted. Then the metaphor of "compulsion" also shifts from specious suggestion of an analogue to physical compulsion, and becomes an impressionistic or metaphorical allusion to a certain kind of mental malfunction. All this is not merely a "matter of words."[34] For the main theme of this study is that although in insanity there *is* "something wrong," something malfunctioning about the person's mind, and although this concept requires analysis and clarification because it is central to exculpation, the legal issues are confused if we analyze this in terms of the quite inappropriate legal concept of "involuntariness."

Perhaps, finally, a last basis for supposing that some desires may be irresistible is the tacit supposition that, underlying the mental impairment (or "mental disease"), is some bodily pathology that makes the conduct in question causally inevitable. Of course, if it can be shown in a particular case that some behavior was a reasonably direct effect of some identifiable bodily pathology, with no mental intervention, the thesis *would* be applicable. For then the behavior at least is not directly voluntary [35] —though it still might be indirectly voluntary, i.e., avoidable by prior direct voluntary action. Physical causation might be demonstrable, for example, in some cases of epileptic clouding of consciousness, of neurologically caused failure of muscular coordination, or of bizarre behavior associated appropriately with an identifiable brain tumor. But here, of course, the insanity plea is not in order; these psychologically meaningless movements *are* genuinely (legally) involuntary and not characteristic of the purposeful conduct of the insane. Unless such specific physical connections that bypass mental control can be shown, there is no scientific warrant to

34. "I believe also there is real merit in the contention that there are more similarities than differences between narcotics and alcohol addicts on the one hand and such other repetitive antisocial defendants as the vagrant, prostitute, homosexual, exhibitionist, and many others. All these conditions and many more present manifestations of emotional illness, but they are not diseases in the same sense that cholera, multiple sclerosis, or diabetes are disease, and the methods of treatment are not as noncontroversial" (Robitscher, 1967, p. 49).

35. See note 19, supra.

assume, and no scientific way to determine, that a particular course of conduct, or more generally that *all* conduct associated with mental malfunction, is to be viewed as beyond the power of mind to control.[36] And of course we exclude as irrelevant to legal analysis the doctrine of determinism and the confused notion that in this respect all behavior is "not voluntary," inevitable, and "irresistible." The fallacies in specific versions of such doctrines, as in the case of the addictions to narcotics and alcohol, for example, are further discussed in detail in Chapters 10 and 11.

It would be foolhardy to hope that the preceding discussions of mental malfunction as related to voluntariness, entering as they do only partway into exceedingly complex issues, would be both translucently clear and completely persuasive to all readers. Though the hope and the effort were present in full measure, success to that degree is not essential. The basic logical role that these discussions serve in the overall argument of this study is much more modest. The basic concern here is with the shift from the paradigmatic criminal law uses of "involuntary" and "not voluntary" to the radically different context of insanity and other irrational but purposeful conduct. The concern has been to show how, in such a shift, we move from simple, readily identifiable structures of fact to structures of fact and inference fraught with complexities, obscurities, and controversies; how we move to different sorts of issues, to different presumptions, to different sorts of inferences, and indeed to a basic shift of orientation. Only metaphor, speculation, and allusive terminology can seem to paper over the confusions; and the paper comes unstuck in too many situations of importance in the criminal law.

36. The reader is again referred to the discussion on addictions in Chapter 9, Section II, infra.

5

"Absence of Criminal Intent" and Conclusion

I: "ABSENCE OF CRIMINAL INTENT"–OTHER CURRENT CONCEPTS

At the outset of this part of the book, the theory to be critically examined was formulated most generally in terms of a mental disability producing criminal irresponsibility by virtue, ultimately, of "absence of criminal intent." The latter phrase has been used in various ways, and the problems of interpretation are notably many and profound. When used in connection with insanity, however, the meaning of the phrase is particularly elusive. That insanity exculpates by virtue, ultimately, of establishing absence of criminal intent is a proposition that, if taken in a certain way, may reach to the tautological. We need only to grant that in insanity there is a relation between mind and act that precludes culpability in criminal law, and then to take "criminal intent" to mean, generally, any relation between mind and act that satisfies the *mens rea* requirements for culpability for the offense alleged.

Such a proposition is verbalistic, however. Rather than twisting and turning the words, we should face the real issues squarely. It is the thesis of this book, of course, that the insane person is not criminally responsible in committing the offending act, and is not culpable in regard to the origin of that irresponsibility at the time of the act. More specifically, the insane person's mental powers are gravely impaired in the respect that such a person, in doing the offending act, lacks the capacity to take into account in a practical way the criminal significance of the act. If one insists on allusion to "criminal intent," one could say that the behavior lacked *criminal* intent even though the psychological intent was present. This is only an obscure way of saying that the lack of responsibility makes *criminal condemnation* on the basis of the intent inappropriate. The finding now expressed in the formula "Not Guilty by Reason of Insanity" would be better expressed, we maintain, by a verdict stating explicitly that the defendant is guilty of having committed a criminally proscribed act, but was mentally so impaired, nonculpably, as to have lacked capacity to act responsibly in regard to the law. The form of verdict that we propose under the D.O.M. doctrine ("Guilty of ———, with Nonculpable Disability of Mind") would express this.

It might be mentioned in passing that not only would adoption of the D.O.M. doctrine result in more helpful instructions to the jury, and not only would the verdict be an unambiguous report of their results, but the change would clear the atmosphere in the public arena, where words play a profound role. Today, the public sees judges and the law announcing verdicts of Not Guilty in some cases where a grievous act, plainly criminally prohibited, was patently committed by the defendant. Under the D.O.M. doctrine, the jury's findings that the defendant was guilty of the offense but suffered Disability of Mind would better express the public intuition. Sitting trial judges should not be insensitive in this regard to the merits of the suggested change.

However, our task in this chapter is not to expound the detail of the Disability of Mind doctrine—which is done in Part V and the Appendices that follow—but to review still other conceptions than those already discussed as to what might have been meant by "absence of criminal intent" in the insanity context. We have now shown at length that the principal candidates—ignorance or mistake as to fact, ignorance of the wrongness of the act or of law, and involuntariness—are all wanting. There remain a few other possible meanings of "criminal intent" that deserve at least brief consideration here if we are to have fully canvassed the doctrines currently invoked in this area of law, and if we are to see why they cannot meet the need.

"Absence of criminal intent" in insanity might, for example, be taken to mean that some specific *mens rea* element essential to the crime alleged was absent.[1] But still it would be necessary to specify the element in

---

1. This is the approach adopted in the proposed Criminal Justice Reform Act of 1975, U.S. Senate Bill S.1. See Chapter 2, note 4.

question. For, expressed in general terms alone, the formula "absence of some specific *mens rea* element" is not a defense but an abstract category or class of defenses. Some relevant mental states (other than those already discussed) whose absence could be exculpatory in appropriate contexts are, for example, premeditation, deliberation, or malice (in murder); intent to commit a felony (in burglary); and intent to take permanent possession (in theft). By the usual tests, such elements of *mens rea,* when relevant to the crime alleged, are quite typically present in the typical criminal insanity trial. An insane homicide, for example, can be intentional, deliberate, and premeditated—as was M'Naghten's. Nor is there anything to suggest that a successful insanity plea must show that the specific intent would be absent in burglary or theft offenses, assuming the usual tests of such specific intent.[2] Of course, such intent can be found "constructively" to be lacking where there is disability of mind.[3] But this is a verbal device to save the "specific intent" doctrine and draw attention from the embarrassing fact that here it is the mental disability that is of the essence in exculpation.

One *mens rea* claim that could have a certain initial exculpatory plausibility, however, is absence of "malice," since the insane person thinks his act justified, or may simply lack any clear sense of its moral character, and in that everyday sense he may not be acting with malice.[4] But of course "malice" is now very much a term of art, and in modern law

2. For example, in a review of all criminal cases between 1954 and 1959 in the District of Columbia, Krash reports ninety acquittals by reason of insanity, and of these only sixteen were murder cases. The other categories were Assaults, Housebreakings, Robbery, Thefts, Forgery, Other Felonies, Municipal Court. Other categories not uncommon generally in this context are arson and rape. The specific intent distinctively required in each of these crimes is almost always present in the case of defendants competent to stand trial at all. See Krash (1961), p. 949.

3. See the full discussion of this tactic in Part III, infra, on intoxication and diminished mental capacity.

4. Murder, which requires "malice," "may be perpetrated without the slightest trace of personal ill-will." The word has a "different significance in legal usage than in ordinary conversation" (Perkins, 1957, pp. 30–31). This familiar point is given particular stress by Michael and Wechsler (1937) in their exhaustive treatment of the law of homicide; they say that "The most striking phase of the development of the English law was the reduction of 'malice aforethought' to a term of art signifying neither 'malice' nor 'forethought' in the popular sense" (p. 707). And in reference to English law, Glanville Williams (1961) speaks of the "commonplace that 'malice' in law generally means intention or recklessness" (p. 72). Indeed, he says, "Malice in law *means* intention or recklessness" (p. 75, emphasis in original).

no longer means that the intent with which the act was done was one that, as judged by some further, moral criterion, was malicious. "Malice" in common law simply is the will to do the act, an act that the law declares to be, in the circumstances, criminal (regardless of how the doer of the act views it, and regardless of whether he knows the law).[5] Since the insane killer typically does plainly intend to kill, and does not believe he has a lawful excuse or justification, he has—in the usual legal sense—malice.[6]

In short, *none* of the specific elements of *mens rea* in any offense are typically absent in the criminally insane person's commission of that offense. Thus, "absence of criminal intent" will not account for the exculpatory force of insanity if the absence in question must be, by the usual tests, absence of some specific mental element of the *mens rea*.

The notion of "absence of criminal intent" could be used to mean absence of "general criminal intent." Absence of *"general* criminal intent" could not refer to absence of an intent to "flout the law." For it is well established that it is the intent to do the act, not the intent specifically to flout the law, that is the most "general" element of *mens rea* in the common law.[7] The intent specifically to flout the law is at most a *specific* intent required only for some crimes.[8]

Could we find a way of construing insane absence of "general criminal intent" by reference to the so-called "general intent crimes"? These are crimes such as assault or manslaughter.[9] But even in these crimes it would seem that the offender must be conscious of what he is doing, and not, in the strict sense, behaving involuntarily. For if this much is not required, it is difficult to see what mental state at all could possibly correspond to "general criminal intent." In any case a successful insanity defense does

5. Perkins (1957), p. 679.

6. See text and notes at notes 10–12, infra.

7. See the discussion of the maxim "ignorance of the law is no excuse," in Chapter 3, supra.

8. E.g., in certain types of cases where the offense must be committed "wilfully." See the discussion of such cases in Perkins (1939), pp. 49–51.

9. It is, unfortunately, impossible to give an adequate definition here, rather than examples. The concept of the "general intent crime" (as distinguished from the "specific intent crime") is inherently vague. It is assigned opportunistically on the grounds of public policy rather than the consistent meaning of the concept. See the full discussions infra in Part III on intoxication, especially Chapter 6. The fact is that "general intent" is a term devised for the special context of intoxication doctrine, to contrast with "specific intent." The terms are obscure enough in that special context, and can hardly be usefully generalized for use in relation to *mens rea* generally.

not require that the defendant have been so mentally confused that he lacked consciousness of the act he was doing. Thus he would rarely lack such a "general" criminal intent.

Hence, absence of "general criminal intent," in any plausibly relevant sense, is not at all what is fundamentally at issue in the insanity defense.

Of course, if one argues that the usual criteria for identifying elements of *mens rea* are inappropriate where there is insanity, the focal point of the argument shifts. One might hold that where mental disability is at issue, the criteria, for example, of "malice," or of "deliberation," must go "deeper." Thus the California Supreme Court held that the deliberation of a mentally abnormal killer could not be "mature and meaningful" enough to count as "deliberation" for purposes of *mens rea*;[10] and more recently the Court enunciated an analogous position with respect to "malice."[11] This, of course, is one more version of the confusing pattern of reasoning that we met with in Chapters 2, 3, and 4.[12] We propose that rather than suggesting vaguely and allusively that some specific element of *mens rea* doesn't "really" exist, it would be more helpful to acknowledge, *as usually defined in law,* the obvious presence of such mental elements—e.g., intent, malice, deliberation—and to assert that the mental disability out of which they arise negates the guilt normally associated with those mental elements. This seems to reflect more correctly the actual moral and legal intuitions we have; it is justified better by the explicit doctrine of Disability of Mind; and it is a natural use of language rather than a strained "constructive" interpretation. A jury of laymen can understand this way of putting matters, and can see how it fits into a coherent perspective on the implications of mental incapacity for assessing culpability.

II: CONCLUDING REMARKS TO PART II

Once the law relating to insanity is relieved of the dubious metaphysics and metaphors about lack of freedom of will in insanity, or about "deeper" forms of knowledge, intent, or other elements of *mens rea,* there should open up the hopeful prospect of a similar freedom in connection with other forms of mental disability as well. For example, the paradoxical and strained legal doctrines related to alcohol intoxication, to drug intoxi-

10. *People v. Wolff,* p. 975. See the discussion infra in Part III on Diminished Capacity (Chapter 8).

11. See Part III (Chapter 8).

12. I.e., another version of the shift to a "deeper" sense of these words.

cation, and to diminished mental capacity, all should take on a new look—as will be seen in Part III. The conclusion proposed here is that wherever a defense is based in substance on Disability of Mind, this should be the defense in procedure and in doctrine as well. One can see, from the outline of doctrine in Chapter 1, that there would be advantages to having a unified, coherent doctrine that covers all defenses where mental disability is at issue.

However, at this point it is important for us to compare, at least briefly, the specific differences that the choice of defense would make in a variety of different cases where total exculpation is at issue—e.g., not only insanity and especially the psychoses, but also comas, seizures, and traumas producing unconsciousness. For all these, the Disability of Mind defense would replace the miscellaneous collection of alternatives now available.

Involuntariness, in the strict sense, is currently a complete defense to any criminal charge, as are "unconsciousness" and "automatism" where those defenses are accepted. Any of these could be developed by showing, as a precondition, that the defendant did fall into unconsciousness. In such cases these defenses would not avoid a showing of Disability of Mind but would presuppose it. There is thus a redundant uneconomy of argument in using these special legal defenses where the Disability of Mind concept is available and the offending behavior is ascribed to such disability.

Moreover, a defense of involuntariness, absence of some element of *mens rea*, or unconsciousness could completely exculpate in a way that, *unfortunately*, avoids the salutary consequences of asserting the defense of mental disability. The latter defense *regularly* includes, as the other defenses do not, an inquiry into the context of origin of the mental unsoundness in order to assess culpability for it.[13] Furthermore, the defense of mental disability must have as a fundamental procedural requirement a post-verdict inquiry to determine whether the previously

13. "[T]his defence of involuntariness should be excluded in cases where the accused either brought about his own lack of power of control, or foresaw that he might lack control and took no precautions. Here culpability and deterrence go hand-in-hand, for we feel that where there was the power of choice at an earlier stage, and the defendant could have helped it, he is culpable; and we also feel that punishment will serve to deter people from similar behavior in the future" (Fitzgerald, 1961, pp. 20-22). Fitzgerald thus sees the need for a Context of Origin inquiry here, though of course he does not phrase it in terms of our generalized doctrine of Disability of Mind.

harmful mental disability is persistent or likely to recur, and if it is, to determine appropriate steps to protect the public and rehabilitate the person.[14] Thus, a coherent doctrine of mental disability will have assurances of justice and of social welfare systematically built into it. By contrast, the defenses of involuntariness, absence of *mens rea,* unconsciousness, automatism, (and intoxication, etc.) do not have such assurances systematically built in. One could, of course, allow for special procedures to be invoked in these various defenses whenever appropriate, i.e., when mental disability is in fact at issue. But this would in substance amount, at best, to a cumbersome form of the mental disability defense; more probably one ends with the erratic congeries of ad hoc provisions that today proliferate and confuse the practitioner. Moreover, if this is the only way to invoke these special procedures, the law suffers from the narrowness of scope of these defenses when applied to mental disability. As we have seen, and will see further below, too many kinds of patently irrational conduct do not fit, or do not easily fit, these concepts. Moreover, the facts pertinent to these defenses sometimes do, sometimes do not, and sometimes may but need not fit the insanity defense.[15]

In general, the existence of these different defenses with their differing burdens of proof, trial procedures, and post-trial consequences leads to a

14. "There are, however, cases where there is no choice at all on the defendant's part, but his condition is such that he is liable to cause harm to others. Epileptics, for example, cannot help the fits they have. But if they know that they are likely to injure others in the course of these fits, it may not be wholly unreasonable to demand that they refrain from engaging in activities where the onset of a fit might lead to disastrous injury to other people.... Similarly a diabetic who fails to take sufficient food and suffers from an insulin reaction may not unreasonably be convicted of driving under the influence of drugs, even though this was not perhaps the type of case originally envisaged by the Road Traffic Acts.... But since he knows of the possible dangers, he should refrain from certain types of activity: and here choice does come into play, for he can choose, for instance, whether or not to drive a motorcar in the first place. He is not, therefore, absolutely justified in saying 'I could not help what happened' " (Fitzgerald, 1961, p. 21).

15. For a discussion of some of the bewildering variety of alternatives opened up by the confusing and often overlapping maze of mental disability defenses today, see Fox (1963), pp. 652–654. Glanville Williams has remarked in connection with the variety of outcomes, including the insanity verdict, that may result from the same facts: "[L]awyers are the prisoners of their conceptual schemes.... One cannot feel satisfied that the outcome of a sleepwalking case should depend upon a medical diagnosis which has no relation to the justice or social necessities of the case" (Williams, 1961, p. 346).

confusing maze of law that is advantageous only to the skilled practitioner who manipulates it for tactical purposes unrelated to justice or social welfare.

We conclude that the inadequacies of these total defenses in the area of mental disability should not be surprising against the background of analysis presented here—analysis showing that the essential "meaningful relation" between the impairment of mental powers and the offending behavior is that those powers were impaired in such a way in relation to that behavior, and in relation to the relevant criminal law norms, that the defendant lacked the mental capacity for rational control of that conduct. Insofar as this deeper condition sets the context out of which arises any particular mental element that would normally establish culpability, that element loses this significance. The result is then that we need not strain logic, facts, and words, trying to deny this or that particular mental element's presence, but need only to acknowledge that in acting this way defendant was not responsible and hence not criminally culpable—i.e., not a fit subject for criminal condemnation or punishment.

In this way, such important common law concepts as knowledge, intent, and voluntariness are left free to keep their traditional roles as used in simpler and impersonal contexts. In these contexts, the normal actor—rational and responsible—is presumed, and the deep complexities of the individual psyche are not at issue. Such complexities are inevitably introduced insofar as the D.O.M. defense is at issue, but at least they are not allowed to permeate illegitimately other fundamental concepts of common law and to sow confusion generally.

On the other hand, the D.O.M. doctrine would bring with it new simplicity: *all* the complete defenses—insanity, unconsciousness, automatism, and voluntariness (due to mental derangement)—would fall into one category and be handled by means of one procedure. This result, which is more fully explained in Part V, provides a rationally based and simple approach to any complete mental disability defense appropriate under our law.

PART III

Current Partial Defenses:
Their Rationales

6
Alcohol Intoxication:
The "Specific Intent Exception"

In a purely formal sense, it can be maintained that in the common law there is no such thing as an "intoxication" defense—indeed the fact that a defendant was intoxicated at the time he committed a crime has classically been rejected as a defense to the commission of that crime. The modern maxim that "voluntary intoxication is no defense" is "so universally accepted as not to require the citation of cases."[1] Early scholars considered that intoxication, far from being a defense, was an aggravation of the crime committed.[2]

In the nineteenth century, however, English and American judges attempted to introduce an element of flexibility into the law to allow partial—but not complete—exculpation of the inebriated offender. The search for such a doctrine resulted in what has become known as the "specific intent exception." Although the specific intent exception was supposedly based on classical principles of criminal law, and although no one would admit to taking part in the birth of a new creation, in fact the nineteenth-century judges constructed a novel and, we shall argue, inappropriate doctrine in an effort to handle the very serious problem of the criminal responsibility of the intoxicated defendant. What began as a

1. "Voluntary Intoxication—Defense," 1966, p. 1240.
2. Coke (125a), for example, stated that drunkenness "is a great offense in itself" and therefore aggravated the defendant's crime.

straightforward acceptance of the idea that intoxication could in fact result in the absence of required elements of a crime became a rigidified doctrine that was arbitrary in its results and capricious in its application. The "exception" became the rule and has been extended by a number of American courts to deal with cases involving mental illness[3] and intoxication by hallucinogenic and barbiturate drugs.[4] What we call the "doctrine" of specific intent has become a time-honored rule which nonetheless fails to recognize the essential reasons for finding that the intoxicated offender is less morally responsible than his sober counterpart. The doctrine does not lead logically to the overall result that was desired—that intoxication may mitigate but should never completely exonerate. The specific intent exception therefore has applications and modifications that are arbitrary and must be learned by rote, since most have little logical relationship to the principles underlying the doctrine—or indeed to the facts the doctrine is often used to cover.

By reviewing the history and (lack of) logic of the currently accepted doctrine of specific intent, we will be better able to see the logic of the alternative approach proposed herein.[5]

The new note of flexibility that members of the judiciary tried to inject into the law concerning the responsibility of the intoxicated offender was sounded simultaneously in England and America. Because it has readily been assumed by most commentators that English law was the more influential and blazed the trail, we shall begin our discussion with an analysis of the English law that generated the British doctrine of specific intent,[6] and we shall examine closely the concept that emerged from the early English intoxication cases.

3. See Chapter 8, infra.

4. See Chapter 7, infra.

5. For the classic critical discussion of the history and logic of the specific intent exception, see Jerome Hall (1944) and (1960). Though Hall brings out problems that are closely related to some presented here, the present discussion is organized in terms of a specific insight, and a correlative solution, that are not Hall's. Thus the object of the present study is not a full historical review for its own sake, but an historical review with a specific analytical objective. We focus here on certain specific issues related to drunkenness and criminal responsibility, and organize the discussion in a way that reveals how these reflect a persistent underlying dilemma. We suggest a fundamental solution. Moreover, case law developments since Hall's essay have revealed in more explicit and acute form the dilemmas here proposed as central. See especially the latter portions of Sections I and II, and Section III, infra.

6. Whether English law in fact influenced the development of American law in this area is a question that we shall hold in reserve for the moment.

I: THE ENGLISH DOCTRINE AND ITS DEVELOPMENT

The fundamental legal principle upon which English judges founded their "exception" to the rule that intoxication is no defense is simple, straightforward, and perfectly general: it is basic law that, before a defendant can be found guilty of any crime, the prosecution must prove beyond a reasonable doubt that all elements constituting the charged offense were present at the time the alleged crime was committed. English judges therefore reasoned that if intoxication resulted in the absence of a required state of mind (*mens rea*) for the alleged crime, the defendant logically cannot be found guilty of that crime.[7]

The practical application of this principle seemed easy enough at first glance: in one of the earliest English cases, a jury was instructed that, where the basic mental state required for conviction of murder is the intent to kill or cause grievous bodily harm,[8] if the defendant had no such intent due to intoxication, he could not be convicted of murder.[9] In another early case, the defendant had allegedly discharged a pistol with intent to kill.[10] The jury was told that, if the defendant had no intent to kill because he was drunk when he fired the pistol, he did not have the

---

7. The first English case in which a judge apparently allowed consideration of intoxication as a mitigating factor was *Rex v. Grindley,* referred to in *Rex v. Carroll* (1835). Judge Holroyd apparently instructed the *Grindley* jury that evidence of intoxication could be considered on the question of whether a homicide was done premeditatedly or with sudden passion. However, Judge Park in *Carroll* rejected the *Grindley* case, stating that it did not express the law, and that if it were the law "there would be no safety for human life" (*Rex v. Carroll,* p. 147).

8. In English law, unlike U.S. law with its degrees of murder and multiplicity of mental elements relevant to murder, the only mental element required for murder is malice aforethought. And malice aforethought in England is, in effect, a matter of intent to kill or cause grievous bodily harm (or foresight that such are the natural and probable consequences of the act). See Smith and Hogan (1973), pp. 225–226.

9. *Reg. v. Cruse* (1838). Here the defendant was accused of killing his wife's child. Judge Patteson instructed the jury that "although drunkenness is no excuse for any crime whatever, yet it is often of very great importance if it is a question of intention. A person may be so drunk as to be utterly unable to form any intention at all, and yet he may be guilty of very great violence" (p. 546). Patteson instructed the jury that if it found no intent, it must find the defendant guilty of assault.

10. *Reg. v. Monkhouse* (1849), p. 56. The judge instructed the jury that it should consider whether the intoxication was of such an extent "as to prevent his restraining himself from committing the act in question, or to take away from him the power of forming any specific intention." The jury should ask: Was the defendant "rendered by intoxication entirely incapable of forming the intent charged?" (p. 56). Judge Coleridge accepted explicitly the basic doctrine in *Reg. v. Cruse,* though with

mens rea for the crime charged and therefore could not be convicted of that crime.

These cases were a logical extension of the basic principle of law that if all the elements of a crime were not present—for whatever reason—then the defendant did not commit the charged offense.[11] Since the *mens rea* for a crime is one of the crime's essential elements, without the presence of the appropriate *mens rea* it seems clear that no crime can have been committed.

If intoxication can negate the presence of *mens rea* in murder and attempted murder cases, cannot the *mens rea* for any crime be absent by virtue of intoxication? Both logic and psychology would imply that the answer is yes, and in the early English cases that conclusion was borne out in practice. In cases of attempted suicide[12] and common assault,[13] for example, judges allowed jurors to consider whether, as a result of intoxication, defendants lacked the necessary *mens rea* for the crimes charged. Since in these crimes, unlike homicide, there is no lesser included offense, the defendants in *Gamlen* and *Moore* were acquitted.[14]

Thus the extension of the concept to crimes other than homicide had a surprising and undesired result: defendants were entirely acquitted by

---

reservations as to the requirement of incapacity rather than mere absence of intent— an issue that we take up in Section IV as going to a central underlying issue.

11. A modern application of this principle can be found in connection with the English Criminal Justice Act 1967, section 8, which requires that when an offense is defined as requiring foresight or knowledge, such foresight or knowledge must be proved. Orchard (1970), p. 133, argues that, if the defendant lacked such foresight, it is irrelevant that it was due to intoxication: "[W]hatever the reason, an essential element of the offence is lacking and he should be acquitted." See *R. v. Sheehan and Moore.*

12. In *Reg. v. Doody* (1845), Judge Wightman instructed that "drunkenness . . . is a material fact in order to arrive at the conclusion whether or no the prisoner really intended to destroy his life" (p. 463). In *Reg. v. Moore* (1852), p. 319, the judge instructed the jury that if the defendant was "so drunk as not to know what she was about, how can you say she *intended* to destroy herself?" The defendant was acquitted.

13. *Reg. v. Gamlen* (1858). The defendant was charged with assaulting another person in a fray at a fair; the defendant claimed that he was drunk and thought he was being assaulted and therefore acted in self-defense. The judge charged that the jury could consider whether the prisoner really believed he was being assaulted, and in doing so, it could consider "that state in which he was" (p. 90). Gamlen was acquitted.

14. See notes 12 and 13, supra.

juries who found that evidence of intoxication negated the *mens rea* for any crime.

As suggested at the outset, outright acquittal for the drunken offender was not the answer for which judges were searching. There is and has been a strongly held belief—and we will argue a *correct* belief—that the voluntarily intoxicated offender should not be entirely exculpated from criminal guilt. Although there exists a split of opinion as to what extent *any* mitigation should be allowed the drunken defendant, there is little or no sentiment for allowing him to get off scot-free. The acquittals that occurred almost immediately, although a logical and practical outcome of the new doctrine, had major repercussions in the subsequent development of the doctrine.

One way to limit the scope of the doctrine—perhaps a natural way for lawyers—was semantical. By happenstance and then by custom, this area of the law developed terminology that was later to be castigated as notoriously ambiguous and meaningless;[15] yet that same terminology, that of "specific intent," has been the crutch on which the Anglo-American law has leaned in its attempts to limit the exculpatory scope of the defense based on inebriation.

The phrase "specific intention" appears first in *Reg. v. Monkhouse.*[16] The defendant allegedly discharged a pistol with intent to kill. Judge Coleridge first asked the jury whether the defendant had been "rendered by intoxication entirely incapable of forming the intent charged,"[17] i.e., the intent to kill. He then instructed the jury to consider whether the intoxication was of such a degree

as to prevent his restraining himself from committing the act in question, or to take away from him the power of forming any *specific intention* [emphasis added].[18]

It seems clear that at this early stage of history the phrase "specific intention" was not a term of art; the judge meant by it nothing more than that the jury had to find that the appropriate *mens rea* (intent to kill) had been present in order to find the defendant guilty. The "specific intention" was simply the *particular* intention or specific *mens rea* needed for the crime of attempted murder alleged in the particular case at issue.

15. See notes 36–38 and 59–68, infra.
16. See note 10, supra.
17. *Reg. v. Monkhouse* (1849), p. 56.
18. *Ibid.*

Judge Coleridge's words, however, in conjunction with later language by Judge Stephen in *Reg. v. Doherty* (1887), have been used as the basis for the formulation of the modern technical concept of specific intent. In *Doherty*, Stephen allowed the jury to consider evidence of drunkenness as it affected "the intention of the party" committing the crime, since that intention "is one of its [the crime's] constituent elements,"[19] and is necessary for commission of the crime.

The importance of the *Doherty* case for English development in this area cannot be overemphasized. There are two primary reasons for the prominence of the case: first, Stephen was a renowned jurist whose many works were and have remained highly influential; second, the *Doherty* charge to the jury was the first discussion of any length in this newly emerging area of law.

Doherty is a homicide case. As we read Stephen's instructions to the jury, it is essential for us to realize that, in accordance with English practice, he was analyzing for the jury the facts of *this* case as he saw them, and therefore putting the law as he viewed it in a specific context.

Stephen instructed the jury that, in this case, they could find that: (1) the defendant had the intention to kill; or (2) he was drunk and fired the shot "vaguely, without any special intent"; or (3) he fired the gun without meaning to, i.e., negligently. If the jury should find (1), their verdict must be murder. Either of the latter two possibilities would establish manslaughter.[20] And of course in either of the latter cases there was no "special intent" in firing the gun, only vaguely violent or negligent behavior.

As Stephen's instructions were closely analyzed and examined by succeeding generations of jurists, his words were removed from their specific context and became the general rule. Those accepting and following that rule believed that Stephen had propounded a doctrine, centering around a technical concept, requiring that only a "specific intent," a *special* kind of intent, could be negated by intoxication. And, moreover, since Stephen indicated to the jury that the defendant in the instant case was, in his opinion, guilty of *at least* manslaughter, later jurists assumed

19. "Although you cannot take drunkenness as any excuse for crime, yet when the crime is such that the intention of the party committing it is one of its constituent elements, you may look at the fact that a man was in drink in considering whether he formed the intention necessary to constitute the crime" (*Reg. v. Doherty* [1887], p. 308).

20. *Ibid.*, p. 309.

that when any defendant was charged with murder and pleaded intoxication as his defense, it was a matter of law that he could *never* be acquitted.[21]

This view of Stephen's decision had one desired result—that intoxication cannot totally exculpate—but the logic is poor. Why cannot the *mens rea* for manslaughter be negated by intoxication, just as it can for murder? It is conceivable that a man may be so drunk as not to have any intent or even knowledge of what he is doing. However, in addition to the apparent boundaries set up by "specific intent" (as distinguished from any other intent), this arbitrary limitation was seen as a second way of marking off boundaries on the intoxication exception.

The double development outlined above was hardened into fixed doctrine in the next important case on the subject, *Rex v. Meade* (1909), the first case to summarize the history of the concept. Stephen's restatement of the newly emerging "exception" was flatly described by *Meade* as established and general "doctrine."[22]

It is ironic that in *Meade,* the first case to generalize the remarks found in *Monkhouse* and *Doherty,* we find the following admonition: "[W]hen a judge sums up to a jury he must not be taken to be inditing a treatise on the law. He addresses himself to *the particular facts of the case then before the jury, and no judge can affect, in those circumstances, to give an exhaustive definition, or one which applies to every conceivable case"* (emphasis added).[23] Unfortunately, the judges in *Meade* failed to heed their own words and proceeded to announce that the preceding cases had established a general doctrine: "[W]here intent is of the essence of a crime . . . intent may be disproved by shewing . . . that . . . the prisoner was in a state . . . in which . . . he was incapable of forming the intent."[24]

21. In the other early English case in which the defendant was accused of murder and pleaded intoxication as a defense (*Reg. v. Cruse*), the court also instructed that if there was no intent to murder because of intoxication, the defendant was guilty of assault. Again, this was undoubtedly a decision by the judge based on the particular facts of that case.

22. *Reg. v. Meade,* p. 898.

23. *Ibid.*

24. *Ibid.* It is important to note, however, that once again the "intent" at issue was specifically the intent to "inflict serious bodily injury" (p. 899). The limitation of possible exculpation to proof of absence of this specific intent, and hence to exculpation from murder but *not* manslaughter, was evident in the entire discussion. The discussion in *Meade* proceeds entirely in terms of the two options, murder or manslaughter, and the court said explicitly that "it is not our duty to say anything

Although this formulation is said to be the "essence" of all that went before (the judges do admit that identical expressions were not used in each case), it is not in fact a good summation. Instead, *Meade* builds in still another limiting concept—incapacity. *In general,* the question that earlier judges had asked was: did the defendant at the time of the act *have* the intent—not was he *capable* of having the intent. This distinction, which is extremely important, will be discussed at greater length below.[25]

The importance of *Meade* for us at this point is the transformation of a specific application of a general principle into a technical and a special legal doctrine.

At the turn of the century, therefore, evidence of intoxication could result in a limited or complete defense. A defendant could show that, due to intoxication, he did not have the requisite *mens rea* for the crime charged. However, in murder cases, evidence of intoxication was arbitrarily limited (following the restrictive interpretation of *Doherty*) to obtaining a reduction of the crime of murder to manslaughter (or assault).

The most influential English case in the twentieth century was, and remains, the case of *D.P.P. v. Beard.*[26] Decided in 1920, and long accepted as the decisive formulation of the intoxication defense, *Beard* exhibits the contradictions and difficulties that have continued to plague English judges to this day as they attempt to apply the specific intent doctrine.

Lord Birkenhead correctly notes in the beginning of his opinion that "[t]he language used by judges has varied and different directions are not

---

which will confer an immunity greater than that which they already enjoy on persons who have voluntarily made themselves drunk" (*ibid.,* p. 899).

25. See Section III, infra. In this context we note another important point made by Stephen in the *Doherty* case. Stephen instructed the jury that if an intoxicated defendant has formed the intention to kill, even though it be a drunken intention, he is "just as much guilty of murder as if he had been sober" (p. 308). Stephen's conclusion, in the context of the development of the specific intent exception, is a logical one. Only *absence* of a required element of the crime can mitigate, since absence of an essential element means no crime was committed; the *presence* of the required state of mind, even if due to intoxication, means that all requisite elements were present, and therefore the defendant is guilty of the crime charged. But the doctrine is less plausible when one explicitly announces, as Stephen did, the logical corollary that the presence of a drunken intent has *no* bearing on culpability. We will propose in Section III that this is morally and psychologically implausible, and will argue that it reflects the basic inadequacy of the rationale here being historically developed.

26. Opinion by Lord Birkenhead (1920).

always easy to reconcile."[27] He then surveys the previous English law on the subject of the defense of drunkenness.

Birkenhead's first conclusion in *Beard* is an important one, for it is a basic modern formulation of the so-called specific intent exception:

[W]here a specific intent is an essential element of the offense, evidence of a state of drunkenness rendering the accused incapable of forming such an intent should be taken into consideration in order to determine whether he had in fact formed the intent necessary to constitute the particular crime.[28]

Here, for the first time, we see the exact phrase "specific intent" used in its technical sense, and in an authoritative context. It is placed in such a way as to indicate that it has some particular and unique significance. This presumption is further strengthened by Birkenhead's firm pronouncement of the associated doctrine:

[T]he law is plain beyond all question. . . . [A] condition of drunkenness . . . can only, when it is available at all, have the effect of reducing the crime from murder to manslaughter.[29]

If drunkenness can only reduce the crime of murder to manslaughter, Birkenhead must perforce consider "specific intent" to be something other than simple *mens rea.* For if drunkenness can negate *mens rea,* why cannot the jury consider evidence of intoxication as it affects the crime of manslaughter? Somehow there must be something *different* about the kind of intent, the "specific intent," needed for murder—something that places it in a radically different legal category from the *mens rea* for manslaughter, since the latter cannot as a matter of *law* be absent by reason of intoxication.

Yet we are given absolutely no idea by Birkenhead what principle of law distinguishes a "specific intent" from the intent needed for any crime. In truth, the only answer is that the distinction is arbitrary—a distinction created ad hoc in order to prevent complete acquittal in the case of murder, a result that would go against the moral grain.

Birkenhead sensed—as have other judges since—that the doctrine was vulnerable to the charge of arbitrariness, and so he compounds the confusion by insisting (with some justice in the peculiar context of *Beard*) that he really meant nothing special by it.[30] In contrasting the *Beard* case (in which the defendant strangled a young girl while in the act of raping her)

27. *D.P.P. v. Beard*, p. 493.
28. *Ibid.*, p. 499.
29. *Ibid.*, p. 500.
30. Williams (1965), p. 43, agrees: "The fourth criticism of Lord Birkenhead's formulation relates to his use of the phrase 'specific intent.' This phrase has some-

with the *Meade* case (in which the defendant battered his wife to death), Birkenhead makes an important distinction. In the *Meade* case, in order to prove the defendant guilty of murder, the prosecution had to prove an intent to cause grievous bodily harm. It was "therefore . . . essential to prove the specific intent; in Beard's case it was only necessary to prove that the violent act causing death was done in furtherance of the felony of rape." [31]

Birkenhead's point is that, in order to convict Meade of murder, Meade *must have intended* to do his wife grievous bodily harm—that was the *minimum* mental state required, i.e., the "specific intent" to do grievous bodily harm. But in *Beard,* where the felony-murder rule was invoked because the defendant was already committing a felony by raping the girl, no specific intent to kill or injure was needed insofar as the crime of murder was concerned. Birkenhead makes it clear that drunkenness as a defense would only benefit Beard if it resulted in an absence of intent *to rape*; and that, Birkenhead holds, was manifestly not the case. [32] Birkenhead concludes:

I do not think that the proposition of law deduced . . . is an exceptional rule applicable only to cases in which it is necessary to prove a specific intent in order to constitute the graver crime—e.g., wounding with intent to do grievous bodily harm or with intent to kill. It is true that in such cases the specific intent must be proved to constitute the particular crime, but this is, on ultimate analysis, only in accordance with the ordinary law applicable to crime, for speaking generally . . . *a person cannot be convicted of a crime unless the mens was rea* [emphasis added] . [33]

If we can accept his words literally, Birkenhead would seem now to be saying that the rule announced (i.e., that evidence of intoxication can negate *mens rea*) is applicable to *any case*. He himself offers as an example

---

times produced the impression that whereas drunkenness is relevant to crimes of 'specific intent' (whatever that may mean), it is not relevant to crimes requiring some intent other than specific intent. This misapprehension was corrected by Lord Birkenhead himself in a later passage." (For the relevant passage, see the quotation from *Beard* in the text directly below.) Cross (1961), p. 512, states: "These quotations [from *Beard*] show that . . . the phrase 'specific intent' was used to describe whatever intent the prosecution may have to prove in the case of a particular charge to which drunkenness is pleaded as a defense."

31. *D.P.P. v. Beard,* p. 504.
32. *Ibid.,* p. 505.
33. *Ibid.,* p. 504.

the charge of attempted suicide—to which, he states, *drunkenness would be an answer.* [34]

The result of the *Beard* case has been to muddy the waters rather than to clarify them.[35] Confusion about the impact of the specific intent doctrine has continued and is, at the present date, still the center of active debate among English scholars, lawyers, and judges.

In 1974, an English court agreed that "it is quite impossible to deal with this matter (the intoxication defense) logically," and once more affirmed the arbitrary rule that intoxication is not a defense against manslaughter, even though the court agreed that logically it should be.[36] In the same vein, a commentary on the English case of *Bolton v. Crawley* [37] remarked that, although the phrase "specific intent" seems "dear to the heart of judges," its meaning is "shrouded in obscurity." The commentator further indicated that he believed "it is surely time that the uncertainty was resolved." [38]

II: THE U.S. DOCTRINE AND ITS DEVELOPMENT

In 1881, six years before the English case of *Doherty*, the United States Supreme Court in *Hopt v. People* held:

The degree of the offense depends entirely upon the question, whether the killing was wilful, deliberate and premeditated; and upon that question it

34. *Ibid.*

35. An additional and important way in which *Beard* has confused matters concerns again the problem of "incapacity" to have intent versus "actual absence" of intent. Birkenhead stressed that the question to be answered is whether the defendant was "entirely *incapable*" of forming the intent charged. "This [Birkenhead's] formulation has not escaped criticism. The apparent requirement that there be evidence that Defendant was *incapable* of forming the requisite intent appears in some, but not all, of the cases preceding *Beard,* and this requirement seems questionable" (Orchard, 1970, p. 133).

36. *Reg. v. Howell* (1974), p. 808.

37. P. 224.

38. *Ibid.* Other commentators in recent English cases have queried the meaning of specific intent. For example: *Reg. v. MacPherson* (1973); *Reg. v. Dodson* (1973). See also: *R. v. Hartridge* (1957); *R. v. Keogh* (1964). The restrictive specific intent doctrine is reiterated in the leading case of *Attorney-General for Northern Ireland v. Gallagher* (1961). However, Section 8 of the Criminal Justice Act 1967 has added a new and somewhat uncertain element. (See the discussion in Smith and Hogan, 1973, pp. 227–229. See, most recently, *R. v. Sheehan and Moore.*)

is proper for the jury to consider evidence of intoxication, if such there be; not upon the ground that drunkenness renders a criminal act less criminal, or can be received in extenuation or excuse, but upon the ground that the condition of the defendant's mind at the time the act was committed must be inquired after, in order to justly determine the question as to whether his mind was capable of that deliberation or premeditation which according as they are absent or present determine the degree of the crime.[39]

The Supreme Court based its decision on a number of earlier American cases,[40] a few of which drew upon several of the English cases discussed above. However, largely as a result of the fact that many states (unlike England) have two degrees of murder, the developing flexibility inaugurated by English judges regarding the intoxicated offender was speedily transformed by American judges.

American common law generally defines the *mens rea* of first-degree murder as being comprised of four elements: malice, premeditation, deliberation, and the intent to kill. In the early American cases relied upon by the Supreme Court in *Hopt,* state judges had allowed juries to consider evidence of intoxication *only* on the question of the presence or absence of premeditation and deliberation. This limitation required, therefore, a conviction of at least second-degree murder.

One of the earliest such American cases was *Pigman v. Ohio,*[41] decided in 1846 subsequent to the earliest English cases moving in the new direction, e.g., *Grindley* and *Cruse.* In *Pigman,* the accused was charged with passing counterfeit bank bills. The trial court had excluded evidence showing that the defendant was drunk at the time. The Supreme Court of Ohio held that, since the act required guilty knowledge or a "deliberate state of the mind ... it is proper to show any state or condition of the person that is adverse to the proper exercise of the mind...."[42] The court concluded that "drunkenness, as anything else showing the state of mind or degree of knowledge, should go to the jury...."[43]

The rationale used by the *Pigman* court is similar to that of the early English cases: it is basic law that if all elements of a crime were not

39. P. 633.

40. Among those cases cited by the court are *Pirtle v. State* (1849); *Keenan v. Commonwealth* (1862); *Pigman v. State* (1846); *People v. Belencia* (1863); and *People v. Williams* (1872).

41. (1846).

42. *Pigman v. State* (1846), p. 557.

43. *Ibid.*

present, the defendant is not guilty. Here, in order to commit the crime of passing counterfeit bills, one must *intend* to pass and know that he *is* passing counterfeit bills.[44] Without that intention, the *mens* is not *rea.*

Unlike *Pigman,* the other American cases that preceded *Hopt* were generally murder cases, and it is in these decisions that the American distinction between first- and second-degree murder becomes crucial as it affects the concept with which we are dealing.

Pirtle v. State,[45] one of the earliest homicide cases and a case that relied explicitly upon *Rex v. Grindley,* above, held that:

[W]hen the nature and essence of the crime is made to depend by law upon the peculiar state and condition of the criminal's mind at the time—and with reference to the act done—drunkenness as a matter of fact affecting such state and condition of the mind is a proper subject for consideration and inquiry by the jury.

The question in such cases is . . . what was the mental status at the time of the act and with reference to the act?[46]

This language would at first glance seem to follow *Pigman* and hold that, if the required *mens rea* was absent, even though it be because of intoxication, the person cannot be found guilty of the alleged crime. However, the *Pirtle* court also made it clear that evidence of intoxication could only reduce the crime of murder to second-degree murder.[47] This arbitrary limitation is a much earlier version of the English rule eventually derived from *Doherty,* i.e., that where the crime charged is homicide, a defense based on drunkenness cannot, as a matter of law, result in complete acquittal. *Pirtle* was decided in the same year—1849—as *Reg. v. Monkhouse*; though the English judge did use the phrase "specific intention," it was in a nontechnical sense, and he made no reference to any doctrine limiting the exculpatory potential of intoxication.

An 1863 California case, *People v. Belencia,* adopted the *Pirtle* analysis limiting evidence of intoxication to a determination of degree. The California Supreme Court held that:

In determining the degree [in murder] any evidence tending to show the mental *status* of the defendant was a proper subject for the consideration

---

44. The court concluded: "[I]f the person was so drunk that he actually did not know that he had passed a bill that was counterfeit, he is not guilty" (*ibid.*).

45. (1849).

46. *Ibid.,* p. 454.

47. *Ibid.*

of the jury. . . . It is necessary . . . to prove that the act was premeditated, which involves, of course, an inquiry as to the state of mind under which the party committed it.[48]

The California Supreme Court reaffirmed its position in 1872 in *People v. Williams,* allowing the jury to consider evidence of intoxication only as it affects the *degree* of the crime, i.e., allowing a choice only between first- or second-degree murder. The California court by 1872 had therefore adopted the rule that a defense based on intoxication, where it is offered to a charge of murder, cannot be a complete defense.

Thus, in 1881, when the United States Supreme Court was faced with the *Hopt* case, it had a fairly coherent line of cases to follow. The Supreme Court held in *Hopt* that, although drunkenness is no excuse to a crime, evidence of intoxication is properly considered upon the question of the presence of premeditation and deliberation. The Supreme Court gave no rationale for its conclusion, but by its formulation it limited evidence of intoxication to one crime—murder—and to only one degree within that crime—first-degree murder.

There is an interesting comparative problem that should be noted at this point as we try to relate the English and American law. In English law, the *only* mental element required for murder is the intent to kill (or cause grievous bodily harm). Therefore the English *mens rea* for murder is simply the intent to kill. The result is that, in English law, an inquiry into the intent to kill is of itself an inquiry into the *mens rea* specific to murder, and since intoxication can establish absence of intent to kill, it can thereby preclude conviction for murder (but requires a manslaughter conviction under *Doherty* and *Beard*). In American law, on the other hand, the *mens rea* for murder is composed of *four* separate elements: focusing on one or two of them is not necessarily to focus on the total *mens rea* specific to murder, but the negation of one element can still result in a reduction of the crime.

Because of the multiplicity of elements in American law, and *in spite of* the Supreme Court's decision in *Hopt,* American judges not only allowed juries to consider whether in murder cases there was, by virtue of intoxication, an absence of premeditation,[49] intent to kill,[50] or malice,[51] but

48. *People v. Belencia* (1863), p. 546.
49. *Latimer v. State* (1898); *Atkins v. State* (1907); *Brennan v. People* (1906).
50. *State v. Anselmo* (1915).
51. *Cheadle v. State* (1915); but see *State v. Potts* (1888).

they further allowed evidence of intoxication to be presented in non-homicide cases.

In view of the many possibilities of the developing approach to the intoxicated offender in both homicide and non-homicide cases, it should be no surprise that, like England, the United States was quickly made aware of the danger of allowing evidence of intoxication: that danger was acquittal. In *Hopt*, the Supreme Court had, by an arbitrary limitation, attempted to forestall such a result (at least insofar as the crime of homicide was concerned); but since the *Hopt* formula worked only for murder, the problem of avoiding acquittals in other cases was not so easily solved.

In order to limit the exculpatory effect of admitting evidence of intoxication in a variety of cases, American courts (as had the English courts) developed a semantic method of straightjacketing the defendant's use of evidence of intoxication. As a result of the focus on the particular "elements" of the crime rather than on the fundamental issue of *mens rea*, American courts were able to introduce a seemingly meaningful distinction between *mens rea* and what was termed "specific intent," i.e., a mental "element" required for some, but not all, crimes. If the court found that a "specific intent" was necessary for commission of the crime charged, evidence of intoxication could be considered as it bore on that intent. If a "specific intent" was not required as an element of the crime, then intoxication could not serve as a defense.[52]

But what *is* a "specific intent"? On what principle is this element distinguished from all other elements of *mens rea*? What is there about specific intent that renders it subject to negation by intoxication, whereas other kinds of *mens rea* elements are legally invulnerable to the effects of alcohol?

52. This "specific" intent was not necessary where the crime of murder was concerned, for first-degree murder had certain mental states that were classically required (i.e., premeditation, deliberation, malice). The creation of a "specific intent" was needed for all other crimes, none of which had the special mental states required by first-degree murder. The result of this dichotomy has been confusion in modern terms: the modern "specific intent exception" is often assumed to cover the crime of murder. In fact, no "specific intent" is required for first-degree murder; evidence of intoxication simply disproves the presence of premeditation or deliberation or malice—not "specific intent." But in all other crimes, it is the "specific intent" that must be shown to be absent by virtue of intoxication.

One of the first key cases in formulating this semantic approach was *Crosby v. People*,[53] a decision handed down in 1891 by the Supreme Court of Illinois. The court held:

It will be observed that all the cases hold, as our statute provides, that drunkenness is not an excuse for crime; and yet the uniform holding is that where *a particular intent is charged*, and such intent forms the gist of the offense, *as contradistinguished from the intent necessarily entering every crime*, as where one crime is thereby aggravated into a higher crime . . . any cause which deprives the defendant of the mental capacity for forming such an intent will be a defense to the graver crime [emphasis added].

The court continued:

[W]here the nature and essence of the offense is by law made to depend upon the state and condition of the mind of the accused at the time, . . . drunkenness, as a fact affecting control of the mind, is proper for consideration of the jury.[54]

This discussion is highly confusing. What is meant by the "intent necessarily entering every crime"? How is it different from the "particular intent . . . charged"? Does it refer to some one item of *mens rea* required for every crime? Or does it refer even more generally to simply a "wicked mind," an intention to act wrongfully? What is different about the "particular intent" for a crime and the *mens rea* for that crime? The two would appear to be identical. Yet, with this vague distinction, the *Crosby* court and others following *Crosby* developed what appeared to be a new and meaningful concept.

In *Schwabacher v. People*,[55] six years after *Crosby*, the jury was told that, where the defendant was charged with burglary, intoxication could negate any intent to steal, the "specific intent" required "before a conviction can be had." In this context, the new technical concept seems vacuous. Since burglary classically requires not only breaking and entering but, in addition, doing so with the intent to commit a felony, absence of the latter intent implies there was not guilt for burglary. Why, then, introduce a technical term with its attendant and dubious doctrine? The limitation of mitigation that the doctrine was intended to assure will

53. (1891).
54. *Ibid.*, pp. 52–53.
55. (1897).

here fail: the result of a successful defense would, under either basic law or the "specific intent" doctrine, turn out to be the same—acquittal on the charge of burglary. Did Schwabacher, if lacking the intent to commit a felony, also lack the "intent necessarily entering every crime"? The vacuity of the distinction here seems evident.

Nevertheless, the formulation proposed by the *Schwabacher* court is one of the earliest versions of the so-called "specific intent exception": "[W]here . . . it is necessary to prove a specific intent before a conviction can be had, it is competent to prove that the accused was at the time wholly incapable of forming such an intent, whether from intoxication or otherwise." Here we have, in a straightforward manner, the modern doctrine—including the shift to incapacity rather than simple absence of intent—more than ten years before the *Meade* case in England was decided.

In 1893, the Supreme Court of Nebraska held that evidence of intoxication could be considered in the case of the defendant charged with forgery.[56] The court held that such evidence could be admitted "where the offense charged embraces deliberation, premeditation, *some specific intent* or the like . . ." [emphasis added].[57] It would appear that if there was no intent to forge, the defendant would be acquitted. Therefore, we have here another example where the original purpose of the specific intent exception is defeated, that is, the purpose of allowing mitigation but avoiding acquittals.

By 1901, the Indiana Supreme Court in *Booher v. State* had enough cases before it to be able to put into capsule form the formulations used by countless other courts to "explain" the specific intent doctrine. The court stated:

Intoxication . . . is admitted only for the purpose of ascertaining the condition of the mind of the accused in order to determine whether he was incapable of entertaining the specific intent charged, where such intent, under the law, is an essential ingredient of the particular crime alleged to have been committed.[58]

56. *O'Grady v. State* (1893).

57. This court explicitly remarks on the conflicting *reasons* for allowing some flexibility in this area of the law. It announced that "as much as we may desire to discourage drunkenness, and deplorable as the habit of drinking, with its train of wrecks and ruin, may be, we must still recognize the frailty of human beings and adapt the law to the actual condition of the party" (*ibid.*, pp. 556–557).

58. *Booher v. State* (1901), p. 160.

This language has become a sort of rote offering when evidence of intoxication in a criminal case is presented, and the crime charged is considered to be a "specific" rather than a "general" intent crime.

Although most courts speak of the "specific intent" doctrine as encompassing a logical and well-settled body of law, the development in this area has met with increasing criticism from scholars and judges alike:

A scholar in search of logic, consistency and clarity of expression in the law would do well to look elsewhere than in the cases involving intoxication as a defense. [59]

This is the harsh judgment of one critic. Another comments that "The trouble seems to be more with the reasoning than with the results reached by the courts."[60] We question the author's conclusion that even the results reached are more than erratic, but, additionally, one should be wary of a formula that makes no logical sense. Upon reading the relevant literature, one is forced to conclude that the prevalent feeling among scholars is that the formula does not "work," either as a logical structure or as a practical tool. [61]

Even more significant than criticism by law review writers and scholars is criticism from the judiciary itself. One of the most vivid examples of judicial acknowledgment that the doctrine of the specific intent exception is untenable came from the California Supreme Court in *People v. Hood*[62] That court was faced with an open conflict in its lower courts as to whether assault and assault with a deadly weapon should be classified as "specific" or "general" intent crimes. The court first summarized the basic dilemma that led to the conceptual morass:

The distinction between specific and general intent crimes evolved as a judicial response to the problems of the intoxicated offender. That problem is to reconcile two competing theories of what is just in the treatment of those who commit crimes while intoxicated. On the one hand, the moral culpability of a drunken criminal is frequently less than that of a

59. Smith (1971), p. 16.

60. "Intoxication as a Criminal Defense" (1955), p. 1218.

61. See: Hall (1944), pp. 1045, 1061; Annotation: "Voluntary Intoxication-Defense" (1966), p. 1246, n. 19; Brooks (1975), p. 250. The American Law Institute Model Penal Code, Comment (Draft #4) par. 2.02, speaks of the concept of "general intent" as "an abiding source of ambiguity and of confusion in the penal law," and the Code abandons it. And see supra, note 38, for analogous criticisms by English commentators.

62. (1969).

sober person effecting a like injury. On the other hand, it is commonly felt that a person who voluntarily gets drunk and while in that state commits a crime should not escape the consequences.[63]

The court then observed that "specific and general intent have been notoriously difficult terms to define and apply, and a number of text-writers recommended that they be abandoned altogether."[64] General intent, the court said, concerns usually "whether the defendant intended to do the proscribed act." Specific intent refers to the "defendant's intent to do some further act or achieve some additional consequence...."[65] The court decided:

There is no real difference, however, only a linguistic one, between an intent to do an act already performed and an intent to do that same act in the future.[66]

In the case of assault, the court's view was that the difference between "general" and "specific" intent is "chimerical," and the court's overall analysis did not give much hope that in *any* case a valid distinction could be made.[67] The court thereupon decided on purely pragmatic grounds that the crime of assault should be classified as one of general intent, because the justices believed that intoxicated offenders should be held fully responsible for such acts, since assault is a crime frequently committed by inebriates.

63. *Ibid.,* p. 455.

64. *Ibid.*

65. This has been one of the standard "distinctions" between "specific" and "general" intent. However, not only is the reasoning illogical—for why should not intoxication be able to negate the "intent to do the proscribed act"—but it has practical flaws. For example, rape is usually considered a "general intent" crime because the act of rape completes the crime; there is nothing further. However, in a recent and controversial English case, *Director of Public Prosecutions v. Morgan, The Times,* May 1975, the court held that the prosecution had to prove that the defendants subjectively believed the woman was not consenting. If *subjective* belief regarding the woman's state of mind is required, then a genuine belief that she consented, although induced by intoxication, should acquit. In connection with drunkenness negating an intent to rape, see Williams (1965), supra note 30 at pp. 47–51.

66. *People v. Hood* (1969), p. 457.

67. Toward the end of its opinion, the court notes that "[t]hose crimes that have traditionally been characterized as crimes of specific intent are not affected by our holding here. The difference in mental activity between formulating an intent to commit a battery and formulating an intent to commit a battery for the purpose of

We therefore reach the unhappy but inevitable conclusion that, after a century and a half of attempts at trying to fix the criminal responsibility of the intoxicated defendant, the law has missed the mark. The lesson to be learned is that we should abandon any further attempt to mold the so-called "specific intent exception" to the psychological, moral, and legal realities; rather we should begin afresh. It is all the more distressing, then, that presumably for lack of a better doctrine, the "specific intent exception" remained in effect, if not in words, reaffirmed in the recent U.S. Senate attempt at comprehensive reform of the criminal code.[68] The time is overdue for a new, rational doctrine in this area of law.

---

raping or killing may be slight, but it is sufficient to justify drawing a line between them and considering evidence of intoxication in the one case and disregarding it in the other" (*ibid.,* p. 458). The court does not explain *why* it is justified to make such a distinction, especially if the difference is "slight." It would appear that in each case two intents are required rather than one. Why should not evidence of intoxication be allowed to show the absence of both intents—since the psychological difference *is* "slight"?

68. Senate Bill S.1, The Criminal Justice Reform Act of 1975, not only embodies the specific intent exception, but also allows for the very result that the exception was supposed to preclude—complete acquittal. The relevant provisions are as follows.

"(a) *Defense.*—It is a defense to a prosecution under any federal statute that the defendant, as a result of intoxication, lacked the state of mind required to be proved as an element of the offense charged if:

    (1) intent or knowledge is the state of mind required; or

    (2) recklessness or negligence is the state of mind required and his intoxication was not self-induced.

Intoxication does not otherwise constitute a defense" (Sec. 523). (The number of cases in which intoxication is not self-induced is minimal. The principal significance of this provision lies in (a) (1).)

Paragraph 302 provides:

"The following definitions apply with respect to an offense set forth in any federal statute:

    (a) '*Intentional*'.—A person's state of mind is intentional with respect to:

        (1) his conduct if it is his conscious objective or desire to engage in that conduct;

        (2) a result of his conduct if it is his conscious objective or desire to cause the result.

    (b) '*Knowing*'.—A person's state of mind is knowing with respect to:

        (1) his conduct if he is aware of the nature of his conduct;

        (2) an existing circumstance if he is aware or believes that the circumstance exists;

        (3) a result of his conduct if he is aware or believes that his conduct is substantially certain to cause the result."

III: A NEW APPROACH

Although the language of the law in this area has not changed very much since the early 1900s, there has been one interesting and revealing development that we have up to this point mentioned only to set aside. This development now deserves careful examination, for a critical analysis will lead to a positive formulation of the basic rationale that ought to govern in this area of law.

As the "specific intent" rule grew in popularity, a split among the courts regarding the ultimate test or standard for intoxication cases became apparent. Perhaps a minority of jurisdictions have held that the guiding test is the lack of *capacity* of the defendant to form any intent due to imbibing alcohol. Many jurisdictions hold, however, that it is the *actual* absence of the required intent as a result of intoxication that is the decisive factor. The mere distinction between actual absence and incapacity may seem on its face to have no major significance, but in fact it goes to the core of the problem with which we are dealing: how to assess the legal responsibility of the intoxicated defendant.

The legal principle upon which early judges allowed a defendant to present evidence of intoxication was the well-worn and fundamental legal

---

Using all terms directly from S.1, it appears that the intoxication defense as applied to the crime of homicide could lead to complete acquittal. Section 303 ("Proof of State of Mind") requires that if "conduct" is an element of the offense described, it must be "intentional" or "knowing." Murder (Section 1601) is divided into two categories: (1) "conduct that knowingly causes the death of another"; and (2) conduct that causes the death of another under "circumstances in fact manifesting extreme indifference to human life." Since "conduct" is required in both categories, it must be either intentional or knowing. If a defendant could show that he did not "know" or "intend" his conduct within the definition of those terms, as a result of intoxication, he cannot be found guilty of murder. Manslaughter (Section 1602) is defined as "conduct that causes the death of another person." Again, if the defendant did not "know" or "intend" his conduct because of intoxication, even if the *result* was the death of another, he is not guilty of manslaughter. Section 1603, "Negligent Homicide," provides for "engaging in conduct that negligently causes the death of another." Once again, could not a defendant argue that, due to intoxication, he did not intend his conduct or know that he was engaging in such conduct, even though its *actual* result was to negligently cause the death of another? In short, the proposed bill, by separating crimes into "conduct" and "result," allows a defendant to achieve complete exculpation by simply showing that one element, "(knowing) conduct," was not present. And it still is based upon *absence* of a particular mental element of the alleged crime—a premise which, as we shall see in Section III, infra, is fundamentally wrong.

concept that *all elements* of a crime must be proven in order to convict a man of that crime. How is it that many courts—both English[69] and American—slipped into the habit of saying that the defendant must show he was *incapable* of having the intent required when, under the fundamental principle at issue, only *actual absence* logically need be shown?[70]

This logically unwarranted demand places a far heavier burden of proof upon the defendant. Under the incapacity test, a defendant has to prove that he was virtually an automaton at the time of the act. For the absence test, a defendant need only prove, by virtue of intoxication, that he did not actually have the requisite intent at the time of the act. The typical "incapacity" standard requires that a defendant's "condition must reveal such degree of complete drunkenness that he is on account of it incapable of forming the requisite intent essential to the commission of the crime charged."[71] Intoxication must, in order to be a legal excuse, result in a "condition so extreme as to suspend all reason."[72]

One wonders why, with such an incapacity test, there is any reason for having a "specific intent" doctrine. If all reason is suspended, surely the defendant would have been unable to form *any* kind of intent or *mens rea*.

The Michigan Supreme Court, one of a number of courts that use the absence test, is aware of the current double standard, and has in fact held explicitly that it is improper to instruct a jury that it could acquit only if the defendant "was not conscious of what he was doing." The test, the court held, is not one of capacity, but whether in fact the defendant *had* specific intent.[73]

One of the paradoxical things about either test is that drunks often—in fact, one might say usually—have the capacity to intend, and do intend to do precisely what they in fact do.[74] In a sense, it is almost always a

69. E.g., *Reg. v. Monkhouse*, p. 56: "[W]as [the defendant] rendered by intoxication entirely incapable of forming the intent charged?"

70. See note 35, supra, regarding discussion of this problem by Lord Birkenhead in *D.P.P. v. Beard*.

71. *State v. Smith* (1971), p. 492.

72. *People v. Williams* (1973), p. 588. See also *People v. Hunter* (1973), p. 486.

73. *People v. Crittle* (1973). The court held that the various rules suggested for jury instructions on drunkenness "all have one thing in common. They refer to a *capacity* standard. Their test is not Justice Cooley's—'The crime cannot have been committed when the intent did not exist.' It is obviously a different standard and not to be followed" (*ibid.*, p. 199).

74. Jerome Hall (1944), p. 1062, remarks in one of his basic works on the inebriate offender that, although complete exculpation was not desired in cases

fiction to say that an intoxicated person can't or doesn't "intend" his actions. However, there is a vital difference between the intent of one who is heavily inebriated and the intent of a sober person—the former is the result of a mind that has been poisoned by alcohol and rendered irrational (even though many mental abilities remain); the latter is the result of a normally functioning mind. Jerome Hall puts it succinctly:

[A] grossly intoxicated person commits the very harm he intends to commit. . . . [T]he salient fact [is] that *there was never an intent to kill or seriously injure by a sober person* [emphasis in original] .[75]

In a way, Hall's statement seems self-evident: how can an intoxicated person have a sober intent when, by definition, he is *not* sober? If the intoxicated defendant *intends* to do what he has done, even though it be a drunken intent, where does that leave the logic of the specific intent rule? It now becomes clear that what we are seeking for conviction is a *sober*—i.e., a rational—intent. By definition, all genuinely intoxicated persons, i.e., persons who have ingested alcohol to an extent that renders the mind irrational, will have an *absence* of—and indeed an incapacity to form—a sober intent. This is the heart of the matter: what is crucial to the assessment of the moral culpability of the intoxicated offender, then, is not absence of intent, or even absence of capacity to form intent, but absence of an intent *formed by a rational mind*—i.e., absence of capacity to *rationally* form the intent, even if that intent can be formed and in fact is present.

To stop at this point, however—as Hall does—is impossible, because the result would be to acquit almost all, if not all, heavily drunken offenders, since in none would the jury be able to find the presence of *sober* intent. Because of this potential result, judges have refused to make any distinction between sober and intoxicated intent, and have held, therefore, that the presence of an intoxicated intent is sufficient to convict. In this way a reasonable proportion of convictions, in spite of drunkenness, has been

---

involving the inebriate, when it occurred it was "posited on an alleged lack of 'specific intent.' " However, Hall continues: "Yet it is commonplace that in most of these cases a criminal intent is present; it is normal restraint that has dissolved in the flowing cup." Frank Remington and Orrin Helstad (1952) also comment that "It is questionable whether intoxication very often operates in a manner so as to render a person incapable of forming a particular intent. It would rather seem to have the opposite tendency in that it relaxes the normal inhibitions against wrongdoing" (p. 669).

75. Hall (1944), p. 1065.

maintained. One decides on extralegal grounds whether mitigation is deserved, and if so, one then invokes whichever of the two available legal formulas will trigger that result—either one finds "absence" of specific intent or "absence of capacity" to form the specific intent, thus allowing mitigation. This is a pragmatic result whose moral desirability has been intuitively and strongly felt.

Thus, those courts opting for the incapacity standard have in effect been attempting to express the intuition that drunkenness, when pled as a special defense, concerns not mere presence or absence of intent but the distinctive effect of alcohol on mental *capacities.* The residual confusion has been, however, that even these courts have supposed that the capacity in question is the capacity to form a "specific intent"—no doubt a result of the dominance of the "specific intent" doctrine in this area of the law.

The concept of incapacity should be a central aspect of any analysis of the intoxicated offender. The confusion arises in supposing that the incapacity in question is the incapacity to *have an intent,* when what is really at issue is the incapacity to form an intent *rationally.* [76] It is clear to everyone that alcohol in some way and to varying degrees "incapacitates" the mind. In some fundamental and intuitive sense, it is evident that we do not expect the same emotional control or the same physical reactions from a person who is under the influence of alcohol as we do from a sober person. This incapacity, when severe enough, may be summed up by what we wish to call "irrationality." It is this incapacity that makes drunkenness a distinctive condition, requiring special treatment in law. This incapacity for rationality is the morally relevant fact that the common law needed (but failed) to bring into focus, not the question whether the "elements" of the crime were present.

It is precisely because we know that the intoxicated mind is disabled and is not functioning normally that we do not desire to find the drunken defendant as culpable criminally as the sober one. The fact that the drunken intent is just that—drunken—is actually the true moral basis, and hence should be the legal basis, for mitigating culpability. Interestingly enough, the intuitive reaction of the very early English judges, who were as yet unconfused by the "specific intent" doctrine, had been to place the

76. Hall approaches this idea in slightly different language, but comes to a similar conclusion: "The solid, unavoidable fact," he says, is "that a harm committed under gross intoxication ought to be clearly distinguished from a like injury by a sober person" (*ibid.,* p. 1061).

inebriated defendant in a category similar to the insane and the child,[77] both of whom almost always intend their acts, but whose intentions spring from unformed or defective minds.

As indicated above, one cannot let the matter rest here. Otherwise, the result of our reasoning would equal this new formula:

To be drunk = to have incapacity for rational thought = to have no criminal culpability

The last part of the equation is not satisfactory; it is *not* our thesis that the drunken offender should be allowed to escape without punishment. As noted earlier, a fundamental cornerstone of this area of the law has been the moral conviction that a person who voluntarily gets himself drunk, makes himself irrational, and in consequence causes harm, has a certain responsibility for the harm.

Austin, the great nineteenth-century jurist, stated that when a man gets drunk "[h]e has heedlessly placed himself in a position, of which the probable consequence will be the commission of a wrong."[78] Although Austin's language may be too strong when he suggests that harm will be the *probable* outcome, there is no question that there is a significant and distinctive kind of increase in the risk of harm as a result of a person's becoming intoxicated. The risk is distinctive and unreasonably incurred just because it is often difficult to foresee, and therefore it is harder to protect against the specific form the harm will take. When a person voluntarily drinks, he should be held criminally responsible at least to the extent that, when originally sober, he voluntarily placed himself in a disabling condition—a condition in which he might harm persons or property, and a condition out of which much of the harm to persons and property does actually arise.

We have therefore to reconcile two important goals in formulating the law in this area: on the one hand, we have the fact that the typical voluntarily intoxicated person can be drunk to the point of irrationality,

77. A person who is exceedingly drunk is "non compos mentis," says Coke (*Beverley's Case*, 1603); "mad," says Blackstone (IV, C.2.S.III); "without understanding or memory," says Plowden (*Reniger v. Fogossa*, 1 Plowden 19). Austin in his *Lectures on Jurisprudence* (1879) says: "The ultimate ground of this exemption [for drunkenness, in Roman Law] is the same as in the case of insanity or infancy" (Lecture 26, sec. 4; p. 512 in 1879 edition).

78. Austin (1879), pp. 512–513.

and therefore not as criminally culpable as a sober person; on the other hand, we have the fact that this state of irrationality is voluntarily[79] assumed with the knowledge that harm is unreasonably risked.

In more fundamental and general terms,[80] we can say that the voluntarily intoxicated person may be suffering a Disability of Mind rendering him nonresponsible in the moment of committing the offending act, but he culpably induced that Disability of Mind.

Actually, once one sees the issues clearly, the remedy follows simply. Here we present only the principle of the remedy, by means of an illustration. Further development of the practical import of this principle will be found in Chapter 15, where the practical implications of the general doctrine of Disability of Mind are elaborated and discussed.

X spends several hours in a bar. Someone accidentally bumps into him and laughs. *X* is infuriated, picks up a bottle near him on the counter, and severely injures the person by hitting him on the head. *X* is charged with aggravated assault and battery. There is wide disagreement between the prosecution and the defense as to how intoxicated and therefore how irrational the defendant actually was at the time. The defense claims that the defendant didn't even know what he was doing. The prosecution takes the opposite view: the defendant could easily "handle" the amount he'd drunk; he is simply a violent man.

The jury can reach one of several conclusions.

(1) It may find that the defendant did intentionally cause grievous bodily harm to the victim—i.e., that he was angry, didn't hold his temper in check, and was not suffering any material irrationality. The defendant is guilty of the crime as charged.

(2) The jury may find that the defendant did intentionally cause great bodily harm, as charged, but also that intoxication played the chief role in his forming and acting on that intent—i.e., that it was by reason of his being intoxicated that he became irrational and was on the whole irrational in his subsequent conduct. The defendant was culpable, however, in the respect that he himself had induced the intoxication. The defendant is guilty of the crime as charged, but was culpably irrational in doing the act. The criminal condemnation and punishment of this defendant is mitigated as compared to that called for had the defendant been rational.

---

79. Cases of involuntary intoxication are so rare as to be almost nonexistent. See Hall's (1944) discussion, particularly at p. 539.

80. That is, expressing the issues in terms of the D.O.M. doctrine.

(3) The jury may find as in (2), except that the irrationality, while significant, wasn't predominant. That is, the defendant's drinking significantly contributed to his forming and acting on the intent to strike and injure the other person; but the intoxication was not plainly the most important contributing factor. The defendant is guilty as in (2) above, but the mitigation will be less.

(4) The jury may find it reasonably possible that the defendant was indeed, as the defense claims, so thoroughly drunk as no longer to know what he was doing when he blindly struck out at his victim. Although the defendant did not know what he was doing, he is culpable of at least criminally negligent behavior because he failed grossly to meet the objective standard of care. Thus, even though there was no *mens rea,* the defense based on intoxication cannot provide an escape hatch from criminal punishment.

In order to insure that no such escape hatch will be available for other sorts of offenses while intoxicated, a broadening of criminal negligence beyond what is provided for by the common law is desirable. In general, common law tends to restrict criminal negligence to the causing of grave bodily injury or death. But when one considers the range of criminally significant acts characteristic of the behavior of intoxicated persons, it becomes clear that certain other acts should probably also be treated in the same way.

So, for example, serious property damage—beyond some dollar figure—should be treated as a crime of criminal negligence when committed while grossly intoxicated. Assaultive behavior while wielding a weapon should probably be at least a crime of criminal negligence if done while grossly drunk. And certain kinds of trespass—e.g., being unlawfully present at night in a building, especially if in possession of a deadly weapon—should be a crime of criminal negligence. Under such a statute, even if the defendant was so intoxicated as to have had no *mens rea,* there would still be a "floor" crime which would insure criminal responsibility and punishment.[81]

81. G. Williams (1965), p. 46, suggests: "One solution would be to create a new statutory offense of being drunk and dangerous (to person or property); and it should be possible to convict of this offense on any charge of inflicting or attempting to inflict injury to the person or damage to property where the defence is one of drunkenness as negativing *mens rea.*" Orchard's (1970) discussion would also seem to indicate that he would favor placing the emphasis on the original course of conduct, i.e., the drinking itself. See also Cross and Jones (1972), p. 96, where the

In summary, then, the aim of reform in this area of law should be to divorce so far as possible two different tasks: (1) making findings of fact as to whether a defined criminal act was committed, and (2) assessing the defendant's rationality at that time. Fundamentally simple and direct application of basic principles of common law should assure the voluntarily intoxicated offender a completely fair and full opportunity to offer evidence as to the role of his intoxication, and the extent, if any, of his consequent lack of responsibility. And similarly fundamental principles— rather than ad hoc and arbitrary devices—will provide the basis for assuring that the inherent culpability of any self-intoxicated and temporarily non-responsible offender will not get lost from sight. This eliminates both the arbitrary exclusions under current law of evidence as to intoxication, and the often arbitrary demand on the jury to consider such evidence, when it is allowed, in relation only to some of the allegations but not to others. This suggested approach would eliminate the pervasive injustice and confusion embodied in current law dealing with the culpability of the intoxicated offender.

---

authors suggest that punishing the intoxicated defendant "for having caused bodily harm while drunk ... should be a separate offence." See the discussion of the "floor" crimes of criminal negligence, in Chapter 15, Section II, #4, infra.

7

Drug Intoxication

I

Defendant X has been charged with the first-degree murder of Y. The facts as proven at trial are the following:

The defendant, while with Y on a camping trip, took an LSD tablet. Shortly after taking the tablet, as X watched his companion sleep, Y made noises that sounded to X like those of a rabid dog which X's father had shot when X was a small boy. Although aware that his companion was not in fact a dog, X took fright and shot his companion.[1]

Testimony by a defense expert at the trial showed that LSD, like other hallucinogens, can produce a range of mental states, including hallucinations, delusions, and partial amnesia. Effects of the drug may range from a loss of time and space perception to panic, paranoid delusions, and reactions very similar to schizophrenia.[2] Another defense expert testified that, at the time of the act, the defendant was not aware of the quality and nature of his act. There was no testimony, however, that the defendant had a mental disease or defect, only that he was in a state of intoxication caused by LSD. It was shown that the defendant had used LSD on previous occasions.

---

1. The basic facts in this example are derived from *State v. Hall* (1974). They have been slightly modified.
2. See note 6, infra.

Defendant *X* asked the trial judge to instruct the jury that if the defendant could not distinguish right from wrong, he is entitled to a verdict of acquittal.[3] Alternatively, he requested instructions to the effect that if, due to drug intoxication, the defendant did not form any one or more of the specific mental states required as an essential element of the crime of first-degree murder, then he is not guilty of that crime. How should the judge rule on his requests?

Since the late 1960s, a number of courts have been confronted with defendants who have committed criminal acts while under the influence of voluntarily ingested mind-altering drugs. Consequently, judges have been forced to deal with complex and fundamental issues regarding the degree of the defendant's responsibility.

Should a person who, like *X*, voluntarily takes a drug with knowledge of its potentially disabling and disorienting effects on the mind, be completely acquitted of a crime on the ground of insanity because, at the time of the act, he could not distinguish right from wrong? The prospect of complete acquittal for intoxicated harmdoers, not surprisingly, has met with great resistance.[4] The absence of "mental disease" provides a logical and traditional basis in law for rejecting this defense.

Is it legally or psychologically accurate to say of a person such as *X*, who was deluded or hallucinatory, yet who intended to kill a person whom he perceived as threatening him, that he did not have the required "specific intent" to kill? The usual effect of this defense, when successful,

---

3. For purposes of this chapter, we use the definition of insanity as advanced in *M'Naghten's Case* (1843), p. 722: a defendant is insane if he "was labouring under such a defect of reason, from disease of the mind, as not to know the nature and quality of the act he was doing, or if he did know it, that he did not know he was doing what was wrong." It will be seen that the problems raised here are not affected by the variant forms of *M'Naghten,* or by the addition of a "loss of free will" clause (*Davis v. United States,* 1897, p. 378; *Parsons v. State,* 1887, pp. 866–867), or by the modernized version of these to be found in the American Law Institute's Model Penal Code insanity test: Model Penal Code S. 4.01 (Proposed Official Draft 1962). All the tests require a finding of "mental disease," and therein lies the crux of the difficulty in ascribing insanity to one who is voluntarily drug-intoxicated. For a general discussion of the insanity tests, see Goldstein (1967) and Fingarette (1972). The criticisms levied against the *M'Naghten* test are chronicled in Student Symposium (1972), pp. 557–560.

4. See, e.g., *United States v. Romano; State v. Cooper; State v. Hall; Commonwealth v. Campbell;* and *State v. Bellue.*

is to reduce the degree of the crime. But, however desirable the result, this defense simply does not fit the facts of most cases involving drug-induced intoxication.

Should a defendant such as X be held to have *no* legally acceptable defense, complete or mitigating, because he is not legally insane (that is, he has no "mental disease"), and because he did in fact specifically intend to kill? The effect of this approach seems both psychologically unrealistic and morally oppressive.

Until recently, there seem to have been only these three alternatives seriously considered [5] (complete acquittal as insane, guilty of a lesser crime because of absence of specific intent, or no defense at all available). Yet clearly a fourth question remains to be asked: Is there another option that both appropriately assesses X's criminal responsibility and also fits readily within the framework of relevant law?

The problem is one that is in urgent need of resolution. In our society there is increasingly common use of hallucinogenic and other types of drugs having consciousness-altering effects significantly different from alcohol.[6] It is the purpose of this chapter to display the inherent contra-

---

5. Although the question of a defendant's criminal responsibility when he commits a crime while drug-intoxicated defines a relatively new area of consideration for legal commentators, there is already a certain amount of literature on the question. Law review writers in general have tended to accept as the only relevant theories the insanity defense and the specific intent exception. Baumgartner (1970) concludes that the specific intent exception will be increasingly used in cases when the defendant acted while under the influence of drugs, because the exception rests on an established body of law and overcomes the problem of unconditionally releasing defendants. The commentator in "LSD–Its Effect on Criminal Responsibility" (1968) accepts both theories as tenable and argues that the applicability of either defense depends primarily on the facts of the individual case. Lunter (1972) approaches the question as one of prosecutorial or defense strategy and suggests what are in essence two opposite views: (1) the prosecutorial view that society could hold criminally responsible anyone who uses drugs; and (2) the defense view that a "toxic psychosis," a psychosis induced by drugs, could result in a successful insanity defense. Other articles have approached the general question of control of drug abuse from the legislative perspective, e.g., Bartels (1973), or from the medical and sociological points of view, e.g., "Contemporary Problems of Drug Abuse" (1973).

6. This article is primarily directed to intoxication from those drugs that tend to have effects which are substantially unlike the effects of alcohol. Drugs of major concern in this context can be grouped into two categories: (1) the aminergic agents (commonly termed hallucinogens and psychedelics), whose best-known representa-

dictions of traditional doctrines when applied to the problem of the drug-intoxicated offender and to show how the D.O.M. approach appropriately assesses the criminal responsibility of such an offender.[7]

II: TRADITIONAL APPROACHES TO
DRUG INTOXICATION: SHORTCOMINGS

A. *The Specific Intent Exception and the Alcohol Intoxication Analogy*

A majority of courts have chosen to analogize the situation of the drug-intoxicated offender to that of the alcohol-intoxicated offender,[8] and therefore to invoke the "specific intent exception."[9]

The intrinsic worth of the specific intent exception—and its usefulness for the area of drug intoxication—cannot be assessed properly unless one examines its historical development.[10] Such an examination reveals that,

---

tives are LSD and mescaline; and (2) the amphetamines, including benzedrine, dexedrine, and methamphetamine (often referred to as "speed"). Both types of drug can induce hallucinations and delusions as well as a toxically produced paranoid schizophrenic condition. Of less concern here are euphoria-producing drugs such as marijuana and hashish (see Gerald, 1974). For further analysis of the effects of various drugs, see DeLong (1972), p. 62, and see Lunter (1972), pp. 738–741. However, any classification of a drug and its effect should be regarded with some wariness, since the effect of any drug on any person is dependent on a number of factors. Among them are purity of the drug, how it was administered, the state of the person's health, his expectations of the drug's effect, and the setting in which the drug is taken (see Blum, Bovet, and Moore, 1974, chaps. 1–3). Much discussion assumes a regular and specific effect of a drug, when in reality one must consider a classification as a "probability" or an "estimate." See Blum (1970), and Blum, Bovet, and Moore (1974).

7. The approach is that proposed in Part V, infra.

8. See, e.g., *United States v. Romano; State v. Clark; State v. Rushing; State v. Nelson; State v. Smith;* and *State v. Roisland.* Just such an approach is explicitly built into the recently proposed Criminal Justice Reform Act of 1975, S.1, 94th Cong., 1st Sess. S 523(a) [hereinafter cited as S.1] :

It is a defense to a prosecution under any federal statute that the defendant, as a result of intoxication, lacks the state of mind required to be proved as an element of the offense charged if: (1) intent or knowledge is the state of mind required. . . .

. . . .

(b) (1) "[I]ntoxication" means a disturbance of a mental or physical capacity resulting from the introduction of alcohol or a drug or other substance into the body. . . .

9. This doctrine is fully discussed in Chapter 6, supra.

10. See Chapter 6, Sections I and II, supra.

even with reference to the area of alcohol intoxication, the specific intent exception has two serious flaws: first, the technical distinctions upon which the doctrine is based are unsound; and second, the practical results are highly inconsistent.[11] Because of the doctrine's severe theoretical and practical flaws,[12] the courts should seriously question the wisdom of expanding its usage to drug-intoxication cases.

The inappropriateness of the specific intent exception is magnified, however, in the case of drug intoxication. The effect of many drugs on the mind and conduct can be very different from the effect of alcohol, and in ways that make the 'specific intent' language even less apt than in the case of alcohol intoxication. The factual discrepancy was at first less evident because the drugs involved, until the 1960s, were mainly euphoric and tranquilizing rather than, for example, hallucinatory or excitatory. This resulted in an almost matter-of-fact extension by the courts of the application of the specific intent exception from alcohol to drug cases.[13] The effects of a euphoric or tranquilizing drug were sufficiently similar to the depressant effects of alcohol for the specific intent exception to be reasonably applicable. With hallucinatory drugs, however, the discrepancies are blatant.

Despite the problems, most courts regard the specific intent exception as the relevant legal principle to apply in drug-intoxication cases. Courts agree that intoxication by drugs should be considered a mitigating factor but should not result in exculpation. Thus, the fact that permitting the intoxication defense often produces a desirable legal outcome has undoubtedly helped suppress disquiet at its blatant inappropriateness as a description of the facts.

For example, in the case of defendant *X*, if the court were to instruct that voluntary drug intoxication may negate the specific mental states essential to the crime, the jury would have to make a determination as to the presence of deliberation, premeditation, malice, and intent to kill—the four mental states essential for first-degree murder—at the time of the act. The jury might well find that all those elements were present; for although *X* was acting under a delusion, he meant to kill and did so deliberately. Even malice, that notably obscure concept, presumably would apply to these facts under most current law. Mere absence of hatred, ill will, or immoral intent is not sufficient to negate malice, and drug intoxication per

11. *Ibid.*
12. See *People v. Corson* and *De Berry v. Commonwealth.*
13. See Chapter 6, supra, and note 8, supra.

se is not an excuse, justification, or mitigation.[14] Since all the requisite specific mental states are thus present, under the specific intent doctrine, X's criminal responsibility would in no way be mitigated if the jury correctly applied the law.

In spite of this, realism requires that we recognize that each and every one of those mental states of X was the product of an irrational state of mind: the intent to kill was a *mad* intent; the deliberation and premeditation were carried out by a mind filled with delusion. Unfortunately for the defendant (and for the cause of justice), the specific intent exception hinges on the *absence* of a mental state; and in X the relevant states were *present*, though the mind that generated them was irrational. Thus X cannot, in logic, take advantage of the rule. A jury that applies the law straightforwardly must entirely ignore the evident irrationality of the defendant at the time of the offense. Or the jury may instead use its common moral sense, ignore the plain meaning of the terms, and find for the defendant, thus distorting the doctrine in order to achieve the desired mitigating effect.

Even in the face of these discrepancies, the specific intent exception in drug-intoxication cases has become sufficiently entrenched in the reasoning of most courts to reduce the rule to mere verbal legerdemain. In 1967, a trial court, faced with a glue-sniffing defendant who killed a companion while hallucinating, held that instructions on the effects of voluntary intoxication in a drug-intoxication case were necessary to carry out the state's duty to "define criminal responsibility in keeping with elementary principles of fairness, justice, and order."[15] The United States Court of Appeals for the Tenth Circuit affirmed, reasoning that although the instruction historically had been concerned with voluntary intoxication from alcohol, there was no constitutional bar to applying it where the intoxication was caused by drugs.[16]

14. Perkins (1969) states: "Despite clear recognition of the non-necessity of any element of hatred, spite, grudge or ill-will, it seems frequently to be assumed that malice, as a jural concept, must involve intent *plus* some matter of aggravation whereas, in truth, the requirement is fully satisfied by intent *minus* any matter of exculpation or mitigation. . . . It is recognized that an intent to cause the particular harm involved in the crime in question without justification, excuse or mitigation, is sufficient to meet the mens-rea requirements of such offenses as murder" (p. 767). (As to the problem of specific intent and delusion, see also note 34, infra.)

15. *Pierce v. Turner*, p. 300.

16. *Ibid.*, p. 113.

However, the blatant inappropriateness of the use of this doctrine for increasingly numerous drug-intoxication crimes has at last induced a degree of uneasiness. Judges recently have begun to recognize the distortion inherent in equating the effects of drugs, particularly those classified as hallucinatory, with the effects of alcohol.[17] Though he spoke in dissent from the majority, Judge Le Grand expressed a recently growing awareness when he said:

Our intoxication rationale as applied to alcohol simply does not fit the use of modern hallucinatory drugs; and it was never meant to. . . . [T]hey *are* dissimilar and should be so regarded.[18]

B. *The Insanity Defense*

An orthodox alternative to the voluntary intoxication defense is the insanity defense. A court faced with defendant *X*, if it accepted his story as true, would be hard put to deny that at the time of the act, *X* was, in at least a loose sense of the phrase, "temporarily insane." Similarly bizarre drug-intoxication crimes suggest the same conclusion: the defendant who killed his girlfriend thinking that she was a nest of snakes;[19] the man who robbed a store, then wandered slowly about, casually trying two locked doors before finally strolling outside.[20] If the condition had been the result of a mental disease, such persons probably would qualify as

17. "In light of the changing state of medical knowledge regarding hallucinogens, we think the district court may have underestimated the unique and potentially dangerous impact that prolonged use of LSD appears to have on the psychological state and behavioral pattern of some users" (*Brinkley v. United States*, 1974, p. 511). Although the trial judge in *Pierce v. Turner* admitted that "[i]ntoxication from glue-sniffing may differ from other types of intoxication," he nonetheless equated glue-sniffing with alcohol for legal purposes (p. 298). "To treat all [drugs] alike simply because each is classified generally as a drug strikes me as a judicial cop-out which completely disregards the realities of the situation," stated Judge Le Grand in *State v. Hall* (1974) (dissent), p. 213. The provisions of S.1. (note 8, supra) thus represent a serious regression. It would fix into federal law an expansion of the "specific intent" intoxication doctrine to cover drug intoxications, and would do so just at a time when there is an emerging awareness that, over and above the inadequacies of the doctrine in its "home ground" of alcohol intoxication, it is specifically unsuited for use in important types of drug intoxication.

18. *State v. Hall* (1974) (Judge Le Grand dissenting), p. 213.

19. *Regina v. Lipman.*

20. *People v. Fanning.*

legally insane. But in cases of drug intoxication there is, of course, no "mental disease" and hence no legal insanity under the tests currently in force.[21]

The majority of courts that have considered the insanity defense in relation to the drug-intoxicated offender have rejected it,[22] not only because of the absence of mental disease, but for one of two related policy reasons.

First, certain courts have determined that public safety demands rejection of the insanity defense in cases such as *X*'s. Although the voluntary consumption of drugs may lead "to a prostration of the defendant's mental facilities, . . . [a] condition so induced cannot lead to acquittal, upon the demands of public security."[23] The very fact that a hallucinogenic drug has effects that are "predictably unforeseeable should require courts to decide in the public interest that this is not legally sufficient to *completely exculpate* a person from murder or any other criminal act."[24]

Other courts reject the insanity defense on a second but related ground: precisely because some drugs are known to produce unpredictable and potentially dangerous effects, a person using such drugs is personally culpable. He deliberately takes the risk that as a result of the ingestion of drugs he may commit a serious harm. It is, after all, common knowledge that drugs have a deleterious effect upon the user.[25] In a recent Arizona case, *State v. Cooper*,[26] the state apparently conceded that the defendant was temporarily insane at the time of the act, but nevertheless argued that because the condition was voluntarily caused by the defendant, the defense of insanity was not available to him. The court agreed:

His subsequent condition after taking amphetamines for several days, leading to his bizarre actions, was a result of an artificially produced state

21. See note 3, supra.

22. See note 4, supra.

23. *State v. Trantino*, p. 122.

24. *Commonwealth v. Campbell*, p. 800. Juries also are reluctant to release defendants who have done serious harm while under the influence of drugs. A defendant who took LSD for the first time and then killed a comparative stranger at a party while hallucinating was found to be sane. "The dilemma facing the jury was that of possibly setting free a person who had committed a serious crime without any sort of punishment or retribution" (Barter and Reite, 1969, p. 536).

25. *Commonwealth v. Campbell*, p. 800.

26. P. 231.

of mind brought on by his own hand at his own choice. The voluntary actions of the defendant do not provide an excuse in law for his subsequent, irrational conduct.[27]

Our hypothetical defendant X, although temporarily insane at the time he shot Y, should not be allowed to invoke the insanity defense. On the facts, he is at least partly culpable: his irrational and hence dangerous condition was voluntarily induced.

C. *The Dilemma—and Diminished Capacity*

The exclusion of the insanity defense, and the inappositeness of the specific intent exception if correctly applied, would appear to leave defendant X with no defense, not even in mitigation. Society has found this outcome morally unacceptable in both alcohol and drug cases ever since the nineteenth century—and rightly so, if common sense is any guide. A defendant like X, who commits an act while in a state of delusion, hallucination, or other gross, chemically-induced derangement of mental faculties, is not rational. Whether he means to kill a human being whom he deludedly believes to be mortally dangerous to him; whether he means to kill but does so only because his ability to assess the act is seriously deranged as a result of massive chemical impact on brain function—whatever the particular facts, the *essential* fact pattern is the same, and the legal and moral significance ought to be the same. Such a person is not fully responsible for his act.

On the other hand, defendant X voluntarily took LSD, knowing from past experience and from common knowledge that LSD, or consciousness-altering drugs generally, have varying effects on the mind; that they can and usually do result in abnormal perception, sensations, and vision; that, in short, they make the mind irrational. By voluntarily taking LSD, typically with the *intention* of producing a significantly altered, irrational state of consciousness, defendant X knowingly and unnecessarily took a risk that he could become disoriented, and hence the risk that he might harm someone or something as a result. For the voluntary risk he assumed, and for the harm resulting, he should receive punishment—but less severe punishment than the person who sanely contemplates and commits the same actual harm.

California attorneys in particular may wish to consider the diminished capacity defense as a possible solution to the problem. Unfortunately, the

27. *Ibid.*, p. 233.

diminished capacity concept, as it has evolved in California case law, has proved a complex and unsatisfactory alternative. In the first place, the diminished capacity applies, generally, only where specific intent is a requisite element of the crime charged.[28] The defense proceeds along much the same lines as the more orthodox specific intent exception, and often uses the same terminology: the defendant must prove that his mental state was so impaired at the time the crime was committed that he lacked the required specific intent.[29] Thus the diminished capacity defense shares the defects of the traditional specific intent exception with regard to crimes involving drug-induced intoxication.[30]

However, the diminished capacity defense introduces still further complications. It is not yet clear how much effect the source of the impairment (alcohol, drugs, mental disturbance not amounting to insanity) may have on the operation of the defense, nor what degree of impairment must be shown in each case; in addition, there is, inevitably, considerable overlap and confusion (indeed, possible conflict) with the separate but related defenses of insanity and unconsciousness.

While recent decisions of the California Supreme Court appear to be broadening the concept beyond the relatively rigid framework of the specific intent exception,[31] a more straightforward solution would seem preferable to the complicated, piecemeal diminished capacity approach.

III: PROPOSAL: DISABILITY OF MIND DOCTRINE AND STATUTES

We believe that the problem posed by criminal acts performed while the defendant is drug-intoxicated should be resolved by keeping distinct the question as to the existence of particular mental elements of the alleged criminal act as normally defined, and the question as to whether the defendant's mental capacities at the time of that alleged offense were so impaired as to render him less responsible, or not responsible, for engaging in such behavior.

28. "Diminished Capacity, Its Potential Effect in California" (1970), pp. 153–154. See generally Cooper (1971).

29. *People v. Nance;* California Jury Instructions, Criminal No. 3.35 (1972).

30. See Chapter 6, supra.

31. See *People v. Poddar* and *People v. Sedeno.* The court appears to hold in these cases that if a person was irrational at the time of the criminal act, he is not fully responsible for that act.

As we have seen, there are cases where one who is drug-intoxicated may have the knowledge, intent, or other requisite mental states essential to the crime alleged. Or the defendant, in some other kinds of drug intoxication, will have been mentally confused or stupefied, and in consequence will in fact not have known what he or she was doing, or will have had no intent to act in the criminally prohibited way or to produce the criminally harmful result. Intuitively one can see that if the defendant was on the whole irrational, then whether this resulted in his forming an intent or having no intent, it should make no difference as to his culpability and punishment.[32] Our proposal reaches just this result.

For example, the defendant took amphetamine pills and was under their influence at the time he got in a fight and caused grave bodily injury. The jury should first determine whether the criminal act was committed, and should do so without introducing such issues as "diminished capacity" or other forms of mental disability issues. One possibility would be that the jury finds that the defendant not only caused the grave injury, but did so intentionally. Then the defendant is guilty of aggravated battery. The jury then turns, under the approach we propose, to consider whether the defendant, in acting as he did, was partially or predominantly irrational,[33] and if so, whether he was culpable as to the origin of that irrationality. They find, let us assume, that the defendant was culpably irrational. The defendant's guilt as charged, *and* his culpable irrationality, are reported in the verdict. The defendant's criminal condemnation and punishment for

32. The trial judge in *Brinkley v. United States,* p. 513 n. 4, gave this charge: "[I]f the act or acts charged as a crime or as crimes are such acts as to require the acting party to *think rationally* or to form a specific intent, and *if his faculties are so impaired by drug use that he cannot think or act rationally* ... then he is not responsible criminally" (emphasis added). Those parts of the charge emphasized here capture the essential nature of the proposal insofar as the concept of irrationality is concerned. However, the present thesis rejects the *Brinkley* judge's conclusion that if by reason of drug impairment the defendant was irrational, he should be found totally nonresponsible.

33. It was noted above (see note 6, supra) that the effect of any drug on any person may vary considerably. It is therefore up to the jury to decide whether, in the case before it, the ingestion of a drug resulted in irrationality in *that* defendant. Even those drugs known as "euphorics" can result in irrationality at times; for example, marijuana, normally a euphoric, can result in acute psychotic reactions characterized by paranoia and hallucinations (Gerald, 1974, p. 348). Therefore, the logic suggested here applies in principle to *any* drug ingested voluntarily, although irrationality will most commonly occur in conjunction with the hallucinogenic drugs such as LSD and the amphetamines.

aggravated battery are mitigated as compared to what such conduct would have warranted had the defendant been rational when he formed and acted on the intent to cause grave harm.

As an alternative possibility, the jury might find that the evidence, taken as a whole, leaves reasonable doubt that the defendant had such an intent; indeed, they might find that the evidence strongly suggests that he was so irrational as not even to know what he was doing at the time. Then the defendant is not guilty of the intentional crime of aggravated battery, but he is obviously guilty of the lesser included "floor" crime of causing grave bodily harm by gross negligence. *Mens rea* is not essential here; the objective standard of care is the criterion. There will be no mitigation of culpability for this crime, because of the defendant's culpability for getting himself into the irrational (grossly negligent) state.

The practical upshot would thus be that the jury has a straightforward set of factual inquiries, in which the issues are not confused; and the jury reports its findings straightforwardly. The defendant is—in *either* case— condemned and punished to about the same extent, which is as it should be.[34]

It would be desirable to regularize and make explicit the principles here outlined; certain statutory provisions could easily do this.[35]

34. It might be worth noting here that a similar result would obtain in *Lipman*. The jury—had it been following our recommended procedure—might have agreed with the prosecution that Lipman understood himself to be killing a human being (in snakelike form); or the jury might have found plausible the defense claim that he thought himself to be killing a snake. But the upshot so far as criminal condemnation and punishment are concerned would have been much the same—either Lipman was guilty of murder but deserved substantial mitigation because of significantly less responsibility in regard to an intentional crime, or Lipman was guilty of manslaughter, for which he was fully responsible and deserved no mitigation, inasmuch as he had, while responsible, brought about the dangerous mental condition.

35. See the discussion at the end of Chapter 6, supra, and more fully in Chapter 15, Section II, infra.

8

Diminished Mental Capacity

After our analyses of the specific intent exception, a defense that is used typically in mitigation and that limits the jury to examination of a legal fiction classified as a mental state, it is only appropriate to study in some detail what at times has seemed an alternative route to the same end—the California defense of diminished capacity. Diminished mental capacity, a concept ambitiously developed by the California Supreme Court, allows examination of any mental disability if it relevantly affects elements of the alleged offense.[1] The label "diminished capacity" originally suggested a

1. Approximately fifteen states have adopted, or at least approved of, forms of the diminished capacity or diminished responsibility concept. However, almost without exception, the defense has been viewed as an extension of the specific intent doctrine and has been considered as particularly applicable to homicide cases. "If alcohol or drugs can legally prevent a person from truly deliberating, then certainly a disease of the mind, which has the same effect, should be given like consideration" (*State v. Padilla*, p. 315). The style of reasoning typical of most courts is fairly well represented by these two decisions: "Defendant in a first degree murder case has the right . . . to establish mental deficiency as bearing upon his capacity to form the specific intent essential [to first degree murder]" (*Becksted v. People*, p. 194). "We believe that failure to recognize there can be an unsoundness of mind of such a character as to negative a specific intent to commit a particular crime is to ignore the great advancements which have been made in the field of psychiatry" (*State v. Gramenz*, p. 289). Evidence of mental abnormality less than insanity, when admissible, is generally considered only to bear on states of mind relevant to murder. Among other states holding that an abnormal mental condition is evidence properly considered by the jury in homicide cases are: Florida—*Gaines v. State*; New Jersey—

radical innovation, a new defense filling the legal limbo between the complete defense of insanity at one extreme, and the highly restricted and unrealistic specific intent defense at the other. Any mental abnormalities not reaching insanity might now establish "diminished mental capacity" and thereby reduce the gravity of the crime.[2] Such an approach seems on its face to promise something more akin to the D.O.M. defense proposed in this book than any other defense yet examined. We shall explore with some care the path that the California Supreme Court took in this matter, for it provides a valuable commentary on the difficulties of a judicially created defense that attempts to answer one of the principal questions

---

State v. Vigliano; Oregon—*State v. Schleigh*; and Utah—*State v. Green*. Colorado, apparently the only state to do so, has enacted a statute which provides that any mental condition may affect specific intent: "[E]vidence of mental condition may be offered in a proper case as bearing upon the capacity of the accused to form the specific intent essential to constitute a crime" (cited in *Gallegos v. People*). The one time it was faced with the issue, the United States Supreme Court, in *Fisher v. United States* (1946), rejected a "partial responsibility" defense. The Court, despite two strong dissenting opinions by Justices Frankfurter and Murphy, held that, since the laws of the District of Columbia did not allow for a partial responsibility defense, the Court could not create it. (For an interesting critique of *Fisher*, see Keedy, 1950.) The District of Columbia Court of Appeals has recently affirmed its rejection of a diminished capacity or diminished responsibility concept in *Stewart v. United States* (1960) and *Stewart v. United States* (1968). The court reasoned that the problems of classifying and analyzing psychiatry and applying it to the criminal law were such that it should be left to the legislature to create a basic framework. Another jurisdiction that has rejected the diminished responsibility concept is Pennsylvania; see *Commonwealth v. Ahearn*. For a full study of those cases allowing consideration of a defendant's mental state in either the guilt-finding or the penalty phase of a criminal trial, see "Criminal Law—Mental Conditions" (1970). The commentator in the latter, and Jones (1967), have each urged adoption of the concept of diminished responsibility for their respective states.

2. In an excellent review, the author of "Criminal Law—Partial Insanity—Evidentiary Relevance Defined" (1961) points out the historic lines of debate on the concept (usually termed diminished responsibility), lines established in the early 1900s. On the one hand, some courts, in accepting the principle, argued that "evidence of any defect, deficiency, trait, condition or illness which rationally bears upon the question" should be allowed to disprove any required element of a crime and result in the defendant's being "found guilty of the basic crime but in a lesser degree" (*ibid.*, pp. 175 and 179). On the other hand, most courts that resisted adopting the principle objected because of "the inability of the courts to determine the mental abilities of an individual, the potential lesser degree of protection to society, and the preference of a legislative treatment of the problem to one supplied by the judiciary" (*ibid.*, p. 179). That division persists to the present.

posed by this book: How do we assess the criminal responsibility of one whose mind, for whatever reason, was partially disabled at the time he committed a criminal act?[3]

Since its inception in 1949, the diminished capacity defense in California has developed along two distinguishable but equally important theoretical lines. One line of development can be termed the *Conley* approach.[4] This approach focuses primarily upon the various specific states of mind essential to one or both grades of murder. According to the *Conley* doctrine, as it came to operate in practice, absence of a specific mental element of a crime, but not of "general criminal intent," can be established by evidence of appropriate mental abnormality not amounting to insanity. Thus, in fact, *Conley* retains the specific intent doctrine, but it expands the scope of the evidence that will be allowed to establish the absence of the mental element: not only intoxication, but also *any* mental abnormality may so serve. The *Conley* approach has gained a sort of "official recognition"; it is this approach that has been largely reflected in the diminished capacity instructions that California judges give in homicide cases.[5]

3. In addition to Hasse (1972), there have been four major articles to date on the California diminished capacity concept: Kay (1967); Leib (1970); Cooper (1971); and Comment, "Insanity, Intoxication and Diminished Capacity Under the Proposed California Criminal Code" (1972). Kay takes an historical approach which, due to its early date of publication, unfortunately does not cover some major developments in the field of diminished capacity. Leib discusses diminished capacity as an alternative to the insanity test and in terms of "status" diseases such as alcoholism and drug addiction. He also suggests extension to include any "specific intent" crime. Cooper gives a good account of the historical development of the concept, but his analysis of the defense is limited in scope since it was written for the benefit of the practitioner. He does, however, note briefly the several different lines of thought by which the Supreme Court has approached the problem. The author of the UCLA Comment discusses the Proposed Model Penal Code sections on diminished capacity, pointing out that, as suggested by the Joint Legislative Committee for Revision of the Penal Code [hereinafter referred to as the Committee], the doctrine of diminished capacity is analogous to the specific intent exception; he further indicates that a primary concern of the Committee was to avoid creating a complete defense when diminished capacity is present.

4. *People v. Conley* (1966).

5. CALJIC 8.77 (1974 Revision):

Diminished Capacity—Ability to Premeditate, Deliberate, Harbor Malice, Or Intend to Kill

If you find from the evidence that at the time the alleged crime was committed, the defendant had substantially reduced mental capacity, whether caused by mental illness, mental defect, intoxication, or any other cause, you must consider what

The second line of development of the diminished capacity concept began with *People v. Wolff.*[6] The *Wolff* test, in addition to inquiring into the defendant's ability to form the mental states classically required for the commission of a crime, focuses on the defendant's ability to understand the moral and social values underlying the laws. It provides in substance, though not in words, for negating the criminal significance of a mental element—deliberation—if it arises out of diminished mental capacity. In a key phrase highlighting this approach, the California Supreme Court referred to the defendant's lack of "moral turpitude."[7] The Court said in this connection that the defendant's diminished criminal responsibility derives from his inability to "maturely and appreciatively reflect" upon his act and to realize the "enormity of the evil" involved.[8] That is, there is established absence of *"meaningful"* deliberation—and hence, for legal purposes, absence of deliberation—even though in the common sense of that term the mental process of deliberation was *present.* Wolff, for example, plainly acted with deliberation, but the court found this not to be "meaningful" because of his diminished mental capacity for moral perception. Thus the focus of *Wolff* is on the defendant's impaired moral perceptions as negating the significance of his deliberation, and consequently on absence of guilt for first-degree murder.

---

effect, if any, this diminished capacity had on the defendant's ability to form any of the specific mental states that are essential elements of murder and voluntary manslaughter.

Thus, if you find that the defendant's mental capacity was diminished to the extent that you have a reasonable doubt whether he did, maturely and meaningfully premeditate, deliberate, and reflect upon the gravity of his contemplated act, or form an intent to kill, you cannot find him guilty of a wilful, deliberate and premeditated murder of the first degree.

Also, if you find that the defendant's mental capacity was diminished to the extent that you have a reasonable doubt whether he was able to form the mental states constituting either expressed or implied malice aforethought, you cannot find him guilty of murder of either the first or second degree. If you have a reasonable doubt whether he was able to form an intention unlawfully to kill a human being, you cannot find that he harbored express malice. Further, if you have a reasonable doubt (1) whether his acts were done for a base, antisocial purpose, or (2) whether he was aware of the duty imposed on him not to commit acts which involve the risk of grave injury or death, or (3) whether he did act despite that awareness, you cannot find that he harbored implied malice.

Furthermore, if you find that as a result of mental illness, mental defect, or unconsciousness caused by voluntary intoxication, his mental capacity was diminished to the extent that he neither harbored malice aforethought nor had an intent to kill at the time the alleged crime was committed, you cannot find him guilty of either murder or voluntary manslaughter.

6. (1964).

7. *Ibid.*, p. 976.

8. *Ibid.*

Distinctive though it is in its recognition of impaired moral perception, and in its acknowledgment that deliberation in the ordinary sense may be *present,* the *Wolff* doctrine has not been clearly and explicitly recognized as such in California by independent jury instructions.[9] Indeed, in our opinion, the importance and full significance of *Wolff* has not yet been fully appreciated by most lawyers, even though in several of its most recent cases dealing with the concept the Supreme Court, after much wavering, has apparently adopted a final analysis based primarily on the thesis originally expounded in *Wolff.*

Whichever of the two approaches has been used—*Conley* or *Wolff*—the constant temptation has been to treat the diminished capacity defense

9. As noted in the 1974 revision of CALJIC 8.77 (note 5, supra), some important new language was added. This added language was: "Further, if you have a reasonable doubt (1) whether his acts were done for a base, antisocial purpose, or (2) whether he was aware of the duty imposed on him not to commit acts which involve the risk of grave injury or death, or (3) whether he did act despite that awareness, you cannot find that he harbored implied malice." This language, although rather awkwardly put, would seem to suggest that an examination by the jury of the defendant's moral awareness is appropriate. In its previous form, CALJIC 8.77 read:

Diminished Capacity—Ability to Premeditate, Deliberate, Harbor Malice, or Intend to Kill: If you find from the evidence that at the time the alleged crime was committed, the defendant had substantially reduced mental capacity, whether caused by mental illness, mental defect, intoxication, or any other cause, you must consider what effect, if any, this diminished capacity had on the defendant's ability to form any of the specific mental states that are essential elements of murder and voluntary manslaughter.

Thus, if you find that the defendant's mental capacity was diminished to the extent that you have a reasonable doubt whether he did, maturely and meaningfully, premeditate, deliberate, and reflect upon the gravity of his contemplated act, or form an intent to kill, you cannot find him guilty of a willful, deliberate and premeditated murder of the first degree.

Also, if you find that his mental capacity was diminished to the extent that you have a reasonable doubt whether he did harbor malice aforethought, you cannot find him guilty of murder of either the first or second degree.

Furthermore, if you find that his mental capacity was diminished to the extent that he neither harbored malice aforethought nor had an intent to kill at the time the alleged crime was committed, you cannot find him guilty of either murder or voluntary manslaughter (CALJIC 8.77, 3d rev. ed. 1970).

It has been suggested by the author of the UCLA Comment, "Intoxication and Diminished Capacity" (1972), that the *Wolff* case was influential in the formulation of the California Proposed Model Penal Code *Insanity* test. The insanity test approved by the Supreme Court in *Wolff* was nothing startling or new, however; it was simply a repetition of the standard jury instructions now given by California courts and accepted by the Supreme Court as an appropriate modern version of the *M'Naghten* test. What distinguishes the *Wolff* case is the novel interpretation of the diminished capacity doctrine as it pertains to the defendant's moral perceptions.

simply as a version of the specific intent exception.[10] Such is the fatal magnetism of the latter doctrine to the judiciary even when a doctrine inherently opposed to it is in the process of birth. Let us see in more detail how this birth and unfortunate transformation took place.

The California Supreme Court laid the foundation for the diminished mental capacity concept in *People v. Wells* in 1949. The Court reasoned that, like any other element of a crime, a specific mental state cannot be presumed but must be proven.[11] The Court broke new ground, however, in holding that evidence of reduced mental capacity tending to show the absence of any mental state essential to the alleged crime should be accepted by the trial court. Thus, whether or not a plea of insanity is entered, evidence of any mental disease or defect must be considered by the trial court as relevant to the question of guilt.[12] This reasoning is based on the same principle of basic law that underlay the early intoxication cases: all elements of a crime must be proven in order to find the defendant guilty.[13] The California jury could thus consider intoxication—and now, with *Wells,* any mental abnormality—to show absence of certain essential mental elements of the crime.

A decade later, in *People v. Gorshen*,[14] the Court formulated the so-called "*Wells-Gorshen* rule," a general proposition that the absence of

10. As note 1, supra, indicates, in almost every other jurisdiction that has accepted a version of the diminished capacity or diminished responsibility doctrine, the concept has been based upon, or is a slight modification of, the specific intent exception. The fact that California, too, fell into the well of the specific intent exception should not, therefore, be too surprising.

11. *People v. Wells*, p. 65.

12. Wells, a prisoner, had been found guilty of assaulting a guard while under an indeterminate sentence, a crime that by statutory definition required malice. At trial, Wells was not allowed to present expert testimony to show that he was in a state of high tension at the time of the crime, and that he had an abnormal fear for his personal safety. Such testimony, as the Supreme Court pointed out, could have established that Wells's fear was genuine and that he therefore lacked malice aforethought (*ibid.*, pp. 61–63).

13. See also "Criminal Law—Partial Insanity—Evidentiary Relevance Defined" (1961), wherein the author notes that the same logic was used as a rationale by those early courts which did allow evidence of mental disability to be considered by the jury.

14. (1959). The defendant, who had been drinking, was involved in a fight with his work supervisor, who had ordered him home because he was drunk. Gorshen went home but returned with a gun, saying that he "had to kill" his supervisor. He did

"a certain specific intent or mental state essential to constitute the crime" can be shown by evidence of an "abnormal mental or physical condition."[15]

The *Gorshen* court also held that voluntary intoxication was a form of diminished capacity and could preclude malice, thereby reducing a charge of murder to manslaughter. This ruling marks a significant policy change, since, as noted above, California courts had previously held, like most other courts, that evidence of voluntary intoxication could be used only to reduce a first-degree murder charge to second-degree.[16]

In *People v. Conley*[17] in 1966, the California Supreme Court gave the concept its present nomenclature and acknowledged the broad proposition

---

so—in the presence of police officers. Gorshen claimed that he heard voices. The defense psychiatrist testified that the defendant suffered from chronic paranoiac schizophrenia and sexual hallucinations; he further testified that the defendant's work as a docker was, to the defendant, a symbol of his virility.

15. CALJIC instructions 3.35, the other standard diminished capacity instruction, represents a formal acceptance of the Wells-Gorshen rule:

Diminished Capacity to Form Specific Mental State (Wells-Gorshen Rule):

When a defendant is charged with a crime which requires that a certain specific intent or mental state be established in order to constitute the crime or degree of crime, you must take all the evidence into consideration and determine therefrom if, at the time when the crime allegedly was committed, the defendant was suffering from some abnormal mental or physical condition, however caused, which prevented him from forming the specific intent or mental state essential to constitute the crime or degree of crime with which he is charged.

If from all the evidence you have a reasonable doubt whether defendant was capable of forming such specific intent or mental state, you must give defendant the benefit of that doubt and find that he did not have such specific intent or mental state.

This instruction reflects the heavy influence of the specific intent exception. What is certainly at issue is the absence of a "certain specific intent or mental state." This instruction, in conjunction with later developments, helps focus the evolution of the diminished capacity concept as a species of the specific intent exception.

16. See Chapter 6, supra.

17. Although *Conley* named the concept, important steps in the growth of diminished capacity had taken place before 1966. In *People v. Modesto* (1963), the court held that it was reversible error to fail to give manslaughter instructions if the defendant showed any sort of evidence purporting to refute malice: "[The defendant] has a constitutional right to have the jury determine every material issue presented by the evidence" (p. 38). In *People v. Henderson* (1963), the court employed the term "diminished responsibility" to describe the *Wells-Gorshen* defense. The Supreme Court held that when a defendant relies upon a "defense of mental illness not amounting to legal insanity" he must be allowed to present that

that evidence of mental abnormality caused either by intoxication, trauma, or disease could support a finding that the defendant did not have a specific mental state essential to the crime.[18] However, the Court immediately began to narrow that fairly general principle by focusing on the particular states of mind essential to the crime of murder: malice, premeditation, deliberation, and the intent to kill. The model jury instructions that the court suggested in the *Conley* case dealt only with an analysis of these four mental states as affected by diminished capacity.[19] The Court apparently did not consider at this juncture the possibility that the defense would be utilized in crimes other than homicide.

As a further result of the *Conley* case, two new nonstatutory crimes were created by judicial decree: nonstatutory voluntary manslaughter and nonstatutory involuntary manslaughter.[20] The fact that the diminished capacity theory gave birth to two new categories of manslaughter added luster to its growing prominence.[21]

---

evidence (p. 490). In *People v. Steele* (1965), a district court of appeal noted that the *Wells* rule is equally applicable to mental states not considered in *Wells*.

18. *People v. Conley*, p. 914.

19. *Ibid.*, pp. 920–921.

20. By its model instructions, the Supreme Court created these two nonstatutory crimes:

If you find that the defendant did not harbor malice, because of his diminished capacity, or have a reasonable doubt whether he harbored malice, you cannot find him guilty of a higher offense than manslaughter.
Manslaughter is the unlawful killing of a human being without malice. Two kinds of manslaughter, the definitions of which are pertinent here, are:
1. Voluntary manslaughter, an intentional killing in which the law, recognizing human frailty, permits the defendant to establish the lack of malice either by
a. Showing provocation such as to rouse the reasonable man to heat of passion or sudden quarrel. . . .
b. Showing that due to diminished capacity caused by mental illness, mental defect, or intoxication, the defendant did not attain the mental state constituting malice.
. . . [I]f you find that the defendant killed while unconscious as a result of voluntary intoxication and was therefore unable to formulate a specific intent to kill or to harbor malice, his killing is involuntary manslaughter . . . (*People v. Conley*, pp. 920–921).

Thus, nonstatutory voluntary manslaughter is the crime in which, because of diminished capacity, the defendant had no malice. Nonstatutory involuntary manslaughter is the crime in which, because of diminished capacity, the defendant had neither intent to kill nor malice.

21. *People v. Aubrey* (1967) endorsed the new definition of nonstatutory voluntary manslaughter and held that instructions on the crime must be given whenever any evidence of diminished capacity is shown. *People v. Mosher* (1969) added

It is evident that marked similarities to the specific intent exception are present throughout this part of the development of diminished capacity: the Court is focusing on the specific mental states of murder—much as the *Hopt*[22] Court had originally done when giving its imprimatur to that portion of the specific intent exception dealing with cases of homicide. Furthermore, the diminished capacity concept looks, as does the specific intent exception, to what is at least verbally construed as the *absence* of required mental states. Finally, as with the specific intent doctrine, the goal of the diminished mental capacity concept is to exculpate partially, not fully.

On the one hand, therefore, the Court in *Conley* broadened the scope of admissible evidence by allowing evidence of any mental abnormality. On the other hand, the Conley case restricted the bearing of that evidence to the four mental states relevant to the crime of homicide, although it did not in absolute terms reverse the broader *Wells-Gorshen* approach.[23]

In 1964, two years before *Conley* was decided, the second approach to the diminished capacity defense emerged in *People v. Wolff.*[24] The Court in *Wolff* faced the case of a fifteen-year-old boy who killed his mother with an axe handle with the expressed intention of thereafter bringing girls home to rape or to photograph. Wolff was found legally sane by the jury, since he had stated, and experts agreed, that he knew the difference between right and wrong. It was evident from testimony at the trial, however, that Wolff was schizophrenic.[25] The Supreme Court ruled that, although he had indeed premeditated and had *intended to kill,* the controlling issue was not simply the nature of the killing but the "quantum of

---

support to the new definition of nonstatutory involuntary manslaughter. Conley was sent back for a third trial when the trial judge failed to give an instruction on nonstatutory manslaughter (1968). *People v. Rodriguez* (1969) held that when any evidence of diminished capacity is introduced, full instructions on diminished capacity (from murder through nonstatutory involuntary manslaughter) must be given *sua sponte. People v. Ray* (1975) corrected the "misunderstanding" that a state of unconsciousness was a prerequisite to a finding of involuntary manslaughter. If diminished capacity rendered a defendant incapable of having malice or the intent to kill, the verdict must be involuntary manslaughter.

22. *Hopt v. People* (1881).

23. The *Wells-Gorshen* rule exists, as noted in note 15, supra, as a separate jury instruction. Its distinctive features are its similarity to the specific intent exception and the fact that it would seem to apply to any crime, rather than just homicide.

24. See note 6, supra.

25. *People v. Wolff,* p. 976.

personal turpitude" involved.[26] A proper test, the Court decided, must include an examination of the defendant's ability to "maturely and meaningfully reflect upon the gravity of his contemplated act."[27] According to the Court, Wolff was vague and detached; thus the "extent of his understanding," his reflection upon the act and its consequences, his "realization of the enormity of the evil,"[28] and his awareness of moral wrongdoing were extremely limited. The real test of deliberation, the Court held, is not the *duration* of reflection upon an act but the *extent* and *depth* of reflection by the defendant.[29]

The requirement that the defendant understand the moral wrongness of a crime is in substance quite different from the *Conley* (and the specific intent doctrine) requirement that the defendant lack the mental ability to form the relevant mental state. For in *Wolff* the Court was asserting in substance that, even if the defendant *did* have the mental ability to form the relevant mental states, i.e., the ability to deliberate and premeditate, the criminal significance of those states was negated because of the lack of moral turpitude and depravity necessary for a first-degree murder conviction. *Wolff* was a radical doctrinal innovation just because all the classical mental elements required for first-degree murder were present. And yet, mental abnormality per se, as *affecting* but *not* showing the absence of one of those states, was held to be the true ground for exculpation. To put *Wolff* in the language of the Disability of Mind doctrine as proposed in Chapter 1: The defendant was materially but not predominantly irrational with regard to the criminal significance of his act (even though the specific mental states defining first-degree murder were present), and he should be

26. *Ibid.,* p. 976.

27. *Ibid.,* p. 975.

28. *Ibid.,* p. 976.

29. The Court derived this important test from two relatively obscure cases: *People v. Holt* (1944) and *People v. Thomas* (1945). In *Holt,* the Court had reasoned that the division of intentional homicides into murder and voluntary manslaughter, and again of murder into two degrees, is a recognition of the difference in the quantum of moral turpitude required for the various offenses. For a homicide to be labeled first-degree rather than second-degree murder, an appraisal involving more than simply the objective facts must be made. In *Thomas,* the Court ruled that merely planning an act did not constitute deliberation because: (1) to deliberate means to "consider the reasons for and against; to consider maturely; to reflect upon"; and (2) for first-degree murder the law requires "substantially more reflection than may be involved in the mere formation of a specific intent to kill" (p. 18). Thus, the real test of deliberation is not the duration of reflection, but the extent of reflection by the defendant.

convicted of "murder in the first degree, with nonculpable partial Disability of Mind." This would entail a substantial reduction of severity in sentencing.

However, in historical fact, *Wolff* could be formulated by introducing and stressing a verbalistic legal fiction as if it were no departure from tradition at all. One can stress that Wolff, because of his schizophrenic condition, was unable to premeditate "meaningfully," i.e., unable to premeditate in the correct legal sense of that term, and that he therefore "lacked" the ingredient of deliberation necessary for a first-degree murder conviction.

It should be no surprise that the appeal of the more traditional language led the Court, in *Wolff* and progressively more so in later cases, to incline toward a formulation in terms of the legal fiction—to focus, in short, on the "absence" of ("meaningful") premeditation. Thus the significance of the new doctrine was almost instantly obscured.

The *Wolff* approach was nevertheless very valuable—so much so that it was employed by the California Supreme Court to modify decisions in three cases following close upon *Wolff's* heels, even though, in each case, the trial court had correctly instructed the jury, applying the *Conley* approach. *People v. Goedecke* (1967), *People v. Nicolaus* (1967), and *People v. Bassett* (1968) were each factually shocking cases[30] in which the Supreme Court invoked *Wolff* to reduce first-degree sentences to second-degree convictions. The three defendants had each been found legally sane. Each had quite deliberately—in the everyday sense of "deliberately"—carried out multiple homicides. Yet the Supreme Court found that each defendant suffered from a mental defect that rendered him so emotionally detached and morally blind that he was unable to deliberate in the legal sense, unable to "meaningfully" deliberate.[31]

Although now framed in terms of "lack of" or "absence of" meaningful deliberation, the underlying implications of the *Wolff* approach remained far broader. For the Court was in substance still saying, "We must look at the overall picture of this man's mind, much as we do for the insanity

---

30. Goedecke brutally, and with great care, murdered his entire family without a sign of remorse; Nicolaus killed his three children to save them from an "intolerable" environment; and Bassett "methodically executed" his parents. Another case typical of this sort of criminal is reported in the *San Francisco Chronicle* of August 19, 1975: a woman charged with killing her two sons, ages 18 and 19, told authorities that "she wanted to kill herself but felt it would be too hard on the boys, so she killed them instead" (p. 3).

31. See, e.g., *People v. Goedecke*, p. 782.

defense, to see if there is a serious gap in his understanding, in his comprehension of the evil he has done"—to see, in short, if he was rational with respect to the criminal significance of his act. Though the Court did not follow through on the logic of *Wolff* in the early days, the logic implied that when a claim of mental disease, defect, or intoxication is made, the jury should be entitled to see how such a disability affects any aspect of the defendant's mental state that is relevant to the criminality of his act, and to discount, for purposes of establishing culpability, that aspect of his mental state.

In fact, in the late 1960s, the Supreme Court lost touch with the substance of this important development, became a victim of its own verbalisms, and abruptly turned completely away from the novel implications in *Wolff*. In a series of three cases, the Court held that if a defendant had sufficient time to consider his act, he had fully premeditated.[32] Forgotten was the clear lesson of *Wolff*: the *amount* of time that a defendant takes to premeditate is unimportant; it is the *quality* of that premeditation, the rationality of the mind that premeditates, which is crucial. These cases represent a reversion to the *Conley* approach: a simple analysis of the presence or absence of the four classical elements of murder, evidence of the underlying condition of irrationality serving only in the ancillary role of showing, in *some* cases, that the specific mental element was in fact *absent*.

It is possible that the Court retreated from *Wolff* and its implications not only out of a conceptual confusion but also out of a growing sense of impropriety. The Supreme Court had been sitting in judgment on an issue that by rights should be the jury's to decide.[33] It is the jury that represents the conscience of the community—the norm of moral behavior.[34] Therefore it is the jury that ought to judge the factual question as to the defendant's moral awareness, his ability to understand the moral significance of his act.

---

32. *People v. Risenhoover* (1968); *In re Kemp* (1969); and *People v. Sirhan* (1972). See also, for example, the Court's opinion in *Sirhan*, where the Court concluded that, because Sirhan had "ample time to reflect upon the killing," and because he seemed "highly alert and intelligent," the defendant must have engaged in mature and meaningful premeditation (p. 1132).

33. The Court noted in *People v. Holt* that the appraisal of that "something more" necessary for first-degree murder is "primarily a jury function and within a wide field of discretion its determination is final" (p. 27).

34. See discussion in Chapter 14, infra.

Additionally, the *Conley* formula, unlike the *Wolff* approach, no doubt has a comfortable feeling of familiarity to the Court. Its logic parallels the specific intent doctrine. That this parallel was attractive to many others besides the Court is made evident by the proposed California Model Penal Code for diminished capacity, which is directly patterned after the specific intent exception and is undoubtedly derived from the *Conley* rather than the *Wolff* reasoning.[35]

It can be no surprise by this point in our discussion that in evolving a test for diminished capacity that was fundamentally the same as the specific intent doctrine, California courts laid themselves open to familiar but insoluble problems. One central problem is the necessity for arbitrary classification of non-homicide cases into "general" or "specific" intent crimes. The arbitrary policy decisions made in the intoxication cases are strikingly paralleled in diminished capacity cases, as is clear from a brief demonstration.

Conley itself expressed the arbitrary limitation in homicide cases, for the opinion explicitly ruled out any verdict less than manslaughter, so far as diminished capacity is concerned. The rationale was based on the familiar (and in this context no less obscure) distinction between "general" and "specific" criminal states of mind—diminished mental capacity affecting, as a matter of law, only the latter.[36] The few reported non-homicide cases also appear to hold uniformly that the diminished capacity defense is available only to negate a specific intent or mental state.[37]

---

35. "Section 540. Diminished Capacity. (a) 'Diminished capacity' means an impairment of mental or physical capacities resulting from mental illness, disease, or defect. (b) *Unless the statute defining a crime expressly requires a specific intent as the culpable mental state,* evidence of diminished capacity is not admissible for the purpose of negating or reducing a person's culpability" (Penal Code Revision Project, The Criminal Code [1972], emphasis added). As a result of this proposed section, one law review writer has concluded that "[t] he [diminished capacity] doctrine is analogous to the defense of intoxication, as evidence pertaining to mental condition may be considered only when the offense includes a specific mental state within its definition" ("Insanity, Intoxication, and Diminished Capacity Under the Proposed California Criminal Code," 1972, p. 575).

36. *People v. Conley,* pp. 323–324.

37. *People v. Glover* (1967): battery on a police officer; *People v. Gentry* (1968): defrauding by issuing checks without sufficient funds; *People v. Mosher* (1969): rape, robbery, burglary; and *People v. Nance* (1972): arson. For a short review of the *Nance* case, see "Diminished Capacity and Arson," 13 *Santa Clara Lawyer* 349 (1972). But see the following cases, which show the possibility of complete acquittal

As with the specific intent doctrine in intoxication, this limitation of the diminished capacity defense is based on neither logic nor psychology;[38] it is a matter of "policy"—the courts simply are unwilling to allow complete acquittal. *People v. Nance* provides a diminished capacity case exactly parallel to the *Hood* (intoxication) case, in which the California Supreme Court held that, for policy reasons, assault and aggravated assault are general intent crimes. The appellate court in *Nance* faced a defendant, obviously mentally ill, accused of arson. The court held that arson was a "general intent" crime, even though malice (a "specific mental state" in terms of *Conley*) was required.[39] This logically arbitrary decision was felt to be required because if the diminished mental capacity defense were allowed, it would be a complete defense, and the defendant pyromaniac would not be subject to any sort of confinement or treatment.[40]

The verbal rationale offered to support these conclusions in *Nance* is as strained as in the *Hood* case. The court, in order to find arson a general intent crime, had to announce that, although malice means the "deliberate and intentional firing of a building, . . . the crime of arson does not require a specific mental state."[41] A certain residual logical embarrassment impelled the court to remark: "Policy reasons weigh in our decision even more strongly than do the technical distinctions between the general *mens rea* and specific intent."[42]

---

still hovering over the courts in cases where intoxication or a mental disability not amounting to insanity might establish absence of a specific intent where there is no "general intent" crime remaining on which to find the defendant guilty: *People v. Calavecchio* (1960): larcenous intent; *People v. Wilson* (1968) and *People v. Chapman* (1968): intent to rob; *People v. Taylor* (1963): burglary—intent to steal; *Schwickreth v. People* (1966): intent to escape; and *Rhodes v. U.S.* (1960): knowingly making a false tax statement.

38. The authors are aware of one unreported case where the defendant admitted that he intended to burgle a warehouse but did so because he wanted to get arrested and be incarcerated: *Hazelaar v. McCarthy* (1974). In his trial, psychiatrists testified that, as a result of his paranoid-schizoid personality, the defendant needed the security of institutional living and was attempting to return to prison. Committing a crime was the most direct way of accomplishing his objective. Therefore the defendant here admitted to the specific intent necessary for the charged crime, but claimed that that specific intent was caused to be *present* by his mental illness.

39. *People v. Nance* (1972), p. 930.

40. "The defense of diminished capacity . . . would be a complete defense to the charge. . . . The pyromaniac would not, under our present system, be subject to compulsory treatment" (*ibid.*, p. 930).

41. *Ibid.*

42. *Ibid.*

In a surprising and unexplained shift, the California Supreme Court more recently returned to the deeper principle espoused in *Wolff*, yet did not reject the trappings of the specific intent formulation. In two 1973 cases, *People v. Sedeno* and *People v. Poddar,* the Court held that the jury must consider whether the defendant "knew of the duty which society imposed upon him and could act in accordance therewith."[43] If the defendant could not comprehend this duty, he lacked malice. Thus the Court in effect asserts the proposition that a defendant can act intentionally, and can premeditate and deliberate, and yet not have acted with the moral turpitude that characterizes the crime of murder. For the Court now uses "malice" to equal that moral awareness which in *Wolff* is called "moral turpitude." Whatever the term, the idea is identical. Since lack of malice defeats either first- or second-degree murder, whereas lack of meaningful deliberation—as in *Wolff*—defeats only the charge of first-degree murder, the new doctrine is a major expansion of the *Wolff* doctrine's effect in mitigation.

At this juncture, we must remember that the series of cases taking the *Conley* approach still stands unrefuted, and by that formulation the defendant can still attempt to show that he lacked not merely deliberation or malice, but also premeditation and intent. Moreover, *Conley* was in fact used, as we have seen, to accomplish the *opposite* result from *Wolff,* i.e., to rationalize a finding of presence of the mental state and therefore of culpability. *Conley* applies also to non-homicide crimes, whereas it is not clear that *Wolff* does.

Lack of consistency, therefore, remains and adds much to further confuse the basic concept of the diminished capacity defense, obscuring its possible novel meaning, i.e., that irrationality of mind may negate the criminal significance of any mental state. To have a variety of such diminished capacity formulas, arbitrarily shifting and even inconsistent with one another, as is the case at present, is unsatisfactory law.

Although the California Supreme Court in its last efforts has moved the pendulum back toward recognizing the basic concept that an irrational state of mind can negate the criminal significance of a mental state, the Court still insists on verbally binding the diminished capacity defense by analogy to the classic—but purely verbalistic—doctrine of specific intent. The result is that legal analysis by the courts remains difficult; and in its task of factual analysis the jury is artificially limited and likely to be confused rather than aided by legal analysis. The Court's new definition of

43. *Ibid.,* p. 759.

"malice," if carefully examined, is in essence a test of rationality with respect to moral and criminal law norms; but because the Court speaks in terms of a particular classic mental state, lawyers and juries will certainly not appreciate the significance of the recent *Poddar-Sedeno* standard.[44]

The diminished capacity defense, as developed by the California Supreme Court, teaches some valuable lessons. It illustrates the extreme difficulties that a court has in developing a well-rounded, well-thought-out technical defense when the real task is to move to a new conceptual foundation, rather than to refine and redefine a more traditional theory. It also illustrates the need for the diminished capacity or some substantively similar test allowing mitigation where there is substantial mental disability. The fact that the *Wolff* rationale emerged against great odds, and that it has struggled back with greater exculpatory force than ever after being buried in a morass of misunderstanding, shows the need for such a test.

Examination of the diminished capacity concept reveals vividly the important role that the alternative doctrine we propose, the Disability of Mind doctrine, can play in the criminal law. The widely felt need to acknowledge lessened responsibility because of an irrational condition of mind[45] is met squarely under the doctrine we propose by allowing the jury, after it has realistically determined the factual issues as to all elements of the crime, to consider the defendant's capacity for acting responsibly at the time of the act.

For example, under the D.O.M. doctrine, if the jury had wished to recognize the obviously bizarre workings of Wolff's mind, but if—as was the case—they were unpersuaded that he was on the whole irrational, they would have had the option of finding Partial Disability of Mind that was Nonculpable in origin.[46] This would be a direct and candid way of providing for the same mitigation of punishment that the California Supreme Court achieved only by the strained finding that there was an absence of ("mature and meaningful") deliberation.

44. Given the court's most recent interpretation of malice, and its realization that a more general sort of examination of the defendant's mind must be made than was previously accepted, we note that the proposed California Model Penal Code test for diminished capacity is already totally inadequate.

45. Note 1, supra.

46. The meaning and significance of the concept of the Context of Origin, as used here, is fully discussed in Part V, infra, and is in substance employed at the end of each of the discussions of Intoxication defenses (Chapters 6 and 7, supra).

Therefore we propose as a uniform policy[47] that, if the jury finds that the defendant was in some relevant and important way irrational at the time of the act, the jury should report this fact, which should warrant mitigation of criminal condemnation and punishment. This captures the real point of the diminished capacity concept, and yet it would not call for distinguishing "true" intent from intent, or "true" deliberation from deliberation, or for maintaining the fiction that the defendant was fully responsible.

47. See Chapters 13 and 15 and Appendix I, infra.

PART IV

Current Controversial Defenses:
The Addictions and Their Rationales

9

Addiction and Criminal Responsibility:
Current Legal Theory

For well over a decade, courts have debated the scope of the criminal responsibility of those addicted to alcohol, narcotics, and other mind-altering drugs.[1] Today the issue remains unsettled. These debates were given a fresh and apparently decisive impetus by the Supreme Court's 1962 decision in *Robinson v. California,* which recognized narcotic addiction as a "disease," and held that criminal punishment of a person thus "afflicted" violates the Eighth Amendment's prohibition of cruel and unusual punishment.[2] Subsequent cases not only took into account the possible bearing of *Robinson* on alcohol addiction,[3] but, more generally,

1. We view alcohol as one of the mind-altering drugs that is "addictive." Hence, generally when we speak of "addiction" and of "drugs" we mean to include alcoholism and alcohol; and this usage is especially appropriate when discussing legal theory pertaining to criminal responsibility, as in the present chapter and in Chapter 12. However, the context or explicit qualification will make it evident that at times we mean to refer specifically either to alcohol and alcoholism, or to narcotics and narcotic addiction; this usage will prevail when we discuss the factual background of each, as in Chapters 10 and 11, infra. The reason for this varying usage, which is not uncommon in the literature, is that there are significant differences in the factual background and medical doctrines relating to these two most widespread, criminally relevant forms of addiction, but it turns out that the legal issues raised in connection with criminal responsibility are the same, as are the conclusions to be drawn.

2. Pp. 666-667.

3. *Powell v. Texas; Driver v. Hinnant; Easter v. District of Columbia.*

discussed the conflicting possible interpretations of *Robinson* itself.[4] All agreed that *Robinson* held, at the very least, that the Constitution precludes criminal punishment of the addict simply for a condition of body and mind manifesting a "bare desire"[5] or "mere propensity"[6] to use the drug. It is over the tendencies to go beyond this "minimalist" interpretation of *Robinson*, however, that controversy flourishes. While the major trend in the courts has been to interpret *Robinson* in the minimalist way,[7] some courts have argued for extension of exculpation[8] to crimes related to addiction.

Arguments of this latter type appear in *Powell v. Texas,* which the Supreme Court decided six years after *Robinson,* and in a series of decisions in the District of Columbia, as well as in other jurisdictions. On a number of occasions these views were stated in powerfully argued dissents in cases decided by narrow majorities.[9] Those who hold the minimalist

4. *People v. Zapata; State v. Margo.*

5. *Robinson,* at p. 679 (Justice Harlan, concurring).

6. *Powell,* at p. 543 (Justice Black, concurring).

7. *United States v. Rundle* (conviction for unlawful use of drugs is not punishment for addiction); *Bailey v. United States* (no error in the refusal to charge that an addiction is a disease creating compulsion under which the defendant is not criminally responsible); *United States ex rel. Swanson v. Reincke* (a statute prohibiting self-administration of narcotic drugs is held constitutional); *People v. Zapata* (imprisonment for possession of heroin for personal use is not cruel and unusual punishment); *Nutter v. State* (addicts may be criminals because they are responsible for acts such as possession and control of a narcotic drug which are crimes even though they stem from the addiction); *People v. Borrero* (penal sanction applied to addicts who committed crimes solely to procure money to purchase drugs is not cruel and unusual punishment); *State v. Margo* (punishment for being "under the influence" of a narcotic, as distinguished from the act of using a drug, is not cruel and unusual punishment); *Rengel v. State* (no error to refuse to instruct the jury to render a verdict of not guilty of possession of narcotics merely because the appellant was an admitted and known addict). See *Powell v. Texas; United States v. Moore.*

8. The term is used here to mean immunity from criminal liability either on the ground that *mens rea* is absent or on the ground that addiction functions as a defense. Whether exculpation takes the former or the latter form is undoubtedly significant both in terms of litigation strategy and in terms of the consequences of a finding of Not Guilty. See Goldstein and Katz, " 'Abolish the Insanity Defense'—Why Not?" Such discussion, however, is beyond the scope of this study.

9. *Powell v. Texas* (Justice Fortas, dissenting); *United States v. Moore,* p. 1236 (vacation of sentences, but not exculpation, for narcotics addict convicted under federal statute for possession of narcotics) (Justice Wright, dissenting); *United States v. Carter* (conviction upheld where there was substantial testimony that the defen-

position to be too restrictive claim either that the addict's use of the drug and some or all related offenses are inseparable from the addict's nonpunishable status or "disease,"[10] or that they are involuntary effects or symptoms of that status.[11]

On the basis of such arguments, some have urged that the *Robinson* immunity should be extended to include the narcotic addict's nontrafficking use, possession, and purchase of his drug; others would go farther and include offenses motivated by narcotic addiction, such as theft.[12] The prospects for expanding *Robinson* so as to apply to alcoholism seemed for a while particularly bright.[13]

---

dant's alleged mental illness and narcotic addiction were not causally connected with the commission of robbery and assault) (Chief Justice Bazelon, concurring); *Watson v. United States* (an insanity plea issue was properly submitted to the jury where the plea was made by a narcotics addict); *Easter v. District of Columbia* (chronic alcoholism resulting in public intoxication is not a crime; holding severely limited by *Powell v. Texas*); *Driver v. Hinnant* (a statute punishing public drunkenness could not be applied to a chronic alcoholic; holding severely limited by *Powell v. Texas*); *Hutcherson v. United States* (a ten-year sentence for a heroin addict convicted of narcotics trafficking is not cruel and unusual punishment) (Chief Justice Bazelon, concurring in part and dissenting in part); *Lloyd v. United States* (denial of petition for a rehearing for an addict convicted of the sale of narcotics) (Chief Justice Bazelon, dissenting); *United States v. Lindsey* (the defendant was unable to show inability to abstain from narcotic drugs which would eliminate *mens rea* for nontrafficking possession of narcotic drug); *United States v. Ashton* (no liability for an addict's nontrafficking possession of drugs); *People v. Malloy* (it is cruel and unusual punishment to charge a certified addict with felony of escape when he is voluntarily incarcerated under a valid civil commitment order for treatment).

10. See *Watson v. United States,* p. 475 (Judge McGowan).

11. See *Powell v. Texas* (Justice Fortas, dissenting), p. 567; *Easter v. District of Columbia* (holding severely limited by *Powell v. Texas*); and *Driver v. Hinnant* (holding severely limited by *Powell v. Texas*).

12. Most of the debate has focused on nontrafficking use, purchase, and possession. At one end of the spectrum, a state court held that *Robinson v. California* did not even cover an addict's "being under the influence" of the drug (*State v. Margo*). At the other end, Judge Bazelon has argued for immunity on the broadest grounds (*United States v. Carter*, p. 202 [Chief Justice Bazelon, concurring]). For a direct expression of disagreement among those who would extend the scope of *Robinson v. California*, compare *United States v. Moore*, p. 1260 (Chief Justice Bazelon, concurring in part and dissenting in part) with p. 1236 (Justice Wright, dissenting).

13. See Hutt, p. 112; Note, "Driver to Easter to Powell: Recognition of the Defense of Involuntary Intoxication?," p. 134. The preceding writers viewed it as "virtually certain" that the decision in *Powell* would accord with *Easter* and *Driver*, "the likelihood of the Supreme Court's rejection of the 'disease concept of alcohol-

However, in *Powell,* where the addiction issues as related to alcoholism were at last taken up by the Supreme Court, there resulted four separate and significantly conflicting opinions. Four dissenting justices argued that *Robinson* and common law principles rendered an alcoholic immune from criminal punishment for public drunkenness by virtue of his addiction.[14] Four justices in the majority rejected this reasoning in affirming the appellant's conviction.[15] The fifth, Justice White, in his concurring opinion, seemed to support immunity from criminal punishment for the chronic alcoholic's drinking or being drunk, but he found that the factual record in the case could not support exculpation based on that principle.[16]

In 1970, in a narcotics case, *Watson v. U.S.,* the Circuit Court of Appeals for the District of Columbia seemed close to a consensus on extending immunity at least to certain behavior distinctively associated with the addictive craving. The court announced that a nontrafficking addict presenting a better factual record than appeared in the case before it ought to be able to invoke *Robinson* to win immunity from punishment for possession. But when the issue arose again in 1973 in *U.S. v. Moore,* the same court rejected, in a five-to-four vote, immunity for possession by an addict. Some of those opposing exculpation for the addict, however, rested their arguments more on the current state of legislation than on a square and self-sufficient rejection of the legal reasoning and factual assumption of those favoring exculpation.[17]

The aim of the discussion in this part of the present book is to seek to dispel the confusion that has arisen in the case law, to clarify the factual

---

ism' being 'infinitesimal.' " Prior to *Powell,* several other alcoholism cases had presented the same or closely related issues. In one such case, public intoxication was said by the court to be *malum prohibitum,* rendering pleas based on lack of *mens rea* irrelevant (*City of Seattle v. Hill*). In a second case, the court upheld a conviction for public intoxication, but there were three separate opinions (*People v. Hoy*). In a third case, the court said that it would be unreasonable to require as a condition of probation that a person who is a chronic alcoholic refrain from drinking if expert testimony establishes that "alcoholism has destroyed [petitioner's] power of volition" (*Sweeney v. United States*).

14. *Powell v. Texas,* at p. 584 (Justice Fortas, dissenting, joined by Justices Douglas, Brennan, and Stewart).

15. *Ibid.,* at p. 514 (Justice Marshall, joined by Chief Justice Warren and Justices Black and Harlan).

16. *Ibid.,* at pp. 552–554 (Justice White, concurring).

17. *U.S. v. Moore,* p. 1159 (Justice Leventhal, concurring, joined by Justice McGowan).

issues, and to draw proper conclusions as to the bearing of addictions on Disability of Mind. This chapter presents an analysis of the typical exculpatory arguments that are based on *Robinson.* It will be seen that, insofar as these arguments attempt to extend the immunity of the addict beyond the minimalist interpretation of *Robinson,* they ultimately rely on the assumption that behavior motivated by addiction is involuntary. The following two chapters then review, in a descriptive way, the factual background of narcotic and alcohol addiction [18] respectively, especially as this background relates to the legal concept of involuntariness. We demonstrate that in each case the assumption of legal involuntariness is unsound. In each chapter we also explore the relevant scientific theories of addiction, and we show that these cannot function as grounds for a valid involuntariness defense in the criminal law. All the exculpatory arguments, whether they originate within or without the legal arena, lead to oversimplified "solutions" to complex and ill-understood problems, thus injudiciously preempting the legislature's role. In Chapter 12, which concludes Part IV, the results are summarized in relation to the issue of criminal responsibility; and some implications of the analysis, especially in relation to D.O.M., are sketched.

The remainder of the present chapter will be organized with reference to three principal lines of argument, often interwoven in the leading opinions. These three lines of argument, purportedly showing that addiction precludes criminal liability, will here be labeled for the sake of convenience as the "status" argument, the "disease" argument, and the "involuntariness" argument.

I: THE STATUS ARGUMENT: A MINIMALIST READING OF ROBINSON V. CALIFORNIA

The issue of "status" is central in *Robinson.* Referring to the statute under which the defendant had been found guilty, the majority wrote:

This statute, therefore, is not one which punishes a person for the use of narcotics, for their purchase, sale or possession, or for antisocial or

18. We shall only occasionally comment specifically on other forms of addiction (e.g., those involving barbiturates, amphetamines, tobacco, and tranquilizers), although we maintain that, so far as the criminal law is concerned, the principal theses of this part apply to all forms of conduct generally collected under the rubric "addiction."

disorderly behavior resulting from their administration. . . . Rather, we deal with a statute that makes the "status" of narcotic addiction a criminal offense. . . .[19]

The Court found that the statute violated the Eighth and Fourteenth Amendments: "We hold that a state law which imprisons a person *thus afflicted* as a criminal, even though he had *never touched* any narcotic drug within the State or been guilty of any irregular *behavior* there, inflicts a cruel and unusual punishment in violation of the Fourteenth Amendment."[20] In arriving at this holding, the Court analogized punishment for the status of narcotic addiction to punishment for affliction with a disease.[21] The analogy can suggest that the term "disease" carries an exculpatory force independent of that of "status."[22] Alternatively, it can suggest that disease is a species of status and is nonculpable simply because it can be so classified. The latter interpretation is in effect taken account of in this section, which is concerned with the supposed nonpunishability of a "status" in *Robinson*.

What, then, is the scope of exculpation for the status of addiction in *Robinson*? Certainly the case cannot be read to do away with all crimes of status. These have a long history in the common law and in statutory law, and they have not been fundamentally challenged by the Court.[23] It is implausible to read *Robinson* as announcing a new constitutional doctrine declaring crimes of status generally to be outside the scope of the criminal law.[24] The text and context of *Robinson* carry no such implication, nor has any court proposed such a reading of the case. It is therefore more

19. *Robinson v. California,* at p. 666. The trial judge made a similar distinction in instructing the jury: he noted that addiction, which the statute made a criminal offense, was a "condition" or "status" while the "use" of the narcotic was an "act." Unlike the act of using a narcotic, said the judge, the status of being an addict is a "chronic" offense that "continue[s] after it is complete" (p. 662).

20. *Ibid.,* p. 667.

21. *Ibid.,* pp. 666–667.

22. This interpretation is discussed in Section II, infra.

23. See generally Amsterdam (1967); Cuomo (1967); and Lacey (1953). Vagrancy, for example, is often characterized as a crime of status. Although a number of vagrancy statutes have been struck down for vagueness in defining the status, nowhere has the claim been accepted that vagrancy is immune simply because it is a status. See *Papachristou v. City of Jacksonville; Edelman v. California.*

24. Amsterdam's exhaustive 1967 survey notes that the questions as to how to construe *Robinson* with regard to status crimes have not even yet been structured (Amsterdam, p. 240).

accurate to read the case as barring punishment for status only insofar as, and just for the reason that, the status excludes any act at all. Indeed, a criminal offense, even though it may not itself be conduct, must generally be defined with some essential reference to conduct.[25] In *Robinson,* the majority emphasizes the absence from the statute at issue of any requirement to prove that there was any drug use, purchase, possession, or sale, or any antisocial or disorderly behavior resulting from drug use.[26] In *Powell v. Texas,* Justice Marshall reads *Robinson* to stand for the proposition that punishment may not be inflicted in the absence of proof of any *actus reus.*[27] Many lower courts have focused on the distinction between status and act in making this, the minimalist argument.[28]

Does this concept of pure status as distinct from acts make sense in the context of addiction? Of course, one may separate addiction status (some distinctive bodily state or mental desire) from the actual use of the drug by mere definition; the California trial court did so in *Robinson* in

25. *Powell v. Texas,* p. 543 (Justice Black, concurring). Justice Black notes that this requirement applies even for "offenses most heavily based on propensity, such as attempt, conspiracy, and recidivist crimes." See G. Williams (1961), pp. 1–2. In *Papachristou v. City of Jacksonville,* p. 170, Justice Douglas's majority opinion quotes with approval an English opinion, *Dean,* that disapproves prosecution and conviction under the Vagrancy Act where there would not be enough evidence to charge the prisoner with an attempt to commit a crime. Lacey (1953), p. 1204, finds that many statutes defining status crimes contain no reference to acts. But he acknowledges that in cases such as "common thief" status, one can argue that "evidence of past conduct is necessary." In analyzing these statutes it would seem clear to distinguish between the *status* (admittedly not itself conduct) and an *implicit reference* to conduct necessarily made because proof of conduct is essential to prove the existence of the status.

26. P. 666.

27. P. 533.

28. In these cases, "status" includes no more than the mere physical and mental state associated with desire: *United States v. Rundle; Bailey v. United States; United States ex rel. Swanson v. Reincke; People v. Zapata; Nutter v. State; State v. Margo; People v. Borrero; Rengel v. State.* But see the following cases and opinions which challenge this use of "status" by arguing either that certain addictive conduct inevitably and involuntarily flows from this immune addictive status or is indeed a part of the status itself: *Powell v. Texas,* p. 554 (Justice Fortas, dissenting); *Watson v. United States; United States v. Carter,* p. 243 (Chief Justice Bazelon, concurring); *Easter v. District of Columbia; Driver v. Hinnant; Hutcherson v. United States,* p. 971 (Chief Justice Bazelon, concurring in part, dissenting in part); *Lloyd v. United States,* p. 243 (Chief Justice Bazelon, dissenting); *United States v. Lindsey; United States v. Ashton;* and *People v. Malloy.*

construing its statutory crime of "addiction."[29] But some would insist that the addict's purchase, possession, and use of the drug are "realistically inseparable from the status of addiction."[30] In this view, California's definition of addiction is unduly arbitrary and unrealistic; regardless of our verbal freedom to define "addiction" only in terms of desire, the possession and use of the drug—and perhaps other acts such as robbing to obtain funds for drugs, or getting drunk in public—are seen as *factually* inseparable from the physiological and psychological status of addiction.

Two arguments have suggested the forms that this alleged factual inseparability takes: (1) the addict's drug use is a symptom of disease; and (2) the addict's use of drugs is an involuntary result of a status that is physiological or psychological, or perhaps both. If the status argument is pushed beyond the minimalist reading to exculpate other behavior associated with the status, it thus resolves into arguments based on disease or involuntariness. These arguments will lead us into complex factual issues about drug addiction that will be explored in subsequent chapters; we turn now to a more narrowly defined examination of the arguments themselves.

II: THE DISEASE ARGUMENT

Robinson opens the door to the argument that "disease" may preclude criminal liability. Justice Stewart's majority opinion recognizes persons addicted to narcotics as diseased or ill;[31] the emphasis on disease is central to his argument. Justice Douglas's concurring opinion asserts that the addict is sick, and that addiction is a disease. Justice Clark's dissent speaks of "cure" and justifies confinement in a penal institution as "treatment."[32] The dissent in *Powell* recognizes it as a "hard fact" that alcoholism is a disease.[33]

Although the theme of disease has remained pervasive in case law on the topic, its exculpatory force remains as ambiguous as it is in the *Robinson* opinions.[34] In applying that theme to the case of addiction,

29. *Robinson*, p. 662.

30. *Watson v. United States*, p. 475 (Justice McGowan). See *Robinson*, p. 686 (Justice White, dissenting).

31. At p. 667 and note 8, citing *Linder v. United States* at p. 18.

32. *Robinson*, pp. 680, 681, and 683. However, Justice Clark insists that the issue which ought to be central is the voluntary quality of the addiction.

33. *Powell*, p. 559. See also pp. 560–561, 567–568; *Driver v. Hinnant*, p. 764; and *Easter v. District of Columbia*, p. 53.

34. But see *United States v. Brawner*, p. 1010 (Chief Justice Bazelon, dissenting).

however, the skeleton of the argument is discernible in at least a generalized form. Its proponents would claim that it cannot be a crime to be afflicted with a disease, that addiction is a disease, and hence unpunishable. Others would argue further that some or all addictive conduct is either part of the disease,[35] "a compulsion symptomatic of the disease,"[36] or an "invariable"[37] symptom of the disease; as a result, such conduct is unpunishable. Two questions must be explored in order to evaluate these arguments: (1) Can the claim that addiction is a disease be usefully adapted to the context of a legal argument? (2) Which, if any, of the phenomena associated with disease are inappropriate as grounds for punishment under the criminal law?

The first question is problematic because the term *disease* is vaguely defined within the medical profession.[38] The term suggests generally that a person manifests some distinguishable complex of abnormal conditions having, or surmised to have, a biological basis.[39] If one seeks to derive a

35. *Watson v. United States,* p. 470 (Chief Justice Bazelon) (appendix to rehearing en banc).

36. *Powell v. Texas,* p. 569 (Justice Fortas, dissenting, quoting findings of the trial judge with approval). Compare *Marshall v. United States,* p. 433 (Justice Marshall) with *Powell v. Texas,* p. 526 (Justice Marshall).

37. *Watson v. United States,* p. 470 (Chief Justice Bazelon; appendix to rehearing en banc).

38. Although Jellinek, one of the greatest authorities on alcoholism, defends the claim that "alcoholism is a disease," he admits that the proposition reflects a labeling decision rather than a discovery of fact: "[A] disease is what the medical profession recognizes as such." The term *disease* is a highly general, handy rubric, not itself the direct subject of any scientific demonstration (Jellinek, 1960, p. 12). Meehl stresses that even in neurology and internal medicine "there is actually no clearly formulable disease-entity model" (Meehl, 1972, pp. 10 and 20). Typical of innumerable medical texts as well as lists of nomenclature is E. Thompson and A. Hayden, *Standard Nomenclature of Diseases and Operations* (5th ed. 1961), which uses the word *disease* as a general rubric but nowhere defines or explains it. The terminological difficulty is not overcome by shifting to the phrase *mental disease.* Challenges to the use of this term are widespread both within and without the medical profession. See generally Fingarette, 1972, pp. 19–52.

39. *Stedman's Medical Dictionary* (22nd ed. 1972) defines *disease* as: "illness, sickness; an interruption, cessation or disorder of body functions, systems, or organs," or "[a] disease *entity,* characterized usually by at least two of these criteria: a recognized etiologic agent (or agents); an identifiable group of signs and symptoms; consistent anatomical alterations, caused by specific micro-organismic alterations." McHugh, 1971, p. 107, states: "The term 'disease' is difficult to define. . . . It is intended to convey the idea that among all the morbid changes in physical and mental health it is possible to recognize groups of abnormalities as distinct entities or

relevant meaning of disease by analysis of the term *addiction,* one confronts a plurality of concepts and definitions describing addiction.[40] Moreover, these are used in varying ways by various authorities within the health professions, sometimes overlapping and sometimes differing significantly in meaning.[41] Unresolved questions, problems, speculation, and

---

syndromes separable from one another and from the normal and that these separations *will prove to have* some biologic explanation when the entities have been thoroughly investigated" (emphasis added). *Taber's Cyclopedic Medical Dictionary* D-47 (12th ed. 1973) defines *disease* as: "a pathological condition of the body that presents a group of symptoms peculiar to it and which sets the condition apart as an abnormal entity differing from other normal or pathological body states." Those in the medical profession tend to use the word *disease* even where they do not yet know the biological basis (if any) of the "disease entity"; they will do so because they assume that one exists. Similar usage of the term in relation to addiction avoids some crucial legal questions. See Chapters 10 and 11, infra.

40. Jaffe (1965a), p. 286.

41. Experts in the field now avoid the term *addiction* (DeLong, 1972, p. 82). For a brief review of these definitional inadequacies, see Lewis (1969), pp. 5–11. For a fuller review, see *National Commission on Marijuana and Drug-Abuse, Drug Use in America: Problem in Perspective* 120–140 (2nd Rep. 1973) [hereinafter cited as *National Commission*]. See generally Eddy, Halbach, Isbell, and Seevers (1965), p. 721. In 1964 the World Health Organization (WHO) formally abandoned the term *addiction* and began to develop a more complex terminology (WHO *Expert Committee on Addiction-Producing Drugs,* Report No. 13) [hereinafter cited as WHO Report No. 13]. Central to the new terminology was replacement of the term *addiction* with the word *dependence.* (The proposed terminology is now widely but by no means universally used in the professional literature.) The Committee distinguished "psychic dependence" and "physical dependence" and classified drugs accordingly. The opiates and alcohol produce both kinds of dependence, and the study provides a set of categories that characterize the degree of dependence, e.g., "overpowering desire" (opiates) and "strong desire" (alcohol-barbiturate types). In a 1969 Report, the concept "drug dependence" is itself defined: "A state, psychic and sometimes also physical, resulting from the interaction between a living organism and a drug, characterized by behavioral and other responses that always include a compulsion to take the drug on a continuous or periodic basis in order to experience its psychic effects, and sometimes to avoid the discomfort of its absence. Tolerance may or may not be present. A person may be dependent on more than one drug" (WHO *Expert Committee on Addiction-Producing Drugs,* Report No. 16 [1969]). The definition is reaffirmed in a 1973 Report, WHO *Expert Committee on Drug Dependence,* Report No. 19. The crucial concepts in the definitions of "dependence" (as distinguished from mere use) are those of "overpowering desire" (the early formulations) and of "compulsion" (1969 formulation and after). But no specific analysis or explanation of these concepts appears in any of the official texts (nor in any other treatises we

controversy abound in this field.[42] Thus it is clear that any claim that narcotic or alcohol addiction is a disease is not made on the basis of a consensus among researchers and health professionals about causes, manifestations, or cure. Obviously the claim that addiction is a disease has its suggestive, rhetorical, and perhaps educational uses. It provides a rationale for allocating public monies to medical research and treatment facilities—a highly important and acknowledged practical reason for the terminological decision made by the profession.[43] But as a scientific claim, it has little substantiated content, and the continuing lack of understanding and controversy that permeates all dimensions of the problem make the claim unsuitable as the premise for tightly reasoned argument leading to fundamental innovation in constitutional or common law doctrine.

Even if theories and definitions were clear and uniform, they would not in themselves make clear which aspects of the alleged disease should or should not be reached by the criminal law. In order to see how the lines of

---

have seen on the topic). The closest approach to such analysis is remote at best: In the 1973 WHO Report, a section entitled "Quantification of Drug Dependence" lists five very general categories of questions whose responses "*may* help to define the *problems* associated with drug taking and provide a basis for quantifying the presence and intensity of drug dependence" (p. 20). Some authorities have tried to replace the subjective and vague notions of "overpowering desire" or "compulsion" with more objective language. Isbell defines dependency in terms of "persistent seeking and undergoing great risks to obtain the drug," use of the drug as the chief means of adaptation to life, and a "strong tendency to relapse after treatment" (Isbell, 1972, pp. 35–42). Lewis (1969), p. 8, suggests defining dependence in terms of observable withdrawal symptoms and behavior. In this book the word *addict* generally refers, as indicated in context, to any one or combination of the following: a person who shows distinctive *physical symptoms* upon abstinence from a drug that he has been using; a person who experiences a powerful *desire* to continue using a drug as a result of frequent prior use; and/or a person who shows through *behavior* a persistent and intense commitment to seeking and using a certain drug, even though lawfulness and analogous socially approved values must be sacrificed.

42. Authorities in the field agree on this point. With respect to the physical aspects, see Goldstein, Aranow, and Kalman (1969), p. 605; Chruscial (1972), p. 79; Jaffe (1965b), p. 285. With respect to addictive life patterns, see DeLong (1972), pp. 79–81; Jaffe (1970b), pp. 230–232; *National Commission* (1973), pp. 369–370. See generally Chapters 10 and 11, infra. Preble and Casey's historical summary (1972), pp. 100–104, shows how heroin use patterns have differed at different times since World War I.

43. In connection with the pragmatic (political, financial, propagandistic) grounds for the medical profession's labeling "alcoholism" as a disease, see the discussion of the "disease concept of alcoholism" at the end of Chapter 11, infra.

argument would be drawn, we list the specific kinds of phenomena associated with the rubric "addiction":[44]

1. *Autonomous somatic states*—specific neurological, physiological, or other bodily states which, though they are effects of repeated use of narcotics, barbiturates, alcohol, or other drugs, can exist even in the current absence of the drug.

2. *Autonomous mental phenomena*—the powerful desire for the drug and the related subjective sensations that can exist after repeated use but in the current absence of the drug.

3. *Autonomous and distinctive patterns of behavior*—the pattern of repeated, persistent, illegal use of the drug, and other behavior distinctively belonging to this pattern, even in the absence of the drug.

It is evident that a minimalist reading of *Robinson* forbids criminal punishment for the existence of the pure status phenomena included in the first category, mere somatic states per se. The phenomena in the second category, mere mental propensities or desires, are similarly protected. Thus, insofar as a disease theory of addiction suggests the existence of autonomous bodily and mental states, criminal immunity is exactly coextensive with that arising from the minimalist reading of the *Robinson* status thesis.

If the disease argument is to broaden the scope of criminal immunity for addiction, it must do so by immunizing the phenomena in the third category, addictive *behavior*.[45] Certainly it is inaccurate to claim that all disease-related behavior can escape the reach of the criminal law.[46] The state can require a nondiseased person to take steps to prevent his catching a specific disease;[47] and it can require the diseased person to isolate or quarantine himself,[48] or to take measures to protect others.[49] But the

44. This categorization is not intended as a definitive one but is formulated for the purposes essential to the argument that follows. It includes each of the main types of phenomena that authorities typically speak of as constituting addiction. See, e.g., WHO Report No. 13. The factual questions that arise in connection with these phenomena are discussed in Chapters 11 and 12, infra.

45. *See United States v. Moore,* p. 1236 (Justice Wright, dissenting).

46. *Robinson v. California; Holden v. Hardy; Slaughter-House Cases;* and *Dowell v. City of Tulsa,* p. 861.

47. *Jacobson v. Massachusetts,* pp. 23–24 (vaccination).

48. See *ibid.,* p. 25; *Holden v. Hardy,* p. 398; and *Compagnie Française v. Board of Health,* p. 387.

49. The classic situation involves a driving prohibition for those who know they may lose control because of their disease. Failure to observe reasonable precautions to protect others from such dangers can warrant criminal conviction if, for example, another person's death results (*People v. Freeman; People v. Decina*).

criminal law may not reach involuntary conduct,[50] and it is this assumption that has formed the basis for arguments for criminal immunity for an addict's behavior.

Since the bodily condition associated with the disease is clearly protected by the status argument, it seems plausible that the addict's conduct can be exculpated insofar as it is an involuntary effect of that criminally immune status. Thus arguments for immunity may describe the addict's behavior in terms that suggest this kind of involuntariness, such as "compulsion symptomatic of the disease."[51]

Involuntariness, however, must in law be demonstrated as a matter of fact. The claim that addictive behavior is a "symptom" of the disease amounts to an attempt to gloss over the issue of involuntariness. There is no reason to assume that whatever is a medically recognized symptom must be legally involuntary. A symptom is simply an indicator or manifestation of the disease.[52] There are some kinds of symptomatic movements of the body that are not directly subject to the will in certain situations— e.g., fainting, tics, or squints. But there are also behaviors that can be symptomatic in medical terms and that can be directly subject to the will.[53] It is, then, a question of fact and not of definition whether symptomatic behavior is voluntary. Where a symptom is a voluntary act, there is no legal basis for declaring that merely because it indicates or manifests a disease, the person cannot be punished for it. Indeed, if such a voluntary act could cause serious social harm, is there any doubt that the state could invoke the criminal law to prohibit it?

50. LaFave and Scott (1972), p. 130.

51. *Powell v. Texas,* p. 569 (Justice Fortas, dissenting; quoting from trial judge with approval); *Watson v. United States,* p. 470 (Chief Justice Bazelon; appendix to rehearing en banc; "Even if an addict retains some minimal 'free will' not to indulge at a particular moment in time, no one would deny that his use of narcotics is largely involuntary—indeed is the essence of his disease"). See *In re Foss,* p. 1080 ("psychological and/or physiological compulsion arising from an addiction").

52. *Stedman's Medical Dictionary,* p. 1231, defines *symptom* as: "Any morbid phenomenon or departure from the normal in function, appearance, or sensation experienced by the patient and indicative of disease." De Gowin and De Gowin (1969, p. 30) say: "Symptoms are those variations from normal sensations or behavior that enter the patient's consciousness. They are *subjective. . . .* Physical examination discloses *physical signs;* these are *objective* manifestations of disease. . . ." *Taber's Cyclopedic Medical Dictionary,* S-140, says: "Any perceptible change in the body or its functions that indicates disease or the kind or phases of disease."

53. One large category of symptomatic behaviors subject to voluntary control includes partial paralyses or failures of bodily coordination symptomatic of various

One variant of the disease argument deserves particular mention at this point; it is the claim, explicit or implicit, that addiction is a *mental disease*.[54] If this is meant to advance the argument by invoking the insanity defense, it only makes the addict's attempt to escape liability more burdensome: the defendant would have to prove both the existence of a mental disease *and* either a lack of understanding related to the offending act itself,[55] or a defect in volitional capacity.[56] Proof that addiction is a mental disease would be difficult; there is no consensus in

---

kinds of neurological or other organic disease or defect. The behavioral malfunction is commonly both evident and symptomatic, but sufficiently limited in degree to be subject to a positive effort of will. For example, in cases where diverging eyes have resulted from partial paralysis of a muscle of one of the eyes, a partial closing of one eye is a typical symptomatic behavior; it can be reversed with some attention and moderate effort of will. The double vision that is distinctively symptomatic of this condition can also be elicited or prevented at will by those who have sufficient use of the muscle to relax it or to activate it sufficiently (Duke-Elder, 1958, p. 617). For other examples of partial paralyses influenceable by effort of will and of voluntary exercises recommended to help in therapy, see the medical treatment discussion of Bell's palsy, and of paralyses due to cerebrovascular accidents in Havard (1970), pp. 454–460.

54. Fifty years ago, when people spoke of "dope fiends," it was possible for a court to accept the notion that a morphine addict was per se insane (*Prather v. Commonwealth*). More recently the claim that addiction is a mental disease had been put forth by defendant addicts either as a generalized claim (*Robinson v. California*, p. 667, n. 8), or with respect to the particular case at issue (*Gaskins v. United States; Rivers v. United States;* see *Hutcherson v. United States,* p. 970 [Justice Burger, concurring] ; *Horton v. United States,* p. 597; and note 58, infra).

55. In *M'Naghten's Case* this lack of understanding is formulated as a defect of reason from disease of the mind, such that "[the accused did not] know the nature and quality of the act he was doing, or if he did know it, that he did not know he was doing what was wrong." This requirement appears as one option for proof of insanity in the Model Penal Code, Section 4.01 (Proposed Official Draft 1962), and is described as a defect resulting from mental disease wherein the person "lacks substantial capacity . . . to appreciate the criminality of his conduct."

56. In *Davis v. United States,* p. 378, the Court described this defect as a condition in which "[the] will, . . . the governing power of his mind, has been otherwise than voluntarily so completely destroyed that his actions are not subject to it, but are beyond his control." The Model Penal Code, Section 4.01, describes this aspect of the insanity defense as an optional alternative to the ground described in the preceding note. Here the defendant "lacks substantial capacity . . . to conform his conduct to the requirements of law." Any trend toward allowing a mere showing that the offending act resulted from mental disease, without a specific showing of lack of knowledge or lack of free will, collapsed with the abandonment of the rule of

the medical profession that addiction is a mental disease.[57] Although courts have shown sympathy for the doctrine that addiction is a disease, they have consistently refused to adopt the doctrine that addiction is a mental disease.[58] Moreover, the very concept of mental disease has been under severe scientific attack and is now plainly a controversial one.[59]

But assume the defendant establishes that addiction is a mental disease. If, for example, he is being tried for narcotic use, possession, or addiction-related theft, or for being drunk in public, the issue of lack of understanding is unlikely to arise. For if an addict committed an act while irrational because of the influence of a drug, the resulting lack of understanding would not suffice to establish the insanity defense; such a lack of understanding would not result in the first instance from the "disease" of addiction, but from the intoxication, the effect of the act of taking the drug on the particular occasion. Proof of defective volition would still be necessary; the addict would have to show that by virtue of his disease he was unable to exert the self-control necessary to refrain from self-intoxication. Use of the insanity defense therefore does not avoid the necessity of

---

Durham v. United States (the act must be the product of a mental disease or defect) in *United States v. Brawner* (adoption of the Model Penal Code test). See generally Fingarette (1972); Goldstein (1967).

57. See notes 40 and 42, supra; Fingarette (1972), pp. 19‒52. Such a consensus would not in any event control the legal concept of "disease" or "defect" as applied in the insanity defense. See *MacDonald v. United States,* p. 851, superseded by *United States v. Brawner.* See also *Powell v. Texas,* p. 541 (Justice Black, concurring).

58. *Castle v. United States,* p. 495 (Justice Burger, concurring). *Robinson* does not assert more than that addiction is a disease, though there is a footnote quoting (without direct comment or clear contextual indication of attitude) the appellee's brief which claimed that heroin addiction is a "state of mental and physical illness" (p. 666, n. 8). Courts have also stated that "a mere showing of narcotics addiction, without more does not constitute 'some evidence' of mental disease . . ." (*Bailey v. United States,* p. 4, citing *Heard v. United States,* p. 44. See also *United States v. Collins; United States v. Freeman; Hutcherson v. United States; Lloyd v. United States;* and *People v. Borrero*). Of course, an addict may make an insanity plea and a showing of mental disease independent of a claim of addiction. This strategy may succeed in a case where addiction exists but the addiction per se is not in itself sufficient even to raise the insanity issue (*Castle v. United States,* p. 494 [Justice Wright], pp. 496‒497 [Justice Burger, concurring]). This approach was used successfully in *People v. Kelly.* But see *Prather v. Commonwealth* (a morphine addict was held insane because of his addictive status).

59. See generally Fingarette (1972), pp. 19‒52.

showing involuntariness; that proof is only one part of the more complex case that such a defendant would have to make.

In summary, the disease argument relies on two assumptions in attempting to exculpate the addict. First, it suggests that his psychological and physiological condition, a pure status, is not punishable; this suggestion is unnecessary because it merely argues the minimalist holding in *Robinson.* Second, it implies that addictive behavior is involuntary. Thus all the arguments directed to exculpating addictive behavior rely, ultimately, on the thesis that such behavior is legally involuntary. The claim that such involuntariness is present has been made explicitly in the case law, and it is explored below.

III: THE INVOLUNTARINESS ARGUMENT

While *Robinson* contains only a brief and cryptic allusion to the involuntariness issue,[60] other cases have extended its implications to directly introduce considerations of involuntariness in ways that would seem to exculpate addictive behavior. Sometimes the argument is that the addictive behavior in question is involuntary;[61] at other times it takes the more complex form that the addictive behavior is the involuntary result of, or condition manifesting, a nonpunishable status.[62] Some forms of the argument use the word *involuntary,*[63] others use the term *compulsion,*[64] and still others use the term *pharmacological duress.*[65] In narcotics cases, the

60. At p. 667. The Court offers two examples in which addiction may result involuntarily. One is the addiction resulting from medically prescribed narcotics; the other is the newborn infant's addiction resulting from the mother's addiction. Both are not only examples of rare types of addiction relative to the total addict population, but are also examples of innocent development of addiction rather than innocent subsequent, self-initiated use of the drug once addiction exists. It is the ability to refrain from use subsequent to addiction that is most commonly at issue when the assumption of the involuntariness of addictive behavior is discussed. The *Robinson* majority opinion says nothing at all on that score, as Judge Wilkey notes in *United States v. Moore.*

61. *United States v. Moore,* pp. 1209–10 (Justice Wright, dissenting).

62. See *Watson v. United States,* p. 475.

63. *Ibid.,* p. 470 (Chief Justice Bazelon, appendix to rehearing en banc).

64. See note 36, supra; and *United States v. Lindsey,* p. 59.

65. *Watson v. United States,* p. 467, n. 18 (Chief Justice Bazelon, appendix to rehearing en banc); *Castle v. United States,* p. 494. See *United States v. McKnight;* and *United States v. Henry* ("pharmacological coercion").

involuntariness is usually said to extend to nontrafficking use, possession, and purchase; sometimes it is said to extend to behavior such as theft, if motivated by the need for money for a personal supply of the drug.[66] The theme of involuntariness has also been pressed vigorously in connection with addiction to alcohol. The premise proposed in the *Powell* dissent, and in the decisions in similarly inclined cases, is that alcoholism (including its "symptom" of appearing drunk in public) is a disease that is involuntarily and nonculpably caused and maintained.[67]

Even where courts have doggedly resisted the exculpatory legal implications of these arguments, they often seem to do so without a firm logical basis. This is because, paradoxically, these courts often seem to acquiesce in the fundamental assumption of involuntariness, or at least fail to challenge it.[68]

On its face the involuntariness argument seems to raise a simple question: Does the addict have any control over the behavior motivated by his desire for the drug? To answer this question we must fully confront a set of deeply rooted myths about addiction. The legal issues can be clarified only if they are reviewed against a carefully redrawn picture of the factual

66. *United States v. Moore,* p. 1210 (nontrafficking possession) (Justice Wright, dissenting); *ibid.,* p. 1260 (trafficking and robbery to obtain funds for purchase of drug) (Chief Justice Bazelon); *Watson v. United States,* p. 470 (Chief Justice Bazelon, appendix to rehearing en banc); *Lloyd v. United States,* p. 245 (purchase and possession) (Chief Justice Bazelon, dissenting); *United States v. Lindsey* (nontrafficking possession). See *Easter v. District of Columbia,* pp. 52–53 (being drunk in public; holding severely limited by *Powell v. Texas*); *Driver v. Hinnant,* p. 764 (alcohol addiction, being drunk in public; holding severely limited by *Powell v. Texas*).

67. *Powell v. Texas,* pp. 560–561, 567–568 (Justice Fortas, dissenting); *Easter v. District of Columbia* (holding severely limited by *Powell*); *Driver v. Hinnant* (holding severely limited by *Powell*). See generally Fingarette (1970).

68. *Smith v. Follette,* p. 961; *Bailey v. United States,* p. 1, n. 4; *United States ex rel. Swanson v. Reincke,* p. 263; *People v. Zapata,* pp. 906–907. If addictive conduct is in truth involuntary, there seems to be no logical basis for the criminal law to deny the addict a blank check to do whatever is necessary to get the drug. Any limitations on that license would simply be arbitrary. The implications for the criminal law are "revolutionary" and disturbing (*Powell v. Texas,* p. 544, Justice Black, concurring; *Powell v. Texas,* p. 534. But see *Powell,* p. 559, n. 2, Justice Fortas, dissenting). Judge Bazelon makes this point eloquently in arguing that a poor and unskilled addict may have no "meaningful choice" but to commit a crime (*United States v. Carter,* p. 210).

background, one that reassesses these myths and stereotypes. In the face of such an analysis, the simple picture of the alcohol or narcotic addict as a helpless slave to the drug disappears. We are left with deeper substantive insight, but also with greater humility, appreciating the extent of our ignorance, the complexity of the problems, and the hopeless inappropriateness of trying to deal with these problems in terms of a blanket concept of involuntariness.

10

Narcotic Addiction:
The Factual Background

A typical layman's view of narcotic addiction is dominated by the myth of the addict's slavery: in this view, drugs typically associated with drug-dependency have powers such that their repeated use, even for a short period, will "hook" the user.[1] Once hooked, he will be unable to voluntarily abstain from use thereafter; he will make any sacrifice to get his daily supply. If he fails to obtain a supply of the drug, he will undergo excruciating withdrawal suffering. If he is forced to abstain for a period of time—as a result of imprisonment or compulsory hospitalization, for example—he will inevitably relapse into addictive use upon his release.

Greater sophistication will no doubt suggest that such an extreme view needs qualification. But the main substance of the portrait is widely accepted even in more sophisticated circles; indeed, the involuntariness argument presupposes acceptance of the myth for all practical purposes. This acceptance accounts for the widespread failure of the courts to

1. In this chapter the emphasis is on narcotic addiction, though much of what is said extends to drug addiction generally. Where some non-narcotic drug addictions differ significantly from narcotic addiction, as for example in the greater severity and danger of sudden withdrawal from deep barbituate addiction, it is commonly the case that in this very trait the non-narcotic addiction is similar to alcohol addiction—which is fully discussed in Chapter 11, infra. For concise and authoritative standard descriptions of the various types of addictions, see Eddy et al. (1965); and DeLong (1972).

challenge the fundamental assumptions of the argument. In this chapter we offer such a challenge. We shall report a number of basic factual considerations that cast doubt on the accuracy of this portrait of addiction. The discussion of narcotic addiction begins by focusing on four aspects of drug use that belie this myth: (1) the existence of a population of drug users who do not become addicts, (2) the successful elimination of addictive patterns among formerly addicted groups, (3) the relative rarity of a heavy physiological addiction in narcotic addicts in this country, and (4) the correspondingly widespread influence of social and psychological inducements to addictive behavior.

I: NARCOTIC ADDICTION: SOME BASIC FACTS

The community's deep concern with the serious social problems associated with addiction undoubtedly focuses attention on those relative few who do take up an addictive pattern of use, thus distracting attention from the larger numbers who use drugs for medical or nonmedical purposes, but who do not take up such a pattern. Narcotics constitute the most effective analgesics (pain relievers) known to medicine, and their use is a widespread and conventional procedure for medical relief of substantial pain.[2] Yet only a small fraction of the many millions of patients who receive morphine ever attempt to take the drug again,[3] and only an exceedingly small proportion of addicts owe their dependence to medically initiated narcotic use.[4] These data alone prove that repeated use of narcotics does not automatically hook users to continued use of the drug.[5] One can

2. See, e.g., Jaffe (1965b), p. 247.

3. Goldstein, Aranow, and Kalman (1969), p. 474 (there is no "valid evidence" that legitimate medical administration of opiates might "create" addicts); DeLong (1972), p. 79; Lasagna (1965), p. 55.

4. Villareal (1970), p. 84; Glasscote (1972), p. 19, report that "iatrogenic addiction [medically induced physical dependence] appears to be an inconsequential component of the drug abuse problems."

5. One important study summarized: "[I]n the population as a whole, very few of those who could obtain morphine or heroin illegally, if they wished, become addicts. It is noteworthy that although D-amphetamine has been used very widely to counteract fatigue and sleeplessness, only an occasional person who used it became habituated to it. And despite the nearly universal exposure of the population to the 'legal' psychotropic drugs (alcohol, caffeine, and nicotine), some become habituated and some do not (Goldstein, Aranow, and Kalman, 1969, p. 474). See generally Hill (1969), p. 288. With regard to opiates specifically, see Geber (1969), pp.

make similar comments about the sedatives and tranquilizers; these can
and do come to be used addictively, but only by a relative few of the
many millions who use such drugs.[6]

Among the minority of drug users who do develop addiction, many give
it up.[7] Contrary to widespread skepticism about drug rehabilitation, there
has been substantial success in measures to control and eliminate addiction
in the United States. Skeptics probably assume that anything less than 100
percent success in achieving total, permanent abstention from narcotics as
the result of exposure to any one program is a failure and proof of the
hopelessness of the task. This conclusion is unreasonable and misleading.
More important than such total successes are the days spent free of drug
use and the direction of the trend for a population even though specific
individuals may relapse on occasion. Impressive achievement in these
latter[8] aspects is often overlooked because attention is focused on the
relapse incidents.

A recent study of Vietnam veterans[9] confirms the notion both that
addiction does not always follow drug use and that addiction can be

---

375–387; Louria (1971), p. 84; and Wald and Hutt (1972), p. 5. Weil (1972), p.
333, discusses the inadequacy of the "addict" stereotype and the individuality of
patterns of use.

6. Goldstein, Aranow, and Kalman (1969), p. 474.

7. With respect to government and government-related programs created for this
purpose, see note 8, infra. Experience in private and purely voluntary residential
programs such as Synanon demonstrates that "many former compulsive drug users
are able to remain drug free and to function productively so long as they remain in
residence" (Jaffe, 1970a, pp. 62–63). Unknown numbers simply quit drug use of
their own volition. DeLong (1972) reports that "there is some evidence that a
substantial number of addicts—perhaps as many as one-third—'mature out' of addiction when they reach their 30's and 40's" (p. 214).

8. Glasscote (1972); Lindesmith (1968), pp. 52–54; Fraser and Grider (1953);
Gearing (1972); Jaffe (1970a); Maddux (1965), pp. 159–176; O'Donnell (1964);
Vaillant (1966a), (1966b), (1966c); Wood (1973). See generally Chapple et al.
(1972); and May (1972), pp. 345–394. In reviewing eleven follow-up studies of
narcotic addiction treatment programs in 1965, O'Donnell noted that high percent-
ages of relapse were valid "only for a highly restricted definition of relapse" such as a
single occasion of use. The studies did not indicate that "most addicts, after a period
of treatment or enforced abstinence, relapse to drugs and continue to use drugs, or
that addicts spend most of their time outside of institutions using drugs" (O'Donnell,
1965, pp. 242–243). One study suggests that there is a reduction in criminal behavior
of patients in treatment (*National Commission on Marijuana and Drug-Abuse*, 1973,
p. 177). Such a benefit is obscured by the "all or nothing" approach.

9. Robins (1973).

eliminated voluntarily. The Vietnam experience was "a natural experiment in the exposure of masses of young men to narcotic drugs,"[10] barbiturates, amphetamines, and marijuana. Pure forms of heroin and other drugs were easily available, and at low cost. In Vietnam in 1971, "almost every soldier had the opportunity to experiment with heroin, and almost all personally knew other soldiers who used heroin with some regularity."[11] In September, 1971, the study examined the entire group of 13,240 young Army enlisted men who were then returning from Vietnam. Eight to twelve months later, this group was re-examined with regard to drug use during the period following their return. Widespread use was not followed by comparable rates of addiction: almost half had tried heroin or opium while in Vietnam, but only about 20 percent developed signs of physical or psychological dependence.[12] Where addictive patterns had developed, voluntary nonaddiction upon return home had almost always followed. Although about 20 percent of the total group of 13,240 had shown actual signs of addiction while in Vietnam, only one percent of the total experienced such signs at any time after their return to the United States.[13] A number of the ex-addicts among these veterans did use narcotics after their return, but without readdiction. The study concluded:

These results are surprising not only in that men who report having been addicted in Vietnam so seldom report any addiction in the United States during the 8 to 12 months since their return, but that many of them avoided readdiction *without* completely abstaining from narcotics. The ability of men formerly dependent on narcotics to use them occasionally without readdiction challenges the common view of narcotic addiction as a chronic and intractable condition.[14]

The phenomenon is not unique to Vietnam veterans.[15] The nature of drug dependency in this country further belies the myth of addict slavery to drugs. It is highly unlikely that much physiological addiction exists in the United States. Drugs sold illegally are usually highly adulterated. In one survey of street drugs in New York, 10 percent of the purchases

10. *Ibid.*, p. 22.

11. *Ibid.*

12. *Ibid.*

13. *Ibid.* Zinberg (1972) essentially confirms this finding on the basis of his surveys and interviews (p. 284).

14. Robins (1973), pp. 22–23.

15. See, for example, Lindesmith (1968), p. 48; and Alarcon et al. (1969), p. 338.

contained no active ingredient whatever, and it has been estimated that illegally purchased bags of heroin typically range from one percent to five percent active material.[16] Thus, if we look solely at the chemical factors involved in drug addiction in this country, we find that the addict's strictly physiological dependence is at most moderate and very often quite mild in degree.[17]

On the other hand, the social inducements to adopt addictive patterns of behavior are often maximal. A very large proportion of new addicts in the United States today are young, psychologically immature, occupationally unskilled, socially uprooted, poor, and disadvantaged. Many engaged in crime before they were addicted.[18] The myth of the addict as a

16. Louria et al. (1967), pp. 1-2. The reports of heroin "overdose" as the leading cause of teenage death in New York City are probably a mark of impurities or special sensitivity, since recent studies show that "overdose deaths" are not usually associated either with high concentrations of the drug or with the usual symptoms of narcotic overdose. See Cherubin (1967); and Chein (1969), pp. 14-15. Wesson et al. (1972), p. 165, speak of the "monumentally poor quality" of the heroin available on the West Coast. A summary of recent studies of "street drugs shows that less than 50 percent of samples surveyed contained the alleged ingredients, and doses varied widely" (Schnoll, 1971-72). At one point the quality of street heroin sold on the Eastern seaboard rose from about 5 percent to a 10 percent concentration; somewhat more intense withdrawal symptoms for addicts resulted (Cohen, 1972, p. 336). Plainly, local fluctuations are common. This variation suggests that the persistence in the life-patterns is not a direct consequence of the physiological action of a certain dose of the drug, but is highly influenced by other (social, psychological, and cultural) factors.

17. "Because of [the highly adulterated doses generally sold] it is now easy to withdraw the majority of heavy heroin users from their drug. Even those using six to eight bags a day (a $30- to $40-a-day habit) often can be rapidly withdrawn without a substitute narcotic, by using mild tranquilizers during withdrawal" (Louria, 1971, pp. 83-84. See also Chein, 1969, p. 89 [discussion remarks]). Physiological dependence may also be moderate among members of the "needle cult," addicts who seem to be addicted more to using the needle on themselves (whether or not there is anything in it) than to the drug itself. See May (1972), p. 370; see also notes 32, 43, and 52, infra. Undoubtedly there are narcotic drug-users in this country who are strongly dependent physiologically as well as psychologically. One cannot say how many. No doubt, significant groups within this class are the health professionals who are addicts, and the "street dealers." See, e.g., Preble and Casey (1972), p. 106; and Chein, supra. Both groups have ready access to reasonably potent concentrations of drugs, but far larger groups do not.

18. *National Commission on Marijuana and Drug-Abuse* (1973), pp. 171-172; Vaillant (1969), p. 347; and Wald and Hutt (1972), p. 6. This is a common finding in many studies, but of course it is related to the nature of the populations among

helpless slave to his habit only lends further strength to the inducements for addicts to continue addictive patterns. It provides such persons with a rationale for ignoring alternatives to crime and the drug culture. Young people who are disadvantaged and alienated may find the foundation of a socially authenticated identity in addiction. For such persons, drug use provides at last a "constructive" focal activity in life, generating its own occupational responsibilities, opportunities for success and achievement, social status, and ideological, philosophical, or religious meaning.[19] The "hustling" required by drug addiction is not always a burden[20] or a separation from a socially productive life; for certain groups it may be one natural outgrowth of the values of an alienated subculture, values that are by definition inconsistent with those of the dominant society.[21] When some writers characterize the addict as one who will seek the drug at "great risk"[22] or "at the cost of unbelievable sacrifices,"[23] the sacrifice in question may be one of values important only to the writer and not to the addict.[24] A person who has developed roots in conventional society and skills for leading a productive life is substantially less likely to find a meaningful social identity in the drug culture, and such a person can more readily abandon addiction once it develops.[25]

Because addiction in this country has far deeper social roots than physiological ones, judicious use of sanctions and threats of sanctions, especially if coupled with suitable constructive aid, can be an effective tool

---

which addictive drug use is currently prevalent. In other epochs, other results would be obtained. See Preble and Casey (1972), pp. 100-104 (historical review); and Weil (1972), p. 340 (cross-cultural review). Similar contemporary statistics are reported from England (May, 1972, p. 381).

19. Ashley (1972), p. 73; Preble and Casey (1972), p. 116. See generally Brecher (1972), chap. 6; Chein (1969); Vaillant (1969), p. 351.

20. See Chein et al. (1964), pp. 36-61.

21. Douglas (1970), p. 52; Feldman (1970), p. 10; Chein (1969), p. 23. See note 49, infra.

22. Isbell (1972), pp. 36-37.

23. Lindesmith (1968), p. 49.

24. Ashley (1972) reports: "Most of what we learn about the heroin user comes from the reports of the police, physicians, psychiatrists, and social workers. As a group they are essentially middle- and upper-middle class, operating under a value system quite different from that held in the urban ghetto . . ." (p. 64).

25. Vaillant (1969), p. 335, finds that addicts with a history of stable work patterns and stable early family matrices were the ones who eventually became abstinent.

in deterring addicts from continuing drug use. Such sanctions may be rooted in the powers of the criminal law; they often are so rooted under present policies (e.g., revocation of parole and use of prison sentences).[26] Sanctions and aid may also be rooted in other values and institutions—for example, in personal freedom, work, or family.[27] What is essential, however, is that the addict perceive both the sanctions and the aid as being such in terms of his own values.[28]

II: NARCOTIC ADDICTION: CURRENT THEORIES

In light of the preceding factual discussion, we now turn to a discussion of the main types of hypotheses used to explain addictive drug use and to prove its involuntary nature. There are basically two types: one explains addiction in terms of physiology, the other in terms of psychology. It might be sufficient for our present purposes simply to point out that there is no generally accepted scientific explanation of addiction,[29] and perforce there is no scientific basis for establishing that addictive behavior is generally involuntary. But if we are to dissolve the myths that dominate

26. These policies are employed in the California Civil Commitment Program and the federal programs at the United States Public Health Service Hospital at Lexington, Kentucky. See Wood (1973); Vaillant (1969); Carrick (1970), pp. 136–152. Vaillant's 12-year follow-up of New York narcotics addicts committed to the Lexington hospital reports: "Effective treatment appears to depend on the compulsory alteration of the addict's behavior for substantial periods of time. . . . [A] long prison term [9 months or more] *coupled with a year of parole* was vastly more effective than short or long prison terms alone, or hospital treatment alone" (Vaillant, 1969, pp. 355–356). Lindesmith (1968), pp. 52–58, reports various studies showing that sanctions, parole, threats of job-loss or license-loss (for physician-addicts) have produced significant results in producing abstinence.

27. For many of the narcotics rehabilitation programs, variable rules of internal discipline allow increased personal freedom as the addict abstains from narcotics and pursues work assignments. See Maddux (1965); Glasscote (1972), pp. 63–241. Far more alcoholics in the United States have well-developed family and career roots than do narcotics addicts. Not surprisingly, the use of carefully worked out family-job sanctions has been showing dramatic success in recent years in dealing with alcoholics. See Pfeffer et al. (1956). Also see Mello et al. (1965), pp. 259–269; Saslow (1970).

28. Lindesmith (1968), p. 53, notes that introducing values that the addict accepts can positively affect the implementation of sanctions.

29. For an elaboration of the various types of hypotheses that have been proposed to account for drug dependence, see WHO Report No. 18, 1970. The

this field, we must go beyond this generalization—logically crucial as it is—and examine specific types of explanations that promote them.

The first type of hypothesis is a qualified version of the simple theory that mere use of a narcotic drug inevitably causes addiction in all persons. According to this hypothesis, the physiological effects of the drug interact with a biological, possibly genetically determined sensitivity found only in a certain subgroup of all users; for this special subgroup the physiological impact of the drug suffices to produce an addictive pattern of conduct.[30]

As a scientific or empirical claim, this type of hypothesis is speculative, neither substantiated by medical evidence nor supported by medical consensus;[31] it hardly warrants reshaping constitutional or common law doctrine. But even if these hypotheses were substantiated to some extent, it is unlikely that such a biological predisposition could account for a

---

generality and range of disciplines covered by these hypotheses reveal the utter lack of specific or definitive causal understanding. They are cast in terms of psychiatric categories, delinquency theories, miscellaneous personal motives (e.g., pleasure, distress and crises, social ambitions, social rebellion), "metabolic lesions," conditioned responses and learning, sociocultural "pressures," and various combinations of these factors. Indeed, a later report states that "these hypotheses are non-specific with respect to drug use" (WHO Study Group, 1973, p. 20). In short, these theories are all very general speculations about social malaises. The analysis which follows in the text does not critically discuss the sociologically oriented hypotheses. The assumption is that the existence of generalized social influences does not amount to the conditions for involuntary behavior in the context of criminal responsibility. It is true that there has been recent argument that for some members of alienated subcultures the social influences may reach the point of establishing irrationality and involuntariness of a kind justifying a finding of absence of criminal responsibility. This novel and highly controversial view admittedly faces formidable obstacles to acceptance in law. In any event no analysis of the bearing of such a doctrine specifically on narcotic addiction has yet been provided. See Floud (1974), pp. 204–221. There is good reason to suppose that social factors are very important in understanding much addictive conduct, but to say this is very different from saying or even meaning to suggest that the conduct is therefore "involuntary." See Chapter 9, text and note at note 42.

30. See, for example, Dole and Nyswander (1968), p. 359.

31. DeLong (1972), p. 212, summarizes the questions concerning the physiological components of addiction and concludes that there are no clear answers and that most scientists are at least skeptical about validating their effects. Goldstein, Aranow, and Kalman (1969), p. 474, raise the possibility that a genetic factor might explain the addictive response in the relative few who become addicts, but acknowledge a "paucity of evidence" for such a view. Specific comments such as those above are also confirmed by the more general acknowledgments that medical science today lacks *any* accepted fundamental understanding of the causes of addiction.

significant portion of drug-related conduct. Biological signs indicate that many of those who demonstrate fullblown, extreme drug-addict patterns of conduct are, at most, only moderately physically dependent. Common addictive patterns of conduct exist in which the known biological aftereffects of the particular drug used are minimal or nil.[32] It is empirically implausible, in the absence of strong independent evidence, that a physiological influence so slight, even if related to unique bodily predisposition, should absolutely and irresistibly transform a whole way of life.

A conceptual incongruity also pervades this type of hypothesis, an incongruity in kind between the supposed biological cause and its supposed behavioral effects. There are, of course, instances where a particular physiological process or directly associated feeling may seem to produce an automatic behavior-response. It seems plausible, for example, that intractable and overwhelming pain, or the last extreme of exhaustion or of hunger, may lead to a kind of immediate, instinctive reflex, an uncontrollable sound or gesture. Yet even in such cases, the notion that this reaction is a direct behavioral effect of a physiological cause, that the mind can play no significant role in mediating the behavior, may be factually incorrect. The biological drive of hunger can be influenced by cultural and psychological factors. Indeed, eating can be suspended altogether to the point of death by the mediation of mind, either by a voluntary hunger strike or by neurotic loss of appetite. Recent medical research has dramatically revealed how much even our extreme pain-distress reactions are complexly mind-mediated rather than direct physical responses.[33]

32. Addictive patterns of conduct are associated with the dependence-producing drugs which WHO lists as *not* producing physical dependence, e.g., cocaine. The addictive pattern of conduct can also exist when no narcotic has been used, such as in the not uncommon cases of addicts who have been unwittingly buying pure milk sugar from their dealers over substantial periods of time. See Vaillant (1969), p. 352.

33. Beecher (1959), pp. 161–166, reports that during World War II two-thirds of the wounded at Anzio did not wish pain-relieving medication, whereas four-fifths of a group of civilians with far less tissue trauma did. The gravely wounded who did not wish medication for wound-pain complained vigorously, however, at inept injections. *"Great wounds with great significance . . . are made painless by small doses of morphine, whereas fleeting experimental*[ly induced] *pains with no serious significance are not blocked by morphine"* (ibid., p. 165). Beecher's experimental reports show that, generally speaking, half the pain-relieving effect of morphine is due to "placebo" reaction, a reaction to the *idea* that a pain reliever has been given rather than to the chemical action; the placebo effect is greater as the stress is greater (*ibid.* See also Grollman and Grollman, 1970, p. 99).

Yet even if one accepts the image of an automatic and involuntary behavioral response to a specific physiological drive, this very limited range of behavior does not constitute the kind of response that could account intelligibly and fully for the typically elaborate addictive lifestyle. A pattern of conduct must be distinguished from a mere sequence of reflexlike reactions. A reflex knee jerk is not conduct. If we regard something as a pattern of conduct, whether criminal or not, we assume that it is mediated by the mind, that it reflects consideration of reasons and preferences, the election of a preferred means to the end, and the election of the end itself from among alternatives. The complex, purposeful, and often ingenious projects with which many an addict may be occupied in his daily hustling to maintain his drug supply are examples of conduct; they are not automatic reflex reactions to a single biological cause.[34]

Nothing in the preceding is intended to deny that chemical predisposition or other biological causes may be some among a number of factors significantly influencing addictive patterns of conduct. But even if such causal factors were shown to exist, it would be implausible to expect that they would be sufficient to resolve the question of the legal voluntariness of the various kinds of complex conduct in which addicts engage. One must conclude that there is no substantiated biological explanation of drug addiction nor is there a reasonable hope that further research in this area could settle the questions of law concerning the voluntariness of addictive conduct and ways of life.

It is therefore necessary to turn to theories that explain addictive conduct by introducing psychological considerations: theories of motivation, learning, or conditioning, or of personality structure and mental pathology. We turn first to theories based on motivation. These explanations of addictive conduct assume that either the drug-induced euphoria or the addict's withdrawal stress or both provide mentally overpowering motives for addictive behavior.[35]

Some would emphasize that either the experience of withdrawal stress or the fear of it can serve as an absolutely overriding motive[36] for continuing addictive patterns of conduct. Immediate total abstention from

34. "[T]hough drugs may have specific physiological effects, their effects upon behavior and experience are largely nonspecific" (Lennard and Bernstein, 1971, p. 57).

35. WHO Report No. 13 (1964), p. 13, uses the phrase "overpowering desire."

36. See, for example, McMorris (1968), p. 1084.

drugs, especially in heavy narcotics users, can be associated with a temporary but intensely distressing reaction that includes chills, muscle twitching, vomiting, diarrhea, and general debility. But "cold turkey" withdrawal from narcotics, in and of itself, is apparently never fatal; its effects are temporary, continuing at worst for no more than several days.[37] Moreover, since most addicts are not heavily addicted physiologically, the reaction is not severe.[38] For the moderately addicted, it is comparable to a bad case of flu.[39] It is not uncommon for young people who think themselves heavily addicted to find that they can withdraw "cold turkey" with only minimal discomfort.[40] And drugs associated with addictive conduct do not always produce withdrawal stress.[41] Most important, there is no need for "cold turkey" withdrawal. The standard, gradual withdrawal procedures used under professional care keep narcotic withdrawal discomfort to a quite moderate and readily bearable level.[42]

Furthermore, it is well-established that withdrawal symptoms (as well as the effects of drug use) are mediated to a great degree by mental attitudes.[43] Not only can the intensity and stress of symptoms vary greatly with changes in the addict's state of mind and the social-psychological setting, but they can even be made to appear and disappear with changes in setting or circumstance.[44] Drug dependence facilities take advantage of this fact: increasing numbers of lay groups, therapeutic

37. A study of the literature written since 1875 found no documented case of opiate withdrawal as "the sufficient cause of death" (Glaser and Ball, 1970, p. 287; also see, for example, Maddux, 1965, p. 168).

38. Glasscote (1972), p. 10. See notes 16 and 17, supra.

39. Wesson et al. (1972), p. 165; Jaffe (1965a), p. 302. See Zinberg (1972), p. 285.

40. Preble and Casey (1972), p. 110.

41. See Deneau (1969), pp. 199−207; Isbell (1972), pp. 36−38; Villareal (1970), p. 97. On the other hand, it should be noted that physiological dependence and consequent withdrawal stress can occur without psychological dependence, without the self-conscious craving to use the drug, and therefore without the addictive life pattern. See Eddy et al. (1965).

42. Blachly (1966); Fraser and Grider (1953); Maddux (1965), p. 168 (withdrawal techniques in U.S. Public Health Service Hospitals).

43. Lindesmith (1968), pp. 34−39, takes it as "conclusively established" that under controlled conditions addicts can be deceived into thinking they have received opiates when they have been given placebos. See generally Lennard and Bernstein (1971), pp. 57−62; Glasscote (1972), p. 34; and notes 32 and 36, supra.

44. Chein and associates report that the distress level in withdrawal depends on the setting: "Alone, it can be an almost unbearable experience. In a hospital ward,

communities, and medical and social welfare agencies provide a variety of withdrawal and postcare settings in which the medical, social, and moral support is maximal.[45]

This discussion suggests that the experience or fear of drug withdrawal cannot render addictive conduct legally involuntary. The criminal law demands that citizens refrain from criminal conduct even at the cost of temporary moderate personal discomfort; fear of such discomfort alone could neither establish a criminal law defense nor an absence of *mens rea* on the ground of involuntariness. Thus arguments for defenses such as "pharmacological coercion"[46] due to drug addiction are fatally flawed. Such arguments implicitly reveal profound factual misapprehensions about the assumed horrors of withdrawal symptoms. The common law defense of coercion requires a showing of reasonable fear of imminent mortal or grave bodily injury;[47] only if one erroneously equates the narcotic addict's withdrawal stress with these dangers could a defense like pharmacological coercion have any legal force.

Moreover, if courts were to make this erroneous equation they would only encourage addictive conduct by validating the myth that withdrawal stress is an agony to be avoided at any cost; the myth often influences addicts themselves.[48] The belief in the myth of addict-slavery can encourage addicts to surrender to, and even to embrace, their "destiny" as helpless victims.[49] This attitude can provide a dimension of drama in a formerly drab or frustrating life. Such beliefs and attitudes, often rein-

---

remarkably little medication often stills the distress associated with quite severe physiological disturbance, e.g., painful cramps and diarrhea. Conversely, patients with minor overt symptoms may be very demanding of medication" (Chein et al., 1964, pp. 247-248; see Phillipson, 1970, p. 1; Lennard et al., 1967).

45. See, for example, Jaffe (1970a), p. 48. See generally Glasscote (1972).

46. *Castle v. U.S.*, p. 494; *U.S. v. Henry*, p. 269. See *Watson v. U.S.* ("pharmacological duress," at p. 447; "physiological duress" at p. 461; Chief Justice Bazelon, concurring and dissenting).

47. *D'Aquino v. U.S.; Gillars v. U.S.*, p. 974.

48. See Freedman (1972), p. 30.

49. Chein et al. (1964), p. 248: "[A]mong adolescent addicts . . . the self-identification as addicts—i.e., as persons who require opiates for comfortable functioning—is an important phenomenon in their developing addiction. . . . There is another aspect to the withdrawal syndrome; it is not merely the bane of addiction to opiates, but also its badge . . ."—a subject of much boastful humor and exaggerated storytelling.

forcing counterculture values, provide a rationale for pursuing a life of crime as a member of an addict culture.[50]

Euphoria is another important effect of drug use that many believe provides a principal motive for addiction.[51] It is obvious that in settings other than addiction prospective euphoria is not a motive that will normally serve to excuse criminal conduct. But one might argue that anticipation of euphoria in the case of drug addiction could be so intense that it could be shown to be overpowering to the point where it negates voluntariness in the criminal law. Even if one strains to entertain the logic of this argument, the facts are otherwise. The narcotic addict typically does not reach or anticipate reaching such an intense level of pleasure. Most addicts in this country cannot amass the money, even through a life of active crime, to buy the quantity of narcotics needed to achieve this kind of euphoria regularly. The orgastic "rush," which may be more common at stages of early use, becomes increasingly rare with the development of tolerance to the drug.[52] Thus a legal defense based on ecstatic drug euphoria would simply have no basis in fact. Nor could the prospect of tranquil euphoria associated with routine drug use preclude criminal liability for addictive conduct; presumably this motive would be even less overwhelming.[53]

Human beings respond to conditioning that influences complex forms of learning. Conditioning and habit-learning can operate without the necessity for (at times with hardly an opportunity for) conscious motivation or reflective choice or will. Could addiction be a form of conditioned or learned "automatic" response that overrides the conscious will? There is no empirical proof that simple pleasure-conditioning or positive reinforcement in operant conditioning can of itself determine a whole way of

50. See, for example, Feldman (1970); Preble and Casey (1972); Chein (1969), pp. 23–24; Ashley (1972), p. 73.

51. See Glasscote (1972), p. 21; Lindesmith (1968), p. 34; Maddux (1965).

52. "[T]he habit size of a long-time heavy user is often not at the level of euphoria but only at a level sufficient to suppress withdrawal or to keep the withdrawal mild" (Holahan, 1972, p. 290). Other commentators confirm this point. See Glasscote (1972), p. 11; Lindesmith (1968), pp. 23–45.

53. In the addict's routine daily injections a relief and calm is achieved. Each new injection abates the tensions and discomforts that emerge as the effect of the preceding dose begins to wear off. During standard withdrawal procedures, with decreased dosages leading to abstinence, this tranquil "euphoria" is normally lost (Jaffe, 1965a, pp. 302–303).

life.[54] Of course, a person may learn to alleviate certain discomforts by the use of a tranquilizing drug such as heroin that has short-run, immediate effectiveness. That person may then develop a strong, habitual propensity to respond to subsequent discomfort in this way. In the absence of strong countermotives, such as a commitment to law or to other cultural values reflected in it, a person who has been positively conditioned to desire and use a drug might indulge this desire persistently, in spite of the illegality of the conduct necessary to do so. But is it plausible that a person who has genuine, urgent contrary values and commitments would find it impossible either to inhibit such a conditioned or learned behavioral response, to substitute another, or at least to take steps that would indirectly bring about extinction of the learned or conditioned response? The availability of any of these measures[55] could establish the legal voluntariness of his drug use. The fact is that there is no independent empirical evidence or generally accepted scientific theory that warrants an assertion that human beings can be conditioned to the point where these options cease to exist. Theories along these lines remain highly speculative and controversial.[56]

Yet another group of psychological hypotheses are based on claims of psychiatric derivation. According to these arguments, whereas mentally healthy persons do not allow the pleasure, fears, or learning associated with drug use to become imperative or paramount in their lives, the addict is psychologically vulnerable. He suffers from "mental illness," "personality defect," "character disorder," or psychic "compulsion." In response to these arguments, one might point to the problems and inadequacies in invoking a generalized concept of disease (including mental illness) that were discussed in Chapter 9. We deal here, however, with what purport to be more specific descriptions of mental illness and how they may relate to the criminal law.[57]

54. For a clear discussion of these concepts, see Skinner (1938) and DeLong (1972), pp. 133–134. Lennard and Bernstein (1971), p. 83, point out that the capacity of the many who reside in such groups as Phoenix House to abstain refutes the hypothesis that addiction is an automatic internally triggered pattern. See Thompson and Pickens (1969).

55. See Jaffe (1970a). See generally Glasscote (1972).

56. See, for example, Skinner (1971). Wald and Hutt (1972), p. 45, conclude that it is a high priority *"question"* whether there is any inborn physiological predilection, drug-induced vulnerability, learned response to external stimuli, *or none of these,* that bear on addiction.

57. The general concept of "mental illness" has no more weight than its more specific forms taken jointly. That is, if "compulsion," "inadequate personality," "character defect," and other psychiatric diagnoses provide no independent proof of

For example, one writer reports that a large portion of addicts suffer from "some form of personality disturbance, . . . [an illness often] manifested by a pattern of anti-social behavior, rather than by observable mental symptoms."[58] This concept of personality disturbance does little to distinguish the addict from other persons who have a tendency to get into difficulties with the law and with their neighbors and who often manifest no discernible mental abnormalities. Nor is it a helpful means of distinguishing addictive disorders to note that addicts manifest personal failings of the sort found in the general population: "The majority of addicts . . . do not fall into clear-cut nosological entities, but rather present mixtures of traits of the kind found in neuroses, character [personality] disorders, and inadequate personalities."[59]

The psychiatric concept of "compulsion" is perhaps the most widely accepted basis for an implicit argument that the addict's conduct is involuntary.[60] The term means something different in psychiatric usage than it does in criminal law. In criminal law, "compulsion" designates what is conceptually and observationally quite simple in commonsense terms: either there is an exterior physical force greater than the person's physical strength to resist, or, if one considers coercion to be a form of compulsion, there is a plain and imminent threat by another person to do grave bodily injury or even mortal harm unless the victim acquiesces.[61]

---

involuntariness, the generic concept, which refers vaguely to some or all of these, can do no more.

58. Bowman (1965), p. 1031.

59. *Ibid.*, p. 1033 (citing an AMA Report on Narcotics Addiction). The labeling process can often simply obscure the legal issues. In *Washington v. U.S.*, the court was confronted with such a situation. It commented: "These labels and definitions were not merely uninformative. Their persistent use served to distract the jury's attention from the few underlying facts which were mentioned. For example, the fact that Washington's difficulties 'in relating adequately to other people are more severe or more extreme than the average [person's]' was immersed in a dispute about whether to classify these difficulties as a 'personality defect,' a 'personality problem,' a 'personality disorder,' a 'disease,' an 'illness,' or simply a 'type of personality' " (*ibid.*, p. 449).

60. Redlich and Freedman (1966), p. 728, find that this characteristic may be singularly descriptive of addicts: "It is questionable, then, whether one can speak meaningfully of an addictive personality beyond the tautological statement that such a person, for one or another reason, has the compulsion to take drugs. At present we are inclined to believe that addicts are a heterogeneous lot."

61. For discussion of the legal concepts of compulsion, coercion, and necessity, see Hall (1960), chap. 12. Of course, a defendant could try to prove that the

However, in psychiatric usage the term means neither of these things. It does have several other meanings, but these, in turn, cannot accurately be used to describe addictive behavior.

In psychiatric terms, being "compelled" is often regarded as the result of tensions among psychic energies or psychic forces within the individual.[62] In this usage, the psychic forces behind the addict's propensity to use the drug are presumed to be quantitatively stronger than any contrary forces. However, they are presumed stronger not because they have been independently measured, but because the theory, *post facto,* merely interprets in those terms the observed fact that the person engages in the repetitive conduct rather than inhibiting it. Thus, in this usage, compulsion is a speculative theoretical construct about human behavior generally, rather than a scientifically identifiable distinctive feature of the individual defendant's behavior.[63]

"Compulsion" may also be used in a more specific, descriptive sense in psychiatry to refer to "an insistent, repetitive intrusive, and unwanted urge to perform an act which is contrary to the person's ordinary conscious wishes or standards."[64] This characteristic definition cannot apply generally to addictive conduct, however, since the drug and the way of life are

---

psychiatric concept of "compulsion" implied a mental disease or defect within the meaning of the insanity defense. Such proof would have to be made independently of a showing of the mere fact of addiction. See Chapter 9, note 56, supra.

62. The doctrine is set out in some of Freud's classic works, and is summarized in Redlich and Freedman (1966), p. 351. See generally Brenner (1973), p. 191.

63. The remarks in the text above do not imply that these general psychiatric doctrines have no use at all. They have uses *within* psychiatry; they can be helpful in gaining an overview of the human psyche, in organizing the specific insights of the clinic, and in guiding research and therapy. Moreover, the psychiatrist can make important contributions in certain aspects of the criminal trial. He or she may have insights into the mind and character of the individual on trial, or at least into a well-understood psychological type to which the defendant demonstrably belongs. However, *specific knowledge* about addicts as a "type" is lacking, although vague, speculative, and often conflicting statements abound in the psychiatric and other literatures. See Redlich and Freedman (1966).

64. American Psychiatric Association, *A Psychiatric Glossary* (1964). This definition would not necessarily preclude a finding of criminal liability. As Justice Black noted: "When we say that appellant's [offending conduct] is caused not by 'his own' volition but rather by some other force, we are clearly thinking of a force that is nevertheless 'his' except in some special sense. The accused undoubtedly commits the proscribed act and the only question is whether the act can be attributed to a part of 'his' personality that should not be regarded as criminally responsible. Almost all of

often consciously and wholeheartedly "wanted."[65] Sometimes, however, psychiatrists define "compulsion" as an urge that *cannot* be inhibited.[66] But on what grounds and in what sense can one say that the addict "cannot" inhibit the impulse? Only two grounds are ever offered: (1) the observation that the addict does not inhibit it, even in spite of attempts to threaten and persuade;[67] and (2) the theory of the balance of conflicting psychic forces, which, as noted above, hypothesizes that the urge that in fact wins out must therefore have been the strongest. But the latter explanation is only a verbal restatement, in the language of the theory, of the already observed fact that the individual does persist.[68] Neither formulation is an independent scientific determination that the individual does so because he *must*.

Moreover, the question of legal voluntariness cannot be resolved until we know, at least, whether the addict had the option of taking some preventive measure that would have either eliminated the compulsive urge or restrained him from satisfying it. These and other questions that are essential in determining legal compulsion are lost sight of when courts employ too readily the psychiatric term; for such questions are simply irrelevant in the psychiatric use of "compulsive."[69] Indeed, psychiatrists themselves recognize that the logical relation between the concepts of "psychic forces" in psychiatry and "will" and "choice" in the law remains unclear.[70] How, then, can the psychiatric formulations of "compulsion"

---

the traditional purposes of the criminal law can be significantly served by punishing the person who in fact committed the proscribed act without regard to whether his action was 'compelled' by some elusive 'irresponsible' aspect of his personality" (*Powell v. Texas,* p. 540 [Justice Black, concurring]).

65. Brenner (1973), p. 191. See notes 49 and 50, supra.

66. English and English (1958).

67. "The universal characteristic common to all types of drug dependence is *psychic dependence,* a psychological compulsion to take a drug. . . . Psychic dependence is difficult to define and measure but is recognized clinically by alterations in behavior such as undergoing great risks to obtain the drug, obsession with maintaining a supply, use of the drug as the chief means of adapting to life and a strong tendency to relapse after treatment" (Isbell, 1972, p. 361).

68. The National Commission on Marijuana and Drug-Abuse urges discarding of the "unidimensional concept of individual loss of self-control which has long dominated scientific and lay concepts of 'addiction' " on the grounds that it is simply inaccurate (*National Commission on Marijuana and Drug-Abuse,* 1973, p. 139).

69. See notes 7 and 8, supra.

70. The eminent psychiatrists Alexander and Staub acknowledge the incongruity of outlook in the two fields: "We may for practical purposes hold the individual

warrant the creation of legal doctrine that labels addictive conduct involuntary?

In the scientifically perplexing context of addiction, all these concepts of mental disorder are mere vague rubrics. They obscure our vast ignorance in this area by imparting an aura of scientific knowledge because of their technical appearance. At most they merely obfuscate familiar facts: when we talk about "addicts," we often have in mind persons with an intense commitment, one that seems unreasonable and excessive, to a pattern of life centering on drug use.

---

responsible for his acts; we assume an attitude as if the conscious Ego actually possessed the power to do what it wishes. Such an attitude *has no theoretical foundation,* but it has a practical, or still better, a tactical justification" (Alexander and Staub, 1931, pp. 72–73 [emphasis added]). See, e.g., Louisell and Diamond (1965), p. 220. Brenner (1973), p. 183, acknowledges that the distinction between the normal expression of character and the abnormal symptom is "necessarily an arbitrary decision" from the purely psychiatric standpoint. Redlich and Freedman (1966), p. 350, say the distinction is "very difficult or impossible" to make. See Fingarette (1972).

11

Alcohol Addiction:
The Factual Background

I: THE "BASIC FACTS"
AS VIEWED IN THE POWELL DISSENT

In *Powell,* Justice Fortas's dissent accepts, without evaluative comment, the trial judge's "findings of fact":[1]

1. That chronic alcoholism is a disease which destroys the afflicted person's will power to resist the constant, excessive consumption of alcohol.
2. That a chronic alcoholic does not appear in public by his own volition but under a compulsion symptomatic of the disease of chronic alcoholism.
3. That Leroy Powell ... is a chronic alcoholic who is afflicted with the disease of chronic alcoholism.

Four of the justices who rejected Powell's appeal agreed that these are not " 'findings of fact' " in "any recognizable, traditional sense in which that term has been used in a court of law...."[2] The first two[3] of the "findings" constitute sweepingly general assertions about a large class of

1. *Powell v. Texas,* p. 521.
2. *Ibid.* The trial judge's "findings" were characterized as "the premises of a syllogism transparently designed to bring th[e] case within the scope of ... *Robinson v. California*" (*ibid.*).
3. Since the trial judge's third finding does not bear on the general issues with which we are here concerned, it will not be further considered.

alcoholics: it is asserted that chronic alcoholism is itself an involuntarily maintained status, and it is further asserted that medical science has demonstrated constant and inevitable relationships between this status and public drunkenness.

It is evident that no reasonable basis for such "findings" could appear either in the testimony of Powell himself or the testimony concerning his personal history. Conceivably the testimony of expert witnesses might justify the findings—yet in Powell's trial only one psychiatric expert testified. While this expert did in fact testify to the effect that a "chronic alcoholic" is an "involuntary drinker," his elaboration of this characterization obscures his meaning.[4] In any event, inconclusive testimony by a single expert witness could hardly justify even the findings as to involuntariness (the expert said nothing of alcoholism as a "disease") unless there were a background of theory so familiar, unambiguous, and unchallengeable as to render further elaboration otiose. A major portion of the dissent consists of an attempt to provide just such an appropriate medical background as a "context" which, as the dissenting opinion avers, an understanding of the case "requires."[5]

With respect to the medical background concerning "chronic alcoholism," the *Powell* dissent acknowledges that "there is a great deal that remains to be discovered," that "many aspects of the disease remain obscure," and that we are "woefully deficient in our medical, diagnostic, and therapeutic knowledge" in both this area and that of "mental disease."[6] Although this admission alone removes much of the ground from beneath the sweeping "findings of fact" of the trial judge, the dissent maintains that there are "some hard facts—medical and, especially, legal facts—that are accessible to us and that provide a context in which the instant case may be analyzed."[7]

One such "hard fact" appears to be that alcoholism is medically recognized as a disease.[8] The dissent also believes it to be a fact that the "core meaning" of the disease concept of alcoholism

---

4. For example, Dr. Wade, the expert witness, testified that individuals such as Powell have "a compulsion, and this compulsion, while not completely overpowering, is a very strong influence . . ." (*Powell v. Texas*, p. 578).

5. *Ibid.*, p. 559.

6. *Ibid.*, pp. 559–560. All of the justices seem to agree that medical knowledge of alcoholism is deficient (*ibid.*, pp. 522–523, 539, 551 n. 3).

7. *Ibid.*, p. 559.

8. *Ibid.*

as agreed by authorities, is that alcoholism is caused and maintained by something other than the moral fault of the alcoholic, something that, to a greater or lesser extent depending upon the physiological or psychological makeup and history of the individual, cannot be controlled by him.[9]

It will be noted that neither of these "facts" mentions public intoxication. This is not because the "core meaning" merely happens to be formulated in the dissent as a very general statement, but because, as we shall see in detail later,[10] its statement can only be a very general one.

Though the "core meaning" is silent with respect to the symptoms or effects of alcoholism, or their voluntariness, it does raise the issue of voluntariness with respect to the causes of the status of chronic alcoholism and with respect to the persistence of that status. However, what it says is not that an alcoholic's condition is involuntary, but that an alcoholic's control over what causes his "disease" will be a matter of "greater or lesser degree"; the degree cannot be assessed in general for all "chronic alcoholics" but will depend upon the individual alcoholic's physiological and psychological makeup and his personal history. Such cautiousness contrasts sharply with the blunt conclusions of the trial judge and of the dissenters themselves that alcoholism is "involuntary."

Even more injudiciously blunt is the judgment that however alcoholism be caused, it is in any event not attributable to "the moral fault of the alcoholic."[11] In fact, of course, moral exculpation is hardly a proper part of medical theory, and to offer it as medically established "fact" is on its face unjustifiable.

Consistently with our overall analysis, we shall here focus on the facts and theories about alcoholism as these bear, in law, on the issue of voluntariness.

II: "LOSS OF CONTROL": CLAIMS AND FACTS

Many of the leading health authorities view "loss of control" as the "hallmark" of alcoholism.[12] The assertion is sufficiently widespread to give the impression of substantial agreement among many authorities on a

9. *Ibid.*, pp. 560-561.
10. See Section II, infra.
11. *Powell v. Texas*, p. 561.
12. Plaut (1967), p. 39; Rip (1966), p. 17; Ullman (1960), p. 8; and Keller (1962), pp. 310, 312-313.

basic fact having near self-evident moral-legal implications to men of goodwill. The *Powell* dissent is not unique in culminating its discussion of "loss of control" by quoting from a medical source: " '. . . the main point for the non-professional is that alcoholism is not within the control of the person involved.' "[13]

However, as we have seen, concepts which center around voluntariness present some of the most complex issues in both law and ethics. We have already noted[14] that everyday phrases like "I couldn't control myself" or "I had no choice" could variously report a strictly physical incapacity, unconsciousness, extreme provocation, extreme temptation, duress, strong habit, bad temper, or—we might add—somnambulism,[15] or "involuntary intoxication" (not associated with addiction).[16] Some of these circumstances could serve in some jurisdictions as a complete defense to criminal liability; others could serve as complete defenses in certain factual contexts, or as "partial" defenses in some degree mitigating culpability; and the remainder would have no legal effect but might mitigate punishment. These very different senses of self-control by no means exhaust the range of meanings. In what sense, then, do the authorities on alcoholism speak of "loss of control" in connection with chronic alcoholism? The *Powell* dissent's categorical claim that alcoholism is not within the alcoholic's control dissolves when one discovers the very different things that authorities mean by the phrase, the different sorts of facts that purportedly justify it, the substantive qualifications ultimately appended, and the authoritative literature in which the phrase is conspicuously omitted or explicitly rejected.

In the first place, it is difficult to sustain *any* categorical statements about alcoholism in light of the multiplicity of diagnostic schemes.[17]

13. *Powell v. Texas*, p. 562.

14. See the discussion and citations on these issues in Chapter 4, supra.

15. *Fain v. Commonwealth*. See also N. Morris (1951).

16. Jerome Hall states that so far as case law is concerned, "*involuntary intoxication is simply and completely nonexistent*" (Hall, 1944, p. 1056, emphasis in original). Although there are a few cases involving involuntary intoxication from drugs other than alcohol, see e.g., *People v. Koch,* we know of only one which involves alcohol, and in this case there was no finding of involuntary intoxication. A conviction was reversed on appeal and a retrial ordered because of the trial judge's refusal to allow presentation of evidence aimed at establishing ignorance as to the effects of drinking on the part of the defendant (*State v. Brown*). See generally: Beck (1967); Fox (1963); Prevezer (1958).

17. See Plaut (1967), p. 41. See also Wallgren and Barry (1970), p. 823: "The alcohol literature is replete with 'explanations' and 'theories' of the causation of

Jellinek distinguishes and lists over one hundred hypotheses about the nature of alcoholism.[18] There is not even any substantial agreement about the region of knowledge from which the best understanding of alcoholism may be forthcoming.[19] As with narcotic addiction, hypotheses range from the genetic through the physiological and pharmacological to the psychological and sociological. More damaging to the "involuntariness" argument, probably no expert would dispute that "variations in the patterns of drinking [among alcoholics] are tremendous";[20] and most would also agree that what alcoholics have in common is simply "a heavy preoccupation with drinking,"[21] which in *some* cultural groups often leads to serious disturbances in social adaptation.[22]

Thus it is not surprising that many authorities who use "loss of control" language ultimately introduce serious qualifications. It turns out, for example, that one of the leading authorities who holds "loss of control" to be the "pathognomonic symptom" of alcoholism does not mean by this phrase that the person cannot abstain or cannot stop once he has started drinking. Rather, we are told, the phrase means that "*it is not certain that* [the alcoholic] *will be able to stop at will.*"[23] Another authority who uses "loss of control" as a "criterion" for diagnosing alcoholism tells us that in various "protected" situations (among them, incidentally, the prison) many alcoholics will with "little or no difficulty"

---

chronic drinking. However, it is impossible to plan good approaches to this 'problem' when there is no satisfactory definition of what alcoholism is."

18. Jellinek (1960), pp. 55–59, 83–86, 113–115. Wallgren and Barry (1970), p. 508, say: "None of the proposed etiological theories of alcoholism seems compatible with the great diversity among alcoholics in physical and personality characteristics."

19. "There is good reason to challenge anyone who claims that he can make a safe prediction about which is the most promising and direct road to advancing our knowledge or understanding [of alcoholism]" (Wallgren and Barry, 1970, p. 831).

20. Block (1965), p. 23.

21. Chafetz (1964), p. 358. "The diversity among alcoholics should be emphasized. . . . [I]t is more accurate to describe alcoholism as a disorder with the behavior of prolonged excessive drinking as the main characteristic all alcoholics have in common, rather than as a unitary disease" (Wallgren and Barry, 1970, p. 508).

22. See the discussion in Jellinek (1960), pp. 13–32. In France and other beer and wine drinking countries a predominant pattern of alcoholism is the constant, daily drinking of wine, with "inability to abstain," but with control over the amount drunk at any one time so that drunkenness or incapacity to carry on with the day's activities is rare. Cessation of drinking does produce withdrawal symptoms, however (*ibid.*, pp. 25–32).

23. Keller (1962), p. 313 (emphasis in original).

abstain or stop.[24] Still other authorities characterize "loss of control" as "not an all-or-none phenomenon"[25] and "a relative and variable phenomenon."[26]

In short, we are told not that the alcoholic has *no* control of his drinking, but that he has greater or lesser control, *widely* varying in degree according to the circumstances and the individual. This consensus conforms with the "core meaning" of the "disease concept of alcoholism" summarized in the *Powell* dissent—that the alcoholic's inability to control his drinking can be of "greater or lesser extent depending on the physiological or psychological makeup and history of the individual"—but is inconsistent with the *Powell* dissent, and also with the *Driver* and the *Easter* decisions, insofar as those opinions assume that chronic alcoholics as a group are, by virtue of their being such, without power to control their drinking.[27]

Thus far we have noted ways in which the notion of an alcoholic's "lack of control" must be qualified. We have not examined just which of the many possible senses of "control" is at issue. As our earlier remarks have recalled, there are a number of reasonable uses of the "loss of control" idiom that exclude neither conscious choice with awareness of the relevant consequences nor legal responsibility.

The frequent reference to alcoholism as an "addiction"[28] has seemed to all but settle the volitional issue; yet when the World Health Organization's Expert Committee on Dependence-Producing Drugs abandoned the term "addiction,"[29] proposing instead a series of terms connoting various

24. Plaut (1967), pp. 39–40.

25. *Ibid.*

26. Glatt (1965). "[N]o clear-cut distinction is possible between the alcoholic and the heavy drinker whose use of alcohol is controlled and nonpathological. Further evidence for lack of a clear-cut distinction is that the progression toward increasing pathology can be halted and reversed at any stage. Some alcoholics have adopted and maintained a pattern of moderate controlled drinking" (Wallgren and Barry, 1970, p. 806).

27. See *Easter v. District of Columbia*, p. 53; *Driver v. Hinnant*, p. 764.

28. Jellinek (1960), p. 70, says that 35 percent of the papers he has worked with which deal generally with the etiology of alcoholism use the term *addiction* or its foreign-language equivalents.

29. *World Health Organization,* Thirteenth Report 9–10 (1964). See generally Bowman, 1965 (discussion of the literature and development of the reasons for case-by-case analysis of the substantial variations in degree and kind of legally relevant dependence in narcotics "addiction"). Bowman's conclusions agree with those of the President's Advisory Commission (1963) to the effect that no general rule, but only case-by-case analysis, can suffice to establish whether or not a

significantly different kinds and degrees of drug "dependence," it classified alcohol and barbiturate addiction under the "strong desire" category.[30] This is not even the "overpowering desire or need" that topped the list and was assigned to narcotic dependencies. This is of particular significance when we recall that, unlike so many typical cases of narcotic addiction, the alcohol addict has typically had ample sources of supply of his drug. Moreover, he generally requires years (as against weeks in the case of narcotics) before continuous heavy dosages develop a genuinely deep physiological dependency.[31] Symptoms of withdrawal, in long-term heavy physiological dependency on alcohol, are substantially rooted in this physiological condition rather than, as appears so largely the case with many narcotic addicts, in psychosocial influences.[32]

"confirmed drug abuser is so impelled by his habit that he is not accountable for his acts under criminal law" (p. 3).

30. The President's Advisory Commission (1963), pp. 13–16. The fourteenth report of the 1967 WHO Expert Committee on Mental Health states that dependence on alcohol and dependence on barbiturates are so similar that they "may be considered under the same heading" (p. 9). Furthermore, dependence of the barbiturate type is classified as producing the intermediate degree of desire, i.e., "a strong desire" (but not an "overpowering" one) in the scale of degrees of dependency announced officially in the World Health Organization's Thirteenth Report (1964), p. 13.

31. See WHO, First Report (1954), pp. 5–7, 9–11. See Wallgren and Barry (1970), p. 725. Aside from the years that it takes for physical dependence to develop, it also deserves note that tolerance levels with alcohol as compared to narcotics remain relatively low.

32. For a recent review of pharmacotherapeutic measures to mitigate the severity and the duration of acute alcohol withdrawal symptoms, see Greenblatt and Shader (1974), pp. 219–222. Though it is generally recognized that risks to life are greater than in withdrawal from heavy physiological dependency on narcotics, the measures available to the alcoholic today make it far safer than continuing to drink. In the most severe cases it is akin to going through an acute but brief illness crisis of several days. Only the most severe cases manifest the symptoms of delirium tremens, and under medical care the rate of mortality is low in this relatively small group. Recently Novotny et al. (1975) report a 2 percent mortality rate in cases of delirium tremens treated with diazepam, the most promising recent drug for this purpose. Moreover, the risks for such far-advanced cases of long-term alcoholism must be balanced against the risks of grave illness, grave injury, or death which such persons face in the course of their daily life as intoxicated and physically debilitated persons. Thus, risk for risk, the risks of medically supervised withdrawal cannot be said to be an unacceptably risky alternative to continued heavy drinking. The end-of-the-road debilitated alcoholic, usually very sick from grave nutritional illnesses and other diseases due to exposure and lack of health care, and often showing marked signs of

Since appeal to labels like "addiction" is not illuminating, we must seek more specific information as to the way and degree in which the alcoholic is thought to be alcohol-dependent.

Among those who incline to the "loss of control" characterization, a number hold for a "physical" or "physiological mechanism."[33] As to the nature of this mechanism, there is a wide variety of opinion. The most one can say by way of generalizing is that these theories postulate genetic, neurological, metabolic, or allergic abnormalities that create a peculiar vulnerability to alcohol. And while the word *physical* would appear at least to exclude meaningful choice, the specific hypotheses, as we have begun to see, are never that simple. Far from excluding volition, most consist of complex models that include volition, more or less explicitly, along with the physical causes.[34]

In fact, there is universal agreement that alcohol is not as physiologically addictive as the morphine narcotics.[35] Beyond this threshold agreement, some theories postulate a physically induced craving for alcohol,

---

mental deterioration or other pathology, may be too mentally disabled to act rationally in regard to self-care and self-cure. But this would then be Disability of Mind, not a basis for an involuntariness defense based on the rationally grounded *coercive* power of withdrawal as a grave threat to life. See Chapter 5, Section II, supra.

33. "After one drink, [the alcoholic] feels a physical demand for the drug so strong that he cannot stop short of intoxication" (*Alcoholism,* U.S. Dept. of HEW [1965], p. 7). But Merry (1966), p. 1257, developed experimental evidence (see note 37, infra) against what he calls the " 'loss of control' myth." Dr. Jack Mendelson (1967), p. 21, Chief of the National Center for the Prevention and Control of Alcoholism of the National Institute of Mental Health, refers to the purported "triggering" effect: "Once an individual has one drink . . . he can't control his alcohol ingestion. . . ." And he says of this: "We do not believe this to be the case." An interesting and concise summary of the more physically oriented hypotheses can be found in Siegler, Osmond, and Newell (1968), p. 581.

34. "Obviously . . . there is little hope of explaining alcoholism on the basis of single biochemical or physiological traits, because whatever else alcoholism may be, it is definitely a form of behavior" (Wallgren and Barry, 1970, p. 823). This central point is usually not explicit in the formulations of physical theories, but a careful reading of the formulations will reveal that they do tacitly presuppose volitional links between the physiological process postulated as "cause" and the actual behavior leading to ingestion of the alcohol. See the listings in Rip (1966), p. 18; and in Jellinek (1960), pp. 82–155, who lists about fifty such hypotheses.

35. In the sense that it takes years, as has been noted, before genuine physiological dependency occurs.

while others speak of craving for the state of intoxication rather than for the liquor. More significantly, some theories hypothesize a physically induced craving to begin drinking, whereas others assume control over the taking of a first drink, but with some loss of control over further drinking. Moreover, while some theorists view compulsion to keep drinking as due to a destruction of certain control centers in the brain, or as an involuntary, conditioned response to incipient withdrawal symptoms, others view this compulsion as only a learned, somewhat controllable preference for continued drinking. Finally, many of the "physical" hypotheses suppose a gradual physical change in an alcoholic caused by his habit, implying that the strength of the compulsion to drink varies over time.

Obviously the moral and legal implications of these various hypotheses may be quite different. If, for example, a physical craving for alcohol triggers a specific, automatic reflex of drinking alcohol, then we exclude by hypothesis any significant volition. To the extent that such a reflex cannot be demonstrated, we are dealing with a volitional response to a desire, more or less strong. With respect to the many hypotheses that postulate no initial physical craving but only a physical mechanism that compels continued drinking, a relevant question may be whether the alcoholic himself believes he can stop, and to what extent that belief is reasonable. The expert in *Powell* testified that many alcoholics have such a belief but that the reasonableness of that belief will vary with particular circumstances. Finally, some hypotheses find volition throughout the drinking pattern, conceiving both the initiation and the continuance of drinking as volitional responses to a more or less compelling desire.

Hypotheses that stress involuntariness must contend with the fact that many alcoholics do choose to abstain or control their drinking—whether only occasionally, as is often true with chronic alcoholics,[36] or in some more permanent way, as by a personal decision to abstain by seeking medical or psychological help, or by joining such groups as Alcoholics Anonymous or Synanon. Of course, capacity to resist the urge to drink on one occasion or for a period of time does not imply that the alcoholic will have such capacity at other times. However, it would at least be more difficult to find "cruel and unusual" the punishment of an alcoholic who enjoyed periods of abstinence or who could be supposed capable of voluntarily subjecting himself to a "cure."

36. "All addictive alcoholics do not always drink in an uncontrolled fashion" (Pattison et al., 1964, p. 624).

It remains a central, though often de-emphasized feature of most of the "physical" hypotheses that the alcoholic, though in some way peculiarly sensitive physically to alcohol, is one who faces a *very difficult and painful choice*. Furthermore, while we do not argue that any of these hypotheses is false, it is important to keep in mind that they often conflict with each other and that none has been confirmed.[37] Our only purpose here is to indicate that "physical" hypotheses do not claim that there is no volition in the alcoholic's excess drinking but that, partly because of physical abnormality, the alcoholic is one who faces a choice that is (increasingly) more difficult than for most people.

Moreover, by no means do all the contemporary hypotheses that are influential in the health professions claim that there is a critical physical factor at work. Many, though they may speak of "loss of control" (quite a number do not), ascribe this to psychological or social conditions rather than physical ones. Here the term *compulsive* or the like may again be used—though some authorities say improperly so [38]—but again we must look behind the metaphor,[39] along the lines already set out in the previous discussion of the narcotic addict's "compulsive" drug use.

One authority speaks of chronic drunkenness as "a means of adapting to life conditions which are otherwise harsh, insecure, unrewarding and unproductive of the essentials of human dignity."[40] Others refer to alcoholism as a "psychosocial behavior syndrome" and assert that the taking

37. "There is no generally agreed upon or accepted etiological pattern in connection with alcoholism. There are, however, many theories but broadly speaking they can be divided into three schools. These three are the *Physiological,* the *Psychological,* and the *Sociological*" (Rip, 1966, p. 18 [emphasis in original]). With respect to physically oriented hypotheses and the often claimed "triggering" effect of the first drink, Merry (1966) reports his experiment in which a group of alcoholics were given a daily dose of vodka, unknown to them, and who throughout the experiment were asked to report their "craving," if any, for alcohol. No deep craving for alcohol was reported, thus tending to confirm the view that "loss of control" or "craving" after the first drink is not an automatic, physically induced phenomenon.

38. Diethelm, cited in Rip (1966), p. 16, argues that it can be confusing to speak of "compulsion" here because it may erroneously suggest that every chronic alcoholic has a compulsion neurosis. Other authorities imply that the vagueness of the term itself calls for caution in its use. For example, see Jellinek (1960), p. 43.

39. "Loss of control is inferred from the drinker's behavior; objective and quantitative measurements are lacking for this criterion [of alcoholism]" (Wallgren and Barry, 1970, p. 806). That is to say, the behavior of heavy drinking is the basis for speaking of "loss of control," and then "loss of control" is used to "explain" the behavior!

40. Pittman (1967), p. 13.

of alcohol is primarily a "central integrative symbol around which the person organizes his life."[41] Or, as another physician puts it: "[A]lcoholism is . . . only a 'common path' in the way of problem solving to a number of adaptational issues. . . ."[42] We should not be misled by the technical psychological and sociological language. This (large) group of authorities is simply saying that, on the whole, the alcoholic, with whatever "inner battles," has elected this way to handle his problems in life. In this view, it may be further supposed that the more he does so, the more he has a stake in this approach and a deep fear of or deep dislike for any other. To say "he can't control it" amounts in this context to saying that mere moralistic appeals of the usual kind by family and friends are no more likely to succeed than subvocal or vocal "resolutions" by the person himself. His values have changed. Excessive drinking has become his "way of life" in spite of such appeals and resolutions. But this does not imply a loss of rationality such that other kinds of appeals or threats having significance for *him,* or a change in life-setting, may not successfully lead him to self-control. A way of life is not easily or casually changed; on the other hand, it is not something beyond volition. Much less is it well-conceptualized in law by classifying it as involuntary. Surely *that* concept is too simple to resolve at one stroke the complex moral and legal issues bearing on responsibility that are posed by a person's law-violating act when that act is an expression of his way of life (or "lifestyle").

Persuasive testimony in support of the view that the right kind of moral, social, or religious appeal or action will elicit restraint or abstinence by the alcoholic comes, paradoxically, from the very advocates of the various "loss of control" hypotheses. For when we look to the therapeutic techniques that they propose or acknowledge as most effective, we see that these involve appeals for the alcoholic to adopt voluntarily one or another course of conduct. They appeal to him to voluntarily enter a "protective setting" such as a hospital and to voluntarily abide by its rules, or they appeal to him to enter voluntarily and cooperatively on a course of the drug Antabuse, or of "reconditioning," or to join Alcoholics Anonymous.[43] Thus the "psychological" and "sociological" hypotheses gener-

41. Pattison et al. (1964), p. 625.
42. Forizs (1965), p. 511.
43. Alcoholics Anonymous maintains that alcoholism is a "disease," but not that drinking is involuntary. On the contrary, the entire approach in Alcoholics Anonymous is to enlist the voluntary cooperation of the alcoholic, to appeal to him on moral-religious-pragmatic grounds to voluntarily abstain from drinking, and to engage in reciprocal self-help along these lines with his brother AA members. According to

ally do not exclude volition but presume it, both in their views of the "etiology" of alcoholism and in their attempts at therapy. Indeed, there are leading authorities who explicitly recommend coercive pressures to get the alcoholic to control his drinking.[44] The effectiveness of nonphysical deterrent measures shows that drinking is to some substantial degree volitional by a test that is peculiarly relevant to the criminal law; for it is reasonable to suppose that for many alcoholics the threat of the criminal sanction may be a factor in controlling such drinking as is likely to lead to criminal offenses.[45]

---

the U.S. Public Health Service, "[r]emarkable success . . . has been achieved" in this way (*Alcoholism,* U.S. Dept. HEW [1965], p. 10). Moreover, there is widespread recognition in the health professions that the AA approach has done at least as much, probably far more, than any other single approach to therapy for alcoholics. "There is no longer any question that Alcoholics Anonymous has been responsible for the sobriety of more alcoholics than any other method, social, religious, or medical. Psychiatrists are now 'believers.' Our 1956 Survey shows that 99% of them approve of Alcoholics Anonymous, and 77% have referred patients to them. . . . Medical practitioners other than psychiatrists are not nearly so partial to Alcoholics Anonymous. . . . In contrast . . . Alcoholics Anonymous is now considered highly respectable and is accepted among most groups working with the alcoholic. . . . For example, 74% of State Hospitals have an Alcoholics Anonymous counselor in their alcoholism treatment program, and 82% rely on Alcoholics Anonymous for follow-up care" (Hayman, 1966, pp. 174–175).

44. "Motivation by coercion is an important technique in inducing the alcoholic to accept help. We can include in this category any reward or punishment which is important enough to the alcoholic to cause him to forego the pleasure and needs of drinking. This could be court probation which, if broken, might lead to jail. It could be the threat of loss of financial support or the loss of a job. . . . [I]n the survey mentioned previously 60% of psychiatrists felt that coercion in the form of legal commitment of alcoholics to state hospitals was beneficial to their treatment. Recovery and improvement rates in industrial clinics where there is considerable coercion are much higher than elsewhere . . ." (Hayman, 1966, pp. 65–66). See also the data on the favorable effect of coercion or duress in deciding to accept treatment in Lemere, O'Hollaren, and Maxwell (1958). Rosenberg and Liftik (1976) report that threats of sanctions (loss of driver's license, etc.) produced a significantly greater participation in an alcoholism program, and that coercive pressures were important to supplement self-motivation even over the longer pull. They, too, make the point that: "coercion is unlikely to succeed when the patient has little to lose by not complying" (p. 65).

45. "The disease concept may also imply that an alcoholic's antisocial behavior is the consequence of a disease, and therefore he is not responsible for such actions as missing work and neglecting his family. . . . Many alcoholics who seek rationalization for their behavior find in the disease concept a perfect alibi—'I'm so sick I couldn't

We may summarize, then, by saying that the *Powell* dissent's formulation of the "core meaning" of the disease concept of alcoholism, vague and cautious as it is with respect to voluntariness, is yet not unduly so. Indeed, quite the contrary. It errs on the "control" issue because it implies too much in the way of current medical knowledge. And it errs in implying that the phrase "loss of control," as used in the medical literature, implies absence of volition in law.

Translating the technical language and including the necessary qualifications, we essay to formulate a statement in harmony with a large number of the influential hypotheses about alcoholism:

Possibly partly due to some abnormal physical condition, the chronic alcoholic is one who for any of a variety of other reasons, often rooted in his past or current patterns of life, has increasingly used drinking as a way of adapting to his life-problems. He has reached the point where the personal and social consequences of his drinking are such that abandoning heavy drinking and the life that goes with it would require him to act in a way which, though usually genuinely practicable, would now be so very distressing and so very difficult, both physically and mentally, that he is unlikely to act that way entirely on his own initiative. He may do so with the aid of special encouragement, professional guidance, and/or coercive influences.[46]

---

help it.' By removing the inebriate from the arrest system we are possibly granting unqualified license to this attitude" (Pratt, 1975, p. 168).

46. This formulation, dating with minor change from 1969, receives an interesting echo in 1975, in the carefully nonvolitional language of the trade, in the formulation by Mark Keller, one of the leading authorities in the field. He summarizes what he believes has been learned to date in regard to understanding alcoholism. He says an "interdisciplinary—wholistic understanding" will incorporate "a genetic or constitutional factor which imposes exceptional susceptibility or immunity; errors of infant relationship or childhood rearing and resultant psychosexual maldevelopment with a possibly defective, especially hyperdependent or dependency-conflicted personality trait; further misfortune in the form of misdirected maturation in the adolescent phase, especially if reinforced by internally well-rewarded drinking experiences; and a subsequent learning or conditioning process, of possibly years-long duration, embedded in culturally and societally determined mores and conditions and directions, with a negative balance of interpersonal relations; and, finally, the pharmacological properties of alcohol assuming a dominant indispensable role in the individual's way of life" (Keller, 1975, p. 144). This seems to say that a person who is physically vulnerable in some way, psychologically weak in some way, with unfortunate life experiences and personal relations, may, over a period of years, find social support for drinking as a satisfying and eventually central response to all life's problems.

It is in part because of ambiguities and confusion inherent in the "loss of control" phraseology that a good many authorities avoid this idiom altogether.[47]

III: "ALCOHOLISM IS A DISEASE": CLAIMS AND FACTS

The "medical fact" that probably has done most to foster the notion that alcoholism is an inappropriate object for criminal punishment is the simple formula "alcoholism is a disease." The dissenting opinion in *Powell* notes at the very outset of its presentation of "hard facts" about alcoholism that

[i]n 1956 [the AMA] for the first time designated alcoholism as a major medical problem. . . . This significant development marked the acceptance among the medical profession of the "disease concept of alcoholism."[48]

To anticipate, it is our conclusion that the widespread (but by no means universal) acceptance in the medical and health professions of the "disease concept of alcoholism" reflects a variety of considerations that are legitimate and important to the *health* professions, but that none of these considerations has any obvious bearing on the legal issue of punishability under the Eighth Amendment.

One such consideration is the underlying judgment, with which we concur, that it is reasonable for the health professions to attempt to help with the problem of alcoholism. Another important consideration, suggested by the first, is the widespread *hope* and *expectation* that the medical profession will someday develop understanding of and remedies for alcoholism. While there is no doubt about the importance and inspirational efficacy of this expectation,[49] and while the reasonableness of the

47. See Block (1965), pp. 23–24; Eddy et al. (1965); Keller (1958);cf. Chafetz (1964), p. 358 (on alcoholism as a symptom of a chronic behavioral disorder). The definitions compiled in the U.S. Department of Health, Education, and Welfare (1965) emphasize primarily the excessiveness of an alcoholic's drinking and his consequent social and personal disabilities, rather than "loss of control." During this discussion we have primarily mentioned only those views oriented toward "loss of control." However, many authorities flatly oppose this orientation, and, while recognizing that there may be physical factors at work, consider it essential that "there is a whole series of voluntary actions in the act of drinking; and there has to be a choice involved . . ." (Myerson, 1967, p. 348; see also the citations in Jellinek, 1960, pp. 58–59, and the remarks of Mendelson, 1967, pp. 21–22).

48. *Powell v. Texas,* p. 560.

49. "The new medical model treats alcoholism as a bona fide disease, without reservations. It is a hopeful model and one which encourages new scientific research.

effort is apparent, these considerations are not obviously relevant to the propriety of punishing alcoholics.

There are certain ancillary practical considerations that also motivate acceptance among doctors of "the disease concept." In the first place, it is evidently in the interest of the medical attack on alcoholism that large sums of money be reliably accessible to researchers and therapists. Adherence within the profession to such formulas as "alcoholism is a disease" (or an "illness," or a "medical problem") does much to provide assurance to such fund-granting organizations as government agencies and foundations that the enterprise is legitimate. Such assurance was no doubt profoundly strengthened when the medical profession in 1956 formally and clearly expressed its concern to assume a responsibility in the area.[50] Similarly, the availability of hospitals for the medical effort against alcoholism was apparently facilitated by the official declaration of the AMA.[51] It is also necessary to the success of the medical effort to motivate more medical men to assume responsibility for treating alcoholics.[52] Apparently this still has a long way to go.[53]

It enables those using it to draw strength from the successful campaigns against other major illnesses" (Siegler, Osmond, and Newell, 1968, p. 584).

50. See Jellinek (1960), p. 161.

51. "Philosophically speaking, alcoholism is not a disease. . . . You want to get hospitals to take in alcoholic problems, but to do so you have to hammer them on the head, to get them to accept it as a disease. So I would agree we should call it a disease. . . . It is a pragmatic definition. It has useful consequences" (Myerson, 1967, p. 348). Jellinek (1960), p. 161, makes a similar point, and says that although there have been great strides in getting hospitals to accept alcoholics in the past few decades, this was more the exception than the rule as of 1944. Hayman, however, reports that his surveys show, as of 1966, that "there are still relatively few hospitals who will admit alcoholic patients on the basis of their alcoholism." This is in spite of the 1956 statement of the American Medical Association, and a subsequent statement in 1957 by the American Hospital Association urging general hospitals to accept alcoholic patients. For example, in 1962, there were only three hospitals in New York City which accepted chronic alcoholics on an in-patient basis (Hayman, 1966, pp. 81 and 130).

52. "[W]e must remember that most planning and policy are for the policy makers and planners rather than for the persons we say we hope to save," says Chafetz (1976), p. 101, in accounting for the controversial "disease concept" of alcoholism.

53. Acknowledgement of the reluctance of both psychiatric and nonpsychiatric medical men to accept chronic alcoholics as patients is a commonplace in the literature. See Hayman (1966), p. 81. Also consult Jellinek (1960), chap. IV, and Blane, Overton, and Chafetz (1963), p. 658.

It is extremely important to concerned doctors that the general public support their efforts.[54] The official AMA announcement and the wide professional use—especially in public discussion—of such formulas as "alcoholism is a disease" have been vital to the growing public support of medical research in the area.[55] The physicians' public use of the phrase has been a powerful influence in combating what many health professionals see as a major cultural obstacle to their efforts—the public's habitual allegiance to "moralistic" approaches. Many health authorities feel that moral, religious, and penal approaches have failed and are bound to fail, and they tend to see public commitment to these approaches as a major diversion of effort, money, and resources from the medical effort.[56] There is also a profound but usually tacit moral judgment on the part of many health professionals that the condemnatory and penal approach is inhumane.[57]

In the discussion of narcotic addiction, we explored the vagueness of the concept of "disease" generally,[58] and its lack of specific scientific content in relation to the issue of voluntariness. Rather than repeat that discussion, which is relevant at this point, we shall only refer to the

54. See Ullman (1960), p. 4. "Why was the disease model attractive and acceptable? Because it was a symbolic mechanism of communication familiar and unfrightening in its acceptability" (Chafetz, 1976, pp. 100–101).

55. See Jellinek (1960), chap. IV.6. On this and other "pragmatic" rather than "medical" reasons for calling alcoholism a disease, see the revealing discussion by T.F.A. Plaut, M.D., Assistant Chief of the National Center for Prevention and Control of Alcoholism, in Plaut (1967), pp. 42–45.

56. "The word 'disease' has been used here as if all the modern experts were agreed that alcoholism is a disease. This is not so. However, the important point for us is that alcoholism is now treated by those who are responsible for the health of the community rather than by those who are responsible for the community's morals" (Ullman, 1960, p. 5). Seeley presents a careful analysis of the concept "disease" in the context of alcoholism, and he makes plain the ineradicable element of moral judgment, the importance of the shift from one set of institutions to another, as a reason for using the concept, and, finally, the "essential" fact about applying the disease label: "that a step in public policy is being *recommended,* not a scientific discovery announced" (Seeley, 1962, p. 593, emphasis in original).

57. "[T]he promulgation of a disease concept of alcoholism has been brought about essentially as a means of getting a better deal for the 'alcoholic,' rather than as a logical consequence of scholarly work and scientific discovery" (Room, 1972, p. 1056).

58. Chapter 10, Section II, supra. See also the discussion of the same topic in Chapter 9, Section II, and Chapter 4, Section IV, supra. For a full discussion, see also Fingarette (1972), Chapter 1; and Swartz (1967).

comment of Jellinek on this issue in the context of alcoholism specifically. As one of the leading authorities in the field, and a supporter of the "disease concept of alcoholism," Jellinek met criticism of this approach[59] by acknowledging the circularity and unhelpful generality of the medical dictionary definitions of *disease,* but then added that

[*A*] *disease is what the medical profession recognizes as such. . . .* [T]hrough this fact alone alcoholism becomes an illness, whether a part of the lay public likes it or not, and even if a minority of the medical profession is disinclined to accept the idea.[60]

59. Jellinek (1960), pp. 11-12.

60. *Ibid.,* pp. 58-59. He cites seven authorities who explicitly reject the disease concept of alcoholism. He goes on to cite approvingly Leopold Wexberg's remarks based on the latter's studies of the physiology of alcoholism: "In no other area of research and social or medical endeavor have slogans so extensively replaced theoretical insight, as a basis for therapeutic action, as in alcoholism. The emotional impact of the statement, 'Alcoholism is a sickness,' is such that very few people care to stop to think what it actually means" (p. 59). Jellinek's list is by no means complete as an inventory of authorities who reject the disease concept of alcoholism. Since his book, for example, Chafetz (1964), p. 358, has said: "I do not believe that there exists a disease, alcoholism, nor a particular set of personality traits we can label 'alcoholic.' " Clancy (1965), p. 314, remarks that "many regard [the American Medical Association statement of 1956] as an opinion and therefore open to challenge. Differences of opinion about alcoholism as a disease still exist in the medical profession." See also Myerson (1967), p. 348. Swartz, a legal scholar who has done extensive work in the area of mental disease and alcoholism, says: "[T]here is considerable divergence of views even among medical men as to whether alcoholism is a disease. . . . I see alcoholism as a violation of conduct norms. . . . Violation of conduct norms . . . would in my view not, of itself, constitute disease" (Swartz, 1967, p. 374). In addition to views such as the above, there are views that are ambiguous, vague, or borderline with respect to the question whether alcoholism is or is not a disease. For example: "At the present time, the consensus of opinion is that the basic problem underlying the addiction to alcohol or other drugs is an emotional one. The nature of it, however, is not a simple matter. Alcoholics do not share the same emotional problems" (Krystal, 1963, p. 707). In the same symposium, at p. 712, Moore, who in many ways takes a view contrary to Krystal's, gives his view of current, sound medical doctrine: "We are not in agreement as to etiology and there is still considerable controversy as to the best treatment techniques. Still, we feel confident that we are dealing with a tangible illness *or pathological life reaction even if we may be reluctant to call alcoholism a specific disease*" (emphasis added). There are interesting comments and data on the "ambivalent medical attitudes about alcoholism as a disease entity," based on careful study of medical practice, as distinguished from theory, in Blane, Overton, and Chafetz (1963), pp. 659-660. The authors themselves do refer to alcoholism in the course of their study as a "disease" or "illness"; but

when one of them in a later paper addresses himself specifically to this question, he rejects the disease concept (Chafetz, 1964, p. 346). The question-begging nature of argument as to whether alcoholism (or any addiction) is a "disease" is plainly evident if one accepts the definition of "disease" of Woodruff et al. (1974): "Any condition associated with discomfort, pain, disability, death, or an increased liability to these states, *regarded by physicians and the public as properly the responsibility of the medical profession,* may be considered a disease" (p. 185, emphasis in original). Woodruff et al. recognize that this makes "disease" a mere "convention" (p. 186), rather than a scientific datum. It should be no surprise to read that "the coalition of interests in the [alcoholism] movement were united [during the past several decades] only in an allegiance to the 'disease concept' of alcoholism, without agreement on what this meant . . ." (Room, 1976, p. 113).

12

Conclusions About Addictions
and Criminal Responsibility

We have seen that in spite of a vast literature, professionals in the field of drug and alcohol addiction acknowledge that no satisfactory scientific understanding of addiction has been reached. Thus there is no medical foundation for adopting the general proposition at the crux of the exculpatory legal arguments, the proposition that addictive conduct is involuntary. On the other hand, massive descriptive evidence indicates that individuals often make choices to abandon addictive conduct or abstain from drug or alcohol use permanently or temporarily. Moreover, authorities observe that in the specific case of narcotic addiction there is often little in the way of chemical or biological influences. Yet such addiction may provide an important individual or group identity for many who lack socially approved skills or are socially alienated. Popular beliefs about the chemically induced hell of narcotic withdrawal agony or the insatiable craving for ecstatic pleasures are profoundly at odds with the facts, though they have deeply colored the thinking of the courts. Since narcotic addiction is officially classified as the most "compelling" form of the addictions, this information forces abandonment of the argument that behavior associated with addiction, whether alcoholic or narcotic, should be regarded as legally involuntary.

Once we conclude that addictive conduct is legally voluntary, however, we do not express a basic substantive insight into addiction, but merely free ourselves from a false idea. Courtroom cliche has obscured the fact

that the problems at issue concern intricate and poorly understood relationships that link character, personality, and mind to upbringing, social
setting, and cultural values, and in turn to biochemical and neuropsycho-
logical processes. Indeed, courts have been ill-served by those psychiatrists
who have promoted the notion that addiction is involuntary and who have
seen this notion as a legal formula that will permit medical models to
supersede the use of criminal sanctions.[1] The very complexity of the
problem calls for legislative determinations concerning rehabilitation, regulation of alcohol and drug commerce,[2] and the general administration of
criminal law in this area.[3]

Undoubtedly there are those who regard possible legal approaches to
addiction in polar terms: either we inflict harsh, punitive, and degrading
measures on the addict, or we declare the person sick and therefore not
responsible for his conduct. What is needed here is the abandonment of
such extreme and fixed positions.[4] Nothing we have said precludes in any
way the many legislative options for establishing rational procedures and
institutions, whether within penal or civil systems, for "detoxifying" the
acutely intoxicated, for counseling, for treating, and for otherwise helping
the addict. Nor is there any support in anything we have said for the
irrational, expensive, and inhumane harassment of addicts, especially those
who have been impoverished and alienated, an approach still so prevalent
today.[5] In the present antipunitive atmosphere in many enlightened

1. This imputation of motive rests upon inferences that seem repeatedly apparent
as one reads the court records and psychiatrists' statements about the irrelevance and
inappropriateness of the criminal law in the areas of mental disease and addiction.
See Fingarette (1972), pp. 37–52; Bazelon (1974).

2. See *U.S. v. Moore*, p. 1159. And see, for example, the review of the enormous
complexities of the problems, and the innumerable unknowns, in Room (1976).

3. See *Marshall v. U.S.*, pp. 427–429.

4. A recent polar formulation reflects a common doctrinaire approach: "Medicine views the drug misuser as a patient who needs treatment; law enforcement views
him as a criminal who must be punished" (*Group for the Advancement of Psychiatry*,
1971, p. 12). Too often such a formulation merely sidesteps a set of complex
personal, social, legal, and spiritual problems: "Oftentime . . . the desire to avoid the
implications of criminality while maintaining formal control has resulted in compulsory treatment of an 'illness' which has never been adequately defined. The Commission warns against the tendency to assume that when its motives are benevolent,
society need not attend to the philosophical and constitutional issues raised by its
actions" (*National Commission*, 1973, p. 257; see also Goldstein and Katz, 1963).

5. With respect both to more rational and humane procedures that have already
been or may be put into effect for alcoholics, without invoking constitutional
doctrine, and with respect to the inhumane aspects of procedures that have been

circles, however, it is appropriate to recall that the lawful and proper threat of sanctions may be not only a pragmatically effective approach, but also a morally humane one. It regards the addict as an autonomous person, responsible for guiding his own life and subject to law.[6]

Of course, the medical approach can also reflect a humane concern, a concern for the weak and ailing and for those who cannot, in some respects, handle their own lives. But by now it is no news that both of these approaches, the medical and the legal, however inspired, can in practice disregard human dignity when ignorance, social prejudice, well-intentioned dogma, lack of funding, or routinization take over. We need to rethink the implications of both approaches against the background of the limited knowledge that we have. Coordinating the attack on the complex problem of drug and alcohol abuse is preeminently a legislative responsibility. For the courts to assume that addictive drug or alcohol use, or addiction-related conduct, is involuntary, and for the courts then to build such an unwarranted assumption into constitutional and common law doctrine would be a grave error.

The fundamental substantive question that the criminal law properly faces here is whether, in a particular case, the defendant's capacity to act rationally in regard to the criminal significance of the act has been so impaired as to have rendered him nonresponsible at the time of the act. At first blush this may look like a more complex question than such apparently limited and technical questions as: Is defendant diseased? or Was the conduct involuntary? But as we have seen, these latter questions are confusing pseudo-simplifications; insofar as they point toward an authentically relevant issue, it is in substance the responsibility issue that is of concern.

There is, unfortunately, no single, simple sign or label that identifies the condition at issue here. Only a review of the defendant's history, conduct,

---

common in recent times, the President's Commission (1967) provides an ample review and bibliography. *U.S. v. Moore* directed itself to these issues in relation to narcotic addiction.

6. See Hart (1968), p. 23: "Criminal punishment as an attempt to secure desired behavior differs from the manipulative techniques of the Brave New World (conditioning, propaganda, etc.) or the simple incapacitation of those with anti-social tendencies, by taking a risk. It defers action till harm has been done; its primary operation consists simply in announcing certain standards of behavior and attaching penalties for deviation, making it less eligible, and then leaving individuals to choose. This is a method of social control which maximizes individual freedom within the coercive framework of law. . . ."

physical health, and general demeanor can provide an adequate picture. This is not a picture that can be read off with scientific precision, or even with science at all, though scientific data may be of help. It is a picture that can only be assembled and assessed from the perspective of practical lay judgment, the judgment of ordinary people who know how to get along in life taking practical account, as they go, of the bearing of law on their conduct. The test they apply to the defendant is a test they themselves pass every day of their lives: Is the defendant, as portrayed up to the moment of the offending act, and in the circumstances of that act, on the whole able to take into account in a practical way, in acting as he does, the criminal significance of his act?

The facts about the life and personality of "addicts" or "alcoholics," as we have reviewed the current state of knowledge, suggest that in some cases there is some impairment of this capacity. Specifically, this is likely to be true of the person who has had a longtime involvement with heavy use of alcohol or other drugs, whose life circumstances by now reveal deep rootlessness and alienation from human contacts, and who also suffers serious physical debilitation and disease in consequence of this unhealthy mode of life. Such persons are typically skid-row "down-and-outers" who have already shown persistent imperviousness to moral values, to rewards or sanctions, or to social pressures. They can readily present the picture of seriously impaired capacity for responsible conduct under law. Given this stage of generalized demoralization, the criminal law should be required to take cognizance of the issue as one touching fundamental criminal law principle, and not merely as a problem properly left to be handled through legislative health and welfare policies more generally. On the other hand, as has been emphasized, mere heavy involvement with drug or alcohol abuse, and related unlawful modes of life, do not per se manifest irrationality. The myth of "slaves to addiction" should not go unchallenged.

In the Disability of Mind doctrine that we propose, the type of resolution suggested above is automatically provided for. Specifically, if the issue comes to trial, the jury has several options. They would look at the total pattern of evidence bearing on the defendant's mind and character. They would decide, on the basis of the particular facts of the case—and not on the basis of labels or diagnostic categories—whether the defendant, from a practical lay standpoint, had the ability to take the law into account in acting as he or she did.

It seems expectable that where the evidence shows that the defendant regularly took into account the criminal significance of the act in a practical way—for example, took intelligible and planned measures to escape police detection, etc.—the jury will not find irrationality in regard to the act. Where, however, the evidence shows genuine incapacity to take such measures, or to take them in relatively regular and reliable ways, or to make simple and obvious plans to carry through even criminal acts efficiently, or to escape detection for them—this, along with the rest of the evidence if it forms a suitable pattern of incapacity for rational conduct, could lead to a finding that the defendant was at least to a material extent irrational. This lack of rationality calls for some mitigation of punishment. The finding would also mandate post-trial medical examination, as well as whatever health, welfare, and safety measures were then applicable under the relevant policies at the time.

Only where there was a finding of irrationality that was both predominant and nonculpable in origin would criminal punishment be entirely precluded, with medical supervision remaining as the sole consequence. Such gross debilitation of character and mind would entail, in practice, significant constraints on the defendant for the safety of the public and for the defendant's own welfare and safety.

A final word may help to show the flexibility of the D.O.M. doctrine in the area of alcohol and drug abuse. Nothing in the doctrine, or in what has been said about addiction to alcohol or other drugs, implies or in any way depends on maintaining our present (U.S.) social policies on these matters. It may well be that we are too lenient in the United States in at least some aspects of regulating use of alcohol; alcohol abuse is probably the single greatest source of domestic and criminal harm. It may well be, however, that we are far too restrictive in the United States in the regulation of narcotic and other drug use. Perhaps *all* drug use—here including alcohol as a drug—should be regulated in the same way, with no radical differentiation as to prohibition or permissiveness. Controversy abounds, but there is certainly weighty argument for abandoning at least our total prohibition against nonmedical use of narcotics. In any case, the D.O.M. doctrine does not prescribe in this or any other area what shall be a crime; it merely sets criteria for criminal responsibility.

PART V

The Disability of Mind Doctrine:
A Proposal

13

Exposition of the Basic
Disability of Mind Doctrine

It has been central to the argument of this book up to this point that there exists a certain basic confusion in the law relating to mental disability and criminal responsibility. And the diagnosis of that central and pervasive source of confusion shows the way to a fundamental cure. The confusion at issue consists at bottom in fusing two very different questions. One question concerns the proof of the essential elements of a defined crime. That is, was the crime as defined actually committed? The second question concerns the rationality of the person: Was the defendant incapable of rational conduct in regard to the criminal significance of the conduct? Once one has disentangled the second question from the first, one sees that still a third question emerges: Is the person, by reason of some earlier conduct, responsible for the occurrence of the offending act as a result of irrationality?

To embody such an analysis in law, as is proposed in the Disability of Mind doctrine, is to introduce a major element of simplification and realism into the law. In this chapter we shall present in a basic, systematic, and constructive way the "cure"—i.e., the correct doctrine implied by the diagnosis of past confusion. In the chapter that follows we shall present a substantial discussion of one of the key concepts in the D.O.M. doctrine— "rationality." And in the last chapter we shall elaborate in more specific, practice-oriented terms how the D.O.M. doctrine would work, how it

compares in particular types of cases with current doctrine, and the impact
on the institutional parties at interest. In Appendix I we present a specific
suggested set of Model Jury Instructions that would replace all the different sets of instructions for the many separate mental disability defenses
currently in use.

I: OVERVIEW AND INITIAL EXPOSITION

Doctrines of law are often expressed in a disarmingly simple way in a
single maxim. The doctrine of Disability of Mind—which we here propose
as the explicit synthesis of the insights gained in the preceding chapters—
can also be expressed in a "maxim": Where there is no *mens* there can be
no *mens rea*. Yet legal maxims are not self-explicating, and the present one
is no exception.

We now present a more precise elaboration of the intuitions that have
been uncovered in the preceding chapters and that give content to this
maxim. We begin by presenting, in the context of criminal law, three basic
propositions, which we shall then develop fully.

1. If a person's mental powers are impaired in such a way as to disable
him at least to some material extent from rational control of his conduct
in respect to the requirements of the criminal law, the person in that
respect acts with materially *lessened* criminal responsibility. If the impairment is of such magnitude that he is in chief part so disabled, he acts in
that respect *without* criminal responsibility. The generic name we propose
for such a condition is "Disability of Mind" (or occasionally "Mental
Disability," and in briefest form "D.O.M.").[1] Where the impairment is
material but not predominant, it is "Partial Disability of Mind."

1. It is evident that findings of Culpable D.O.M. and of Partial D.O.M. (whether
culpable or not) are suggestive of what has at times been referred to as "partial
responsibility," or "diminished responsibility," or "diminished capacity." There has
been some resistance in U.S. law to the concept of "partial" or "diminished"
responsibility, but the Supreme Court, in *Fisher v. U.S.* (1946), held only that it was
a matter for legislative decision as to whether to allow such defenses. In any case, it is
important to understand that the D.O.M. concepts are not conceptually equivalent to
the concepts usually at issue in the U.S. law when these phrases have been invoked.
For example, in *Fisher,* the Court makes plain that when it speaks of "partial
responsibility" it means to indicate "responsibility for a lesser grade of offense." It is
made explicit and very plain that the Court here has in mind the traditional
theory—of which we have been fundamentally critical—that in order to establish

A defense in which this legal disability is an essential element is hereafter referred to as a Disability of Mind defense. However, deciding the question as to the existence of a Disability of Mind is only the first step of a D.O.M. defense. There is a second step.

2. Assuming the defendant did suffer a Disability of Mind, there still remains the question of whether there was culpability in regard to the context of origin of the D.O.M. For brevity's sake, we shall speak of "culpable D.O.M." One common form of such culpability exists when the offending act has its origin in voluntary gross intoxication.[2] Another, but less common, form of culpable D.O.M. exists when the defendant fails to take reasonable precautionary steps to avoid a foreseeable loss of consciousness, from an illness he knows to exist, while driving a car or operating dangerous equipment. It is this culpability in the context of origin that the law must systematically take into account (as commonsense morality does, but as the common law has not) when assessing ultimate culpability in connection with criminally offending acts committed by a person suffering Disability of Mind. Where Disability of Mind is culpable in origin, that element of culpability in the context of origin is not negated by the subsequent D.O.M.[3] But where there is not culpability in the

---

"partial responsibility" one can only do this by finding absence of guilt for the graver crime charged, and finding guilt along with *full* responsibility for a lesser crime. D.O.M. verdicts would avoid such confusion. "Lesser responsibility" becomes just that—lesser responsibility for the crime actually committed.

2. This intuitively evident point was lost from sight in the *legal* analyses of the nineteenth century. Prior to that, Coke had seen that voluntary intoxication (leading to harm) introduced a distinctive element of culpability—culpability for having voluntarily put oneself into a criminally dangerous condition. This insight led him, unfortunately, to conclude that voluntary drunkenness *aggravates* the crime; he failed to appreciate the implication of his own remark that a man who is exceedingly drunk at the time is "non compos mentis" (*Beverley's Case*) and hence in *that* respect *less* culpable than were he of sound mind in committing the harm. The detail of the moral calculus here is not simple, but the principle is. And the principle is surely not one of simple addition of culpability for getting drunk *plus* full culpability for the harmful act as if one had been of sound mind in doing it. In any case, early English law did not accept the "aggravation" doctrine of Coke, but neither did it allow negating *any* culpability because of drunkenness. These issues are taken up more specifically in the discussion in Section III, infra, of "culpability in the context of origin" of the D.O.M. The issues are explored thoroughly in Part III, supra (Intoxication and Criminal Responsibility).

3. The key concepts in this second basic proposition are discussed fully in Section III, infra.

context of origin—as in nonculpably caused chronic irrationality ("insanity"), or non-negligently caused accidental trauma—the D.O.M. condition does negate responsibility for the conduct to which it pertains.

In the light of the two theses presented above, it is easy to formulate what is distinctive, for example, about the culpability of the person who gets himself very drunk, and then, while in that state, gets in an argument, decides to kill his antagonist, and sets about, successfully, to do so. Intuition tells us that in this relatively common form of homicide, the killer is typically more culpable than the genuinely insane harmdoer, but less culpable than the sober deliberate murderer. The "Disability of Mind" and "Context of Origin" concepts make explicit the ground of this intuitive judgment: the grossly drunken harmdoer conceives and carries out his project while suffering Disability of Mind—criminal irrationality— unlike the sanely deliberate killer who kills while rational and conscious of what he is doing. It is in this respect that the typical grossly drunken killer is less responsible, and hence less to be condemned than the sane deliberate killer. But since (typically) the drunken killer has culpably induced his Disability of Mind, he is in that respect unlike the insane killer, whose Disability of Mind in so acting is, by implicit definition, not the result of prior conduct while rational, and who is therefore not culpable for being in the criminally irrational condition.

3. Finally, it is evident that insofar as a person's mental powers are impaired to the point of Mental Disability, that person, by the hypothesis, cannot act as an adequately responsible person under criminal law. The post-verdict implication of this is of special interest. If a defendant suffered from a certain D.O.M. that eventuated in a criminal offense, it is reasonable to take steps to determine, on conclusion of the trial, whether the defendant is still suffering from that Mental Disability, or is still subject to recurrences of it. Thus, unlike currently used defenses, with their varying effects upon post-verdict disposition, a successful defense to the effect that a criminal harm arose out of a Disability of Mind always warrants such post-trial mental examination of the defendant. Even if the D.O.M. was not culpable, it must nevertheless be determined whether the defendant still remains subject to that D.O.M. Defendants for whom a D.O.M. verdict has been rendered, and who have been subsequently determined to be likely to have recurrences of the condition, should be subject, under appropriate policies, to measures designed to promote the welfare and safety of the defendant and of society. Such measures could be independent of, or concurrent with, any statutory penalties if the

D.O.M. was culpable. Thus an habitual drinker might have imposed upon him a combination of punishment and of medical-social rehabilitative measures.[4] A completely nonculpable epileptic who caused a criminally prohibited harm by reason of that disability might be required to conform to a medically prescribed regimen, even though no punitive measures are justified.

In short, neither culpability *nor* "dangerousness"[5] to self or others are ignored, once D.O.M. is accepted as a defense.

The three basic propositions express the substance of long-persistent intuitions of common sense that have only erratically been explicitly expressed in the common law. The intuitions have a validity that is self-evident, even while questions of exact wording, clarification, proof, and implementation still are numerous. The great task in what follows will be to avoid distortion in elaborating and commenting on their meaning and their justice.

It is important to notice that although a D.O.M. defense poses three main questions, concerning three significantly different issues, the answers to only two of the questions directly affect the finding as to the culpability of the defendant. The first question, bearing centrally on culpability, but only erratically acknowledged in current law, concerns the existence and degree—partial or predominant—of the Disability of Mind.[6] Upon a finding of D.O.M., there arises the second question, also bearing centrally on culpability, but even less systematically acknowledged in current law than the first: Was there culpability in the context of origin of the D.O.M.? Only the third question does not bear on culpability: Is the mental impairment that amounted to D.O.M. still in existence, or is it likely to recur; and, if so, what rehabilitative-protective regimen, conforming with applicable law, is best suited to the circumstances?

Since the first and second questions raise fundamental issues bearing on criminal culpability, justice requires—and D.O.M. doctrine assures—that

4. This combination is, in fact, one of the effective rehabilitative combinations. See the full discussion in connection with alcoholism (and also narcotic addiction) in Part IV; and see Fingarette (1970) and (1975).

5. See the discussion in the text following note 6, infra.

6. It is assumed here, and through the discussion in this essay generally, that the defendant is found to have committed the criminal act; for in the absence of such a finding the question of Disability of Mind becomes irrelevant to the verdict—which must be, of course, a simply Not Guilty.

these questions will be integral to the trial and definitively resolved by the verdict; for the trial is the forum specifically designed to assure due process and justice in rendering society's judgment on the defendant's criminal culpability. It is to these first two questions that the D.O.M. doctrine is specifically addressed, and to which we almost entirely restrict our comment.

It is equally plain that the third question, though it has dimensions that significantly affect legal rights of the individual, is not one essential to the trial process. This question poses problems that are primarily medical and custodial rather than legal; the concerns are prospective rather than, as in the trial, retrospective; the problems call primarily for expert consensus rather than adversary argument or moral judgment; and the issues are primarily those of public safety and of human welfare rather than justice. This third question is therefore best separated from the accusatory trial process and should be treated subsequent to the trial in a nonaccusatory forum.[7]

It should be emphasized that the D.O.M. doctrine contains no implication whatsoever about the specific nature of the post-verdict diagnostic, protective, or rehabilitative measures, or about the specific policies of law that should apply; nor does the doctrine promise anything as to the ultimate efficacy of such measures. We shall have nothing to say about such specific matters in this book. It is not for us, in developing a doctrine of criminal responsibility, to presume to propose techniques or doctrines of psychology or medicine, or to propose social or legal policies concerning rehabilitation of the mentally disabled or protection of the public welfare and safety. The third thesis of the D.O.M. doctrine of criminal responsibility merely makes plain a basic principle: a finding of D.O.M. is in substance a finding that a mental condition constituting a distinctive danger to the community existed (the defendant was unable to take into account the criminal significance of his conduct), and this in fact led to a criminally prohibited act. Moreover, normal corrective responses of the law—condemnation and punishment—are inappropriate.

It is justified, therefore, to take reasonable steps to determine whether overt manifestations of the mental condition still exist or are likely to recur. For if so, it is reasonable to take steps—other than condemnation and punishment—to protect the individual and society against the crim-

7. Professor Glanville Williams (1961) proposes substantially this division of roles, the jury assessing past responsibility, the medical experts assessing current dangerousness in the light of past conduct and present diagnosis (pp. 351–352).

inally dangerous consequences. What specific steps are reasonable to take will depend upon the state of our technical knowledge in such matters, the practical availability of specific measures, and the legal and social policy decisions that finally balance costs, estimated efficacy, and the requirements of human rights. But the principle established by the D.O.M. doctrine, if adopted, would ensure evenhandedness: *all* defendants whose verdicts include reference to D.O.M. would be subject to the diagnostic, safety, and welfare measures according with legal and social policy at the time.

Having said this much, we now turn our full attention back to the two main questions relevant to culpability: Did D.O.M. exist? Was it culpable in origin?

The questions are formulated, not in technical scientific terms, but in legally ultimate, classic terms of guilt, responsibility, and rationality. They are questions to be settled in a judicial setting, by use of disinterested lay judgment.[8] In a D.O.M. defense, medical, psychological, or other expert testimony may be relevant to the question of rationality. The aim is to provide, not medical diagnoses, but factual information about the defendant that can give laymen a better insight into the defendant's personality and mind as these would be understood and assessed by laymen. The aim is to aid the lay fact-finder to make an independent judgment on the substance of the issue, not to force reliance on authority. Since the defense is not cast in terms of "disease," or scientific causality, or specific medical categories, and since its key conclusory terms do not belong within the terminology of medical expertise, there is no reason to allow—as is now the case—conclusory comment by experts.[9] Thus the expert's role should be less portentous; it should be a role less troublesome to courts—*and* to experts—than it has been under present doctrines.

The essential issue posed by the D.O.M. doctrine is relatively narrow—in contrast to the many different and obscure issues that may be posed by current doctrines, which allow a plurality of alternative and logically

8. See Chapter 14 for a full discussion of the rationale for this thesis. This point of view is, of course, not restricted to the specific views in the D.O.M. doctrine. Increasingly, courts have come to feel, if only on pragmatic grounds and in spite of the lack of a unitary doctrine, that the "complicated . . . intertwining moral, legal, and medical judgments" involved (*King v. U.S.,* 1967, p. 389) must rest on the jury as the community surrogate applying the underlying sense of what is essential for responsibility. See the majority opinion of Judge Leventhal in *U.S. v. Brawner,* 1972.

9. A forceful statement of this approach is to be found in *Washington v. U.S.* (1967).

disparate defenses. Could the defendant act rationally at the time with regard to the criminal prohibitions bearing on his conduct; and, if not, did the defendant culpably induce the Mental Disability?

We should perhaps emphasize certain important psychological obstacles to acceptance by the courts of the general proposition that irrationality necessarily vitiates responsibility. This proposition has historically evoked from judges widespread anxieties on two quite distinct grounds. One source of anxiety has been a moralistic one—the fear, at times justified under traditional common law doctrine, that such a principle could be used to completely excuse the harmdoer who commits the harm while voluntarily intoxicated with drink or drugs.[10] The D.O.M. doctrine's concept of "culpability in the context of origin" is the basis for allaying that fear.

The second source of anxiety is that, moralistic considerations aside, a verdict of Not Guilty for the criminally irrational will free them, or (as some have argued) ought logically to free them from the clutches of the criminal law. Such defendants would then go forth into the community again, often while they are still dangerous to society.[11] It should now be evident that the legitimacy of this anxiety is also recognized, and the grounds for the anxieties also dissolved. The D.O.M. doctrine makes it explicit that a D.O.M. finding implies that the defendant was, or may at least reasonably be supposed to have been, mentally incompetent in a criminally harmful way, and therefore the defendant cannot reasonably be released into society until there is an appropriate disposition in regard to medical, welfare, and safety issues.

II: THE EXCULPATORY LOGIC OF D.O.M.
AND ITS BASIS IN IRRATIONALITY

We turn now to examine the concept of Disability of Mind specifically. It is a legal concept, very broad in scope, the aim being to identify general

10. Precedent is overwhelmingly against allowing intoxication to serve as a complete defense to criminal charges. See Chapter 6, supra.

11. In English law, when the first stirrings of the new approach to allowing mitigation of culpability in cases of intoxication had become evident (in *R. v. Grindley,* referred to in *R. v. Carroll,* 1835), they were almost immediately followed (in *R. v. Carroll*) by Justice Park's rejection of the idea for fear that if such were the law "there would be no safety for human life" (p. 145). See Part III (Intoxication), supra, for a fuller discussion of the significance of these anxieties.

and basic legal issues. Thus "Disability of Mind" may, from a psychological standpoint, designate any kind of individual mental abnormality, pathology, impairment, defect, or disorder, and from whatever origin. But the concept is precise and specific in that the impairment must be related specifically to the particular criminal conduct alleged. It is not enough for the trier of fact to judge that the defendant's mental powers had been impaired at the time of the alleged crime. Those powers must have been impaired in a way and in a degree that at least materially disabled him from rational control of his conduct specifically with respect to the crime alleged, even though the physical act alleged was performed by him. It is irrelevant to the assessment of criminal responsibility whether the defendant may have been irrational in any other respects. This specific linkage between the mental condition and the criminality of the act is deeply rooted in the tradition of the common law, and in the D.O.M. doctrine it remains entirely valid.[12]

The concept of rational control of conduct with respect to the criminal significance of the act is of course central here; it will be explicated briefly below, and then more fully and generally in the following chapter. But it is important to stress at the outset our claim that whatever the merits or defects of details in our admittedly exploratory analysis of it, the concept itself has in fact been what men have had in mind and *used,* with all its everyday language vagueness, and even if only on an intuitive basis, when assessing mental disabilities and criminal responsibility.[13] This being so, we must use the concept, try to clarify it, and perhaps refine it for the more technical purposes of law. But its lack of perfect clarity in everyday use cannot warrant rejecting it as a "wrong" concept—any more than concepts such as "justice," "due process," "voluntary," or "cause" are dispensable or wrong because the task of defining them presents problems.

In the relevant sense of "rational," all criminality is rational. As the D.O.M. doctrine states, insofar as there is irrationality there is *not* crimi-

12. See Chapter 2, Section I, supra.

13. Once one has been "sensitized" to the aptness of this concept here, one will notice the occasions when, in their less formal moments, writers on insanity and other mental disabilities will easily and naturally resort to the term *rationality* and its close variants as the criterion of mental disability in any of the major dimensions of mental function. One example, taken from a discussion of psychoses generally: "[The psychotic's] thinking and behavior are disproportionately influenced by irrational beliefs, perceptions, and impulses. . . . The swings between rationality and irrationality can be better understood if we bear in mind that psychoses are sometimes acute and sometimes in remission" (Goldstein, 1967, pp. 28–29).

nality, though of course irrationality can be dangerous and lead to harmdoing.[14]

Law addresses itself to those who have reached relative maturity and are acting in their right mind. That is, in their conduct they must be mentally able to take into account, in a practical way and at least in the essentials, the relevance to that conduct of certain basic norms of criminal law. It makes no sense to speak of the law as addressed to the month-old infant unable to respond intelligently; and in consequence the whole panoply of associated moral sanctions is not applicable to the infant. The upshot is the same in the case of the mentally disabled adult, the adult impaired in mental ability so as to be unable to take into account in practice the bearing of some or all of the injunctions of law.

The possession of such an ability or capacity by no means amounts to complying with law, nor with acting prudently or wisely in regard to the law. A distinctive feature of law is the recognition that among persons in their "right mind," i.e., persons who are able to take into account effectively the bearing of criminal law standards on their conduct, there are some who nevertheless wilfully, recklessly, or negligently disobey. They may be evil, or rebellious, or thoughtless, or foolish. But they are at least minimally *able* to take into account in a practical way the criminal significance of their conduct, although they on occasion ignore it or choose to act in a way that they are conscious is criminal. It is the existence of this group, of course, that gives particular point to the sanctions of the law. Such persons, being response-able, are held responsible.

There are those, however, who in acting as they do at a particular time are in some respect mentally incapable of a practical grasp of the bearing of some criminal law norm that is relevant to their conduct at that time. They are in that respect "outside" the law. But to be "outside" the law in this way differs radically from the outlawry of the response-able person. The latter is "outside" the law in the sense of having been accused of law violation and found guilty. The former is "outside" the law in the sense that the accusatory process is inappropriate.

14. It is a platitude of psychiatric lore that even those who show serious irrationality are usually not irrational in *all* respects and at *all* times. What is at issue in the text is the group who are at some time irrational in respect to criminal law norms, or who are subject to recurrences of such irrationality. Many of those who are in this group may in fact commit no criminal harm, but the *danger* that they will do so exists in a special way that singles them out from the rational criminal on the one hand, and the rational law-abiding citizen on the other.

In the criminal trial, all defense strategies (except those based on Mental Disability) are directed to *defeating* an accusation—by offering disproof of the act, or by offering some specific excuse or justification, or by a showing that the act alleged in a particular accusation, even if it took place, would not constitute a violation of law. The claim of nonresponsibility, however, is not the offering of an excuse. In offering an excuse, one responds to a legitimate accusation by offering a particular reason why one should not be condemned.

The Disability of Mind defense is more fundamental than any of these. Insofar as there is a claim of Disability of Mind, the claim is that the person, being nonresponsible, need not respond to a particular accusation because, even if the act was committed, the whole apparatus—accusation, denial, excuse, justification, condemnation, and punishment—is misplaced and inappropriate. More briefly put, the D.O.M. plea is not a challenge to the prosecution's case but a plea to circumvent the prosecutory process (entirely or in some limited respect).

This has important implications that have hitherto been only erratically and obscurely manifest in the form of the verdicts as now presented. And the ambiguity of the phrases *Guilty* and *Not Guilty* contribute to the confusion. A person may be guilty of committing a specified criminal act, but not criminally responsible and hence not "guilty" in an accusatory-condemnatory sense. We have repeatedly alluded to the obscurity created by confusing the question of commission of the defined act with the question of criminal responsibility. The D.O.M. doctrine suggests a simple and total clarification of all these issues: the finding of a Disability of Mind should never be confusingly reported as "Not Guilty." If a defined criminal act was committed, this should be unambiguously reported by a verdict of "Guilty"; if there is not proof of all the elements, the verdict should likewise be unambiguous: "Not Guilty." If the defendant did commit the criminal act as defined by law, then the finding as to Disability of Mind, unconfused with the former question, should *also* be reported. Where the jury finds full Disability of Mind that is nonculpable in origin, this finding amounts to a finding of complete lack of criminal responsibility. It entails that even though the alleged act was proved, no criminal condemnation or punishment is warranted, and that the social problems posed should be resolved in a suitable, nonaccusatory process.[15] If,

15. See Chapter 15, Section II, infra, and Appendix I, infra, for a full development of these questions.

however, the D.O.M. is only partial, or is culpable in origin, there is significant criminal responsibility for the act.

Another implication of this way of seeing the nonresponsibility defense arises in connection with the question of burden of proof, a question we mainly postpone to a later discussion in a more practice-oriented context.[16] The gist of the matter may be set out here, however. When viewed in the way just suggested, the question of rationality or irrationality is not one that pertains to proof of guilt, or excuse therefrom. The burden should probably be on the defense to show that in some respect the normal accusatory process and its consequences should be set aside because of nonresponsibility.

It should be stressed that although Disability of Mind is defined in terms of a defect of mental capacity, the capacity here in question differs significantly from the capacity at issue in the American Law Institute's Model Penal Code test of insanity. The Model Penal Code test misidentifies the capacity that should properly be at issue. That test calls for "substantial lack of capacity to conform conduct to the requirements of law."[17] However, it is quite typical that even the obviously mentally disabled offender is capable of electing to do what happens in fact to conform to law, or even capable of purposely conforming to the law. But even the individual who could purposely conform if he so willed is unable, because of the irrational condition of mind, to form his will rationally. He is unable to go beyond the purely formal aspect of the matter and take into account, while forming his intentions, the criminal significance of what is at issue. In consequence, the irrational individual may end up purposefully and even skillfully bent upon conduct that he knows does not conform to the rule of law.

This is not at all unusual in offenses arising out of paranoia, some kinds of schizophrenia and psychotic depressions, and some kinds of deep intoxication. Such persons may be able to give correct verbal answers about the formal prohibitions of law. But we see that, because of their deranged thinking or moods or feelings, the norms embodied in these legal prohibitions have lost their significance. The law is for them *mere* verbal rules: it defines the *word* "crime," but no longer signifies *crime.* In such

16. See Chapter 15, Section I, infra.

17. "A person is not responsible for criminal conduct if at the time of such conduct as a result of mental disease or defect he lacks substantial capacity either to appreciate the criminality (or wrongfulness) of his conduct or to conform his conduct to the requirements of law" (American Law Institute, Model Penal Code, Sec. 4.01, 1961; see also the discussion of "involuntariness" in Part II, infra).

cases, the fact-finder's intuition is that nonresponsibility existed at the time of the offense, even though the offender *could* have conformed to the rule if he wished. This intuition squarely conflicts with legal formulas such as the Model Penal Code's. By contrast, the capacity identified by the D.O.M. doctrine is the capacity for rational (i.e., responsible) shaping of beliefs, moods, intentions, decisions, and actions[18] in regard to criminal law standards.

Analogously, it may be recalled in regard to the *M'Naghten* type of test that if we remain with ordinary English usage of "know"—and with typical legal usage of "know" in all other areas of law—it is typically plainly true to say that the mentally disabled offender *does* "know the nature of his act" and that it is considered to be against the law. The trouble—as recognized in the D.O.M. doctrine—is that in arriving at the will to act in this way, in spite of the knowledge that the rule of law forbids it, the offender's mind worked irrationally.

III: THE CONCEPTS IN THE DOCTRINE: "CULPABILITY IN THE CONTEXT OF ORIGIN"

When we raise the "context of origin" question, we in effect raise a special form of the very general question of law as to whether there is *mens rea.*

18. In addition to the cognitive confusion or delusions most readily accepted under the *M'Naghten* rule, plausible claims of criminal insanity under *M'Naghten,* or other insanity definitions such as the Model Penal Code definition, can be based on severe (schizophrenic) deficiency of feeling-emotion responses to other human beings, on psychotic depressive and destructive impulses toward self or others, or on manic-psychotic extremes of hyperexcited elation and feelings of aggressive power. For discussion, illustrations, and citations of cases bearing on the various forms of mental pathology as related to criminal insanity, see generally: Brooks (1974), chap. 4, sec. A; Goldstein (1967), chaps. 4, 5, and 6; and Fingarette (1972), chap. 3. In this context the remarks in the Report of the Royal Commission on Capital Punishment (1955) reflect the facts well: "We have been struck, for example, by the large number of cases where the offender was undoubtedly insane both at the time of the crime and afterwards, but clearly showed . . . that he knew what he was doing and that it was punishable by law" (p. 103). "In many cases, such as those of melancholia, . . . the sufferer . . . experiences a change of mood which alters the whole of his existence. He may believe, for instance, that a future of such degradation and misery awaits both him and his family that death for all is a less dreadful alternative. Even the thought that the acts he contemplates are murder and suicide pales into insignificance in contrast with what he otherwise expects. The criminal act, in such circumstances, . . . may be coolly and carefully prepared; yet it is the act of a madman" (*ibid.,* p. 110). The Commission adds that similar states of mind are likely to lie behind criminal acts arising out of schizophrenia or paranoid psychoses.

The basic idea is simple and general,[19] but the specific form of the question will depend upon the nature of the Disability of Mind, the circumstances under which it arose, and the extent to which the offending act is attributed to it.

It is evident that culpability in the origin of a Disability of Mind can be of various kinds and degrees. But no novel concepts are needed except for "context of origin": the same mental elements that are required for the alleged or some lesser included crime will also determine, if present in the context of origin, the nature of the culpability for the D.O.M. That is, we ask whether the defendant, by his prior conduct while responsible, brought about, or unreasonably risked bringing about, *either* the Disability of Mind *or* the condition of being in a position to cause a criminal harm because of such a Disability of Mind, or both. These possibilities call for brief discussion.

To cause or unreasonably risk the occurrence of Disability of Mind—for example, by self-intoxication, or by failing to take prescribed insulin medication—is in effect to cause or unreasonably risk a state of mind in which one is inherently grossly unfitted to observe a reasonable standard of care. In short, this is to be responsible, at the very least, for what is by

19. The basic idea proposed here has been implicit in various proposals, more narrow in scope, made by various writers. Hall (1960) states it in quite general terms in his analysis of *mens rea* (p. 188). See Hart and Honore (1959), pp. 70, 301; Perkins (1957), pp. 726, 789–790; Prevezer (1958); G. Williams (1961), pp. 13–14, 571; Smith and Hogan (1973), p. 157; *Johnson v. Alabama* (1905); *Thebo Meli v. R.* (1954); and *Attorney General for Northern Ireland v. Gallagher* (1963). Perkins (1957) casts the issue as to the relation of *mens rea* and *actus reus* as one of causality (p. 726), whereas Hall (1960) casts it in terms of "concurrence" and "coalescence," but analyzes these ultimately as rooted in a moral relation between the *mens rea* and the *actus reus* as well as a causal one (pp. 185–188). Some commentators hold that temporal simultaneity of *actus reus* and *mens rea* is essential; and some of these have made statements seeming to imply the contrary as well. See Williams (1961), p. 2; Smith and Hogan (1973), p. 51; and see generally Marston (1970). The wavering and apparently inconsistent formulations seem to derive from an inclination to keep *mens rea* and *actus reus* contemporary, and, on the other hand, from the pressure of common sense in certain cases, e.g., "Dutch courage" cases or the *Thebo Meli* kind of case, where the earlier state of mind so plainly determined the subsequent outcome in spite of intervening irrationality or action-out-of-ignorance. One can say that the entire sequence is only one "transaction." This seems inadequate as a general concept to cover all culpable D.O.M. "Context of origin" is a frank acknowledgment that even where, as in casual drinking, there was not in any evident sense "one transaction," subsequent harmdoing *is* significantly dependent on the earlier decision to drink.

objective standards gross negligence in regard to any relevant criminal norms. Here there is no specificity in the context of origin as to the nature of the norm that might later become applicable. More will shortly be said about this kind of culpability in the context of origin.

However, one may have caused oneself to be, or unreasonably risked being, in the position where one would commit a specific criminal harm by reason of D.O.M. Such a person would be one who, knowing he is unpredictably susceptible to syncope or coma from epilepsy or heart failure, nevertheless drives a car or operates highly dangerous machinery and in consequence of such coma causes the death of another. This is at the very least criminal negligence in regard to that specific criminal harm. It would probably be recklessness in that regard.

More gravely criminal, though still rare, is the case where the individual intentionally causes the D.O.M. with further intent or recklessness as to bringing about the harm. Here the typical example would be the person who drinks or uses a drug, either in order to build up "Dutch courage" to carry out a specific criminally prohibited act, or in order to gird up "nerve" to take action that risks eventuating in a specific criminal harm.

The jury, in reporting whether there was D.O.M., should specify any such recklessness or intent in the context of origin of the D.O.M.[20] If, however, the defendant was neither negligent nor reckless as to the producing of D.O.M., and also as to the possibility of its occurrence in a situation where it would produce harm, there is no culpability in the context of origin.

By far the most common kind of case is that in which the culpability of the D.O.M. is nonspecific as to the ultimate harm. Here, typically, the defendant gets himself drunk without any intention as to the consequences, without even any awareness or negligence in regard to any specific risk of criminal harm. Then, after having become drunk to the point of irrationality, he conceives and executes some criminally prohibited act—perhaps a homicide conceived in drunken rage and brooding. Though such a person would not be criminally responsible at the time of

20. Though the rationale offered here is distinctive and falls within a unitary theory quite general in scope, the result is not unorthodox, for "no amount of argument can obscure the fact that homicide resulting from a deliberate and premeditated intent to kill is a deliberate and premeditated killing" (Perkins, 1957, p. 790). In England, see *Attorney General for Northern Ireland v. Gallagher* (1963), pp. 349, 382. See also the theory proposed to this effect in Smith and Hogan (1973), pp. 156–157.

the homicide, if indeed his act arose chiefly out of Disability of Mind,[21] there still would be culpability in the context of origin, and he would not, therefore, be free from criminal condemnation and punishment. The degree of condemnation and punishment would, however, be less than that for a deliberate homicide by a rational person.

While it is easy to see the criminal guilt in cases where culpability in the context of origin is specific as to the harm caused, fuller comment is needed on the thesis that merely getting oneself intoxicated[22] itself suffices to establish culpable D.O.M. Of course, one may take an intoxicating substance and yet hope and expect to abide by the law. But this in itself would not exclude all guilt for harms that result. Inadequately grounded hopes or expectations leading to the taking of unreasonable risks are the very stuff of gross negligence and recklessness. The reckless driver, for example, may hope and expect and intend not to harm anyone as he careens through the apparently isolated countryside at 100 miles per hour, into the opposite lane, and around the curves and over the hills. Many such drivers are not "indifferent" to the danger; they may indeed be intent upon avoiding any accidents—provided the danger can be avoided while careening at 100 miles per hour.

Such a driver may try to justify the risk by arguing (with some plausibility) that, from a "statistical" standpoint, even reckless driving rarely causes death. The issue, however, does not rest on such "statistical" considerations, nor does it dissolve in the face of our inability to specify exactly what the eventual harm, if any, will be, or how or when it will come about. It is plain that this driver is unreasonably adding a real risk of

21. It should be emphasized that the mere fact that the defendant had been drinking and was, as a consequence, boisterous or reckless or combative does not per se constitute the material impairment of rationality adequate to establish D.O.M. The intoxication must in fact cause irrationality. "[N]o man may be allowed to expose the public to the danger of harm or violence caused by his own misconduct in voluntarily rendering himself dangerous" (*Boswell's Case,* quoted in *Johnson v. Commonwealth,* 1923).

22. Not all culpable D.O.M. is due to casual self-intoxication. However, by far the most common crimes with culpable D.O.M. are crimes committed while intoxicated. The discussion will therefore be carried through in those terms. There is no problem in generalizing the theses, e.g., to the case of the person who during his rational periods knows himself to be subject to periodic mental disorder amounting to irrationality, and who commits a criminal harm while irrational as a result of failing to take the medicine he has been told he must take. See *R. v. Quick* (1973).

harm, even of death, to himself and others. If he thinks about the matter, and still goes ahead, he is wantonly reckless; if he never even thinks of it, he is criminally negligent.

Analogously, the person who takes substances in amounts that can quickly produce a material loss of rationality cannot logically argue that there is no unreasonable risk of grave harm because many people do this and produce no harm, or because he himself never until now caused such harm while intoxicated, or because the range of possible harms risked is too broad to have warranted foresight of any specific harm such as death. The fact that the harm in question is so unspecifiable, unpredictable, and hence uncontrollable beforehand is precisely wherein much of the risk and its unreasonableness lie. To say that there was culpability as to the origin of D.O.M. is to say that the individual, while rational, so acted as to bring about a condition of mind in which any of a broad range of criminal harms were unreasonably risked—either out of intention, or out of recklessness or gross negligence.

The development of new and more potent forms of intoxicating drugs underlines the urgency of this type of risk-situation for the law. It is a distinctive type, not analyzable adequately in terms of intent, or knowledge, or even negligence in the usual context (negligence with respect to a *specific* harm risked). Moreover, the development of new nondrug techniques[23] for manipulating the mind and affecting its modes of consciousness in as yet unpredictable ways requires us to face the issue in its most general form.

We propose as fundamental, therefore, that the irrational state of mind at the time, if culpably induced, should provide no cover of excuse from the usual tests of criminal negligence or recklessness. This places a "floor" under any mitigation of condemnation or punishment where there is culpable Disability of Mind. For if the jury finds so gross an irrationality as to establish doubt that there was intent or knowledge as to the specific nature of the behavior and harm caused, it will then commonly and

---

23. Among nondrug consciousness-altering techniques currently already used by many are "meditational" practices derived from Asian traditions, "biofeedback" learning, hypnotism, intensive use of fasting, and perceptual and sleep deprivation. Given what is already known about the alterability of consciousness by chemical, physical, and behavioral means, and the widespread persistent interest on the part of religious, scientific, therapeutic, and other groups, one must expect the proliferation predicted in the text.

obviously be the case that by objective standards the defendant was either reckless or grossly negligent.[24]

On the other hand, if the gross lack of reasonable care did arise chiefly out of Disability of Mind, but if the defendant was not culpable as to the origin of that condition, then it seems fair—and the D.O.M. doctrine clearly establishes this—that the defendant should not be held criminally responsible for the harm committed.

The upshot, then, of the systematic use of the "context of origin" concept would be to raise to explicit and clear legal status the reasons why we do correctly see culpability in certain types of conduct where the offender is at the time grossly irrational, lacking *mens rea* in the usual sense, and incapable of responsible conduct. There would be no "escape route" for such persons even when their mental disability at the time of the act is fully and candidly taken into account.

IV: CONCLUSION: THE BASIC D.O.M. FORMAT

The doctrine of Disability of Mind proposed here has been developed only in its essentials; its key concept of "rationality" and its practical import have only been adumbrated and not yet elaborated. However, it is one of the major merits claimed for the D.O.M. doctrine that it can readily and logically be elaborated, adapted, and refined to suit complex circumstances and the demands of a body of law that is ever growing and adapting to new and unforeseen circumstances. This ready manageability results from the fact that the doctrine is rooted in the basic moral and legal intuitions that have inspired the criminal law in this area. The doctrine takes as central the psychological realities to which the intuitions are relevant, rather than replacing or blurring the realities by introducing legal constructions and fictions. There is a single, basically simple doctrine to be mastered—not, as now, a multiplicity of overlapping unrealistic, and arbitrary doctrines.

The upshot is that both the lay juror and also the law professional should be able to genuinely think through problems within the framework

24. Of course, in those cases where, regardless of the irrationality, there is *not* gross failure to conform to reasonable standards of care, then criminal negligence in regard to those acts would not exist—but then in such cases this seems the fair result. After all, a defendant should not be criminally penalized *merely* for drinking, even though a harm was committed, if the harm was not due to any gross negligence on the defendant's part.

of the D.O.M. doctrine, and indeed should be aided by it in their thinking. Such thinking is now hindered by the artificialities and obscurities of the specialized defenses such as insanity, diminished mental capacity, absence of specific intent due to intoxication, unconsciousness, automatism, and involuntariness due to mental malfunction; and of their would-be cousins— such recently proposed defenses (for alcoholism and addiction) as "pharmacological coercion" or constitutionally nonpunishable "disease"; and also of the cluster of controversial subconcepts such as "knowing the act was wrong" and "compulsion." All of these could be swept from the scene into the limbo of an unhappy chapter in the history of the criminal law. And yet a fundamental principle of common law justice—that a person may not be criminally condemned for harms for which he is not responsible—would be preserved intact, as well as formulated simply and coherently, and with due regard to social protection, in relation to disabilities of mind.

14

The Concept of "Capacity for Rational Conduct in Regard to Law"

The concept of lack of capacity for rational conduct in regard to the criminal significance of the conduct plays a central role in the understanding of Disability of Mind. It is, we maintain, the concept that underlies the long history of practical intuitive judgments that some people are so mentally disabled as to be nonresponsible. Our systematic use of it here requires explicit analysis and explanation.

The terms *rationality* and *rational* have, unfortunately, significantly varied uses in English. They can take on the sense of *logical, prudent, judicious, wise, reasonable,* or *effective.* But there is a concept that is different from any of these, and that in English is also expressed by *rational* and *rationality.* The particular concept that is here relevant is the concept of capacity for rational conduct. It is the absence of this capacity that is central to what we wish to express when we speak of someone as "out of his mind," "out of touch with reality," "mentally incompetent," "crazy," or "mad." The task here, of course, is to develop with explicitness and precision the sense of this concept in the context of criminal responsibility. In doing this, we are not defining or inventing a new concept, but explaining the concept that has actually been at the center of the practical intuition that mental disability negates responsibility.[1]

1. For a fuller discussion of alternative uses, see Fingarette (1972), pp. 179-186. It will be noticed by the reader who compares the discussion in the 1972 work with

I: SOME ANALOGIES

In order to see more deeply into the meaning of the concept of rationality in relation to specific crimes, it will help to begin with some analogies. The analogy with color blindness can be helpful. In a variety of contexts, one is required to take into account, by direct vision, the colors of objects. In those contexts, the color-blind person is incapable of taking into account in his conduct the bearing of certain relevant features of his situation. He may try to compensate for his lack by indirect means; for example, he may make use of verbal labels that indicate the color, or of conventional associations of objects and colors (as in the red, white, and blue of the American flag). But whenever he is called upon to discriminate colors *by direct color vision,* he is blind, in other words, not able to respond, not response-able. [2]

This radically differs from the case of the person who *is* able to discriminate red from green, but who, for example, is negligent about attending to the traffic lights, or who sees the red light glowing but nevertheless wilfully crosses the intersection. Such a one is the nonconforming but response-able and hence responsible offender. In ascribing nonresponsibility, it is not a question of whether the discriminative capacity is actually exercised: "I did not look to see what color the traffic light was" is no excuse. The question is whether the capacity to discriminate existed: *Had* you looked, *could* you have told red from green?

We can now consider some analogies that approach more nearly to the specific notion of criminal irrationality. For example, we may imagine experimentally induced emotional "blindness" and consequent lack of relevant response-ability. [3] An experimenter might use selective electrical

---

the discussion in the present chapter that, whereas the present chapter begins in the spirit of the earlier discussion, it moves into far more explicit and deeper analysis of the issues, more systematic relating of them to legal concepts, and, in consequence, into a new way of explicating the concept itself.

2. Of course, the color-blind person can be held responsible for taking reasonable steps to avoid situations in which his incapacity could result in harm. The analogy with *People v. Eckert* (1955) and *People v. Decina* (1956) is clear. In these cases, the defendants knew they were subject to recurrent attacks of mental disability (epileptic seizures) but nevertheless undertook to drive an automobile (no medication or preventative being available).

3. The following hypothetical illustrations centering on control of mental processes by electrical stimulation of the brain are inspired by the rapidly proliferating technical powers being achieved in the area of physical and chemical control of the

stimulation of the brain, or selective neuroactive drugs or neurosurgery, to block the range of emotional responses that are essential to feelings of compassion, sympathy, and pity. The subject in such an experiment would still be able to conduct himself rationally in many respects. But wherever there were social or environmental conditions normally having some bearing on the arousal or subsidence of the selected range of feelings, the subject would manifest a materially defective sensibility, or for practical purposes, a "blindness." To a material degree, perhaps to a prevailing extent, he would show what psychiatrists call "flatness of affect."[4] He might happen to engage in conduct, even if it were initially innocent, that finally issued in acts of irrational cruelty or purposeless grave bodily harm. For the feelings that are normally important restraints would be absent. Even an intellectual awareness that such acts are "wrong" might sooner or later cease to play a significant inhibiting role because of the pervasive incapacity to feel that such things really make any difference one way or another.

Such an experimental subject would then be remarkably reminiscent of a certain type of schizophrenic criminal who, perhaps with emotionless methodicalness, kills purposelessly, though with otherwise "rational" efficiency, in the course of committing robbery, or who is unnecessarily and pointlessly brutal.[5]

Given substantial irrelevance of response—whether in the dimension of emotion-feelings or desire, or in the dimension of cognitive relationships, or in any relevant mental dimension—the resulting intentions and conduct

---

mind. The mind-controlling techniques supposed here for the purpose of bringing out the theoretical point at issue are realistic in the sense that they (or closely analogous techniques) are already existent. For full discussions, see generally Delgado (1969) and London (1969).

4. See note 5, infra.

5. In their review of problems of schizophrenia diagnosis, description, and explanation, Carpenter, Strauss, and Bartko (1974) report that the single most discriminating operationally identifiable sign of schizophrenia is "restricted affect" (p. 46). This has long been considered a classic sign of schizophrenia. In the review this condition is keyed behaviorally, in examining a patient, to the presence of a "blank, expressionless face," and "very little or no emotion shown when delusional or normal material that would *usually* bring out emphasis is discussed" (p. 76, emphasis in original). See the description of "Schizophrenia," category #295, and "Schizoid Personality," #301.2, in the American Psychiatric Association's *Diagnostic and Statistical Manual of Mental Disorders,* 2nd ed. (1968). And see also the fuller descriptions and illustrative criminal cases in Brooks (1974), pp. 39–52.

will be to that extent irrational and will often have a bizarre appearance. However, the rational capacities of the person in other dimensions of his mental powers may enable him to "rationalize"[6] away what even he realizes strikes others as strange. Thus, our experimental subject, having been challenged for unfeelingly harming someone, may assert by way of excuse, perhaps "sincere" in his own eyes, that some movement on the part of his victim had revealed assaultive intent requiring emergency self-defense. Moreover, it may have surface plausibility to the subject and to the casual observer who knows nothing further of the circumstances.[7] However, a closer observation of the manner and degree of the brutality might reveal that, even as a misguided case of self-defense, the conduct was bizarre and reflected unresponsiveness to those features of the situation that normally evoke some feeling of compassion or pity. The careful observer thus need not know the cause, as we observers of the experiment do, but if enough of the relevant facts are available to him he can see the effects on conduct—which, after all, is the decisive aspect of the matter in the law.

The notion of "blindness" and the analogy of the emotion desensitizing experiment may suggest *absence* or passivity of response, or apathy to socially relevant circumstance, but this suggestion that the response out of "blindness" must be negative can be misleading. The irrational respond in many respects with clear purpose—but in so doing they will not be responding to some relevant standard.

One could see this phenomenon clearly if, for example, the experimenter were to produce states of rage in the subject at arbitrarily selected times. The result would then be that the rest of the perceptions, motives, thoughts, and conduct of the otherwise rational subject would be profoundly colored and shaped by the states of rage that emerged (and disappeared) without relevance to (out of "blindness" to) the conditions in the subject's social situation that are normally relevant to rage evocation or reduction. Since his rage states were produced by the electrical impulses

6. It perhaps merits emphasis that "rationalize" is used here in the familiar sense that implies "*pseudo*-rational"—the offering as one's reasons what were in fact not one's reasons but a (false) facade of reasons or seeming reasons.

7. It is a familiar result in experimentally induced or pathological brain malfunction, and in hypnosis, that the subject, unaware of the true cause of his strange conduct, will endeavor to rationalize it with apparent sincerity. This phenomenon throws light on the rationalizations of neurotics and psychotics that we see, more generally, as "symptoms." See Fingarette (1969), Appendix on surgical severing of the connections between the two hemispheres of the human brain.

arbitrarily activated by the experimenter, they would, from the standpoint of relevant social norms, be "arbitrary," "irrelevant," "meaningless," and "bizarre." This might or might not be immediately evident to an innocent observer. For even in his rage, the subject might retain enough other elements of rationality to act with clear and relevant intent to injure someone, and to do so with a superficially plausible rationalization.

Here the parallel case of the paranoid schizophrenic readily comes to mind. What is it that eventually leads us to conceive of a pattern of conduct as paranoid, and of ideas as delusions? There may at first be an air of intelligibility or "rationality" about the ideas and conduct. And, indeed, if one assumes the truth of the delusory belief, the paranoid's desperate measures *are* intelligible; some would even say "rational."[8] But eventually we come to see that what governs is the deluded person's deep, persistent, ultimately quite unfounded (i.e., *irrelevant*) feelings of fear and enmity. We realize that the objective events or demeanor of others that would normally be relevant to arousing such fear and hatred play no practical role here. Under pressure of events, the initial plausibility of the paranoid schizophrenic's rationalizations eventually dissolves in the face of proliferating rationalizations, inconsistencies, and the increasingly bizarre character of the "explanations" designed to reinterpret whatever happens in a way that will conform to the intractable and dominating fearfulness, anger, and suspiciousness. The beliefs are not merely false, they are for *practical* purposes immune, though often not verbally so, to evidentiary relevance insofar as it enables one to discriminate threatening situations from nonthreatening ones. It is this immunity of the beliefs and attitudes, their life independent of relevant evidence or circumstance, that constitutes what we call *delusion* rather than mere erroneous belief. It is the irrefutable axiom of the subject's emotional life that he is profoundly threatened by others. Nothing has any practical bearing for him on that; everything else must be made to fit. The typical and dramatic sign of it is that *any* belief, however bizarre—even if it requires supposing that the forces of the cosmos are in league against him—will be adopted if needed to explain away what would otherwise be evidence relevant to, and counting against, the delusion and fear and aggression.[9] The paranoid is *in practice* blind to the relevance of certain kinds of circumstance.

8. See the criticisms along this line of my use of "rational," criticisms therefore missing the point of my usage, by Morris (1974), p. 352, and Walker (1975).

9. See Brooks (1974), pp. 41–44, for a brief but illuminating description, with illustrations, of paranoid states and related crimes.

Up to this point we have been casting the analysis in terms of analogies, metaphors, and illustrations that help to bring "lack of capacity for rational conduct" into proper focus. Now it is time for more systematic and direct comment.

In particular we need to see as sharply and deeply as possible how "lack of capacity for rational conduct" is a concept of a somewhat different logical kind, and a far deeper and more global significance, than such traditional concepts as "intent," "knowledge," "deliberation," and "voluntariness," and why such concepts lose their normal criminal significance insofar as the individual is irrational.

Mental capacity for rational conduct is what we have elsewhere called a "cross-dimensional" concept.[10] That is to say, one of its logical dimensions concerns certain normal *presumptions of fact*; but another calls for *decision* as to the applicability of those presumptions in the particular case.

We shall eventually consider the decisional element; but first we shall examine at some length the presumptions of fact that hold true where there is capacity for rational conduct. We shall see how these normal presumptions—extremely complex in nature—underlie the crucial criminal significance of such relatively easily identifiable mental states as "intent," "knowledge of the act," and "deliberation."

II: PRESUMPTIONS OF FACT UNDERLYING "RATIONALITY"

Since so many classic "mental elements" of crime can play a crucial role in homicide, we can develop our analysis by considering homicide in some depth.

When a person has allegedly murdered, once the physical elements of the crime are proved, the focus of attention normally turns to certain mental states that signal, in a crucial way, criminal culpability.[11] *Why* do these states have crucial significance?

A. *The Factual Presumptions Underlying the Significance of "Deliberation"*

The community expectation of most specific relevance to the crime of first-degree murder is that the individual not deliberately kill another

10. This notion, whose meaning is briefly indicated in the text that follows, is more fully explicated in Fingarette (1972), pp. 37–43.

11. In this discussion of the crucial role of certain mental states, it will always be assumed for the sake of brevity that we have to do with cases where the defendant's behavior has in fact been found to have been, as alleged, the physical cause of death.

human being. The basic moral ground for the community's imposing this expectation as positive law is the community assessment of murder as an evil—a "crime" in a moral sense. It is because the act is seen as a "crime" in a prelegal, essentially moral sense, that it is and deserves to be prohibited by positive law. Murder is, in short, *malum in se,* crime in the moral sense, not a merely legal wrong, *malum prohibitum.*[12] Though murder is legally prohibited because it is a moral crime, the instituting of the legal prohibition adds new and important dimensions of criminality to the act. It becomes criminal in law as well as in morality; and since there is at least a prima facie moral duty to abide by the law, it becomes in this still further, derivative sense, a moral wrong.[13]

The universality of this condemnation of murder—what shall here be referred to as the community perception of murder as a wrong or *malum in se*—reflects a crucial fact. Among members of the community, in spite of their many differences, there is a certain nexus of basic feelings, customs, values, and social relationships, and this nexus constitutes the valuational background out of which emerges the common response to murder. Some individuals respond more to the pragmatic dimensions of this shared background-nexus,[14] others more to the considerations of principle, others more to direct humane feeling, and still others respond very largely out of habit and custom. Some respond keenly and sensitively; others dully. In the upshot, however, without some such minimum shared background-nexus of basic perceptions and values, which provide the basic standards relevant to criminal *mala in se,* there would, of course, be no community. This is the background-nexus against which the community views and sees as wrong such acts as assault, rape, arson, and theft.[15]

12. These terms are used in the sense evident in this paragraph. They are not used as terms presupposing or implying any specific legal doctrine or philosophy associated with them.

13. We see here the ambiguity of the word *criminal*—its implication of both moral *and* legal wrong—that has caused much confusion in the controversies, in U.S. and in English law, over the meaning of *wrong* in the *M'Naghten* test. See *People v. Schmidt* (1915); *R. v. Windle* (1952); and Fingarette (1972), pp. 142–157, 238.

14. See the discussion in Goldstein (1967), pp. 12–13.

15. This concept of a shared nexus, conceived as essential to community, and having a content that at least includes the perception of nonconforming violence and some property offenses as basic wrongs, receives support not only on broad anthropological and historical grounds as one surveys known human societies, but also in certain law-related theories—e.g., the traditional "natural law" theories. However, as Professor H. L. A. Hart (1961) has argued independently of such metaphysical

The basic factual presumption, then, that underlies our expectation that people should not deliberately kill, is that each individual in the community shares in a practical awareness of this background-nexus of basic perceptions and basic values; and against this background, killing a human being is perceived as, broadly speaking, gravely criminal unless certain kinds of excuse or justification are present.

It has been argued in recent years that such a foundation for responsibility under law has been eaten away because values are no longer widely enough shared and our society is no longer a community, or is rapidly losing this status.[16] Deeply alienated subgroups and subcultures have become, it is said, so predominant a feature of our society that we cannot presume a background of shared values and perceptions as to the basic significance of certain kinds of acts such as killing or injuring human beings, destroying or thieving property, fraud, and treachery. But such attacks on the concept of responsibility under law rest on a confusion.

Of course, there may be differences of view within a community about the moral quality of particular acts, or classes of acts, or institutions. Some persons and groups are loyal to particular values or institutions that are the "official" ones; others may rebel against "official" values and institutions; and still others may be indifferent. This, however, does not of itself entail the absence of the shared background-nexus necessary if responsibility under law is to be a viable basis for law in that society.

For example, an individual or a group may be so alienated from the law and what it stands for as to hold that certain unlawful homicides are excusable, or even justifiable. The violent revolutionary, or the member of an ill-treated segment of the society, may not care, or may even approve, if someone kills a representative of the purportedly oppressing classes or institutions. The impoverished urban youth, convinced that local merchants have been exploiting him, may feel no qualms of conscience in turning to looting when an electric power breakdown blacks out the city. But even such persons, for whom the extant law represents an alien or even enemy power, have reasons why that particular killing or thieving is

---

theories of law, any adequate system of law must include a certain "minimum content" of law as a matter of "natural necessity," given that men are constituted as they are. Men, says Professor Hart, are constituted, everywhere, with a need for certain "minimum forms of protection for persons, property, and promises..." (p. 195).

16. See Floud (1974). And see the concern along these lines expressed by Judge David Bazelon (1974).

to them justified or excusable. They recognize that totally indiscriminate killing or thieving is wrong. Their "code" may be different from the code of law, but there *is* a code, a code identifying killing and taking the possessions of others as kinds of acts that call for excuse, justification, or special pleading of some kind.

What should we think, however, of someone who sees nothing in homicide per se that calls for justification or exculpatory explanation? For this person, killing human beings poses in itself no issue. This person truly fails to share the background-nexus we have spoken of. If a collection of human beings consisted entirely of such persons, there could be no community.

A person who can kill and yet sense no need for certain kinds of relevant excuse or justification is a person with no inner touchstone by which to assess conduct rationally in regard to law. Indeed, even the significance of the criminal law as an institution would be invisible to such a person. This complex perceptual-valuational background is the essential background for the spontaneity of everyday life. One must be able to identify and weigh from moment to moment the relevance of the multifarious, ever-changing, and always unique complexes of circumstances; and one must be able to do so in the spirit of the law as it applies to that unique situation. The lawyer knows only too well that the application of law to life cannot be set out in a rigid set of rules, or learned by rote. It calls, in the last analysis, for practical intuitive judgment by one who has a direct, basic appreciation of the deeper issues at stake. Only against such a background can our occasional deliberation make real sense.

So we need to contrast two different kinds of person here. First, there is the person who has a *practical* grasp of the general moral significance of killing, and who has the sense that it calls for excuse, justification, or special pleading, that it is an issue of deep concern to the law, and generally forbidden—but who may make the personal judgment that a particular unlawful killing is acceptable or even desirable. Such a person is rational in regard to the law, even though—perhaps on moral or political or religious grounds—in disagreement with it. Such a person may be socially alienated, but is not irrational. In sharp contrast is the person who does not sufficiently share in the background-nexus to perceive the nature of the issue—or even, perhaps, that there is an issue at all. Such a person is not rational in regard to law.

So the basic presumption underlying the significance of "deliberation" in homicide arises out of these facts. In broadest terms, the presumption is that a deliberate, premeditated killing is the fully conscious affirmation of the act by one who has, in some fundamental way, the ability to perceive its criminal significance. In purposefulness arising out of such awareness lies the highest degree of culpability in regard to law prohibiting killing. Therein lies the essential ground for proclaiming that *deliberation* typically signals the gravest form of murder.[17]

But deliberation has this significance only if the person *is* rational—more specifically, only if the presumption of fact as to the shared background-nexus holds true.

For a variety of mental conditions this normal presumption of fact does not hold true. The presumption may not hold true, for example, in certain criminal acts arising out of schizophrenic "flatness of affect,"[18] or depressive psychotic states of absolute despair and guilt.[19] The presumption may fail temporarily in regard to a grossly drunken person, or permanently in regard to a person of very low intelligence (e.g., a low-grade moron).

Such persons may know the verbal formulas, but they do not share the background required to identify and weigh—in practice—the relevant factors, and the possible justifications and excuses. So they cannot apply the verbal formulas in a practical way. They—and their deliberation—are in that respect irrational.

Of course, deliberation and premeditation are essential to culpability only for first-degree murder. We turn now to consider other elements of crime essential not only for first-degree murder but for murder generally.

B. *Presumptions of Fact Underlying* *"Knowledge," "Intent," and "Voluntariness"*

The crime of second-degree murder implies a different kind of expectation, based on somewhat different background presumptions of fact. Specifically, when the law declares that the knowing, intentional killing of

17. Michael and Wechsler (1937) fail to see the significance of deliberation because they do not include culpability as one of the reasons for which the criminal law ought to concern itself with the behavior of individuals. Their entire focus is on deterrence and reformation (p. 1283). In the following discussions that touch on the concept of first-degree murder, we speak of "deliberation" and "premeditation" as its distinctive mental elements. This simplification is justified because we argue that, regardless of variations in statutory definitions of murder, there is one criterion—degrees of moral guilt—that is essential to the degrees-of-murder distinctions. We believe our argument holds generally wherever degrees of murder are recognized in any of the common law and statutory variations.

18. See note 5, supra.

19. See the illustrative case history of a depressive mother who kills her children (Livermore and Meehl, 1967, Case #7).

a person can be a crime, even if there was no deliberation or premeditation, the law is embodying the community expectation that we not kill—not merely that reflection or deliberation should lead us to abstain from killing. What presumptions of fact underlie such an expectation?

Can we reasonably expect a person to refrain from indulging the impulse to kill—even *before* he has deliberated on the question? Of course, we can and do expect this. It is axiomatic that it is no excuse that one acted before one thought (though it may be less culpable than acting after thinking). Far from being an unreasonable demand, this is a simple, natural, and extremely common type of expectation. Human life could not go on if, before each and every act, we had to contemplate it and be explicitly conscious of the inherent *malum* or *bonum* of the act, and then deliberately choose whether to do it.

Plainly, life in society rests on the fact that, even without having deliberated, human beings can be reasonably expected to learn to do many required things and not to do many impermissible things; to curb certain wishes or impulses and to indulge others; to intuitively identify relevant circumstances and norms, and to weigh them intuitively; to understand (without "thinking about") the basic meanings of gestures, demeanor, conduct, and speech; and to be skilled in spontaneously responding in kind, intelligibly and relevantly. In addition to all this, we are expected to develop, and generally do develop, a basic core of motivations and attitudes essential to the social context of such skills and social attitudes. One must have some capacity to appreciate friendship and enmity, intimacy and nonacquaintance; and one must have some sense of when to intervene or interrupt or respond, whether in speech or work or any other basic dimensions of social intercourse. Without such immensely complex learning and associated attitudes, social intercourse would be impossible; indeed it *does* break down when an individual suffers a serious failure or loss in some area of this complex web of learning and attitude. This web of learning, with its associated motivational influences, is an essential condition for ongoing community life—even if, in restricted contexts, there may be differing views or habits regarding a particular act, or kind of act, or pattern of conduct.

All this is so very fundamental that we take it for granted—as well we may do in most cases. Even children of five or six have achieved a great deal of this learning and acquired the basic attitudes—they are, as we say, "socialized" to a substantial extent by then, though not enough so to be responsible under law.

It is because of the *presumption of fact* that we all share this background that we can efficiently focus our attention in the criminal law on a very few highly significant features of relevant conduct. We can ask: Did the person *know* (realize, believe) that the behavior was causing a certain harm (or likely to cause it)? Did the person *intend* to cause the harm? Did the person act *voluntarily?* Such questions are significant if we presume that, at the time the belief developed and the intent was formed, the person effectively shared, at least to some minimal extent, in the web of social learning and attitudes that give such beliefs and intentions their usual basic significance.

We may imagine a homicidal person—for example, a person with paranoid delusions—who is suffering a gross disruption of the skills and attitudes that enable most of us to respond intelligibly, even if at times mistakenly, to the friendship-neutrality-enmity dimension of social intercourse. Such a person may be aware of the unlawfulness of killing, and may sufficiently share in the common background-nexus of values to recognize the need for excuse or justification. But he believes that he *has* justification. The bizarre nature of his "justification" leads us to recognize his underlying derangement. It leads us to recognize that the normally presumed skills for discriminating friend and enemy are in him deranged. And we also recognize his derangement in regard to the normally presumed range of certain basic emotions and attitudes to people. The paranoid knows that he is killing a person, knows that it is contrary to the law, and still he deliberately and intentionally does it. Such knowledge, deliberation, and intent have lost their full significance as "mental elements" of crime because the usual presumption of fact about the background context of skills and attitudes is radically inapplicable here. These elements no longer reflect the ability to respond to legal norms that we usually presume; they do not reflect response-ability.

Or, again by way of example, we can imagine a person whose intense manic or depressed mood has from some cause or other become so intractable and dominant that he no longer can bring countervailing moods or emotions to bear, no longer can weigh the relevant social and environmental factors. The hypothetical experimental subject discussed earlier would be a case in point: when the experimenter activates the electrical current in the subject's brain, the subject becomes overwhelmed with anger (or anxiety, or fear, or pleasure—all are producible). A person in a deep, agitated psychotic depression would illustrate such mental disturbance, as would a person in full-blown manic excitement. Some persons with brain damage or pathology are subject to fits of overwhelming blind fury or aggression. They may be "rational" enough to form intentions consistent with their fury, and to act in a more or less coherent manner on such intentions. But they are utterly unresponsive to anything relevant to arousing other moods, or to allaying fury—and in that regard their intention and their conduct are throughout permeated by irrationality while the fit of anger continues.[20]

The other side of the coin is that a lack of some specific mental capacity does not always permeate and subvert all other aspects of the mind's workings. Human beings have enormous powers of compensation and adaptation. Even gross and demonstrable brain damage can occasionally be partly or fully compensated. Only the most acutely disturbed or chronically dilapidated persons approach *total* nonrationality. An assessment of the background learning and attitudes of a person must therefore take into account not only his weaknesses but his strengths.

This in turn forces a far more general distinction that, however obvious it may be, cannot go unmentioned here. It is the distinction between lack of capacity and mere failure to exercise—or to exercise diligently enough— capacities that exist. Here we have to do with mundane flaws of character as well as specific pathology. The law expects us to compensate for such traits as quick temper, weakness of will, cruelty, greed, ambition, and hatred. These are paradigmatic sources of the crimes to which the law and its sanctions are most directly addressed. It is normally reasonable to expect us to compensate for such character traits when they generate impulses to unlawful conduct. Moreover, we can often compensate for defects that are more patently pathological. So a delimited lack of capacity need not amount to a lack of capacity on the whole; it merely calls for more diligent exercise of other compensatory capacities, if such exist.

We also need to distinguish between: (1) a child's normal lack of the background web of learning and attitudes; (2) a lack of such background that is due to having been brought up in a radically alien culture; and (3) the lack that is due to either a personal mental incapacity ever to develop the skills, or individual mental pathology that has led to a temporary or

20. This may be the place to note for the record that the narcotic "addict" who thieves in order to get money to buy his day's supply of the drug does *not* belong in the category just discussed. The example of the addict used in an analogous context in Fingarette (1972), pp. 189–190, was in error. The image of the "heroin addict" that governed that 1972 discussion was later recognized to be myth rather than reality (Fingarette, 1975). See also Chapter 10, supra.

permanent loss of such skills. The first type of case would be exemplified
by a five-year-old girl who is convinced that there are bears that roam the
house at night. We consider this a normal childhood lack of the background learning and attitudes. An adult from a backlands African village,
completely steeped in the cultural lore about witches and witchcraft,
could illustrate the second kind of lack. Such a person might emigrate to a
Europeanized community and in "self-defense" attack someone who
shows all the standard signs of casting mortal spells. Here, we may
suppose, the background web of learning and attitudes is so different from
the Europeanized norms and beliefs, so permeated with a different understanding of the world, that even the voluntary, knowing, intentional, and
even premeditated killing of the "witch" simply does not have the significance it otherwise would. This immigrant is a grave social danger, but
criminal condemnation hardly seems fitting.[21] It is the third kind of case,
individual pathology, that is at issue in these discussions of Mental
Disability.

C. *Summary of the Discussion About the Presumptions of Fact*

In broadest terms, then, there is a deep and tacit presumption that an
individual shares, at least to some minimal practical extent, in a background of basic concepts, perceptions, values, skills, and attitudes common
to the members of the community. This is not at all the same as presuming
that any individual agrees with, or responds in the same way as, everyone
else or even anyone else, or that all individuals always act in the same way
or support the same specific policies or institutions. When these presumptions are valid, then we can simply assess conduct by asking: Did the
person do that voluntarily? Was it done intentionally? Did the person
know the particular facts material to that particular act as relevant to
standards of law? A few basic questions tell all—or at least enough for the
purpose of the serious matters contemplated by law. For the intention is
seen against a (presumed) background of shared understanding and skills
and attitudes.

But when there is real doubt as to the existence or integrity of this
background of skills, attitudes, and perceptions, then we cannot take for
granted the usual crucial significance that these particular features of
conduct have for assessing responsibility. It works the other way around as

---

21. See *R. v. Machekequonabe* (1898), in which the deliberate killing of an "evil
spirit" in human form was held by the judges to be manslaughter.

well: when, after reviewing the circumstances, we come to realize that we have serious doubt whether we can take a person's intent or knowledge or deliberation to be criminally significant in the usual way, *that* is the sign that we have come to see irrationality, come to see that somehow the background skills and attitudes are gravely awry. The discovery is typically not one of temporal sequence but of an emerging awareness simultaneously that the "mental elements" don't have their usual significance, and that the background mental processes are grossly flawed or deranged.

D. *The Jury Decision: Are the Presumptions of Fact Applicable in the Particular Case?*

We have said that rationality has two basic dimensions: there is the dimension that concerns certain presumptions of fact, and there is the dimension of decision as to the applicability of these presumptions in a particular case. The decisional dimension now needs comment.

The jury must first make a complex comparison of a factual kind. On the one hand, it must take into account the specific facts as to the mental powers of the individual in question. On the other hand, it must set this, by way of comparison, against the framework of powers normally presumed and essential for responsibly law-abiding conduct in the circumstances. To some extent these things can be measured quantitatively by tests; and, qualitatively, they can be richly described or implied in narratives of personal history and conduct. But the innumerable variations and nuances in these many different capacities as they are relevant to particular circumstances are ultimately utterly beyond our powers to describe fully, or even to list or explicitly identify fully. Crucial as this complex of powers is for normal social intercourse, there is ultimately only one way we can—and in everyday life do—assess what is needed, what powers a person actually has, and the relation of the two. We do this, ultimately, by a practical judgment, made in the light of the fullest possible information, by someone who is in practice already possessed of the capacities, i.e., the responsible lay person.

Such decisions are not uncommon in the serious occupations of life. We expect expert practitioners—whether in the professions, business, or practical arts—to use their practical mastery as a basis for evaluating apprentices in the field. The apprentice's supervisor may be able to collect some precise or even quantified information about the subject's abilities, but the final judgment is a practical one, not a conclusion rigorously deduced from precise data. We rely on such practical judgments in all aspects of life—

from our most intimate personal affairs to the selection of our political leaders. And we do so knowing that such judgments are fallible.

But there are more than complex factual judgments to be made here. There is a policy decision. The discrepancy between a defendant's actual capacities and those normally presumed must be assessed in the light of the specific circumstances of the particular act. The jury must decide whether the discrepancy is enough, and of suitable kind, to ascribe nonresponsibility. This requires getting a good grasp of the facts of the particular case and having a sense of the larger context. Against that background the policy aspect of the decision takes the form: Is it still reasonable, in the context of crime and punishment, for society to expect responsible conduct of such a person in such circumstances?—Or is it more reasonable in this particular case to give up such otherwise normal expectations and deal with the problem in a different perspective?

The members of a jury—not legal or medical experts—constitute the body best qualified to make such a decision when the matter is in dispute. They are qualified by reason of their status as responsible lay members of the community sworn to use their practical mastery of the art of responsible conduct under law in everyday life; and they also reflect lay attitudes. They need not have each been always perfectly law-*abiding,* of course; but they have the capacities required to act responsibly in regard to law. They are expected to use these capacities as the basis for judging the capacities of others—and, if narrative news and informal reports are to be believed, it appears that they usually make the effort sincerely.

It is not, after all, as if such a factual-decisional "finding of fact" by the jury were unique in the law.[22] Examples of the same sort of dual factual-decisional jury role in legal "fact-finding" are to be seen in the application of such concepts as "due care" and "the reasonable man."[23] "Rationality" is one more such concept.

22. See *King v. U.S.* (1967), p. 389.

23. "There is a limit to the 'concretisation' of the negligence issue. . . . For instance, the rule that a motorist should not proceed at an excessive speed can hardly be stated in a helpful form. . . . What is an excessive speed depends upon factors too numerous to be exhaustively catalogued" (Williams, 1961, p. 105). Speaking of the concepts of negligence and of due care and caution under the circumstances, Perkins says that the number of variables is so great "that it would be futile to attempt to establish a rule for each possible combination. The only possibility was to test such conduct by a standard and the standard formulated was that of a reasonable man under the circumstances" (Perkins, 1957, p. 665).

III: "DEGREES" OF IRRATIONALITY

How finely can discriminations as to rationality or irrationality be made in connection with criminal responsibility? How finely *should* they be made?

We propose that there be three options available to the jury: (1) *Disability of Mind*—in the conduct in question, the defendant for the most part lacked the capacity for rational conduct in regard to the criminal significance of the act; (2) *Partial Disability of Mind*—the defendant was for the most part rational but did suffer a material lack of the kind; or (3) *No Disability of Mind*—no material lack of rationality.

Our reasons for establishing these three options are as follows: (a) The whole thrust of our argument is, of course, that under a system of law based on personal responsibility, it is vital to make *some* distinction between rationality and irrationality. (b) The complexities of a criminal trial generally are so great as to compel the maximal degree of simplification when submitting ultimate issues to the jury. This would suggest as an ideal a simple yes-or-no option. (c) As a practical matter, however, there are many kinds of criminal mental disability cases where the two-option set leads to conclusions that are unacceptably extreme. A middle term seems urgently needed. (d) Related to this latter point is the fact that in actual practice, in one legalistic guise or another, juries do distinguish an intermediate condition in regard to the presence or absence of mental disability. Sometimes this is done openly and is recognized by the court, as when the "diminished capacity" or "diminished responsibility" concepts are applied.[24] More often it is done covertly, either by use of legalistic facades such as finding guilt for a lesser crime because of purported "absence of specific intent,"[25] or by simply defying the legal formulas, as

24. The "diminished responsibility" defense in England allows a verdict of manslaughter in place of what would otherwise be a conviction for murder if the defendant "was suffering from such abnormality of mind (whether arising from a condition of arrested or retarded development of mind or any inherent causes or induced by disease or injury) as substantially impaired his mental responsibility for his acts and omissions in doing or being a party to the killing" (Homicide Act, 1957, s.2(1); see generally Edwards, 1958, and Appendix II, infra). In the United States the concept of "diminished responsibility" has not met with acceptance, but the closely related concept of "diminished mental capacity" has been accepted in one or another form in a number of jurisdictions, California being one that has developed the defense at some length. See the full discussion of such defenses in Part III, supra. See generally Goldstein (1967), pp. 194–202; Dix (1971); and Hasse (1972).

25. The reference here is, of course, to the so-called "specific intent exception," which in one variant or another has been available in England and the U.S. as a defense based on intoxication, and aimed at mitigation of culpability, since the

when juries simply fly in the face of evidence *and* the legal definitions, and arbitrarily bring in a conviction on a lesser crime because they cannot find any other way to recognize the role of the mental disability at the time of the offense.[26]

Of course, it is true that even aside from the complexities of current concepts, juries (or judges in the role of fact-finder) often have difficulty in settling upon the substance of the appropriate option. This is because the "easy" cases are often disposed of without the necessity of formal trial. The fact-finder's burden is the heavy one of making crucial distinctions where no rule provides the answer.

IV: SOME "HARD" CASES

There are two kinds of personalities that often turn up in the criminal law context—the "psychopath" and the hardened professional criminal—that may seem to be inherently "hard cases" if one tries to apply the concept of "capacity for rational conduct in regard to the criminal significance of the act." We can gain deeper insight into that concept by examining the questions such cases evoke.

The difficulties that seem to arise do so, broadly speaking, in the following way. Individuals with such personalities may manifest a bizarre insensitivity or a purposefully cultivated but now deep-rooted callousness that enables them to commit crimes of peculiarly inhuman or cruel kinds. Could it be said, then, that on the whole each "lacks capacity for rational conduct in regard to the criminal significance of the act" because of a gross incapacity for emotional responsiveness? And if one did make such a

---

mid-nineteenth century at least. See the systematic discussion in Part III, supra. On intoxication as a mitigating defense, see generally J. Hall (1960), Chapter 14. It is widely recognized that the "specific intent" doctrine was acceptable on policy grounds because it seemed to provide a device for mitigating but not negating the culpability of the drunken offender. It has also been widely assumed that the device is based on legally sound reasoning keyed to absence of an essential mental element of the crime, and not on the mere ad hoc desire to allow mitigation. The latter assumptions, however, have been increasingly challenged by modern commentators and (recently) by some English and American courts. Part III, supra, presents a systematic demonstration of the invalidity and pragmatic unreliability of the legal reasoning on which the "specific intent exception" is based, in spite of the fact that the result sought can be seen intuitively to be desirable. The D.O.M. doctrine brings out a proper and reliable legal rationale for an intoxication defense in mitigation. See Chapter 13, Section III, supra.

26. See Goldstein (1967), pp. 62–63.

judgment, and if it was also conceded that such persons could not be held culpable for having originated this incapacity, would this not, under the D.O.M. doctrine, preclude criminal condemnation and punishment for such conduct? And would not this result, in turn, be so scandalously unacceptable to our conscience as to amount to a refutation of the validity of the D.O.M. concept for assessing criminal responsibility?

The beginning of insight here is to go beyond a merely schematic consideration of such categories in the abstract. Let us consider first the question of the professional killer.

Presumably it is established that the defendant killed in a manner showing gross and ingrained insensitivity to the human significance of the act; it is this characteristic insensitivity that would presumably raise the "incapacity" issue. But no *one* such contextually isolated characteristic can establish incapacity in the relevant sense. For understandable reasons, many persons develop a role-specific or context-specific ability to exclude certain responses—emotional or otherwise—that would normally be present in human behavior: the medical student learns to dissect cadavers without experiencing the emotional reactions that are natural for most people; the surgeon learns to cut up living human bodies without responding emotionally in the way others normally would; the soldier can learn to be with the wounded and dead, or to wound and kill others, without the feeling-shock that initially is ubiquitous. We may approve, or at least accept, such immunity in some individuals and deplore it in others. We do not consider these people irrational, however. The failure to respond in a sensitive way has a larger context that we intuitively recognize to be relevant. The D.O.M. concept calls for us to look at that larger context. In the kinds of persons cited as examples, the remainder of their mental powers, together with the consciousness they have of their special circumstances, makes it possible for them to rationally apply the relevant criminal law standards. So we would by no means view the surgeon as criminally nonresponsible if he were to injure another person maliciously.

The professional killer may also be, in the relevant sense, a rational person. He may have developed the ability not to be distracted by humane feelings—to be simply unresponsive, rather than having to "control" them—when ordered to kill for money in the course of "business." This alone should not lead us to say that he lacks adequate capacities to grasp the practical bearing of the criminal law on his conduct. Indeed, a jury might very well find in some cases that this callousness was his own doing, a consciously cultivated trait, and hence something in regard to which he was culpable. But in any case, one who led an otherwise emotionally responsive social life could not adduce such a cultivated, specialized insensitivity as proof of irrationality.

On the other hand, we might find that such a criminal's choice of career is itself rooted in deep-seated blindness to the significance of human life, as is reflected in many other ways, directly and indirectly, in the individual's life history. If the facts do show chronic generalized failure to develop human relationships—i.e., a generalized incapacity to respond with feeling to the sufferings, agonies, or death of human beings—then we do indeed have grounds to view the individual as criminally irrational. This is likely, in real life, to be a judgment supported by other features characteristic of such personalities, for such a deep blindness cannot exist in isolation; it will pervade and corrupt generally all activities in which the worth of human life and feelings are at all central.

The professional criminal who really does show such broad signs of irrationality is not going to be a callous but otherwise psychologically normal person; instead, he will in fact often fall into such medical categories as "schizophrenic" or "sociopathic personality." Schizophrenic disorders can be blatantly expressive of irrationality. But the "psychopathic" pattern may seem to be a "hard case" to classify in regard to rationality. The categories of persons variously referred to under such vague rubrics as "psychopathic personality," "sociopath," "antisocial personality," and "severe character disorder" are persons whose daily lives are pervaded by signs of failure to respond to human values or moral norms or even to evident prudential considerations of a selfish kind. Yet these persons do not clearly show the range of other characteristics associated with such diagnostic categories as "schizophrenia"—e.g., hallucination, withdrawal from human relations, flatness of affect, and thought disorders.

The inchoate and fluctuating nature of these sociopathic personality patterns is evidenced by the "wastebasket" nature of the concept itself as officially defined.[27] Certainly the law should not be seduced into reifying such abstract and controversial categories of personality. The problems

27. The *Diagnostic and Statistical Manual of Mental Disorders* (1968) of the American Psychiatric Association now states that the term *antisocial personality* is to be used in reference to "individuals who are basically unsocialized and whose behavior pattern brings them repeatedly into conflict with society. They are incapable of significant loyalty to individuals, groups, or social values. They are grossly selfish, callous, irresponsible, impulsive, and unable to feel guilt or to learn from

posed are real for the criminal law, but the medical categories are not the basis on which to make the legal decisions. The practical point is that it is a truly difficult task to decide whether an individual who suffers some significant lack of capacity to take into account in his conduct relevant moral, legal, and prudential norms still retains enough other powers of mind to compensate adequately. The "wastebasket" psychiatric categories used in this area of "personality disorder" tell us nothing on this question. And certainly the myth that what is at issue is *simply* a propensity to repeated violations of law—a myth unfortunately perpetuated in the ALI Model Penal Code insanity test[28]—has not helped understanding of the problem.

The question can only be settled case by case in the light of all the facts about each particular case and in the context of the expectations on which criminal law, as applicable in everyday life, is based. This can only be settled by persons who do have a practical mastery of what it takes to get along responsibly in everyday life—the jury. They must decide whether in the particular case it is reasonable to expect responsible conduct of a person such as has been portrayed to them, or whether it is more reasonable to forego such expectations and to deal with the problem from a different perspective than that of responsibility under law.

A final caveat may be in order. Irrational behavior, though it is in lay terms irrational, may in some scientific contexts be "intelligible," i.e., explicable. For some policy purposes these explanations may be important to society. But this is in no way to say that the behavior is intelligible in terms of the norms and practices of everyday social intercourse and its associated morality and common sense. Yet it is the latter kind of intelligibility that is at issue here. It is the latter kind of intelligibility on

---

experience and punishment. Frustration tolerance is low. They tend to blame others or offer plausible rationalizations for their behavior. *A mere history of repeated legal or social offenses is not sufficient to justify this diagnosis*" (p. 38, emphasis added). The three conditions that should be met for applying this diagnosis are: (1) "the disorder should begin before the age of 15"; (2) "the clinical picture should be of antisocial behavior involving multiple areas of social functioning"; (3) "*there should be no other psychiatric illness that could explain the symptoms*" (Freedman et al., 1976, p. 650 [emphasis added]). Woodruff et al. (1974), pp. 145–146, state that "satisfactory data on the prevalence of antisocial personality are lacking. This is partly because of the failure to reach general agreement about a definition"—or, we might add, failure to reach general agreement even about a *name* for the condition.

28. Section 4.01, and Comment (Tentative Draft #4, 1955).

which the law is based and addressed to the community; and it is that perspective—a perspective that, by definition, all responsible laymen share—that is essential, therefore, if responsibility and culpability are to make sense.[29]

29. "For the criminal law is not a mere happenstance or a technology remote from the main stream of human history. It is an institution which represents more than 700 years of thoughtful experience in dealing with the primary problems of society. It was not imposed by a hereditary elite, but is instead the product of the commerce of many keen minds with popular ideas. Not only were custom and public opinion the original sources of the common law, but laymen also participated in the processes of criminal law as members of legislatures, grand and petit juries, and the police force. Lawyers, judges, and the writers of treatises mediated between science and the flow of daily life. Unlike the physical sciences and technologies, the law of crimes therefore represents the layman's thought and values clarified by the sensitivity of bench and bar to the progress of knowledge" (Hall, 1964, p. 1045; see also Fingarette, 1972, pp. 55-59).

15

The Practical Implications and Impact of
the Disability of Mind Doctrine

I

Law is so inherently concerned with the practical conduct of human affairs that even a study of fundamental doctrine must inevitably, at some point, raise such questions as: How does the theory translate into specific provisions of law and trial process? How does it work when applied to standard cases and to significant borderline or controversial kinds of cases? What would be the major practical impact on the principal interests involved? Will it weigh on the side of the defendants or the prosecution? Will it benefit the legal profession specifically? Society as a whole? To such questions, at least in overview, we now address ourselves.

In this final chapter we shall translate the D.O.M. doctrine into language closer to specific provisions of law and trial process, illustrating specifically the expectable results and comparing them with the workings of current doctrine. Then, finally, we shall discuss the overall impact of such a shift in terms of various major perspectives—the defense, the prosecution, the legal profession, social welfare and safety, justice, and our legal system as a whole. In Appendix I, which follows this chapter, we present a set of suggested Model Jury Instructions intended to serve for *any* kind of case where the defense is based, partly or wholly, on the claim that Mental Disability, of whatever kind and from whatever source, played a material role in the allegedly criminal conduct.

The following outline and discussion are designed to explain the setting that would make it possible, under the D.O.M. doctrine, for the trial jury to make an extremely simple sequence of basic decisions. The gist of that sequence is this:[1] The jury first decides the question as to guilt or innocence on each count. There are no artificial restrictions as to what evidence they can consider—they can consider *any* evidence genuinely bearing on the question whether an essential element of an alleged criminal act existed, even if the evidence was offered in connection with the D.O.M. issue. Having determined guilt or innocence on each count, and if the defendant is found Not Guilty of all, the jury have finished their task. Only if the defendant has been found guilty on at least one count do they proceed to consideration of the D.O.M. issue. They then ask the two basic D.O.M. questions: Was the defendant mentally disabled at the time of the criminal act; and if so, was this disability culpable in origin? When they have answered these two questions they have completed their task. They report their findings as to guilt and innocence on each count; then they report the finding as to D.O.M.

Such a process conforms to the basic analysis we have presented. It keeps separate two questions: (1) Were the essential elements of a defined criminal act present? and (2) Was the defendant, in performing that act, so mentally disabled as not to be criminally responsible? This simple basic pattern is conceptually sound. As a practical matter it is far more simple to grasp and to apply than are the current doctrines, which interweave the issues and do so in ways that are logically arbitrary and psychologically unrealistic.

II: STATUTORY FRAMEWORK

We have argued that the D.O.M. doctrine is profoundly in tune with basic common law principle.[2] We believe that in substantial measure it could be implemented on that basis. Nevertheless, if one is introducing reform aimed at simplicity, universality, and reliability, it seems desirable to make certain aspects of the matter statutorily explicit and to tie up certain loose ends. We therefore propose certain kinds of statutory support for imple-

---

1. See the full discussion in Section III, infra, the theoretical background discussion in Chapter 13, supra, and the suggested Model Jury Instructions in Appendix I, infra.

2. See Chapter 13, supra.

menting the D.O.M. doctrine. We shall list the types of statutory action proposed, and then discuss each in turn.

1. The question of burden of proof in regard to proving D.O.M. should be settled by statute.
2. There should be provision for automatic remand for mental examination of those found to have suffered Disability of Mind. Provision also should be made for authority to take welfare and protective measures where appropriate, under suitable guidelines.
3. Explicit provision should be made for appropriate mitigation of punishment of those found to have suffered partial or full Disability of Mind.
4. The "floor" crimes—offenses of criminal negligence—should be statutorily explicit in regard to D.O.M. Statutory action should also assure that such crimes are adequate in scope in regard to the different kinds of acts covered. Some of the issues connected with these statutory proposals have been amply discussed elsewhere in this book. Such discussion will be cited here but not belabored. There are a few issues that call for elaboration here, however.

1. *Burden of Proof*

We of course assume the usual principle that the prosecution must show beyond a reasonable doubt all the specific elements going to show culpability. But we shall also consistently assume that the defense has the burden of showing by a preponderance of the evidence the existence of any mental incapacity for rational conduct asserted at any stage of the defense argument.

This stance is not logically necessitated by the D.O.M. doctrine. The entire burden could be placed on the prosecution (as is currently the case with the Insanity defense in the Federal courts) to prove beyond a reasonable doubt the absence of the claimed mental disability. But we believe that our earlier analysis strongly suggests the attitude we have adopted.[3] The reasoning that we have offered is, briefly, that to claim exemption under the D.O.M. doctrine from the presumption of rationality is neither to deny nor to admit any particular element of the offense charged, nor is it to offer argument, excuse, or justification in direct response to the accusation. It is, broadly speaking, to claim partial or total exemption from the criminal accusatory-condemnatory process itself. Thus a claim of Disability of Mind is not, per se, a challenge to the prosecution's case. It is a plea to circumvent, at least in some respect, the prosecutory process and aim.

---

3. See Chapter 13, Section II, supra, main text between notes 14 and 16.

Therefore, though not logically necessitated, it seems reasonable that all claims as to irrationality of mind should be a special burden on the defendant. As is then normally the case, this should require only a showing on the preponderance of the evidence. On the other hand, wherever a specific link in the chain of culpability is at issue—as in showing culpable origin of the D.O.M.—the burden of proof beyond reasonable doubt should as usual lie with the prosecution. An analogous pattern is used in many state jurisdictions.[4] This pattern works out readily and intelligibly in the D.O.M. context. (As might be imagined, the pattern is logically even simpler if the burden remains always on the prosecution throughout; but we do not present such a version here.)

There is indeed a surface paradox in calling on the prosecution to prove culpability as to the origin of the D.O.M. if, as would often be the case, the prosecution is also denying that the D.O.M. existed. But the air of paradox depends on looking at the matter in abstraction from the trial realities. For example, where D.O.M. consisting in intoxication is claimed by the defense, the prosecution will typically not challenge that defendant had been drinking or using an intoxicating drug; what it may well challenge is that the amount used, under the conditions, sufficed to induce irrationality to such an extent as constituted Disability of Mind. So the prosecution can attempt to prove, with a clear logical conscience and perfectly good common sense, that insofar as the defendant was intoxicated—and the jury will ultimately decide as to that—the intoxication was due to the prior voluntary use of intoxicants, which is admitted on all hands, and indeed insisted on by the defense.

On the other hand, the defendant may succeed in showing a condition of Mental Disability, for example a state of gross mental confusion, and yet offer no explanation as to how it came about. Or the defense may propose the theory that the confusion had its origin in some nonculpable way such as a temporary derangement of brain function due to an arteriosclerotic condition. It should then be incumbent on the prosecution

---

4. In the insanity defense, about half of the states call for the defense to carry the burden of going forward with the evidence and persuading by a preponderance of the evidence. About half of the states, and most Federal courts, require the defense to go forward with evidence to raise the issue, but then require the prosecution to prove absence of insanity beyond a reasonable doubt. See Goldstein (1967), pp. 110–115; Brooks (1974), pp. 304–307; and, generally, "Modern Status of Rules as to Burden and Sufficiency of Proof of Mental Irresponsibility in a Criminal Case," 17 A.L.R. 3d 146.

to prove—if it so claims—that in truth the confusion was precipitated culpably, e.g., by prior heavy drinking. If the prosecution cannot prove beyond a reasonable doubt that, insofar as such mental confusion did exist, it was the outcome of prior drinking, then the defendant is of course entitled to the benefit of the doubt, and the fact-finder should not find culpability in the context of origin of the D.O.M.

2. *Post-Trial Welfare and Safety Measures*

A result regularly distinctive of the D.O.M. doctrine would be that any finding of D.O.M. that would appear in the verdict would assure a post-verdict medical examination to determine—*outside* an accusatory process—if the D.O.M. was of a kind that has persisted and still constitutes a comparable danger of criminally offending conduct. The reader is referred to the discussions of this issue elsewhere in this book.[5] It should suffice to say here, then, that we have no specific proposals for this highly complex and controversial area of mental disability law. Our only concern is the principle that whatever the policies deemed best for dealing with mentally disabled offenders, they should be applicable evenhandedly, by statutory requirement, to *all* offenders who are found by a jury to have suffered Mental Disability of whatever kind and from whatever cause.

3. *Mitigation*

While it is true that for the most part judges do have significant discretionary powers in regard to sentencing those culpable for criminal acts, it would be desirable to establish explicit public policy, and to formulate guidelines, in regard to the specific mitigatory implications of a D.O.M. finding. The general principles here can be stated simply enough, and they are obvious. The precise details would have to be worked out in relation to the actual current sentencing policies in the particular jurisdiction.

The general import of a finding of D.O.M. is that there is lesser or no criminal responsibility. However, this must be assessed in context. No completely numerical rule is possible. So, for example, a finding of full D.O.M. implies less responsibility, and hence greater mitigation of condemnation and punishment, than a finding of partial D.O.M. A finding that the D.O.M. is culpable, however, will *always* entail that the defendant was to some extent responsible, culpable, and hence punishable. A finding that

5. See the main text following note 7, Chapter 13, supra; and see also the further discussion, infra, in Section IV of this chapter.

the D.O.M. was nonculpable will increase the mitigatory implication; and if there is full Disability of Mind that is nonculpable, then of course there is no criminal responsibility whatsoever, and hence no basis for any criminal condemnation or punishment at all.

The baseline from which mitigation is measured is always in principle the sentence that would normally be appropriate for the kind of crime in question when D.O.M. is not an issue.

Obviously the judge will have to exercise discretion under the above general guidelines to adapt the sentence—if any—to the particular circumstances.

Such judicial discretion is important in all cases, but it would be particularly so in the relatively rarer cases where the defendant, in the earlier causing of the D.O.M., was either reckless as to the specific harm ultimately risked, or even intended to cause that harm.[6] Such cases would include, for example, the man who stops off at a bar on his way to work as a railroad train operator, drinks heavily, and subsequently causes a wreck because of his negligence. Here recklessness has its root in the awareness that existed, at the outset of drinking, of the danger of causing just such accidents as a result of drunkenness. Another example is that of the man intent on a criminal project who drinks or uses a drug to "nerve" himself, and is found to have taken enough to have been partially Mentally Disabled on the occasion of successfully carrying out the project. It is plain that the facts as stated establish crimes of recklessness or intent respectively, and do so independently of the D.O.M. doctrine. Instructions defining the criminal acts will have made this clear. But the D.O.M. statute pertaining to mitigation must make it explicit that where such knowledge or intent (or other requisite mental element of the crime) was already present in the *causing* of the D.O.M., *no* mitigation is called for in spite of the D.O.M. finding. This is readily accomplished by a special Jury Instruction,[7] to be used only where the defendant is found guilty of such a crime. Such an Instruction must call for the amplified report that there was partial or full Disability of Mind, "Culpably Caused with Recklessness" (or with Intent, etc.).

4. *The "Floor" Crimes of Criminal Negligence*

It has been pointed out elsewhere in this book[8] that a condition of Disability of Mind is inherently a criminally dangerous condition. The

6. See Chapter 13, Section III, supra.
7. Appendix I, Instructions 16a, b, c, infra.
8. Chapter 13, Section III, supra, main text at note 22.

defendant may take active measures to cause death, for example by shooting, stabbing, or purposely striking the victim. In such a case, the defendant will be found guilty of the intentional crime (murder or voluntary manslaughter), and may also be found to have suffered D.O.M. But where there is full Mental Disability, we may see, for example, the patently *un*intentional, *un*cognizant conduct of the person who is "blind drunk." Such a person—psychologically speaking—has no *mens rea.*

It is essential to the D.O.M. doctrine that one who causes harm while culpably suffering D.O.M. shall not escape criminal condemnation and punishment, no matter how "unconscious" he was at the time of the offense.[9] Since the defendant manifests, in such extreme cases, no mental states pertinent to crime, it remains essential—and is perfectly logical— that he be held culpable by reference to objective standards of care. In short, the gross negligence of the defendant in causing the harm establishes the offense as criminal.[10]

The common law provides for crimes of criminal negligence in regard to the causing of grievous bodily injury or death. But it is reasonable, in the context of D.O.M. offenses, to make explicit and clear by statute that a wider range of acts, when performed in a grossly negligent way, are criminal offenses. So, for example, the causing of substantial property damage (at some specified dollar level or above) should be a criminal offense if done with gross negligence. In this way, one who was culpably Mentally Disabled—grossly intoxicated, for example—and who caused such damage without any intent or even adequate awareness of what was happening, could still be held criminally culpable for the "floor" offense of criminal negligence, rather than being allowed to escape on the ground of absence of any *mens rea.* Similarly, one who breaks and enters at night, particularly with a deadly weapon, or who flourishes a deadly weapon in an assaultive way, should not be allowed to escape punishment by a showing of gross intoxication to the point where intent necessary for burglary, or for assault, can be doubted.

As to such cases of extreme intoxication, the law should be made clear in appropriate statute: one who deviates grossly from a reasonable objec-

9. The fundamental importance of this principle is brought out, for example, in the discussions of LaFave and Scott (1972), p. 331, and Goldstein (1967), p. 199.

10. Of course, if the defendant was not by objective standards grossly negligent in causing the harm, then there would be no finding of criminal negligence—nor in all fairness should there be. To hold otherwise would amount to making it criminal *merely* to drink and cause harm, even where the behavior might have conformed perfectly to appropriate standards of care.

tive standard of care—as such defendants plainly have done—and who does so in ways that either constitute criminal harms or are peculiarly closely related to such harms, should be held criminally culpable. The only exception would be, of course, if the D.O.M. is nonculpable in origin, as it is not in the case of voluntary intoxication.

Given a suitable range of such "floor" offenses of criminal negligence, the judge would then instruct the jury on the criminal negligence offense relevant to the case, and would do this, of course, as part of the normal sequence of instructions as to the counts on which the defendant may be found guilty.

The result of the preceding approach is then, in a nutshell, as follows: If the defendant is found to have unlawfully committed the physical act or caused the particular result, as contemplated in the statute, the defendant *must* then either be found guilty on one or more counts of intentional or knowing crime as alleged, *or* be found guilty of the relevant count of criminal negligence. There is no escape from this much.

If the defendant is found to have committed the crime of criminal negligence and to have had culpable D.O.M., *no* mitigation is in order. The defendant may have had full D.O.M. that was *non*culpable, however. Then the verdict would be: "Guilty of [the offense of criminal negligence], with Nonculpable Disability of Mind." This means, as usual, that the defendant did commit the defined criminal act but was not criminally responsible and is therefore not to be criminally condemned or punished.

III: FORMING THE D.O.M. VERDICT:
THE PATTERN IN OUTLINE

We can now systematically analyze the specific impact of the D.O.M. plea in various kinds of factual contexts. We shall do so by laying out the pattern for forming these verdicts. This pattern is here presented in an expository form; it is presented in more specific terms in the Suggested Model Jury Instructions in Appendix I.

The jury should have had read to it, prior to any comment on D.O.M., the main body of the usual instructions appropriate to each of the counts. This will always include, of course, the "floor" count of criminal negligence. Typically the judge will instruct the jury as to the elements of each of the counts, and he will inform them that it is the burden of the prosecution to prove beyond a reasonable doubt the existence of all such elements. The jury is instructed to reach a determination as to Guilty or

Not Guilty in regard to each of the counts by considering all the evidence, including evidence of mental condition insofar as it genuinely bears on the existence of any element of the crime.

The jury should be instructed to proceed to consider the plea of Disability of Mind after completing all determinations as to guilt or innocence; and it should consider D.O.M. only if the defendant has been found Guilty on at least one count. Lacking a finding of Guilty on any count, the jury need not enter upon any consideration of the D.O.M. plea.

The jury, if it does proceed to the D.O.M. issue, can make one of the four basic D.O.M. findings.[11] After it reports all the verdicts as to guilt or innocence, it will report its D.O.M. finding. The four basic D.O.M. findings are:

1. Nonculpable Disability of Mind
2. Culpable Disability of Mind
3. Nonculpable Partial Disability of Mind
4. Culpable Partial Disability of Mind

Each possible finding will shortly be defined and discussed, but in order to give a more concrete sense of the pattern we shall first present five brief illustrations.

Illustration 1. The defendant is charged with first-degree murder—he allegedly had an argument with the deceased, went home to get a gun, returned, and shot the deceased and killed him. The defendant enters a D.O.M. plea based on evidence as to gross intoxication. In considering whether the defendant deliberated, the jury will take into account *all* the evidence insofar as it realistically bears on the issue. The evidence shows beyond a reasonable doubt that the defendant did deliberately kill the deceased. All other requisite elements of first-degree murder are found. The defendant is found Guilty of first-degree murder. Having found the defendant Guilty of the alleged crime, the jury then examines the evidence in order to make a D.O.M. finding. The jury finds that the defendant was grossly intoxicated, to an extent constituting lack of mental capacity for conduct that is rational in regard to the criminal significance of the act he committed. The jury finds that this played the chief role in the defen-

11. The only variation on these basic findings occurs in the rare cases where recklessness or intent as to the ultimate specific offense existed prior to the D.O.M. and in causal relation to it. In addition to the discussion supra in the present Section, see the discussion in the main text of Chapter 13, Section III, supra, between notes 19 and 20, and Instructions 16a, b, c, in Appendix I, infra.

dant's acting as he did. The jury finds culpability as to the context of origin, since the defendant, initially sober, brought about the disability by his prior conduct (i.e., his drinking or drug use). The jury therefore reports: "Guilty of First-Degree Murder, Culpable Disability of Mind." The defendant's condemnation and punishment will be substantially miti- gated as compared to what would have been normal for first-degree murder committed by one who is perfectly sane and sober. The defendant is also remanded for medical examination to determine whether he is still Mentally Disabled or subject to recurrence. (This could be particularly important where intoxication is due to heavy doses of certain drugs such as LSD or amphetamines, which can result in periodic recurrence of derangement even without further drug use. It is also of special pertinence where the defendant is a heavy, frequent drinker. The issues of alcoholism and addiction are taken up below.)

Illustration 2. The defendant, stumbling about in patent gross intoxica- tion, takes umbrage at a casual bump from a bystander, picks up a heavy object, and strikes the bystander heavily, killing him. Charged with second-degree murder, the defendant enters a D.O.M. plea. The jury, taking all the evidence into account, finds reasonable doubt that the defendant intended to kill, or even that he knew what he was doing at the time. The defendant is therefore found Not Guilty of Second-Degree Murder, or of Voluntary Manslaughter. But the defendant is of course found Guilty of the "floor" crime—causing death by reason of criminal negligence. The jury then takes up the D.O.M. issue, and finds Disability of Mind, Culpable in Origin. Therefore the defendant *is* criminally responsible in regard to the offense of criminal negligence. No mitigation is entailed. The defendant is sentenced accordingly, and is also remanded for medical examination, etc.

Illustration 3. The defendant shouted mortal threats at the victim while flourishing a gun. A plea of D.O.M. is entered to the charge of Assault with a Deadly Weapon. The defense offers evidence of a history of recurrent episodes of acute mental confusion and hallucination, with periodic hospi- talization (diagnosis—schizophrenia). The jury, on the basis of all the evidence, finds reasonable doubt that there was intent to assault a person or even that the defendant knew what he was doing at the time—the evidence as to confusion and hallucination suggest that he may not even have been aware of where he was, or that it was a human being he was addressing. Therefore the jury finds Not Guilty on the assault charges. But the jury finds the defendant Guilty of the (statutory) "floor" crime of flourishing a deadly weapon within range of others and in a grossly negligent manner. The jury finds that the defendant suffered Nonculpable Disability of Mind. The defendant is thus Guilty of having committed a criminally prohibited act while not at the time criminally responsible. Therefore criminal condemnation or punishment is precluded. The defendant is remanded for medical examination, etc. (Had the defendant's confusion been due to gross intoxication, the same Guilty verdict would have been returned, of course. But the finding of *Culpable* D.O.M. would have meant that the defendant *is* criminally responsible, at least for the offense of criminal negligence.)

Illustration 4. The defendant, having just seen his child killed by a reckless driver, ran into his house, came back with a gun, and shot the driver dead. A plea of D.O.M. is entered. The jury finds that, as charged, the defendant did deliberate and did intentionally and with malice kill the driver. The defendant is Guilty of first-degree murder. The jury finds that the defendant temporarily suffered lack of mental capacity for conduct that was rational in regard to its criminal significance, and that this lack played a material role, but not the chief role, in the defendant's acting as he did. The D.O.M. finding is: Nonculpable Partial Mental Disability. The defendant's criminal condemnation and punishment are mitigated. (Conceivably, the jury could find full Mental Disability—thus precluding any punishment. But proper jury instructions are essential here. They should, in this special kind of case, emphasize that the law does not contemplate absolving members of the community from criminal responsibility for anything they may wish to do, even to the extent of taking the law into their own hands and killing others, just because they have been themselves caused deep sorrow or anger or frustration. The jury should be reminded that although we may understand and in a certain way sympathize with the actions of a distraught parent, this is different from saying that the parent genuinely and preponderantly lacked the capacity to take into account the criminal significance of the act.)

Illustration 5. The defendant, having broken into and entered a residence at night, is found with his pockets filled with jewelry belonging to the residents. Charged with burglary, the defendant enters a D.O.M. plea. Evidence as to D.O.M. shows the defendant to have been a regular and heavy user of narcotics, amphetamines, and other drugs over a period of at least some five years. The defendant has no legitimate occupation or source of income, has no residence, and often sleeps in one-night skid-row rooms shared with others. The defendant has a history over the past few years of being picked up by the police for various offenses, particularly in connection with drug sales and purchases in small amounts but on a regular basis. The defendant has been seriously ill and hospitalized several times recently. He is at present physically debilitated and suffering from anemia and malnourishment. The jury finds that the defendant did break and enter at night with the intent to steal; the defendant is found Guilty of burglary. Turning to the D.O.M. issue, the jury finds that the defendant suffered Partial Disability of Mind—in acting as he does, the defendant has *some* significant capacity to take account, in a practical way, of the criminal significance of his acts; but he also suffers a significant lack in this respect, too. The D.O.M. is found to be culpable in origin—the result of the defendant's prior conduct when still rational. The defendant's punishment is mitigated, and he is also remanded for medical examination, etc. (No doubt such cases as this would usually not go to trial but would be settled on the basis of a bargained plea of Guilty of Burglary, with Culpable Partial D.O.M.)

We now proceed to a consideration of the four possible D.O.M. findings, with explanation of the meaning and effects of each, and illustrative categories of specific disabilities.

1. *Disability of Mind, Nonculpable*

The jury has found (a) that there was a lack of mental capacity for rational conduct in regard to the criminal significance of the act, (b) that the lack played the chief role in the defendant's commission of the act, and (c) that the defendant is not culpable as to the origin of that irrational condition.

The Effect of the Finding. This finding implies total lack of criminal responsibility for the act, even for the "floor" crimes of criminal negligence. If all the essential elements of a defined criminal act were present, this will be unambiguously reflected in the finding of Guilty that results from the earlier phase of the jury's deliberations. This finding will be joined with the D.O.M. finding in the verdict: "Guilty of ———, with Nonculpable Disability of Mind." If, however, there was reasonable doubt as to whether a particular criminal act as legally defined was committed, the defendant will simply be found Not Guilty of that crime. Of course, the fact that there is a D.O.M. finding presupposes that the defendant was found Guilty on at least one count—normally the "floor" offense of gross negligence.

This D.O.M. verdict precludes any criminal condemnation or punishment for the act. But where D.O.M. is reported in any verdict, post-trial nonaccusatory measures in relation to any remaining potential criminal irresponsibility are automatically applicable.

This way of reporting the verdict—analogous to the old "Guilty but Insane" verdict—has an important practical impact. If the defendant did in fact commit a particular criminal act, then the verdict "Guilty . . . with Nonculpable Disability of Mind" makes this perfectly explicit. Although in itself only a verbal change from the present *"Not* Guilty by Reason of Insanity" verdict, this should be a real benefit, as many a judge will have felt, especially where the commission of the act is patent and the act itself shocking. The public understanding and sympathy for the process of law is often lost when such a person is held *Not* Guilty—even if the insanity clause is added. On the other hand, the present insanity verdict is ambiguous in its public impact—paradoxically, it can be taken to imply that the defendant *was* proved to have committed the criminal act, whereas in truth it is intended to mean that the physical act but not the criminal act was committed. The D.O.M. form of the verdict clarifies this—if the defendant is not proved to have had the particular mental states requisite to the offense as defined, then he is held *Not* Guilty of that offense. And now "Not Guilty" unambiguously means *not guilty.* The defendant will typically be found Guilty of at least the "floor" offense of gross negligence, with Nonculpable Disability of Mind.

The Types of Cases Covered. Verdicts reporting "Nonculpable Disability of Mind" would appear in the types of cases where at present the defense successfully establishes either *Insanity,* or *Unconsciousness,* or *Automatism,* or *Involuntariness* (when due to mental derangement). In all these kinds of cases there is a mental incapacity for rational conduct in regard to law that predominates in the conduct, and that arises out of mental disability typically associated with such medical conditions as psychogenic or organic psychoses, epilepsy, organic brain damage from tumor, trauma, or other physio- or neuropathology. Of course, the existence of any such medical condition does not in itself establish D.O.M. And under the D.O.M. doctrine there is also the possibility of showing incapacity for rational conduct arising out of conditions that are not so precisely defined medically. What counts is not diagnostic categories but specific information, so far as available, about the defendant's capacities, in committing the act, for taking account practically of its criminal significance.

Another category of possible—though not probable—eligibles for this full D.O.M. finding would be people who have been very long and very deeply involved with drugs or drink, and who have been leading so unwholesome a life as to be significantly malnourished, physically ailing, socially alienated, and rootless. Such are the debilitated skid-row habitués—alcoholics and addicts of long standing and demonstrated gross incapacity to take care of themselves. They can present a bedraggled and self-destructive picture that reveals, on the whole, a loss of capacity to act rationally in regard to criminal law norms. This would be for the fact-finder in the trial to determine—but probably the determination would in practice be made far more often at the police or prosecutory level. All things considered, we believe that those who come to trial would very probably be found to suffer only a state of *Partial* Disability of Mind, a prospect discussed further under that heading, below. If full Disability of Mind is found, and it is found nonculpable, then condemnatory and punitive treatment is entirely precluded; but nonaccusatory medical and other appropriate welfare and safety intercession is mandatory as specified in the relevant policies at the time.

2. *Disability of Mind, Culpable*

Here the finding is again that (a) the defendant had a Disability of Mind that (b) played the chief role in the commission of the criminal act, but (c) was brought about by the defendant's own prior conduct while not suffering Disability of Mind.

The Effect of the Finding. The verdict "Guilty, with Culpable Disability of Mind" unambiguously reflects that the defendant was guilty and culpable, and yet on the whole nonresponsible *at the time* of the act. The defendant's criminal condemnation and punishment should be mitigated in regard to crimes requiring intent or knowledge. The exception to the mitigating import of this verdict is in regard to the "floor" offense of criminal negligence. In the latter case, the standard of care is objective, and the defendant was responsible for the condition of mind amounting to incapacity to observe due care. Therefore the defendant was responsible for—and hence fully punishable for—the negligent behavior.

The Types of Cases Covered. Culpable Disability of Mind would be typical of voluntary self-intoxication to the point where, at least temporarily, the rational capacities are largely destroyed—e.g., the person who is deeply drunk, either in a mad but purposeful fury or a wildly reckless or "blind" drunk. Another example would be the "pill-popper" who is in a state of acute mania while hallucinating or suffering delusions. Many of these persons would be Guilty of acting with intent, and if so would be found Guilty of the appropriate offense. The D.O.M. finding would then have a mitigatory import. But many of them, because of the gross intoxication, will have reached a condition where the existence of any definite intent or awareness of what is happening is genuinely to be doubted. In the latter cases, the defendant will be found Guilty of the "floor" crime of criminal negligence; in which case the Culpable D.O.M. finding will have no mitigatory effect, but will trigger automatic remand for mental examination, etc.

3. *Partial Disability of Mind, Nonculpable*
and
4. *Partial Disability of Mind, Culpable*

Here the jury finds that (a) there was D.O.M. that (b) played a material role but not the chief role, and (c) was Nonculpable (or Culpable) in origin.

The Effects of the Verdicts. The general effect is one that overlaps with what is accomplished by present concepts such as "diminished capacity," "diminished responsibility," and the "specific intent exception." The *Partial* D.O.M. finding implies less mitigation than full D.O.M. Where the crime is one of criminal negligence, the Culpable Partial D.O.M. finding implies no mitigation, whereas if Nonculpable it does.

Types of Cases Covered. In the Culpable category would fall defendants who were intoxicated from drink or other drugs, or affected by any other self-induced disabling of the mind. The evidence could show that they were evidently and significantly unclear about their circumstances. It would show that they were disordered or confused or slow-thinking enough to have become unreliable, erratic, and deficient in their capacity to grasp the significance of their actions. Yet these would be defendants who were not so drunk or otherwise intoxicated or disabled as to lack, on the whole, resources to inhibit behavior that (typically) is patently criminal.

Defenses based on long-term and heavy drug or alcohol abuse, *supported* by other kinds of evidence about mental capacities showing lack of capacity for rational conduct, would be appropriate. But the heavy alcohol or drug user who leads a purposeful and reasonably organized life, whether criminal or not, would not—in our analysis—qualify as being in any legally relevant way nonresponsible; the mere invocation of labels such as "addict" or "alcoholic" cannot justify ascriptions of lack of capacity for rationality.

The finding of Partial Disability of Mind allows the jury the opportunity to recognize candidly what so often we do want to recognize in real life: that some persons cannot fairly be viewed as acting with full responsibility while in certain conditions of reasonably heavy intoxication, or when affected by a past history of chronic intoxication and consequent general debilitation. Under such circumstances, inhibitions as to violent or antisocial conduct are chemically and physiologically weakened; yet, at the same time, there does remain significant capacity to inhibit patently criminal conduct—all the more so if the individual is by habit and character genuinely committed to respecting law. The Partial D.O.M. finding would allow the jury to express this intermediate-range assessment, crudely but effectively enough to provide a proper juridical framework for sentencing.

Under current law, the jury has only two equally unsatisfactory options in cases of the kind described. They can press for mitigation by "finding" that a "specific intent" (for example, the intent to injure grievously) was absent, even though the evidence patently shows it to have been present. Or the jury can stick to the truth—that the intent was present—and thus have to find the defendant guilty of the graver so-called "specific intent" crime. In the latter case the jury is unable to differentiate their finding from the finding that the defendant soberly and calculatingly committed the crime. Yet, criminal as the act may be in either case, a fair-minded jury rightly is reluctant to lump them together, and is just as rightly reluctant to fly in the face of the evidence in order to "find" absence of an intent that was clearly present.

Nonculpable Partial Disability would suit several categories of cases that are very troublesome under current law. In general it would at least cover the cases for which "diminished capacity" and "diminished responsibility" are now intended, when the mental condition is of the kind that is nonculpable in origin.

One such group includes the borderline mental disorders that, when full-blown, are patently conditions of irrationality—for practical purposes this turns out usually to mean borderline psychotic conditions, whether "functional" or of known organic origin. Such cases are currently handled in trial, either by use of the insanity defense or, where available, by use of the diminished capacity (or, in England, diminished responsibility) defenses. When the insanity defense is used in these cases, the results are inherently erratic—the "in-between" nature of the case, for which no provision is made in the insanity defense, can only be responded to by a full acquittal based on a finding of insanity, or by a full conviction because the jury does not find that the condition amounts to insanity. It is partly in response to this dilemma that diminished capacity defenses have been introduced in some jurisdictions. But, as we have shown, the diminished capacity defenses have become inextricably confused with the "specific intent" exception. Instead of acknowledging that the borderline irrationality undermines criminal responsibility to a degree but not totally, the current law sets juries on the metaphysical quest of determining whether the defendant's intent, or deliberation, or malice was "really" intent, or deliberation, or malice, in view of the disordered condition of mind in which he entertained the criminal plan and purposefully executed it.

Nonculpable Partial Disability, in addition to fitting the borderline psychotic case perfectly, would also fit the hitherto highly troublesome cases often characterized by psychiatrists with such labels as "character disorder," "personality disorder," "psychopathic personality," or "sociopathic personality." There has been strong resistance to allowing this as a basis for any exculpation from criminal guilt. Psychiatrists have vacillated as to whether or not to label these "mental diseases" for purposes of applying the criminal insanity tests. Some of the criminal responsibility tests have been intended to exclude such conditions by adding an explicit proviso that mere repeated criminal conduct shall not in itself be considered as constituting a mental disease for purposes of the insanity defense. But such provisos reflect unfortunate confusion. We need not here dive into the complexities of these diagnoses and their significance. It suffices for our purposes to recall that the D.O.M. finding is not a medical finding. It is inconceivable that a jury would find incapacity for rationality in one who in every respect—even in his criminal conduct itself—acts with understandable motives and in intelligibly responsive ways to his circumstances, but who makes a living by robbing people. What is essential for a D.O.M. finding is substantial evidence (in the way the crime is committed, along with the defendant's history and conduct generally) that shows a mental incapacity to take into account the criminal law norms in shaping conduct. *Mere* repeated criminal acts could prove no such thing.

The Partial D.O.M. finding would, however, seem applicable to the "drifter" or person in perennial "difficulties" who not only causes trouble for others but engages in obviously self-defeating and self-injuring escapades, or rash and imprudent impulsive ventures, who may tend to drinking bouts, and who reveals a longtime pattern of inability to "learn from experience." Such persons *do* have a certain degree of ability to get along, and yet, in the long run, seem incapable of avoiding difficulties. The finding of Partial D.O.M., Nonculpable, amounts to finding the defendant

Guilty of the criminal act, properly subject to criminal condemnation and punishment—but somewhat less so than the fully rational person—and evidencing a criminally dangerous mental condition warranting nonaccusatory medical, welfare, and protective measures under the policies applicable. Here, too, would fall many of the longtime "down-and-outers," skid-row habitués, and longtime debilitated alcoholics and addicts. "Partial D.O.M." would offer mitigation but not exculpation, and authorize medical intercession.

Finally, a third broad category of persons found to have *Nonculpable Partial Disability of Mind* would probably be those who, because of a unique and extreme overwhelming personal crisis, become temporarily overwrought and in that condition commit a criminal act. Here the Nonculpable Partial Disability of Mind finding, along with the Guilty finding, amounts to a verdict that might be paraphrased: "Guilty—but deserving of mercy because of the overwhelming stress on the mental capacities for rational conduct." Such a finding seems apt for such cases— candid and explicit as to what has been found. Under present law such a result is in substance possible only by use of legal subterfuges of the kind we have already discussed above.

5. *No D.O.M. Finding*

If there was no incapacity for rational conduct, or if such as there was did not play even a material role in the commission of the physical act, then there is no D.O.M., and the jury merely reports its finding as to guilt or innocence.

IV: SOME REFLECTIONS ON THE LARGE IMPACT OF THE D.O.M. DOCTRINE

Having reviewed the D.O.M. pattern of verdicts in some detail, we may now attempt to explore the larger impact of adopting the D.O.M. doctrine—its impact generally on defendants, prosecution, the law itself, and society. We cannot pretend to do more here than to give a brief, speculative, and highly general analysis; to attempt more would require a second volume. Certainly no one can reliably predict in detail the outcome of adopting such a new doctrine.

Fundamental to our proposing the D.O.M. doctrine is our belief in a doctrine based squarely on the psychological realities and on principles of justice. We believe that such a doctrine is bound to produce more reasonable and just results, with less controversy and more efficiency, than do the arbitrary, disconnected, and often downright unintelligible doctrines that are current today.

We should say at once that we do not see an overall advantage to any particular "special interest." Defendants will not find the D.O.M. doctrine a wide-open escape hatch to freedom, and the prosecution will acquire no great new strategy to convict. Each will gain by working with a simpler legal doctrine whose growth and development can be more rationally predicted. Professionals in other affected fields such as forensic psychiatry will be liberated from the burden of testifying in conclusory terms on legal issues, and free to participate in a more modest but appropriate trial role. And society will gain by being more reliably protected from potentially dangerous offenders. Rather than biasing the trial process to the advantage of special interests, the D.O.M. doctrine would embody greater realism. Greater justice would both be done and be seen to be done.

Of even more fundamental significance to our legal institutions and philosophy, such a reversal of present confusion could also reverse the current trend to radical disillusionment with the very idea of individual responsibility as the basis of law. As we noted in Chapter I, the arbitrary, unrealistic, and erratic workings of the present law have led many scholars and professionals to propose, out of frustration, that we sweep away all concern in the criminal law with the concept of responsibility, and also with the *mens rea* concept (or major elements of it).

If the concept of individual responsibility under law is to be retained, we must confront the challenge to it in the touchstone area of criminal responsibility and mental disability. Generalized philosophical arguments can no longer suffice. The present shambles of confusion and injustice must be met head-on with basic and specific conceptual reform that promises uniform, intelligible, realistic, and evenhanded treatment of all offenders in this general category. If we cannot show that there really is a basis for such law, the practical result will be that the concept of responsibility as a basis of law, already seriously threatened, may soon be so undermined as to allow the purely technological and social-control orientations to dominate in the law. Some would welcome such a change. We, however, strongly believe that the concept of individual responsibility under law must remain a foundation stone of our society.

Nevertheless, even given these fundamental objectives, questions naturally arise as to how the shift to the D.O.M. doctrine would quantitatively affect the disposition of mental disability cases. While we believe there would be some desirable localized statistical changes if the D.O.M. doctrine were adopted, we also believe there are no good grounds for expecting any gross change.[12] There is some evidence to suggest that, on balance, and whatever the legal formulas used, a certain small number of offenders persuade attorneys, judges, and juries that some recognition of defective responsibility is warranted. The current erratic results as to specific types of cases seem ultimately to balance out so as to keep overall figures reasonably stable. We suspect the overall figures would remain comparable under D.O.M. because we believe that the basic but unexpressed intuitions that have on the whole governed past results would still govern, but in a far more reliable and intelligible way, case by case. This is no minor benefit: overall social statistics have little human impact on the individual defendant or participant in a particular trial; but under the

12. Statistics are few and difficult to interpret, being at most suggestive. In England there seems to have been a shift in homicide dispositions, as a result of the introduction of the Diminished Responsibility defense. As the number of Diminished Responsibility verdicts increased, the number of Insanity verdicts decreased, the overall total remaining fairly steady. This may suggest that there was a shift to the more punitive verdict and hence to greater severity towards defendants. But Walker (1965), who reports this, also reports that under the new Diminished Responsibility defense there was a noticeable group of defendants who succeeded who would not have qualified for an Insanity defense in any case. Thus the overall impact of the new defense is ambiguous and unclear; and in any case we are dealing with a very small absolute number—some thirty persons per year for all of England. See also Sparks (1964), pp. 31-32. In the U.S. the *Durham* rule led to an initial upsurge in Insanity verdicts, and then, quickly, to a decline. In any case, the absolute numbers are small, ranging from three to sixty-six, but settling down to around twenty-five per year out of total cases ranging from around 1,500 to 2,500 (see LaFave and Scott, 1972, p. 269; and Arens, 1974, p. 17). Goldstein (1967) says that the move to alternative defenses to insanity that are based on "subjective" theories is not likely to produce serious problems so far as increasing the numbers of lighter sentences is concerned. He believes that so long as the possibility of conviction on crimes such as manslaughter remains, the mitigation of punishment—as compared to punishment for murder—should not significantly affect deterrence (p. 199). However, Goldstein does express concern that there must be a lesser offense of some sort on which to convict those held "partially responsible," for such offenders may be objectively dangerous and should not be allowed to go free (p. 202). LaFave and Scott (1972) express a similar view in connection with doctrines taking cognizance of degrees of culpability, and they state a formula to which the D.O.M. doctrine directly and fully responds (pp. 331-332).

D.O.M. doctrine the individual would see the rationality and justice of the judicial process as it affects a particular human being's claim to have been unable to act responsibly.

Perhaps the D.O.M. provision allowing for "Partial D.O.M." would result in a certain increase in the number of Guilty verdicts calling (by virtue of "Partial D.O.M.") for some modest mitigation of punishment. And perhaps a group of crimes associated with borderline irrationality— e.g., borderline pathology or serious but not gross intoxication—could be more readily plea bargained by offering to accept a Partial D.O.M. plea along with the Guilty plea. We cannot estimate what the net result would be in regard to the number of additional D.O.M. pleas that would go to trial as compared to the number of trials avoided through plea bargaining, but we believe that the proportion of cases going to trial would not greatly change.

One significant result—again more a matter of evenhandedness and clarity of principle rather than gross statistical change per se—would arise out of the provision that *any* D.O.M. verdict automatically mandate at least a post-trial medical examination in a nonaccusatory context, and authorize—under the relevant policy guidelines—such protective and welfare measures as are deemed reasonable.

The D.O.M. doctrine, as was emphasized earlier, implies *nothing* about the specific nature of such policies or measures, nor about their efficacy. These are problems of legal and social policy, and of scientific and related expertise. They pose, of course, immense problems faced by our criminal justice system today. But the D.O.M. doctrine is not a panacea. It does establish a basic principle hitherto only erratically recognized. It makes explicit that a verdict reporting Disability of Mind is a positive finding that social interests which the criminal law is designed to protect have been threatened or harmfully affected, and that this threat or harm has been found to be inextricably associated with nonresponsibility arising out of an irrational mental condition. Therefore the basic responsibility and authority of the criminal law remain pertinent, even though the normal accusatory-punitive process is less fitting, or not fitting at all, as the means to resolving the matter. But—as we again emphasize—the D.O.M. doctrine in itself does not prejudge the social, legal, and technical decisions following upon a D.O.M. verdict. Such decisions will depend on the values of the community and the state of the sciences at any particular time. The doctrine only provides that insofar as there are social policies designed to deal with the problem of the nonresponsible criminal offender, the population subject to those policies will consist of *all* persons found to be nonresponsible criminal offenders—an obviously desirable result that we are far from achieving today.

We also believe that, as law professionals become accustomed to using the D.O.M. doctrine, the "tyranny of the experts" in the courtroom—as unwelcome to many experts as it is to judges and attorneys—would disappear. It would become firmly fixed in the minds of all that the determination of Disability of Mind is to be made by the jury, since the decision has to do with the everyday capacity of the ordinary citizen to take account in a practical way of the bearing of the rudimentary principles of criminal law on conduct in the particular context. Experts could testify, but they would do so for the purpose of giving to the lay fact-finder additional facts or deeper insight, in lay terms, concerning the particular defendant's mind and personality. The aim would be to aid the fact-finders to form, by their own independent thinking about all the circumstances, their own answers to the conclusory questions. Whether expert witnesses agreed on such generalized issues as the medical diagnosis of a condition, or as to whether it is or is not a "mental disease," would neither settle nor seem to settle the question whether in the particular circumstances the defendant, in acting as he did, lacked material capacity to take into account the criminal significance of that act.

Thus, to summarize, we maintain that great benefits would accrue to law professionals generally, that all persons swept up in the criminal justice system would receive, and be seen to receive, greater justice, that society would be better protected, and that our traditional conception of individual responsibility as basic to law would again be seen as well grounded in the area of law where it has most recently been subject to widespread and influential challenge.

Appendix I

Suggested Model Jury Instructions
for Disability of Mind

These instructions should be studied in close conjunction with the expository discussion in Chapter 15, Sections I, II, and III. As explained there, these instructions would be presented after the normal instructions to the jury covering general matters, defining the counts on which the defendant could be found Guilty (including the "floor" crimes of criminal negligence), and explaining the prosecution's burden of proving each element of an offense beyond a reasonable doubt.

It is intended that these D.O.M. instructions be presented as a set, since they constitute a unified treatment of a distinct topic.

Typographical conventions used here are as follows: when a phrase is set in brackets, it is intended that the specific act or circumstance in question be inserted in place of the more general phrase in the brackets. For example, "If you find that the defendant did [commit the alleged harm]" would be read, assuming that the allegation concerns a homicide by stabbing: "If you find that the defendant did stab and thereby cause the death of the deceased. . . ."

In order to provide more specific insight into the practical translation of the D.O.M. concepts, we have provided as Addenda specific sets of coordinated phrases illustrating main types of mental disabilities and origins thereof. At the appropriate bracketed phrases—specifically, in Instructions 10 and 15a—we have placed asterisks after the phrases. Refer-

ence to the Addenda, as asterisked, will illustrate how to replace the
bracketed phrases with sets of coordinated specific phrases characterizing
the factual circumstances as to D.O.M. and its origin.

INSTRUCTIONS FOR THE JURY

1. The defendant has entered a plea of Disability of Mind. Before
you take up this issue at all, you should have completed your
consideration of the proof as to each count, and you should have
determined, in regard to each, whether the defendant is Guilty or
Not Guilty.

2. In coming to your determination as to the defendant's guilt or
innocence in regard to each count, you should consider any evidence
that in your judgment bears on the issues of guilt or innocence, even
if that evidence may have been offered in connection with the issue
of Disability of Mind.

3. If you should find the defendant Guilty of none of the alleged
criminal acts, or lesser included offenses which I described previously,
you should not enter into deliberations on the question of Disability
of Mind. You should simply report your verdict. Only if you find
the defendant Guilty on at least one count should you proceed to
consider the issue of Disability of Mind, and you should consider
this issue only in relation to the count or counts of which you found
the defendant Guilty.

4. *Burden of Proof:* Before I explain to you the possible findings
as to Mental Disability, and their meaning, I want to inform you that
wherever a claim as to Disability of Mind is asserted, the burden of
proof is on the defendant to prove this claim by a preponderance of
the evidence. This is a shift of the burden of proof from the
prosecution to the defense; but the defendant has this burden *only*
in connection with any claim made by the defendant that Disability
of Mind existed. Further, whereas the prosecution must establish its
proof beyond a reasonable doubt, the defense burden as to Disability of Mind is a lesser one, since, as I have said, the defendant need
only show proof by a preponderance of the evidence.

5. Proof by a preponderance of the evidence is proof by such
evidence as has, when weighed with that opposed to it, more
convincing force and the greater probability of truth.

6. Now I will explain to you what the possible Disability of Mind
findings are, and then I will explain the terminology.

7. *Possible D.O.M. Findings:* As to findings in regard to the Disability of Mind plea, you may find Disability of Mind, or you may find Partial Disability of Mind, or you may find neither. If you do find Disability of Mind or Partial Disability of Mind, you must also make a finding, in the manner I will shortly explain, as to the defendant's culpability or nonculpability in regard to the origin of the Disability.

8. *Definitions:*

a. The phrases *Disability of Mind* and *Partial Disability of Mind* both refer to a condition or state of mind consisting of a lack of mental capacity for conduct that is rational in regard to the criminal significance of the act.

b. There was Disability of Mind if there was such a lack of capacity for rational conduct, and if it played the chief or the predominant role in the defendant's committing the alleged criminal act.

c. There was Partial Disability of Mind if there was such a lack of capacity for rational conduct, and if it played a material role but not the chief or the predominant role in the defendant's commission of the alleged criminal act.

I will explain the terms used in these definitions, and then, after that, I will discuss how you determine whether any Disability you may find is culpable in origin, or not.

9. *Disability of Mind* and *Partial Disability of Mind* are terms of law. They are not medical or psychological terms. The object of allowing expert medical or psychological testimony is to provide you with additional specific information that may provide you with a better understanding of the defendant's mind and personality; it is for you, basing your judgment on all the evidence you have heard, and not only on the testimony of experts, to reach your own independent judgment as to whether Partial or full Disability of Mind, as defined by law, existed.

10. By the phrase *lack of mental capacity* the law means something very different from a mere failure to exercise a capacity, or a mere unwillingness to make the effort to exercise it adequately. In this particular case it is for you to distinguish between a failure or inadequate effort to [correct the mental disability claimed***] and an actual lack of mental capacity to do so. The law expects those who have capacity for rational conduct in regard to law to make the fullest effort to exercise it, difficult as this may be for some persons

or under certain stressful circumstances, and tempting as it may be at times to be satisfied with less than such fullest effort. (Where circumstances are appropriate, language as suggested in Section III of Chapter 15, at the end of Illustrative Case number 4, may be desirable.)

11. The phrase *capacity for conduct that is rational in regard to the criminal significance of the act* refers to practical capacity, not to some purely theoretical or intellectual capacity in itself. It concerns whether, in the commission of the criminal act, the defendant was able, in a practical way, to take account of the criminal significance of such act. This does not necessarily mean that the defendant had to take *conscious* account. Responsible law-abiding citizens take practical account, in every moment of their social life, of the limitations set on conduct by the law, but relatively rarely do they have to think explicitly about this.

In taking account of the law in a practical way, one may need to use the intellectual faculties, or perceptual or emotional or other mental faculties. No one list or formula will apply to all circumstances. It is for you as responsible lay persons, considering all things together, to assess whether the defendant, in acting as he (she) did, lacked mental capacity under the particular circumstances to take the criminal significance of the act into account.

12. When I speak of *the criminal significance of the act,* I do not mean, of course, that the defendant had to be able to take the law into account in all its complexities and technicalities, such as a lawyer would know it. This phrase refers only to that broad practical knowledge that every responsible person has: the awareness of the wrongfulness of such things as stealing, killing, rape, and arson, and, in this particular case, of [committing the alleged harm].

Nor do I mean that the defendant had to agree in his (her) own personal moral judgment that the act forbidden by law was truly wrong. We are not free under law to disregard the law if we disagree with it, no matter how sincere or fervent our belief. The question of Mental Disability asks whether, as a minimum, the defendant had mental capacity, at least in a practical way, to take the standards of law into account; it does not ask whether the defendant agreed or not with those standards.

13. The phrase *the chief or the predominant role,* as applied to the lack of mental capacity for rational conduct, means that this lack

played the single most significant role, being for practical purposes the major factor in the defendant's acting as he (she) did in committing the alleged crime.

14. The phrase *plays a material role* means that the lack of capacity for rational conduct, though it may not have played the chief role, was nevertheless a significant, important influence in the defendant's coming to act the way he (she) did. A material role is not a minor or merely incidental role.

15. *Application to the present case:*

a. The general concepts and definitions that I have given you would apply in the present case as follows: In order to find lack of mental capacity for conduct that is rational in regard to the criminal significance of the offending act, you must find by a preponderance of all the evidence that the defendant, at the time of the act, suffered a lack of mental capacity arising out of [specify the claimed conditions of origin*]. You must further find that the lack of capacity manifested itself at the time of the act in [specify the claimed manifestations of irrationality**]. And you must find, further, that this lack of capacity was of such a nature as to render the defendant lacking in ability to take rational account of the criminal significance of that act.

b. If you do so find, and if you find that this irrational condition played the chief role in the defendant's commission of the act, you should find the defendant to have been suffering Disability of Mind.

c. If you find that there was such an irrational condition of mind, and that it played a material role in the defendant's acting as he (she) did, but that it did not play the chief or the predominant role, you should find the defendant to have been suffering Partial Disability of Mind.

d. If you find no such irrational condition of mind, or if you find that any such condition as did exist played no material role in the defendant's commission of the act, then there was no Mental Disability as defined by law.

16. *Culpability as to the Context of Origin of the Mental Disability* (*One* of the following is to be used, according to particular circumstances):

a. *The Defendant Caused the Disability or Failed to Take Reasonable Precautions to Prevent It.*

The prosecution alleges that insofar as the defendant may have suffered any Mental Disability at the time of the act, it was the defendant's own prior conduct, specifically the defendant's [specify the conduct], that was chiefly responsible for the existence of that Mental Disability. If the evidence leaves a reasonable doubt that it was the defendant's prior conduct that was chiefly responsible for the existence of the Mental Disability, you should give the defendant the benefit of that doubt and hold the defendant Nonculpable in regard to the origin of the Disability of Mind. If, however, the evidence shows beyond any reasonable doubt that the defendant's own prior conduct was chiefly responsible for bringing about the Disability, then you should find the defendant Culpable as to the origin of that Disability [add, if applicable:]—unless you also find that a preponderance of the evidence proves, as the defendant claims, that even at the time of that earlier conduct the defendant was already suffering a Disability of Mind, in which case you should find the defendant Nonculpable.

b. *Recklessness in the Context of Origin of the Disability of Mind.*
The prosecution alleges that the defendant was reckless in regard to [the harm allegedly done]. Specifically, the prosecution alleges that, *prior* to being [Mentally Disabled] the defendant was aware of the risk of later becoming so and in consequence causing just such a kind of harm as did allegedly result. The prosecution alleges that nevertheless the defendant did proceed [e.g., to drink; to drive without having taken prescribed medication; to drive in spite of knowledge of susceptibility to fits of fainting; etc.].

If you find the defendant Guilty as to [the alleged crime of recklessness] based on this allegation of awareness of risk prior to becoming Mentally Disabled, then you should report this explicitly in your verdict as to Mental Disability. You should do this along with your verdict that the defendant suffered Disability of Mind, or Partial Disability of Mind, by adding that this was "Culpable and Reckless."

c. *Intent, etc. in the Context of Origin of the D.O.M.*
(This Instruction applies particularly to the "Dutch Courage" situation.)

The prosecution alleges that even in [the conduct leading up to the D.O.M. and the alleged harm] the defendant did throughout [with malice, deliberately, premeditatedly] intend to [commit the alleged criminal act]. If you find the defendant Guilty as to any count on the basis of any such intent [malice, deliberation, premeditation] existing prior to the Mental Disability, you should report this explicitly in your verdict as to D.O.M. You should do this by adding to the rest of your finding as to Mental Disability a reference to each such prior mental state you find proved; for example, if you find that prior to the condition of D.O.M. there already existed an intent to [commit the crime], then you should state that the defendant suffered Disability of Mind, or Partial Disability of Mind, "with Culpability and Intent."

17. *Reporting the Verdicts:* Having made your finding as to the defendant's Culpability or Nonculpability in regard to the context of origin of the Disability, you will have completed your consideration of the questions pertaining to the plea of Disability of Mind. As I have already said, you will have previously completed your determinations as to whether the defendant is Guilty or Not Guilty in regard to each count. You are now, therefore, prepared to report your verdicts. You should report your verdicts by taking up each count in turn and stating how you find the defendant, Guilty or Not Guilty. Having completed your statement as to all counts, you will then conclude by stating your full finding as to Disability of Mind, if you have made any such finding. You would, therefore, state nothing about Disability of Mind if you have found neither Partial nor full Disability of Mind as legally defined. If you find Nonculpable Disability of Mind, or Nonculpable Partial Disability of Mind, you should so state at the conclusion of your entire verdict. Likewise, if you find Culpable Disability of Mind, or Culpable Partial Disability of Mind, you should so state ([add if applicable:] including any findings you may have made as to Recklessness in the context of origin of the Disability [or Intent; Deliberation; etc.]).

18. *General Significance of a D.O.M. Verdict:* If you do find the defendant Guilty as to one or more of the charges, and if you then also find that the defendant did suffer Disability of Mind, or Partial Disability of Mind, in regard to the criminal act, your verdict as to the defendant's mental condition will be taken into account in

connection with sentencing of the defendant. I would like to explain briefly to you the general effect of such a verdict.

a. Any verdict in which you report some finding of Disability of Mind will result in the defendant's being subject, when this trial is completed, to mental examination by appropriate experts, under overall supervision of the court. If the court then, upon receiving the advice of the experts, determines that the mental disability in question exists now, or is likely to recur, the court will, upon advice of appropriate experts, and with due regard to the defendant's legal rights, order measures to be taken to protect the welfare and safety of society and of the defendant, and, if possible, to alleviate or eradicate the mental disability.

b. Also, if you report in your verdict either Disability of Mind or Partial Disability of Mind, this will be taken into account as a possible mitigating factor by the court in sentencing the defendant for any crime of which he (she) was found Guilty. The exact amount and kind of mitigation, if any, will depend upon whether you found full or Partial Mental Disability, and upon the verdict as to the defendant's culpability or lack of it in regard to the context of origin of the Disability. In determining mitigation, the court will view your findings in the context of the particular circumstances of this case.

c. A finding of full Mental Disability that is Nonculpable automatically excludes any criminal condemnation or punishment for the act, since it implies that the defendant was not criminally responsible for his (her) conduct at the time of the offending act. But it is only Nonculpable full Mental Disability that has this effect; none of the other possible verdicts referring to Mental Disability calls for a total exclusion of punishment.

ADDENDA   *   **   ***

Specific Language Describing Some
Typical Kinds of D.O.M.

The following language is not meant to be obligatory but only to illustrate typical language that might appear in place of the bracketed phrases in Instructions 10 and 15a. For any category of Mental Disability indicated by the lettered headings below, the set of asterisked phrases under a heading could be substituted uniformly in Instructions 10 and 15a, as indicated by the corresponding asterisks in the Instructions.

(a) *Drug or Alcohol Intoxication*

    * the defendant's having (injected, swallowed, drunk) (a specific quantity of the substance) (at a specific time prior to) (the physical act)

    ** a mental apathy, or dullness of perception or sensibility; or: a mental confusion; or: a state of intense and pervasive mental excitement and excitability

    *** think more clearly, to pay more attention to the circumstances, to take account of the circumstances; or: curb and inhibit the violent impulses that arose

(b) *Trauma*

    * the defendant's having been (struck a blow . . . ; fallen and . . . ; subjected to . . . ;) shortly before (the physical act)

    ** the defendant's being (mentally confused about; out of touch mentally with) the (time; place; setting; meaning) of (the physical act) so as to be lacking in ability to take rational account of its criminal significance

    *** think more clearly, pay more attention, take more careful account of the circumstances, take extra precautions in view of the blow that was suffered and the effects felt

(c) *Chronic Mental Disorder*

    * the defendant's abnormal mental condition which had existed for (approximate duration); or: which had manifested itself recurrently in times past; or: which had suddenly developed because of abnormal, pathological processes of his (her) mind and body, and not as a reasonably expectable result of some particular act or acts of the defendant

    ** the defendant's being subject to (delusions; hallucinations; or: mental confusion; or: mentally disruptive emotions; moods of ———; or: mental apathy or insensitivity in regard to human life or suffering)

    *** pay more attention to the nature of the act and the circumstances, and the criminal significance of the conduct

(d) *"Character Disorders," "Addictions"*

     * severe, long-persisting habits and ways of living, including persistent, regular use of (drug, alcohol) over a period of (———) amounting by the time of (the physical act) to a generalized mental (and physical) disorganization (or dilapidation) of the mental faculties (and physical health); a deep and pervasive and often self-destructive failure to take obvious prudential care for harmful or noxious consequences to self and others

     ** imprudent unawareness or reckless unconcern for the safety of self or others, or for property, or for the requirements of law or orderly social intercourse

     *** exert more effort to take careful account of the circumstances and the criminal significance of the conduct

Appendix II

The English Law Context of
the Disability of Mind Doctrine:
"Diminished Mental Capacity
as a Criminal Law Defence"*

I. INTRODUCTION

My remarks pertain to a congeries of *ad hoc* defences: insanity, diminished responsibility, drunkenness and other forms of chemical intoxication, mental defect, automatism, and "unconsciousness."

It is intuitively evident that all these notions appearing in criminal law belong in some one large but significant category. Roughly, each rests on the thesis that aberration of mind may partly or wholly negate criminal guilt. This underlying unity is not coherently reflected in current law.

*This Appendix consists of the original text, with no changes except those needed for editorial uniformity with the rest of the book, of a paper published by H. Fingarette in the *Modern Law Review* (London) in 1974. It presents a version of the D.O.M. doctrine (the first version published) in the context of English criminal law. As such it has the value of relating the theses of Chapter 1 in a systematic way to current English law. There are some details in which the general theses of this article differ from the later version formulated in Part V. A principal difference, however, is that when this paper was written, the author was (as the text of the article reveals) still unwittingly under the spell of the "specific intent" doctrine as a tool of legal analysis. It was only after the analyses of the intoxication defenses

The establishment of the Butler Commission[1] suggests that the time is ripe for a review of the law in this area. I shall focus primarily upon the conceptual issues, though I do not deny that there are other important problematic issues—not only other legal ones, but also medical, administrative, social, and political issues.

What I do in the following may be thought of as an attempt at a rational restatement, and in some details as a proposal for rational reconstruction, of a core doctrine unifying this particular area of the criminal law. It will be seen that to a substantial extent the actual law in its effects does fall within the logical format here outlined. However, the actual law is more restrictive, more of a patchwork, and in a few instances positively inconsistent with the proposed doctrine. I will begin with some introductory remarks to sketch the direction I will take, and then proceed in sections II and III to a more precise and systematic discussion.

The concept which I propose as central, as generic to the entire domain of the relevant law, indeed as defining that domain, is *diminished mental capacity*. A second, related concept, also basic to the analysis, is that of the *context of origin* of the diminished mental capacity. Both these concepts take their sense, as will be seen, in a legal context, the context of assessing criminal responsibility. They are not medical concepts, though medical evidence may be relevant.

The entire legal doctrine based on these concepts is, I believe, an elaboration of deeply rooted and entirely reasonable commonsense intuitions. These might be rendered explicitly, though somewhat formally, as follows. A person's mind may be deranged in ways that make him unable to conduct himself rationally with respect to some standard. If so, he is

---

(Chapters 6 and 7) and of the "diminished mental capacity" defense (Chapter 8) had been fully worked out that the "specific intent" doctrine was exposed to us as fundamentally irrelevant to a D.O.M. defense of any kind. Part V definitively abandons the last remnants of reasoning based on differentiating specific elements of *mens rea* as determinative for assessing irrationality. Part V clearly recognizes the fundamental point in D.O.M. doctrine—that specific elements of *mens rea* lose their criminal significance when Disability of Mind exists, and have their different and specific kind of criminal significance only when the mind is rational.

It will be evident that in this Appendix the phrase *diminished mental capacity* corresponds to and was subsequently replaced by our phrase *Disability of Mind*, which for a variety of reasons we have thought better for the purpose than the earlier phrase.

1. *The Times*, June 29, 1972.

not responsible in his conduct with respect to that standard. If, when we look to the context in which this irrationality had its origin, we find that he became irrational in this way through no fault of his own, he should not be held responsible at all for the conduct in respect of that standard. Therefore he cannot be in that respect culpable. However, if he was culpable with respect to the origin of this condition of diminished mental capacity, then he cannot totally escape responsibility and culpability for his offending conduct. In the latter case, the specific kind and degree of ultimate culpability will depend, systematically, on the way in which his originating culpability is related to the impaired state of mind, to the resulting offending act, and to the relevant standards. Finally, whether the verdict is that the diminished mental capacity originated through the accused's own fault or not, this prior irrationality with respect to a criminal law standard warrants appropriate court-imposed restraints and medical regimen unless and until the likelihood of any further such diminished mental capacity is past.

This central intuition, which will be explored and elaborated in the remarks that follow, is the proper basis on which to achieve doctrinal coherence and realism in assessing culpability where there is diminished mental capacity. It also allows a significant simplification of the forms of verdict, and hence of trial strategies—but not at the expense of fundamental legal rights and principles.

Thus justice requires that the jury should be concerned with *any* aspect of the accused's state of mind as it bears on his culpability, but *only* as it bears on culpability. As I shall show, this means that the jury need not be compelled, as it is by the law at present, to decide the medical and pseudo-medical questions built into such concepts as "insanity," "automatism," and "diminished responsibility." Juries should not need to answer arcane and medically dubious questions such as whether the confusion caused by an arteriosclerotic condition is a genuine "disease," or whether it is a "physical" or "mental" disease. The jury's question in the latter case, for example, should be whether, in the light of the behavioural, circumstantial, and medical evidence, the accused was in fact gravely confused about what he was doing and was so without culpability on his part.

The diminished mental capacity doctrine implies that once culpability has been assessed, and provided the verdict as to this rested on a finding of diminished mental capacity, all further questions of exact diagnosis, prognosis, post-verdict restraint, and medical regimen should be explored fully and without the inappropriate restraints of the adversary proceedings in a trial as to culpability. After the verdict and prior to sentence, the court can take advantage of the fullest professional advice, and include its own judgment with respect to any appropriate punishment or restitution.

This "division of labour" implied by the diminished mental capacity doctrine differs, for example, from that proposed by Lady Wootton, which excludes consideration of *mens rea* during the trial.[2] Exclusion of the *mens rea* issue from the trial goes counter to the central tradition of all legal systems rooted in English law. On the other hand, my proposal differs also from such a counterproposal as Professor Hart's. This provides for exploring during the trial the *mens rea* issues except as these relate to mental abnormality,[3] the latter issue alone to be solely a matter for post-verdict assessment by experts. I suggest with respect that this purportedly "moderate" compromise amounts to excluding by fiat, and counterintuitively, the possibility that a just determination of culpability can crucially depend upon whether the person's mind was abnormal at the time of the act.

In the next section, I will develop the general doctrine of diminished mental capacity. Section III will deal with important types of cases and current defences to which the doctrine would apply.

II. "DIMINISHED MENTAL CAPACITY":
DEFINITION AND GENERAL DISCUSSION

If some specific mental state of the accused is an essential component of a relevant[4] crime, and if it is shown that the accused's mind was in that respect abnormal, i.e., that he was in that specific respect mentally incapable of rational control of his conduct,[5] then the mental abnormality in question is "diminished mental capacity." A defence to a criminal charge, when based on a showing of diminished mental capacity can, by

2. Wootton (1960); Wootton (1963), pp. 58–90.

3. Hart (1968), chap. 8. This proposal has in effect been tried and found wanting in California, and for just the reasons in the argument of the text above. See Goldstein (1967), p. 222; and see Wasserstrom's (1967) critique of Hart. See also Jacobs (1971).

4. The phrase *a relevant crime* is used to refer severally to each of the crimes in connection with which the fact-finder properly entertains the questions of the accused's guilt.

5. For discussion of *mentally incapable of rational control of his conduct*, see note 14, infra, and at much greater length: Fingarette (1972), chap. 4; and Chapter 14, supra.

extension, be called a "diminished mental capacity defence." The use of this defence always requires further inquiry into the "context of origin" of the diminished mental capacity in order to discover whether or not there was a culpable origin and, if there was, the specific interrelations of the culpable origin to the impaired state of mind and the resulting offending conduct.

Some comments on the significance of these concepts are now in order.

Diminished mental capacity *always,* by definition, affects the nature or degree of guilt and responsibility. But abnormality of mind, of itself, and no matter how grave, need not have this effect. For "a person may be both insane and responsible for his action. . . ."[6] If there is to be nonresponsibility, it is necessary that the abnormality have a certain specifiable and essential role in the allegedly criminal conduct.[7]

For example, a person whose mental abnormality consists in periodically suffering from states of schizophrenic confusion cannot legitimately claim lesser criminal responsibility for conduct which took place in a period of "remission," when he was quite free from any attack of his psychotic confusion. The psychosis would have to be seen to have actually infected the offending conduct in question in some specific way that is related to guilt or responsibility[8]—for example, the accused's failure, from psychotic confusion, to realise that he had a gun and was firing it at a human being.

The concept of "diminished mental capacity" is thus designed to link a specific mental abnormality in a legally relevant way to some essential mental component of crime, e.g., in the above example, knowledge of the nature of the act. Moreover, designing the concept this way distinguishes it from the concept of the "context of origin," which fills in the further information necessary for a final determination of culpability. Thus a particular kind of diminished mental capacity—e.g., the responsibility-

6. *Russell on Crime* (1964), p. 118.

7. See Williams (1961), p. 446; *Russell on Crime* (1964), p. 118; *R. v. Davis* (1881), p. 564; and *R. v. Porter* (1936), p. 189, per Dixon, J. With respect to diminished responsibility, see Homicide Act 1957, s.2(1). With respect to drunkenness, see *D.P.P. v. Beard* [1920], the leading case concerning lack of "specific intent" from drunkenness. Among earlier cases in relation to drunkenness, see *R. v. Monkhouse* (1849), p. 56, per Coleridge, J.; and *R. v. Letenock* (1917). And specifically in relation to provocation, see additionally the more recent *R. v. McCarthy* [1954]; *R. v. Wardrope* [1960]; and Homicide Act 1957, s.3. In regard to self-defence and intoxication, see *R. v. Rose* (1884) and *R. v. Chisam* [1963].

8. See the general discussion of this issue of specific "causal" relation in Jacobs (1971), pp. 31–32.

impairing mental confusion about the gun—could in some instances have its origin in psychosis; yet in other instances this same kind of confusion could have its legally relevant origin in voluntary self-intoxication. Or this same kind of mental confusion might have had its origin in the nonculpable taking of an improper dosage of insulin.[9] Or, again, this same kind of diminished mental capacity might have originated in a blow to the head.[10]

Each of these alternative origins of the same kind of diminished mental capacity could lead to different ultimate legal outcomes. These I will discuss in Section III.

I turn now to discussion of a central feature of the intuitive theses enunciated earlier—that where conduct flows from abnormality of mind in relation to a criminally relevant standard, the person is in that respect not criminally responsible. If we are to place this very central intuition on a more explicitly intelligible basis, what now calls for clarification is the sense of the key term, "abnormal."

Byrne [11] states: " 'Abnormality of mind' . . . means a state of mind so different from that of ordinary human beings that the reasonable man would term it abnormal."[12] Such a "definition" seems almost circular. And yet it tells us quite enough, especially in the context of the statutory diminished responsibility phraseology which it is intended to explicate: ". . . such abnormality of mind . . . as substantially impaired his mental responsibility. . . ."[13]

Procedurally, these propositions tell us that we must have the reasonable man represented, in effect, by the juryman. He is to give his judgment as to whether the "difference" from ordinary human beings was of such kind and degree as to lead him to characterise it as "abnormal." He is to decide this question specifically in the light of those facts, and only those facts, bearing in his judgment on the accused's state of mind as it was different from the ordinary person's, and different in ways that are conducive to impairing responsibility. This sets important constraints upon the jury. Of course, it gives the jury no exact *rule* for automatically deriving the final judgment from the facts. There are, however, helpful remarks to be found in several leading cases, of a kind which can well be

9. *R. v. Clarke* [1972].
10. *Cooper v. McKenna, ex parte Cooper* [1960].
11. *R. v. Byrne* [1960].
12. *Ibid.*, p. 403.
13. Homicide Act of 1957, s.2(1).

brought to the attention of the jury.[14] Nevertheless, the doubtful case calls for a practical, reasonable man's judgment. This is not a question that falls within the scope of science or any other expertise.

The "inference" from abnormality to nonresponsibility is akin to that from negligence to fault. Negligence entails fault because in the last analysis "negligence" means a failure, *to the point of fault,* to take care. The varieties of ways in which a person can fail to exercise reasonable care are, like the varieties of ways in which minds can be abnormal, too indefinitely various to be captured in a rule.[15] But the concept of "negligence" focusses the jury's deliberations on the relevant facts—the facts about the care taken and relevant standards of care. The concept of "abnormality," in turn, focusses the jury's attention on the kinds of facts relevant to assessing the accused's mind as "different" in ways that impair capacity to respond to elementary standards of criminal law. Thus the "circularity" built into these concepts constitutes no conceptual or procedural flaw.

We can now say something more explicit and substantive about the kind of "difference" that is at issue: any specific mental abnormality, in the present context, must amount to a mental incapacity for rational control of conduct with respect to a relevant criminal law standard.

The justification and significance of this assertion I have set forth at great length elsewhere.[16] However, at least a few words of comment are in order here. First, let it be noted that central to the formula is the concept of rationality, a concept deeply rooted in the relevant law and moral tradition.

14. Lord Parker, in *Byrne* [1960], asserts that the phrase *abnormality of mind* is "wide enough to cover the mind's activities in all its aspects..." (p. 403). But although abnormality may appear in any *aspect* of mind, it is not enough of a "difference" merely to show "that an accused person has a very short temper, or is unusually excitable or lacking in self-control" (*H.M. Advocate v. Braithwaite* [1945], J.C., p. 55). Or, as Dixon, J. in *Porter* (1936): "Mere excitability of a normal man, passion, even stupidity, obtuseness, lack of self-control, and impulsiveness are quite different things from [mental disease, disorder, or disturbance]" (p. 188).

15. See Williams (1961), p. 105: "There is a limit to the 'concretisation' of the negligence issue. . . . For instance, the rule that a motorist should not proceed at an excessive speed can hardly be stated in a helpful form. In itself it is nothing but a tautology, for it means merely that he ought not to go at a speed at which he ought not to go. What is an excessive speed depends upon factors too numerous to be exhaustively catalogued."

16. Fingarette (1972), chap. 4. This formula is akin to that of Professor Hart (1968), pp. 44–49: ". . . informed and considered choice"—respect for which he holds to be "very central to the notion of justice." It is this, not "compassion" or

Secondly, though the term "rationality" has a range of meanings, the relevant concept of rationality, as expressed in the above formulations, emphasises conduct as central, not merely intellect.

The gloomy mood of a person in the depths of depressive psychosis is irrational, for example, and so is the conduct motivated by such gloom (e.g., killing one's children and oneself). In such a case, effective execution of the project can show that the intellectual processes are sound enough; it is motive and mood and conduct that are irrational.

Thirdly, the formula about "capacity for rational control of conduct" expresses aptly what the usual legal formulae obscure. The paranoid killer, motivated by his bizarre delusions, "knows the nature of his act"—that he is killing. He "knows it is wrong"—that his act is contrary to law, and contrary to the moral views of mankind. If these *M'Naghten* phrases were strictly applied, few, if any, would be found insane by a jury. But in fact what the juries have tacitly appreciated is that persons such as Daniel M'Naghten[17] and James Hadfield[18] lacked the mental capacity, by virtue specifically of their delusions, to conduct themselves rationally with respect to the criminality of their conduct at the time.[19]

The depressive or manic killer is not acting out of an "*ir*resistible impulse"; he is often well in control, wholeheartedly committed to acting as he does. But the impulse is irrational; he lacks *rational* control of his conduct.[20]

The schizophrenic who calmly inflicts bizarre and grievous bodily injuries on another is not "*incapable* of conforming to law."[21] He could act otherwise if he wished, but he *wishes* to act in a way that he *knows* is in fact *non*conforming. The true problem is that his wishes are irrational, his decision as to whether to conform to law or not is formed irrationally, and his conduct is irrational.

As one would infer from the previous discussion of the equivalent though less explicit concept "abnormal," the use of the fuller formula,

"sentiment," as Walker (1968) claims (p. 253), that is relevant to culpability. See Kadish (1968).

17. *M'Naghten's Case* (1843).

18. *Hadfield's Case* (1800).

19. The phrase in *M'Naghten* that does correspond to this formula, as I would interpret it, is *defect of reason.* See Fingarette (1972), pp. 178, 198.

20. Sparks (1964) explains mental abnormality in terms of incapacity to control one's thoughts and acts "in certain respects, as normal men can do" (p. 11). But he subsequently (pp. 11, 13, 23) refers to capacity for "*rational*" control of conduct.

21. Section 4.01 of the American Law Institute's Model Penal Code, Draft 4. This test has received increasing acceptance in U.S. courts. See Fingarette (1972), pp. 242–244.

"mental incapacity for rational control of conduct with respect to criminality," requires a commonsense judgment, not a technical or scientific one. It expresses explicitly, formally, the essence of a basic concept of common sense and morality. Expressed more informally, the question is whether the accused was mentally able to conduct himself intelligibly enough within the elementary "rules of the game" of everyday social intercourse. As to such a question, the appropriate umpire is the man whose "game" it is—the reasonable layman.

I turn now to discuss a fundamental conceptual confusion that has arisen because the special verdicts of Not Guilty in insanity[22] and automatism are too often conceptually equated with the more usual Not Guilty verdict. Normally, a Not Guilty verdict wipes the slate clean of criminal flaw. But the criminal slate is not wiped clean when the verdict is based on a finding of diminished mental capacity. An insane person who kills someone is doing what criminal law is intended to deter men from doing. His defect with respect to criminal law is grave, in spite of the misleading Not Guilty verdict. The point here is not that he is guilty, nor that he is innocent—but that his radical incompetence is such that he should not be morally judged at all. The claim of such diminished mental capacity is *a fortiori* the admission of a lack of qualification to be treated as a free and responsible person under law. It is this which warrants treating such a person as a ward of the state, even though "not guilty," until the flaw is remedied.

With these general remarks as setting, I shall turn to consider specific applications of the doctrine to various types of defences and types of cases.

III. CURRENT DEFENCES AND TYPES OF CASES

The defence of so-called "automatism"[23] has usually been expressed as amounting to a defence based on "unconsciousness" and "involuntari-

---

22. The original verdict of Not Guilty in cases of insanity was changed by the Trial of Lunatics Act 1881 to Guilty. The form of the verdict was changed back to Not Guilty by the Criminal Procedure (Insanity) Act 1964, s.1. Right of appeal *against* this Not Guilty verdict was paradoxically (yet sensibly) assured by the 1964 Act and the Criminal Appeal Act 1968, s.12, thus reversing *Felstead v. R.* [1914], which had held that no appeal against a Not Guilty verdict could lie.

23. *R. v. Charlson* [1955]; *R. v. King* [1963]; *Hill v. Baxter* [1958]; and *Bratty v. Atty-Gen. for N. Ireland* [1963]. See Prevezer (1958); Edwards (1958); Cross (1962); Williams (1961), pp. 12–15; Smith and Hogan (1973), pp. 34–37; and *Russell on Crime* (1964), pp. 25, 36–40.

ness,"[24] the latter in particular having been widely remarked upon as precluding any criminal guilt.[25] It would seem generally acknowledged, but is only rarely expressed because of the lack of doctrinal clarity, that there must be no culpability in the context of origin of the automatism if it is to serve as a complete defence to criminal charges.[26]

Current law concerning automatism suffers from the use of vague and ad hoc concepts that are used neither in a strict medical sense nor a strict legal sense. Favourites—"unconsciousness," "automatic," and "involuntary"—often are plainly inaccurate as descriptions of the crucially relevant features of the behaviour. These terms are usually used, in effect, as mere code words to trigger a desired legal outcome.

For example, it confuses rather than clarifies if, as in *Charlson*, we characterise a man's conduct as "unconscious" or "automatic" when he picks up a child, beats him, carries him over to a window, and manages successfully to throw him out of the window.[27] Charlson's conduct was without motive, but he was not unconscious. It would be more appropriate to say that Charlson was suffering an "*altered* state of consciousness." But "altered" in what way? There are very many legally irrelevant kinds of alterations of consciousness. Charlson's altered state of consciousness was legally relevant because the "alteration" consisted in a change from capacity for rational control to lack of capacity for rational control of his conduct.

One who is caused to lose control of his automobile when suddenly attacked by a swarm of bees is not "unconscious" nor is this in the strict sense a "reflex." Yet this could amount to automatism.[28] Again, what is really at issue here is a momentary loss of rational control.

---

24. Prevezer (1958), p. 363; Edwards (1958), p. 383. See Morris and Howard (1964), pp. 61–70, emphasizing Australian and Commonwealth law.

25. My argument implies that "voluntariness" is not of the essence in the automatism defence, but irrationality is. This approach avoids the difficulties in the general doctrine that all "acts" are, in law, necessarily "voluntary." See Hart (1968), chap. 4; and see the American Law Institute Model Penal Code, Draft 4, Art. 2, 5.2.0 (2)—where an inventory of "nonvoluntary" acts is plainly inadequate to deal with automatism. See also Williams (1961), pp. 12–15; Smith and Hogan (1973), pp. 34–38; *Russell on Crime* (1964), pp. 25, 36–40; and Edwards (1958), pp. 379–383.

26. *Hill v. Baxter* [1958]; *R. v. Sibbles* [1959]; Prevezer (1958), p. 364; and the remarks of Lord Denning in *Bratty* [1963], p. 410.

27. *R. v. Charlson* [1955]. See also *R. v. Kemp* [1956], in which the accused killed his wife by attacking her (not by accidentally hitting her) with a hammer.

28. *Hill v. Baxter* [1958], p. 286. I must say, with respect, that Professor Hart's (1968) analysis of the situation as one of "bodily movements . . . not 'governed by will' " (p. 105) seems to me unsatisfactory.

The often elaborate, intelligent, and purposeful conduct of a person in an epileptic fugue state can only as a legal fiction be described as unconscious or involuntary. The psychological experts have gone along with this terminology in the vague belief that it is the appropriate exculpatory language in a court of law; and the courts have gone along with it, erroneously supposing it to be a scientific description.[29] Critical analysis of the concepts has given way before the intuitive consensus in paradigm cases that the person was not culpable and should be acquitted. The legally distinctive features of epileptic fugue behaviour can correctly be characterised, however, by noting that though the person shows control in his conduct, he has lost *rational* control of his conduct.[30]

In the upshot, the automatism defence turns out to depend not on false descriptions or dubious distinctions such as "physical" versus "mental" disease, but on these conditions jointly: the accused suffered from diminished mental capacity with respect to any crime on the occasion of his allegedly criminal conduct, and his diminished mental capacity was of nonculpable origin.

In the insanity plea, the same conditions are in principle at issue prior to the verdict, as the doctrine of diminished mental capacity reveals. Anything extraneous to these conditions is either ad hoc limitation, or it is a consideration that ought to play its role subsequent to the verdict as bearing on technical questions of deterrence or rehabilitation rather than on culpability.

For example, as we have already noted, although M'Naghten did know the nature of the act he was committing and that it was unlawful, his mental condition, for purposes of assessing culpability and criminal responsibility, did fulfill the conditions set out above. He was nonculpably incapable of *rational* control of conduct with respect to any criminal standard when motivated by his delusions of persecution having their origin in his paranoid psychosis.

Of course, terms such as "psychosis," "schizophrenia," and "mental disease" should have no decisive legal force. Along with all the other

29. A similar, mutually reinforcing failure of communication has resulted in the frequent assumption that "mental disease" in legal tests is equivalent to the psychiatric concept "psychosis." See Fingarette (1972), p. 31.

30. Walker's (1968) characterisation is true to the facts here: ". . . complex sequences [of movements] . . . which are normally carried out with a purpose, and by a person who is paying some attention to what he is doing, but which seems to involve the person concerned in doing things which are quite inconsistent with his normal desires and behaviour, and of which he afterwards has no recollection, or only a faint and inaccurate memory" (p. 165).

testimony bearing on the accused's condition of mind, such terms, if explained, may help the jury to make a reasonable man's commonsense judgment whether the accused's mind was so different from others as to be called abnormal with respect to the criminality of his conduct.

Finally, a last remark on *M'Naghten,* though this is not the place to discuss that insanity test in detail. In centering on "knowledge" rather than will or emotion, *M'Naghten* seems restrictive as compared to the general doctrine of diminished mental capacity. However, a renewed emphasis on the *M'Naghten* phrase "defect of reason" could accomplish much to bring the meaning of *M'Naghten* back to where I think it originally was—directed to a central concern with an essentially legal concept, the lack of mental capacity for rational conduct. The true point of saying, in *M'Naghten,* that the defect of reason must be "from mental disease" was not, I suggest, to tie the legal concept to a medical concept but to require that the "defect of reason" have a nonculpable context of origin.[31]

We are now prepared to turn to the defence of "diminished responsibility."[32] The rationale for the diminished responsibility defence typically used to be expressed by noting the fact that the defence was a "device to enable the courts to take account of a special category of mitigating circumstances in cases of murder, and to avoid passing sentence of death in cases where such circumstances exist."[33] Subsequent to the abolition of the death penalty, this rationale has been rerationalised to suggest that it is the fixed life sentence which needs mitigation. This still leaves the defence as a device, ad hoc, to mitigate one particular penalty—in a system of law wherein all other penalties are mitigable by quite other means such as distinguishing among similar crimes of different gravity and providing for flexibility in sentencing. The defence of diminished responsibility thus appears as an anomaly.

However, this defence, when viewed in the context of the diminished mental capacity doctrine, no longer appears merely as an invocation of mercy prior to the verdict. The defence of diminished responsibility falls

31. See note 19, supra. See generally Fingarette (1972), chaps. 1 and 4.

32. Homicide Act 1957, s.2; *R. v. Byrne* [1960]; Sparks (1964); Wootton (1960); Wootton (1963), pp. 58–90; Walker (1971), pp. 279–280; Williams (1961), pp. 541–558. For a review of the defence as it originated in Scotland, see Walker (1968), pp. 138–146.

33. Report of the Royal Commission on Capital Punishment, Cmnd. 8932, p. 144. See also "Murder: Some Suggestions for the Reform of the Law Relating to Murder in England" (*Heald Report,* 1956); and Sparks (1964), pp. 14–16.

entirely unexceptionably within the pattern of diminished mental capacity defences. Wherever, with respect to some graver crime in a set of related crimes, the accused's mind was abnormal with respect to a mental element essential in the graver crime, and yet not abnormal with respect to the mental elements essential to a lesser crime, then of course the accused has diminished mental capacity with respect to that graver crime,[34] but not with respect to the lesser crime.

In the case of murder, for example, as distinguished from manslaughter, the distinctive mental element is "malice"[35] —which is typically signalled by the presence of the psychological intent to kill. However, the presence of the intent does not necessarily establish that what would otherwise be manslaughter is murder. For example, in spite of the intent to kill, there is not murder if the context of the intent shows provocation, a suicide pact, or, of course, diminished responsibility.[36] Given these special circumstances, the psychological intent does not reflect that particularly "heinous kind of homicide"[37] which is signalled by the phrase "malice aforethought."[38]

Specifically, the diminished responsibility defence is an acknowledgement that the powers of rationality were not adequate to "reflect meaningfully and maturely" enough upon the purport of the act if there was to be that extra "quantum of moral turpitude,"[39] that extra "heinousness" which distinguishes murder from manslaughter. The irrationality of mind out of which the intent arose precluded a rational awareness of the gravity of criminality of such an intent.

34. The concept of diminished responsibility as I analyse it here has a more general scope, logically, than crimes of homicide. Such a defence is in effect applied with generality in some Continental jurisdictions. See Royal Commission Report on Capital Punishment, Cmnd. 8932, pp. 143‒144.

35. For a full discussion of the terms *malice* and *malice aforethought,* see, for example, Williams (1965), chaps. 2 and 3.

36. That "malice in law *means* intention or recklessness" (Williams, 1961, p. 75) is, I propose with respect, an overstatement.

37. "[I]t has always been true that [manslaughter], although blameworthy, is a less heinous kind of homicide than [murder] . . ." (*Russell on Crime,* 1964, p. 598).

38. The extra "heinousness" of murder is not, of course, to be identified necessarily with "an ulterior evil motive" (*R. v. Solanke* [1969], p. 1385, per Salmon, L.J.). Objective evil does not necessarily correspond to subjective motive. See *Russell on Crime* (1964), p. 32.

39. The analysis here has roots in the leading California case, *People v. Wolff,* (1964). See especially Hasse (1972), and Chapter 8, supra.

On the other hand, the diminished responsibility defence implies that the accused did have sufficient rationality to grasp the criminal purport of his conduct up to a significant point, though not in its full heinousness. When stated thus abstractly this may seem to be an overly abstruse distinction. Yet it is precisely the practical distinction we do want to make when we hold a mentally disturbed person culpable for manslaughter but not for murder. We intuitively appreciate his lesser culpability. We are inclined, confusedly, to think in terms of a special need for "mercy." Yet the requirements of coherent legal doctrine require us to distinguish between finding culpability for a lesser crime and offering mercy to one who has committed a graver crime.

I turn now to intoxication crimes.[40] I will discuss and illustrate these in relation to homicide, where the full spectrum of possibilities most clearly appears.

A first major subclass consists of the cases of what might be called intoxication to the point of *partial* irrationality. The accused is mentally abnormal with respect to a mental element essential only in the graver of a set of related crimes. For example, the accused is mentally confused in such a way that he is incapable of forming any such precisely defined intention as the intent specifically to kill a certain person in a certain way. Yet he *is* intentionally violent and assaultive. This is the classical "absence of specific intent" treated in the case law.[41] Or, on the other hand, the accused may have been intoxicated in such a way that he was irrational enough to *form* the intent to kill. In the latter case it will be of the essence, of course, that the intent came out of an intoxication-disordered mind rather than mere unusual excitability due to the drug. Common sense, embodied in the diminished mental capacity doctrine, tells us that a person may be so drunkenly irrational that although he forms and acts on the intent to kill, he may be incapable of rational awareness of the full criminal gravity of his act, and thus significantly less culpable than the cold-blooded murderer. He still may have retained enough rationality to grasp the criminality of his act up to a point—the point we mark off as the crime of manslaughter. We can now see that this case is, up to this point in the analysis, the logical equivalent of the diminished responsibility case.

40. See generally note 7, supra.

41. This defence was acceptable, particularly if going to show lack of mental capacity to form the intent, and not merely absence of the intent, as early as *R. v. Monkhouse* (1849), p. 56. See the leading case of *D.P.P. v. Beard* [1920], p. 499. Also see Orchard (1970), p. 211.

The significant difference emerges when we turn to the question of culpability in the context of origin.

For example, if the intoxication had a culpable origin consisting in the prior intent (or foresight) that it would produce just such a death, as when a sober and sane person with the specific homicidal intent or foresight begins to drink as a step toward "nerving" himself to do that specific killing,[42] then the specific mental intent (or recklessness) requisite for murder is present. More typically, however, the intoxication will have had its origin in a mere intent to "have a good time," in which case there would never have been a murderous intent, and the proper verdict is manslaughter. This is indeed the classic actual result in the "absence of specific intent" cases as cited above. There is an "intermediate case," not clearly settled in law, where the accused may have been grossly negligent in voluntarily intoxicating himself. For example, he may have been drinking heavily on the job, even though his job included regular and frequent responsibility for handling highly lethal materials. He could then be guilty either of murder or of manslaughter, depending on how one interprets the law of murder-manslaughter, currently not well settled with respect to gross negligence.[43]

The second major subclass of intoxication-induced diminished mental capacity cases contains all cases of voluntary intoxication where the intoxication produces not partial but *complete* absence of capacity for rationality of conduct with respect to criminality.

Such complete irrationality could—at least in theory—have its origin in an earlier specific intent, or recklessness, or gross negligence. The remarks above in connection with such cases and partial intoxication would hold here as well.

Of most practical importance, however, is the most common type of totally drunken homicide: here, heavy drinking, without any specifically

---

42. *Attorney General for N. Ireland v. Gallagher* [1963]; *Thebo Meli v. R.* [1954]. See Smith and Hogan (1973), p. 157; Williams (1961), pp. 13–14; Hart and Honore (1959), pp. 70, 292, 301; and Prevezer (1958). All these sources argue for special versions of the generalised principle propounded here. However, some commentators, including at times authorities cited just above (!), hold that temporal simultaneity with the *actus reus* is of the essence in *mens rea*. See Williams (1961), p. 2; Smith and Hogan (1973), pp. 52–53, 157, 217–219; *Russell on Crime* (1964), pp. 54–55, 466; Coke 3 Inst. 51. See generally Marston (1970), especially at p. 210.

43. Turpin (1962) concludes that "the great weight of authority [is] to the effect that causing death by gross negligence is manslaughter" (p. 201).

criminal motive or intent, goes to the point of total irrationality; this in turn leads to a brawl with enemies (or friends, or strangers) that results in a killing which, initially, hardly could be specifically foreseen.

The tendency of the courts in dealing with these extreme intoxication cases has been to stress "the general proposition that drunkenness is no excuse for crime."[44] Yet it is also held that the "law is plain . . . that . . . drunkenness . . . can only . . . [reduce] the crime from murder to manslaughter."[45] This suggests, at least, that drunkenness really does excuse, but only partially. Unfortunately for the sake of clarity, it is also said that the rule regarding drunkenness "is only in accordance with the ordinary law applicable to crime . . . [that] a person cannot be convicted unless the *mens* was *rea*.[46] Why must he even be guilty of manslaughter if the latter is the operative principle? How could there even be negligence at the time of the act if, at that time, the accused was totally irrational and therefore incapable of paying proper attention and exercising due care?[47] Even in so-called "strict liability," some minimal element of knowledge of the nature of the act is essential.[48]

There is indeed a valid moral rationale, as well as the practical one of public safety,[49] underlying our commonsense judgment that even the unplanned and unforeseeable drunken killing should not go unpunished. This rationale, however, requires reference to the context of origin, as we shall see. Confusion has arisen in the courts because they have strained, at the price of conceptual confusion, to locate all the elements of culpability within the very harm-causing act itself, and even though the accused may have been totally irrational at the time of the act.

44. *D.P.P. v. Beard* [1920], p. 506.

45. *Ibid.*, p. 500.

46. *Ibid.*, p. 504. Williams (1961), pp. 559–560, 570. But see the conflicting views of Lord Denning in *Gallagher* [1963], p. 381, and in *Bratty* [1963], p. 410. Confusingly, the drunken man is spoken of by Williams as "acting," and yet is analogized to the automatistic sleepwalker (pp. 12–13). *Russell on Crime* (1964), p. 596, says that drunken total irrationality—as in the *Gallagher* examples—cannot be *mens rea* and justify a manslaughter verdict.

47. See Williams (1961), pp. 102, 118, 529; Smith and Hogan (1973), pp. 151–152; Orchard (1970), pp. 217–218. *Kay v. Butterworth* (1945); *R. v. Sibbles* [1959]; *R. v. McBride* [1962]; and *Gallagher* [1963].

48. *R. v. Prince* (1875); *Gleeson v. Hobson* (1970); *Hill v. Baxter* [1958]; *Warner v. Metropolitan Police Commissioner* [1969]; and *Sweet v. Parsley* [1970]. See Jacobs (1971), pp. 104–105.

49. Park, J. in *R. v. Carroll* (1835); Stephen, J. in *Doherty* (1887), p. 308.

Lipman, invoking *Church,*[50] attempts to escape the dilemma by avoiding any reference to the subjective mental capacity of the accused at the time of the act. *Lipman* does require, however, that harm result from an unlawful act; yet we are not told what was the nature of Lipman's "unlawful act."[51] How could there have been an unlawful act of any kind if Lipman, who had taken LSD, was hallucinating and had no idea at all of the nature or consequences of his conduct, or even that it was a human being he was harming?

To find the proper basis of culpability, we must turn from the intoxicated act itself to its context of origin. Lipman, while sane and sober, deliberately set about to intoxicate himself, and in doing so he foreseeably, materially, and unreasonably increased the risk of substantial loss of his mental capacity for rational control of his conduct with respect to the law (and indeed with respect to any rational norms).

Of course, one may take intoxicating substances and yet hope and expect to abide by the law. But inadequately grounded hopes or expectations, leading to the taking of unreasonable risks, are the very stuff of gross negligence and recklessness. The reckless driver, too, may hope and expect and intend not to harm anyone as he careens through the apparently isolated countryside at 100 miles per hour, over the hills, into the opposite lane, and around the curves. Many such drivers are not "indifferent" to the danger; they may indeed be intent upon avoiding any accidents—provided the danger can be avoided while careening at 100 miles per hour.[52]

Such a driver may rationalise the risk by arguing (truthfully) that, from a "statistical" standpoint, even reckless driving rarely causes death. The issue, however, does not rest on such "statistical" considerations, nor does it dissolve in the face of our inability to specify exactly what the eventual

50. *R. v. Lipman* [1970]; *R. v. Church* [1966], p. 70; and *Bolton v. Crawley* [1972]. See Orchard (1970) and Glazebrook (1970).

51. Lipman was completely involved in hallucinating, but Cruse (1838), though intoxicated, was still mentally capable of committing the unlawful act of assault, even though too drunk to commit murder. See also, in connection with attempted suicide, *R. v. Moore* (1852) and *R. v. Doody* (1845). In *R. v. Lamb* [1967], the absence of any independently unlawful act such as assault, had the deceased not been killed by the supposedly unloaded gun, established that the unintended killing was not manslaughter. *Lipman* accepts *Lamb* but differentiates it on the ground that the latter did not involve intoxication. But this fact is irrelevant to the principle involved—whether the killing was the result of an otherwise unlawful act.

52. See Williams (1961), pp. 53–54.

harm, if any, will be, or how or when it will come about. It is plain that this driver is unreasonably adding a real risk of harm, even of death, to himself and others. If he thinks on the matter, and still goes ahead, he is reckless;[53] if he never even thinks of it, he is criminally negligent.

Analogously, the person who takes substances in amounts which can quickly produce a grave loss of rationality cannot rightly argue that there is no unreasonable risk of grave harm because many people do this and produce no harm, or because he himself never until now caused such harm while intoxicated, or because the range of possible harms risked is too broad to have warranted foresight of any specific harm such as death.[54] The fact that the harm in question is so unspecifiable, unpredictable, and hence uncontrollable beforehand is precisely wherein much of the risk and its unreasonableness lies. In short, diminished mental capacity constitutes a situation of high risk with regard to a broad range of harms, though low risk with respect to any very specific harm.

New and more potent forms of intoxicating drugs are increasingly being developed and becoming available. This fact should underline the urgency of this distinctive risk-situation for the law. Moreover, there are significant developments in the area of new nondrug techniques for manipulation of the mind and for affecting its modes of consciousness. Such developments present the issue in even more general form: one who knowingly and unreasonably risks loss of his powers of rationality with respect to criminal law, whether by chemical or any other means, should—I propose—be viewed as committing a crime of criminal negligence.

In spite of the justice of this basic proposition, there is a notable degree of community tolerance for excessive drinking, as is also the case in regard to driving offences. This is not currently the case with regard to other drugs, but tolerance for these, too, may develop. Juries may be, and in the case of alcohol probably will be, reluctant to see as criminal negligence with respect to death or grievous bodily harm the fact that an ordinary person, with no ulterior motive or advertence to the risk, had got himself grossly drunk or otherwise intoxicated. Facing this fact, I suggest that statutory provisions, akin to those in driving offences,[55] could easily be

53. " 'Recklessness' with regard to a foreseen consequence connotes the *unjustified* assumption of a risk . . ." (Cross, 1961, p. 510, italics added).

54. Walker (1965), p. 32, cites reports indicating the important role that drunkenness plays in many dangerous offences, not only driving offences but also crimes of violence and sexual assaults.

55. E.g., s.1 of the Road Traffic Act 1960: "Causing death by reckless or dangerous driving."

formulated to cover the basic offence of causing harm by virtue of voluntarily induced diminished mental capacity. This proposal is a generalised concept under which fall various ad hoc proposals to be found in the recent literature.[56]

The essence of any such statutory provisions would be this: the accused must have been charged with a crime (other than a crime under the present statute) which includes causing death or bodily harm as essential elements. The accused must be proved to have caused such death or harm. The *mens rea* of any such crime must have been negated by a showing of voluntarily induced diminished mental capacity. All this being the case, the accused is guilty of the crime of "causing death, or of causing (grievous, or nongrievous) bodily harm, by reason of voluntarily induced diminished mental capacity," and is subject to the appropriate penalty.

Plainly, rare types of cases such as *in*voluntarily drug-induced diminished mental capacity would count as nonculpable diminished mental capacity.

It can be seen that the diminished mental capacity doctrine, when applied to intoxication, introduces unity, coherence, and generality to the issues. Moreover, it introduces greater realism, psychological and moral, neither insisting misleadingly that intoxication "cannot excuse," nor allowing (at the other extreme) that the person who is thoroughly intoxicated should be viewed as "totally lacking *mens rea*"[57] and hence guilty of no crime. Stating the matter positively, the diminished mental capacity doctrine, as it bears on voluntary intoxication, conforms (in my opinion) to basic intuitions expressed in English law from earlier times: a man who is exceedingly drunk is "non compos mentis,"[58] "mad,"[59] "without understanding or memory."[60] The relevant *culpable* mental state, however, is not that madness but the original, avoidable "folly" which led him, when sober, to drink to the point of madness.[61]

56. See Cross and Jones (1972), p. 96; Williams (1961), p. 573; Orchard (1970), p. 211; and Cross (1962), p. 243.

57. See, for example, *Russell on Crime* (1964), p. 596.

58. *Beverley's Case* (1603).

59. Blackstone, IV, c.2, s. III.

60. *Reniger v. Fogossa.*

61. *Ibid.* See also Smith and Hogan (1973), pp. 252–257; Cross and Jones (1972), p. 91; Austin (1879), Lec. XXVI, s.4.

TABLE OF CASES

293

BIBLIOGRAPHY

"Admissibility of Subjective Abnormality to Disprove Criminal Mental States." 1959. *Stanford Law Review* 12:226.

Alarcon, R. de, N. H. Rathod, and I. G. Thomson. 1969. "Observations on Heroin Abuse by Young People in Crawley New Town." In Steinberg, Hannah: 338.

Alcoholism. 1965. United States Department of Health, Education, and Welfare.

Alexander, Franz, and Hugo Staub. 1931. *The Criminal, the Judge and the Public: A Psychological Analysis.* New York: Macmillan.

American Law Institute. 1962. *Model Penal Code,* proposed official draft.

American Psychiatric Association. 1964. *A Psychiatric Glossary.* Washington, D.C.

Amsterdam, Anthony C. 1967. "Federal Constitutional Restrictions on the Punishment of Crimes of Status, Crimes of General Obnoxiousness, Crimes of Displeasing Police Officers, and the Like." *Criminal Law Bulletin* 3:205.

Archbold: Pleading, Evidence, and Practice in Criminal Cases. 1973. London.

Arens, Richard. 1974. *Insanity Defense.* New York: Philosophical Library.

Ashley, Richard. 1972. *Heroin—The Myth and the Facts.* New York: St. Martin's Press.

Austin, John. 1879. *Lectures on Jurisprudence.* London: J. Murray.

Bartels, Robert. 1973. "Better Living Through Legislation: Control of Mind-Altering Drugs." *University of Kansas Law Review* 21:439.

Barter, James T., and Martin Reite. 1969. "Crime and LSD: The Insanity Plea." *American Journal of Psychiatry* 126:536.

Baumgartner, Kenneth C. 1970. "The Effect of Drugs on Criminal Responsibility, Specific Intent and Mental Competency." *American Criminal Law Quarterly* 8:118.

Bazelon, David L. 1974. "Psychiatrists and the Adversary Process." *Scientific American* 230:18.

Beck, S. M. 1967. "Voluntary Conduct: Automatism, Insanity and Drunkenness." *Criminal Law Quarterly* 9:315.

Beecher, Henry. 1959. *Measurement of Subjective Responses.* New York: Oxford University Press.

Biggs, John, Jr. 1955. *The Guilty Mind.* New York: Harcourt Brace.

Blachly, Paul H. 1966. "Management of the Opiate Abstinence Syndrome." *American Journal of Psychiatry* 122:742.

——— (editor). 1970. *Drug Abuse: Data and Debate.* Springfield, Illinois: Thomas.

Blackstone, Sir William. Various editions. *Commentaries on the Laws of England.*

Blane, Howard T., Willis F. Overton, Jr., and Morris E. Chafetz. 1963. "Social Factors in the Diagnosis of Alcoholism." *Quarterly Journal of Studies on Alcohol* 24:640.

Block, Marvin A. 1965. *Alcoholism.* Belmont, California: Wadsworth Publishing Company.

Blum, Richard H. 1970. *Society and Drugs.* San Francisco: Jossey-Bass.

Blum, Richard H., Daniel Bovet, and James Moore. 1974. *Controlling Drugs: International Handbook for Psychoactive Drug Classification.* San Francisco: Jossey-Bass.

Bouvier Law Dictionary. 1589. Rawles' Third Revised.

Bowman, Addison M. 1965. "Narcotic Addiction and Criminal Responsibility Under Durham." *Georgetown Law Journal* 53:1017.

Brecher, Edward M. 1972. *Licit and Illicit Drugs.* Boston: Little, Brown.

Brenner, Charles. 1973. *An Elementary Textbook of Psychoanalysis.* Garden City, New York: Anchor Books.

Brooks, Alexander D. 1974. *Law, Psychiatry and the Mental Health System.* Boston: Little, Brown.

Btesh, Simon (editor). 1972. *Drug Abuse: Non-Medical Use of Dependence-Producing Drugs.* New York: Plenum Press.

"California Jury Instructions, Criminal No. 3.35 (1970)." 1972. *Santa Clara Lawyer* 13:249.

California Penal Code (West). 1970.

California Vehicle Code (West). 1971.

CALJIC—*California Jury Instructions, Criminal.* 1970, 1974.

Carpenter, William T., Jr., John S. Strauss, and John J. Bartko. 1974, Winter. "An Approach to the Diagnosis and Understanding of Schizophrenia." *Schizophrenia* 11:35.

Carrick, Robert W. 1970. "The Government's Role in Affecting Change in the Treatment of Narcotic Addiction." In Blachly, Paul H.: 136.

Chafetz, Morris E. 1964. "Who Is Qualified to Treat the Alcoholic?: Comment on the Krystal-Moore Discussion." *Quarterly Journal of Studies on Alcohol* 25:347.

———. 1976. "Comment on 'The Uniform Alcoholism and Intoxication Treatment Act.'" *Quarterly Journal of Studies on Alcohol* 37:100.

Chapple, Peter A. L., David E. Somekh, and Marilyn Taylor. 1972. "A Five Year Follow-Up of 108 Cases of Opiate Addiction." *British Journal of Addiction* 67:33.

Chein, Isidor. 1969. "Psychological Functions of Drug Use." In Steinberg, Hannah: 14.

Chein, Isidor, Donald L. Gerard, Robert S. Lee, and Eva Rosenfeld. 1964. *The Road to H.* New York: Basic Books.

Cherubin, Charles E. 1967. "The Medical Sequelae of Narcotic Addiction." *Annals of Internal Medicine* 67:23.

Chruscial, T. L. 1972. "Perspectives in Pharmacological Research on Drug Dependence." In Btesh, Simon: 79.

Clancy, John. 1965. "Who Is Qualified to Treat the Alcoholic?: Comment on the Krystal-Moore Discussion." *Quarterly Journal of Studies on Alcohol* 26:314.

Cohen, Sidney. 1972. "Patterns of Drug-Abuse—1970." In Zarafonetis, Chris: 336.

Coke. *Institutes.*

"Contemporary Problems of Drug Abuse: A National Symposium." 1973. *Villanova Law Review* 18:787.

Cooper, Grant. 1971. "Diminished Capacity." *Loyola Law Review* 4:308.

Criminal Appeal Act. 1968. (England).

Criminal Justice Reform Act of 1975. S.1, 94th Congress, First Session.

"Criminal Law: Abnormal Mental Conditions and Diminished Criminal Responsibility." 1970. *Oklahoma Law Review* 23:93.

"Criminal Law: Demise of 'Status-Act' Distinction in Symptomatic Crimes of Narcotic Addiction." 1970. *Duke Law Journal:* 1053.

"Criminal Law—Mental Conditions." *Annotated Law Reports* 3d: 22:1228.

"Criminal Law—Partial Insanity—Evidentiary Relevance Defined." 1961. *Rutgers Law Review* 16:174.

Criminal Procedure (Insanity) Act. 1964. (England).

Cross, Rupert. 1961. "Specific Intent." *Criminal Law Review* 510.

———. 1962. "Reflections on Bratty's Case." *Law Quarterly Review* 78:236.

Cross, Rupert, and P. A. Jones. 1972. *Introduction to Criminal Law.* London: Butterworths.

"The Cruel and Unusual Punishment Clause and the Substantive Criminal Law." 1966. *Harvard Law Review* 79:635.

Cuomo, Anthony A. 1967. "Mens Rea and Status Criminality." *Southern California Law Review* 40:463.

Davidson, Henry A. 1956. "Irresistible Impulse and Criminal Responsibility." *Journal of Forensic Science* 1.

Dealing With Drug Abuse: A Report to the Ford Foundation. 1972.

De Gowin, Elmer L., and Richard L. De Gowin. 1969. *Diagnostic Examination.* New York: Macmillan.

Delgado, Jose M. 1969. *Physical Control of the Mind.* New York: Harper and Row.

DeLong, James V. 1972. "The Drugs and Their Effects." In *Dealing With Drug Abuse: A Report to the Ford Foundation:* 62. Staff Paper Number 1.

Deneau, Gerald D. 1969. "Psychogenic Dependence in Monkeys." In Steinberg, Hannah: 199.

Diagnostic and Statistical Manual of Mental Disorders. 1968. Washington, D.C.: American Psychiatric Association.

"Diminished Capacity and Arson." 1972. *Santa Clara Lawyer* 13:349.

"Diminished Capacity, Its Potential Effect in California." 1970. *Loyola Law Review* 3:153.

Dix, George E. 1971. "Psychological Abnormality as a Factor in Grading Criminal Liability: Diminished Capacity, Diminished Responsibility and the Like." *Journal of Criminal Law, Criminology, and Political Science* 62:313.

Dole, Vincent P., and Marie Nyswander. 1968. "Methadone Maintenance and Its Implications for Theories of Narcotic Addiction." In Wikler, Albert. *The Addictive States*. Association for Research in Nervous and Mental Diseases. Baltimore: Williams and Wilkins: 359.

Douglas, Jack D. 1970. *Youth in Turmoil*. Chevy Chase, Maryland: National Institute of Mental Health Center for Studies of Crime and Delinquency.

"Driver to Easter to Powell: Recognition of the Defense of Involuntary Intoxication?" 1967. *Rutgers Law Review* 22:103.

Dubin, Gary V. 1966. "Mens Rea Reconsidered: A Plea for a Due Process Concept of Criminal Responsibility." *Stanford Law Review* 18:322.

Duke-Elder, Sir Stewart. 1958. *System of Ophthalmology*. London: H. Kimpton.

Eddy, Nathan S., H. Halbach, Harris Isbell, and Maurice Seevers. 1965. "Drug Dependence: Its Significance and Characteristics." *Bulletin of the World Health Organization* 32:721.

Edwards, J. LL. J. 1958. "Automatism and Criminal Responsibility." *Modern Law Review* 21:375.

English, Horace B., and Ava C. English. 1958. *A Comprehensive Dictionary of Psychological and Psychoanalytic Terms*. New York: Longmans, Green.

Feldman, Harvey W. 1970. "Ideological Supports to Becoming and Remaining a Heroin Addict." *Drug Dependence* (HEW), March:10.

Fingarette, Herbert. 1969. *Self-Deception*. London: Routledge and Kegan Paul.

———. 1970. "The Perils of Powell: In Search of a Factual Foundation for 'The Disease Concept of Alcoholism.' " *Harvard Law Review* 83:793.

———. 1972. *The Meaning of Criminal Insanity*. Berkeley: University of California Press.

———. 1974. "Diminished Mental Capacity as a Criminal Law Defence." *Modern Law Review* 37:264.

———. 1975. "Addiction and Criminal Responsibility." *Yale Law Journal* 84:413.

Fitzgerald, P. J. 1961. "Voluntary and Involuntary Acts." In Guest, A. G. *Oxford Essays in Jurisprudence*. London: Oxford University Press.

———. 1962. *Criminal Law and Punishment*. Oxford: Clarendon Press.

Floud, Jean. 1974. "Sociology and the Theory of Responsibility: 'Social Background' as an Excuse for Crime." In Fletcher, Ronald. *The Science of Society and the Unity of Mankind*. London: Heinemann: 204.

Forizs, G. 1965. "Comment." *Quarterly Journal of Studies on Alcoholism* 26:510.

Fox, Sanford J. 1963. "Physical Disorder, Consciousness, and Criminal Liability." *Columbia Law Review* 63:645.

Fraser, H. F. and James A. Grider, Jr. 1953. "Treatment of Drug Addiction." *American Journal of Medicine* 14:571.

Freedman, Alfred M., Harold J. Kaplan, and Benjamin J. Sadock. 1976. *Modern Synopsis of Psychiatry/II*. Baltimore: Williams and Wilkins.

Freedman, Daniel X. 1972. "Non-Pharmacological Factors in Drug Dependence." In Btesh, Simon: 30.

Gearing, Francis R. 1972. "Methadone Maintenance: Six Years Later." *Contemporary Drug Problems* 1:191.

Geber, Beryl A. 1969. "Non-Dependent Drug Use: Some Psychological Aspects." In Steinberg, Hannah: 375.

Gerald, Michael C. 1974. *Pharmacology*. Englewood Cliffs, New Jersey: Prentice-Hall.

Glaser, Frederick B., and John C. Ball. 1970. "Death Due to Withdrawal of Narcotics." In Ball, John C., and Carl D. Chambers. *Epidemiology of Opiate Addiction in the United States*. Springfield, Illinois: Thomas.

Glasscote, Raymond. 1972. *The Treatment of Drug Abuse*. Washington, D.C.: Joint Information Service of the American Psychiatric Association and the National Association for Mental Health.

Glatt, Robert. 1965. "Normal Drinking in Recovered Alcohol Addicts." *Quarterly Journal of Studies on Alcohol* 26:116.

Glazebrook, P. R. 1970. "Constructive Manslaughter and the Threshold Tort." *Criminal Law Journal* 21.

Goldstein, Abraham S. 1967. *The Insanity Defense*. New Haven: Yale University Press.

Goldstein, Avram A., Lewis Aronow, and Sumner M. Kalman. 1969. *The Principles of Drug Action*. New York: Wiley.

Goldstein, Joseph, and Jay Katz. 1963. " 'Abolish the Insanity Defense'— Why Not?" *Yale Law Journal* 72:853.

Goodman, Louis S., and Alfred Z. Gilman. 1965. *Pharmacological Basis of Therapeutics*. New York: Macmillan.

Greenblatt, David J., and Richard I. Shader. 1974. *Benzodiazepines in Clinical Practice*. New York: Raven Press.

Grollman, Arthur, and Evelyn F. Grollman. 1970. *Pharmacology and Therapeutics*. Philadelphia: Lea and Febiger.

Group for the Advancement of Psychiatry, Drug Misuse. 1971.

Guttmacher, Manfred S. 1961. "A Historical Outline of the Criminal Law's Attitudes Toward Mental Disorder." *Archives of Criminal Dynamics* 4:647.

Hale, *Pleas of the Crown*. 1736. London.

Hall, Jerome. 1944. "Intoxication and Criminal Responsibility." *Harvard Law Review* 57:1045.

———. 1960. *General Principles of Criminal Law*. Indianapolis: Bobbs-Merrill.

———. 1964. "Science, Common Sense, and Criminal Law Reform." *Iowa Law Review* 49:1044.

Hall, Livingston, and Selig J. Seligman. 1941. "Mistake of Law and Mens Rea." *University of Chicago Law Review* 8:641.

Harris, Robert T., William M. McIssac, and Charles Shuster, Jr. 1970. *Drug Dependence*. Austin: University of Texas Press.

Hart, H. L. A. 1961a. *The Concept of Law*. London: Oxford University Press.

———. 1961b. "Negligence, *Mens Rea* and Criminal Responsibility." In Guest, A. G. *Oxford Essays in Jurisprudence*. London: Oxford University Press: 29.

———. 1968. *Punishment and Responsibility*. London: Oxford University Press.

Hart, H. L. A., and A. M. Honore. 1959. *Causation and the Law*. Oxford: Clarendon Press.

Hasse, Ann F. 1972. "Keeping Wolff from the Door: California's Diminished Capacity Concept." *California Law Review* 60: 1641.

Havard, Cyril W. H. 1970. *Current Medical Treatment.* London: P. Stapler.

Hayman, Max. 1966. *Alcoholism–Mechanism and Management.* Springfield, Illinois: Thomas.

Heald Report. 1956. "Murder: Some Suggestions for the Reform of the Law Relating to Murder in England." London: Her Majesty's Stationery Office.

Hill, Sir Dennis. 1969. "Chairman's Introduction." In Steinberg, Hannah: 288.

Holahan, John. 1972. "The Economics of Heroin." In *Dealing With Drug Abuse:* 290.

Holmes, Oliver. 1963. *The Common Law.* Boston: Little, Brown.

Homicide Act. 1957. (England).

Hutt, Peter B. 1967. "The Recent Court Decisions on Alcoholism: A Challenge to the North American Judges Association and Its Members." In President's Commission on Law Enforcement and the Administration of Justice. *Task Force Report: Drunkenness:* 110.

"Insanity, Intoxication and Diminished Capacity Under the Proposed California Criminal Code." 1972. *UCLA Law Review* 19:550.

"Intoxication as a Criminal Defense." 1955. *Columbia Law Review* 55:1210.

Isbell, Harris. 1972. "Pharmacological Factors in Drug Dependence." In Btesh, Simon: 36.

Jacobs, Francis G. 1971. *Criminal Responsibility.* London: Weidenfeld and Nicholson.

Jaffe, Jerome H. 1965a. "Drug Addiction and Drug Abuse." In Goodman, Louis S., and Alfred Z. Gilman: 285.

———. 1965b. "Narcotic Analgesics." In Goodman, Louis S., and Alfred Z. Gilman: 247.

———. 1970a. "Development of a Successful Treatment Program for Narcotic Addicts in Illinois." In Blachly, Paul H.: 48.

———. 1970b. "The Implementation and Evaluation of New Treatments for Compulsive Drug Users." In Harris, Robert T., William M. McIssac, and Charles Shuster, Jr.: 230.

Jellinek, Elvin M. 1960. *The Disease Concept of Alcoholism.* New Haven: Hillhouse Press.

Jones, Warren L. 1967. "Diminished Responsibility and Psychiatric Testimony in Pennsylvania." *University of Pittsburgh Law Review* 28:679.

Kadish, Sanford H. 1965. Book Review of Morris and Howard, *Studies in Criminal Law. Harvard Law Review* 78:907.

———. 1968. "The Decline of Innocence." *Cambridge Law Journal* 26:273.

Kadish, Sanford H., and Monrad G. Paulsen. 1969. *Criminal Law and Its Processes. Supplement 1973.* Boston: Little, Brown.

Kay, Stephen. 1967. "Diminished Capacity." *California State Bar Journal* 42:385.

Keedy, Edwin R. 1908. "Ignorance and Mistake in Criminal Law." *Harvard Law Review* 22:75.

———. 1950. "A Problem of First Degree Murder: Fisher v. United States." *University of Pennsylvania Law Review* 99:267.

———. 1952. "Irresistible Impulse as a Defense in the Criminal Law." *University of Pennsylvania Law Review* 100:956.

Keller, Mark. 1958. "Alcoholism: Nature and Extent of the Problem."
Annals 315:2.

―――. 1962. "The Definition of Alcoholism and the Estimation of Its
Prevalence." In Pittman, David, and Charles R. Snyder. *Society, Culture
and Drinking Patterns.* New York: J. Wiley, 310.

―――. 1975. "Multidisciplinary Perspectives on Alcoholism and the Need
for Integration." *Quarterly Journal of Studies on Alcohol* 36:133.

Kenny's Outlines of Criminal Law. 1966. London: Cambridge University
Press.

Krash, Abe. 1961. "The Durham Rule and Judicial Administration of the
Insanity Defense in the District of Columbia." *Yale Law Journal*
70:907.

Krystal, Henry. 1963. "Who Is Qualified to Treat the Alcoholic?: Comment on the Krystal-Moore Discussion." *Quarterly Journal of Studies
on Alcohol* 24:705.

Kuh, Richard H. 1962. "The Insanity Defense." *University of Pennsylvania Law Review* 110:771.

Lacey, Forrest W. 1953. "Vagrancy and Other Crimes of Personal Condition." *Harvard Law Review* 66:1203.

La Fave, Wayne R., and Austin W. Scott, Jr. 1972. *Handbook on Criminal
Law.* St. Paul, Minnesota: West.

Lasagna, Louis. 1965. "Addicting Drugs and Medical Practice." In Wilner,
Daniel M., and Gene G. Kassebaum: 55.

Leib, Charles. 1970. "Diminished Capacity: Its Potential Effect in California." *Loyola Law Review* 3:153.

Lemere, Frederick, Paul O'Hollaren, and Milton A. Maxwell. 1958. "Motivation in the Treatment of Alcoholism." *Quarterly Journal of Studies
on Alcohol* 19:428.

Lennard, Henry, and Arnold Bernstein. 1971. *Mystification and Drug
Misuses.* San Francisco: Jossey-Bass.

Lennard, Henry L., Leon J. Epstein, and Bertram Katzung. 1967. "Psychoactive Drug Action and Group Interaction Process." *Journal of Nervous
and Mental Disease* 145:69.

Lewinstein, Stephen R. 1969. "The Historical Development of Insanity as
a Defense in Criminal Law Actions." *Journal of Forensic Science*
14:275.

Lewis, Aubrey. 1969. "Introduction: Definitions and Perspectives." In
Steinberg, Hannah: 5.

Lindesmith, Alfred R. 1968. *Addiction and Opiates.* Chicago: Aldine
Publishing Company.

Livermore, Joseph M., and Paul Meehl. 1967. "The Virtues of M'Naghten." *Minnesota Law Review* 51:789.

London, Perry. 1969. *Behavior Control.* New York: Harper and Row.

Louisell, David W., and Bernard L. Diamond. 1965. "Law and Psychiatry:
Detente, Entente, or Concomitance?" *Cornell Law Quarterly* 50:217.

Louria, Donald B. 1971. *Overcoming Drugs.* New York: McGraw Hill.

Louria, Donald B., Terry Hensle, and John Rose. 1967. "Major Medical
Complications of Heroin Addiction." *Annals of Internal Medicine* 67:1.

"LSD―Its Effect on Criminal Responsibility." 1968. *De Paul Law Review*
17:365.

"Lunacy and Idiocy: The Old Law and Its Incubus." 1951. *University of Chicago Law Review* 18:361.

Lunter, Gary W. 1972. "The Effect of Drug-Induced Intoxication on the Issue of Criminal Responsibility." *Criminal Law Bulletin* 8:731.

McHugh, Paul R. 1971. "Psychologic Illness in Medical Practice." In Beeson, Paul B., and Walsh McDermott. *Textbook of Medicine.* Philadelphia: W. B. Saunders Company: 107.

McKevitt, James D. 1969. "The 'Untouchable' Acts of Addiction." *American Bar Association Journal* 55:454.

McMorris, S. Carter. 1968. "Can We Punish for the Acts of Addiction?" *American Bar Association Journal* 55:1081.

Maddux, James F. 1965. "Hospital Management of the Narcotic Addict." In Wilner, Daniel M., and Gene G. Kassebaum: 159.

Marston, Geoffrey. 1970. "Contemporaneity of Act and Intention." *Law Quarterly Review* 86:209.

May, Edgar. 1972. "Narcotic Addiction and Control in Great Britain." In *Dealing With Drug Abuse:* 345.

Meehl, Paul E. 1972. "Specific Genetic Etiology: Psychodynamic and Therapeutic Nihilism." *International Journal of Mental Health* 1:10.

Mello, Nancy K., Jack H. Mendelson, and H. Brian McNamee. 1965. "An Experimental Approach to the Drinking Patterns of Alcoholics." In Steinberg, Hannah: 259.

Mendelson, Jack H. 1967. *Social Welfare and Alcoholism:* 21. United States Department of Health, Education, and Welfare.

Merry, J. 1966. "The 'Loss of Control' Myth." *The Lancet* 1:1257.

Michael, Jerome, and Herbert Wechsler. 1937. "A Rationale of the Law of Homicide." *Columbia Law Review* 37:701.

"Modern Status of Rules as to Burden and Sufficiency of Proof of Mental Irresponsibility in a Criminal Case." *Annotated Law Reports* 3d series, 17:146.

Morris, Arval. 1968. "Criminal Insanity." *Washington Law Review* 43:583.

Morris, Herbert. 1968. "Punishment for Thoughts." In Summer, R. S. *Essays in Legal Philosophy:* 1. Berkeley: University of California Press.

———. 1974. "Review Discussion: Criminal Insanity." *Inquiry* 17:345.

———. 1976. *On Guilt and Innocence.* Berkeley: University of California Press.

Morris, Norval. 1951. "Somnambulistic Homicide: Ghosts, Spiders, and North Koreans." *Res Judicatae* 5:29.

———. 1968. "Psychiatry and the Dangerous Criminal." *Southern California Law Review* 41:514.

Morris, Norval, and Colin Howard. 1964. *Studies in Criminal Law.* Oxford: Clarendon Press.

Mueller, Gerhard O. W. 1961. "M'Naghten Remains Irreplaceable: Recent Events in the Law of Incapacity." *Georgetown Law Journal* 50:105.

Murphy, Jeffrie G. 1971. "Involuntary Acts and Criminal Liability." *Ethics* 81:332.

Myerson, David J. 1967. "Institute on Modern Trends in Handling the Chronic Alcoholic Offender." *South Carolina Law Review* 10:305.

National Commission on Marijuana and Drug-Abuse, Drug Use in America: Problem in Perspective. 1973. Second Report 120–140.

Newman, Lawrence, and Lawrence Weitzer. 1957. "Duress, Free Will and the Criminal Law." *Southern California Law Review* 30:313.

Novotny, V., et al. 1975. "Our Experiences with the Treatment of Delirium Tremens with Diazepan." *Quarterly Journal of Studies on Alcohol* 36:1658.

O'Donnell, John A. 1964. "A Follow-Up of Narcotic Addicts." *American Journal of Orthopsychiatry* 34:948.

———. 1965. "The Relapse Rate in Narcotic Addiction: A Critique of Follow-Up Studies." In Wilner, Daniel M., and Gene G. Kassebaum: 242.

Orchard, Geoffrey F. 1970. "Drunkenness, Drugs, and Manslaughter." *Criminal Law Review* 132.

Penal Code Revision Project. *The Criminal Code.* 1972. (California).

Pattison, E. M., E. B. Headley, G. C. Glaser, and L. A. Gottschalk. 1968. "Abstinence and Normal Drinking." *Quarterly Journal of Studies on Alcohol* 29:610.

Perkins, Rollin M. 1939. "Ignorance and Mistake in Criminal Law." *University of Pennsylvania Law Review* 88:35.

———. 1957. *Criminal Law.* New York: Foundation Press.

———. 1969. *Criminal Law.* New York: Foundation Press.

Pfeffer, Arnold, Daniel J. Feldman, Charlotte Feibel, John A. Frank, Marilyn Cohen, M. Freile Fleetwood, and Sidney S. Greenberg. 1956. "A Treatment Program for the Alcoholic in Industry." *Journal of American Medical Association* 161:827.

Phillipson, Richard V. 1970. *Modern Trends in Drug Dependence and Alcoholism.* New York: Appleton-Century-Crofts.

Pittman, David J. 1967. "Public Intoxication and the Alcoholic Offender in American Society." In President's Commission on Law Enforcement, *Task Force Report.*

Platt, Anthony, and Bernard L. Diamond. 1966. "The Origins of the 'Right and Wrong' Test of Criminal Responsibility and Its Subsequent Development in the U.S.: An Historical Survey." *California Law Review* 54:1227.

Plaut, Thomas F. A. 1967. "The Cooperative Commission of the Study of Alcoholism." *Alcohol Problems* 39.

Pratt, Arthur D. 1975. "A Mandatory Treatment Program for Skid Row Alcoholics; Its Implication for the Uniform Alcoholism and Intoxication Treatment Act." *Quarterly Journal of Studies on Alcohol* 36:166.

Preble, Edward, and John J. Casey, Jr. 1972. "Taking Care of Business: The Heroin User's Life on the Street." In Smith, David E., and George R. Gay: 100.

President's Advisory Commission on Narcotic and Drug Abuse. 1963. *Final Report.*

President's Commission on Law Enforcement and the Administration of Justice. 1967. *Task Force Report: Drunkenness.*

Prevezer, S. 1958. "Automatism and Involuntary Conduct." *Criminal Law Review* 361.

"Punishment of Narcotics Addicts for Possession: A Cruel but Usual Punishment." 1971. *Iowa Law Review* 56:578.

Redlich, Frederick C., and Daniel X. Freedman. 1966. *Theory and Practice of Psychiatry.* New York: Basic Books.

Remington, Frank J., and Orrin L. Helstad. 1952. "The Mental Element in Crime—A Legislative Problem." *Wisconsin Law Review* 644.

Rip, Colin. 1966. *The Alcoholic and the Group.* Praetoria, South Africa: Academica.

Road Traffic Act. 1960. (England).

Robins, Lee N. 1973. *A Follow-Up of Vietnam Drug Users.* Special Actions Office for Drug Abuse Prevention, Executive Office of the President.

Robitscher, Joan. 1967. "Psychiatry and Changing Concepts of Criminal Responsibility." *Federal Probation* 31:45.

Room, Robin. 1972. "Comment on the 'Alcohologist's Addiction.'" *Quarterly Journal of Studies on Alcohol* 33:1049.

———. 1976. "Comment on 'The Uniform Alcoholism and Intoxication Treatment Act.'" *Quarterly Journal of Studies on Alcohol* 37:113.

Rose, Earl F. 1970. "Criminal Responsibility and Competency as Influenced by Organic Disease." *Missouri Law Review* 35:326.

Rosenberg, Chaim M., and Joseph Liftick. 1976. "Use of Coercion in the Outpatient Treatment of Alcoholism." *Quarterly Journal of Studies on Alcohol* 37:58.

Royal Commission on Capital Punishment, 1949–1953. 1955. Report, Cmd 8932. (England).

Russell on Crime. 1964. London: Stevens.

Saslow, George. 1970. "Where Do We Go From Here?" In Blachly, Paul H.: 247.

Sayre, Francis B. 1932. "Mens Rea." *Harvard Law Review* 45:974.

Schnoll, Sidney H. 1971–72. "Drugs and Therapy—How to Interpret What You Read and Hear." *Contemporary Drug Problems* 1:15.

Seeley, John. 1962. "Alcoholism Is a Disease: Implications for Social Policy." In Pittman, David, and Charles R. Snyder. *Society, Culture and Drinking Patterns.* New York: J. Wiley, 586.

Siegler, Miriam, Humphrey Osmond, and Stephens Newell. 1968. "Models of Alcoholism." *Quarterly Journal of Studies on Alcohol* 29:571.

Skinner, Burrhus F. 1938. *The Behavior of Organisms.* New York: D. Appleton-Century.

———. 1971. *Beyond Freedom and Dignity.* New York: Knopf.

Smith, Charles W. 1971. "Intoxication as a Defense to a Criminal Charge in Pennsylvania." *Dickinson Law Review* 76:15.

Smith, David E., and George R. Gay. 1972. *It's So Good Don't Even Try It Once.* Englewood Cliffs, New Jersey: Prentice-Hall.

Smith, J. C., and Brian Hogan. 1973. *Criminal Law.* London: Butterworths.

Sparks, Richard F. 1964. "'Diminished Responsibility' in Theory and Practice." *Modern Law Review* 27:9.

Starrs, James E. 1967. "The Disease Concept of Alcoholism and Traditional Criminal Law Theory." *South Carolina Law Review* 19:349.

Stedman's Medical Dictionary. 1972. Baltimore: Williams and Wilkins.

Steinberg, Hannah. 1969. *Scientific Basis of Drug Dependence.* New York: Grune and Stratton.

Student Symposium on the Proposed California Criminal Code. 1972. *UCLA Law Review* 19:550.

Stumberg, George. 1937. "Mistake of Law in Texas Criminal Cases." *Texas Law Review* 15:287.

Swartz, Louis H. 1967. "Compulsory Legal Measures and the Concept of Illness." *South Carolina Law Review* 19:372.

Taber's Cyclopedic Medical Dictionary. 1973. Philadelphia: F. A. Davis.

Thompson, Edward T., and Adaline C. Hayden. 1961. *Standard Nomenclature of Diseases and Operations*. Chicago: Physicians' Record Company.

Thompson, Travis, and Roy Pickens. 1969. "Drug Self-Administration and Conditioning." In Steinberg, Hannah: 177.

Trial of Lunatics Act. 1881. (England).

Turner, J. W. C. 1936. "The Mental Element in Crimes at Common Law." *Cambridge Law Journal* 6:31.

Turpin, C. C. 1962. "Mens Rea in Manslaughter." *Cambridge Law Journal* 200.

Ullman, Albert D. 1960. *To Know the Difference*. New York: St. Martin's Press.

Vaillant, George E. 1966a. "A Twelve Year Follow-Up of New York Addicts, Part I." *American Journal of Psychiatry* 122:727.

———. 1966b. "A Twelve Year Follow-Up of New York Addicts, Part II." *New England Journal of Medicine* 275:1282.

———. 1966c. "A Twelve Year Follow-Up of New York Addicts, Part III." *Archives of General Psychiatry* 15:599.

———. 1969. "The Natural History of Urban Narcotic Drug Addiction— Some Determinants." In Steinberg, Hannah: 347.

Villareal, Julian E. 1970. "Contributions of Laboratory Work to the Analysis and Control of Drug Dependence." In Blachly, Paul H.: 97.

———. 1974. "Recent Advances in the Pharmacology of Morphine-Like Drugs." In Btesh, Simon: 84.

"Voluntary Intoxication—Defense." 1966. *American Law Review* 8:1236.

Wald, Patricia M., and Peter B. Hutt. 1972. "The Drug Abuse Survey Project: Summary of Findings, Conclusions and Recommendations." In *Dealing With Drug Abuse:* 5.

Walker, Nigel. 1965. *Crime and Punishment in Britain*. Edinburgh: Edinburgh University Press.

———. 1968. *Crime and Insanity in England*. Edinburgh: Edinburgh University Press.

———. 1971. *Crime and Punishment in Great Britain*. Edinburgh: Edinburgh University Press.

———. 1975. "Comment." *Modern Law Review* 38:119.

Wallgren, Henrik, and Herbert Barry. 1970. *Actions of Alcohol*, Vol. II. Amsterdam and New York: Elsevier Publishing Company.

Wasserstrom, Richard. 1967. "H. L. A. Hart and the Doctrines of Mens Rea and Criminal Responsibility." *University of Chicago Law Review* 35:92.

Wechsler, Herbert. 1955. "The Criteria of Criminal Responsibility." *University of Chicago Law Review* 22:367.

Weihofen, Henry. 1954. *Mental Disorder as a Criminal Defense*. Buffalo: Dennis.

Weil, Andrew T. 1972. "Altered States of Consciousness." In *Dealing With Drug Abuse:* 333.

Wesson, Donald R., George R. Gay, and David E. Smith. 1972. "Treatment Techniques for Narcotic Withdrawal." In Smith, David E., and George R. Gay: 165.

Williams, Glanville L. 1961. *Criminal Law–The General Part.* London: Stevens.

———. 1965. *The Mental Element in Crime.* The Hebrew University of Jerusalem: Lionel Cohen Lectures, 11th Series.

Wilner, Daniel M., and Gene G. Kassebaum. 1965. *Narcotics.* New York: McGraw-Hill.

Winfield, Percy H. 1943. "Mistake of Law." *Law Quarterly Review* 59.

Wood, Roland W. 1973. "18,000 Addicts Later: A Look at California's Civil Addict Program." *Federal Probation* 37:26.

Woodruff, Robert A., Donald W. Goodwin, and Samuel B. Guze. 1974. *Psychiatric Diagnosis.* London: Oxford University Press.

Wootton, Barbara. 1960. "Diminished Responsibility: A Layman's View." *Law Quarterly Review* 76.

———. 1963. *Crime and Criminal Law.* London: Stevens and Sons.

———. 1968. Review of "The Insanity Defense" by A. Goldstein. *Yale Law Journal* 77:1019.

World Health Organization Expert Committee on Addiction-Producing Drugs. 1964. Report Number 13. (Technical Report Series Number 273).

World Health Organization Expert Committee on Addiction-Producing Drugs. 1969. Report Number 16. (Technical Report Series Number 407).

World Health Organization Expert Committee on Alcohol. 1954. First Report. (Technical Report Series Number 84).

World Health Organization Expert Committee on Drug Dependence. 1970. Report Number 18. (Technical Report Series Number 460).

World Health Organization Expert Committee on Drug Dependence. 1973. Report Number 19. (Technical Report Series Number 526).

World Health Organization Expert Committee on Mental Health. 1967. Report Number 14. Services for the Prevention and Treatment of Dependence on Alcohol and Other Drugs. (Technical Report Series Number 363).

World Health Organization Study Group, Youth and Drugs. 1973. (Technical Report Series Number 516).

Zarafonetis, Chris. 1972. *Drug Abuse.* Philadelphia: Lea and Febiger.

Zinberg, Norman E. 1972. "Rehabilitation of Heroin Users in Vietnam." *Contemporary Drug Problems* 1:263.

INDEX

311

Composition/Omega Repro
Lithography/ Publishers Press
Binder / Mountain States Bindery

Text/ IBM Press Roman
Display/Compset Times Roman
Paper/50 lb. P&S offset vellum
Binding/Johanna Arrestox B 34620